I'LL BLAME IT ON THE WIND

To my wonderful wife and three great kids to whom I owe more than I can ever describe.

Mathew Colbert

I'LL BLAME IT ON THE WIND

AUSTIN MACAULEY
PUBLISHERS LTD.

A CIP catalogue record for this title is available from the British Library.

ISBN 978 184963 747 3

www.austinmacauley.com

First Published (2014)
Austin Macauley Publishers Ltd.
25 Canada Square
Canary Wharf
London
E14 5LB

Printed and bound in Great Britain

Prologue

You know, not all that long back I read a book. Now is that a fact you say, like you and how many millions of others? Perhaps something in the way of an explanation is required. For me to have taken the time required to read a book was quite an exception, something that hadn't occurred in a very long time. Not mind you, that I make this admission with any pride, willingly accepting that many more books should have been read, with my wisdom and general knowledge being enhanced accordingly. But for a variety of reasons I'm forced to admit this hadn't happened, that was until my oldest daughter kept on absolutely insisting I should take the time to read that book.

Now speaking of reading, there's someone who can read, and looking back, it's as if she was almost born reading was that child, but now a child no longer, and with all that reading and acquired knowledge behind her, I decided her constant pleading had to carry some weight, so finally admitting defeat, I gave up the uneven battle and read that book.

And as so often happens in similar circumstances, it turned out I was glad that I did, because I completely fell under its spell to a point where I couldn't put it down until that last thought provoking line was read. However, not all that long after, towards the end of what had proved to be a rather chaotic day, I wandered into our lounge and settled comfortably into my favourite chair, relishing the thought of a few blissful, uninterrupted moments, until yet another of the requirements of a somewhat hectic life demanded my involvement.

The television was on, offering a strong hint that one of our three children had conveniently ignored one of the family rules; that being absolutely no television at that time of the day, then added to their indiscretion by failing to switch off as the culprit probably glided silently away. The picture on the screen was that of some indiscriminate woman on some equally indiscriminate channel, one that was rarely if ever watched. In desperation I groped frantically for the remote, and as always failed to locate it, so after a faint surge of irritation I gave up, preferring to concentrate on the comfort available in the form of leather bound relaxation instead.

But gradually, through the fog of tiredness it started to register, the topic under discussion was my recently completed piece of literature. So with my attention finally activated, I watched and listened as her opinion became perfectly clear. She obviously didn't hold the book in all that high regard, and accordingly, couldn't really understand the attention it appeared to be creating.

It seemed like half a lifetime back since it had been strongly suggested I should consider writing, a wonderful cleanser the medical professional had said at the time, but just the thought alone had left me highly amused. Someone as professional with words as my daughter perhaps, but definitely not I, with the faintest of consideration quickly having been obliterated by the turmoil created by the combination of my business and family life.

But now, as I sat back and listened, I realised a flicker of interest in that direction was gradually being reactivated. Finally the discussion concluded, and with perseverance resulting in the remote being located, a touch brought that longed for peace and quiet. Sitting back in the soft, late afternoon light, I thought long and hard about that book and the message I felt it offered, and as I did, sure enough it was happening again. For the countless time I found my memory digressing as it stumbled back down that chain of my life, the links of which irrevocably led back to the dreadful purgatory, suffered through those few terrible years. I still found it slightly incredible that the pain and humiliation and gut wrenching fear experienced in childhood, could still flicker in the adult. The strain associated with living with the stress caused by the constant threat of unjust and unwarranted exposure, and this was combined with the fear of never ending and poisonous ridicule, all of which I was convinced could only end in total rejection and the most scathing of disbelief. Yet as I sat alone in our lounge, I was forced to accept that in some minute way it was still all there, and it took quite a concentrated effort to force my thoughts back down their original path.

So as I did my best to assess the situation, I decided whether it was a good book or something rather less, the author had written it as he had for one very good reason. Nothing could change fact, that was the way the story of his life had unfolded. So hopefully, allowing for my total inexperience, and with my decision irrevocably made, as I attempt to write about the good and the bad and what manages to fill the gaps between those in my life, I write it like this, because this is the way that it was. As a twelve year old, it was beyond me to try and comprehend why my life, good as it was, suddenly took the path it did, as seemingly out of nowhere, those dark years of abject misery descended. As a young boy, any attempt at rectification seemed to pose an impossible and insurmountable problem, but looking back with the wisdom of an adult, the remedial action, even allowing for what could have proved to be dreadful ramifications, was all so painfully clear.

Chapter 1

I was born in that delightful harbour dominated city of Auckland, but my parents were of English origin and as very young children, emigrated to Australia with their families, who settled around the Sydney suburbs of Hurstville and Penshurst. As the years past, they both emerged as representative tennis players, and as their sporting commitments decreed they started to see a lot of, and as a result, became attracted to each other, it was apparently soon accepted by those who knew them, that marriage was a forgone conclusion. When this happy event finally occurred, they honeymooned in New Zealand, then for a reason I was never to find out, apparently forgot to go back, and for the next forty odd years my father constantly reminded my mother that as far as he was concerned, this meant their honeymoon had never ended. However, as a few years past, and I started to become slightly more familiar with the strange ways of the adult world, I began to suspect my mother did not quite share my father's degree of so called wedded bliss.

I became convinced the main reason for this was that as far as their personalities were concerned, they forever remained a world apart. Also, constantly hovering in the background was this strange decision not to return to their Sydney roots, but whenever I dared to raise this matter with them, my probing was always discouraged in a most emphatic way. This had the effect of leaving me all the more convinced that a story of some kind lay hidden in one of their lives, with my suspicions always aimed directly at my father.

He was a man of no more than average height, with in those early days a thick head of dark brown hair that he brushed straight back in one of the approved fashions of the day. Very well built, with a slim waist setting off to perfection a set of broad and extremely powerful shoulders, he moved at all times with a smooth, rhythmic grace that to my mind, only elite sportsmen seem to so naturally achieve. Once reasonably settled in their new, chosen environment, he was apparently welcomed with open arms by the local sporting fraternity, due entirely to the fact he excelled at tennis and badminton to the extent he did, and one of my earliest memories relating to sport, which was destined to play a dominant role in my own life, was that of sitting with my fingers entwined in the wire around one of the Nicholson Park tennis courts. From my vantage point I would watch intently as my father glided gracefully from one side of the court to the other, blazing back power laden ground strokes, then moving into the net with the speed of a striking snake, from where he'd invariably finish off the point with one of his deadly volleys, and in the process winning A Grade tennis matches with regular monotony. This acted as a natural incentive for my own early involvement with the sport, where I also experienced some junior success, much to my father's enthusiastic delight.

Casual acquaintances usually assessed him as being relaxed and openly friendly, which most of the time he most certainly was, but those with whom he was more constantly involved soon discovered, sometimes to their detriment,

that he possessed a will of iron and bitterly resented his decisions and opinions being questioned in any way. He was employed as a departmental head at the country's largest window manufacturer, being in charge of their architectural metalwork division, and during the latter part of my preschool years, there were few things I enjoyed more than being able to visit him at the factory, where I would wander around, well out of harm's way as I'd been taught, and watch his staff as they created what to me were little short of architectural masterpieces. The majority of these tended to be installed in the front entrances of the city's many banks and insurance companies, where it was hoped they would help to entice the local population into their luxurious interiors, from where they would hopefully proceed to commit themselves and their finances accordingly.

But as far as my father's workplace was concerned, above all else, I did my best to manipulate my mother so as our visits happened to coincide with the midday soccer matches. These were played during the staff lunch break on the company's lengthy and wide tar sealed driveway, and with the sporting genes I'd inherited starting to gradually emerge, my foremost wish was to grow up fast enough so as to be eligible to compete in these truly bloodthirsty and barbaric contests. Anything remotely relating to rules and generally accepted sportsmanship was totally non-existent, with the primary objective of all concerned being to score goals by the use of any devious and underhand method that had ever been devised.

Needless to say, with the combination of the lack of rules and the rough, tar sealed surface on which they were playing, the demolition wrought amongst the contestants was without doubt bloodcurdling to behold. So on completion of these murderous confrontations, many of the contestants would drag themselves back to work sporting a great variety of battered and bleeding bodily parts, but remaining completely undeterred, I still couldn't wait for the time to arrive so as I could be deemed old enough to be included.

However, according to my mother, with my father showing something of an indifference to my youthful existence, which she conveniently blamed on the fact that he was struggling to find enough hours in the day to accommodate his variety of interests, let alone being able to find the time to assist in the upbringing of a young son, it meant this responsibility lay predominantly with my mother. Naturally, this is a situation that exists in many families, and it suited me quite admirably, because I found her laid back attitude to life far more acceptable, in comparison to my father's rather full on approach.

Following my arrival, she had given up playing representative tennis, but due to those many years of competing at such a high level, remained more than competent on the end of a racquet herself, and still excelled while playing the occasional social game. During one of these sojourns, I happened to hear one of the younger male members of the club describe her as a raven haired beauty, and as a result, I sat back and gave his comment some deep thought, finally coming to the conclusion it did qualify as a reasonably apt description. But I felt that to add to this compliment, she also possessed legs that would have done justice to any movie star, and a pair of deep brown, beautiful eyes, that as far as I was concerned, seemed to possess the ability to look into the depths of your soul.

These features were finally complimented by a tone to her skin that was butter smooth, the origin of which I remain convinced was developed during her early childhood in England. Later, the Southern Hemisphere sun combined to add the finishing touches, blending her skin to a soft, silken bronze. However, I had to agree her crowning glory was that beautiful head of hair, and occasionally I'd compare it with my father's dark brown colour and be left wondering where my own thick, blond mop could possibly have originated from.

Chapter 2

The first steps I can recall with any clarity, that could be classified as breaking away from that all enveloping parental protection, was my friendship with the Gossini children. The family were of Swiss-Italian extraction, and the oldest child was a girl named Irene. She was a number of years older than I was, and during at what times proved to be a rather volatile relationship with her three brothers, her natural nursing instincts and all round sensible competence were often required to treat the variety of bruises and other superficial damage that occurred as a result of confrontations, occasionally of the pugilistic kind. These however, did not include Michael, my natural sense of self preservation assured that. He was the oldest of the three boys, and possessed a right hook I was convinced could fell a bullock. Peter, the middle son, was within a few months of my own age, then came Damien, who was that little younger again.

They lived across the street from us in a large, weather beaten old bungalow, that possessed as far as I could estimate, enough bedrooms to accommodate a small army. I assessed it would have proved to be difficult to conquer in times of strife, because the house was perched high above the street, and any experienced soldier such as myself was well aware, they who hold the high ground, hold the advantage. Normal access to the property was by way of a conventional concrete path, but sometime in the past, Mr. Gossini had undertaken the back breaking task of forming the front bank into a series of stone terraces.

As far as the children in the street were concerned, their preferred option was to leap from one terrace to the next, that was until you reached the top where a major detour was required, because that's where you were confronted by Mr. Gossini's vegetable garden. This was without fail always carefully skirted, because one foot placed on this hallowed ground put one at risk of the direst of consequences, as I was duly and painfully destined to find out.

During the period I was associated with the family, circumstances were to determine that the old man's wisdom and all round common sense approach to life was to have a profound effect on me, equally as much as my own parents. After a period of slowly getting acquainted with and then finally being accepted as virtually a member of the family, I gradually started to look on him as something approaching that of a second father.

He was employed on the Auckland wharves, working as I'm sure as he did around their property, doing the work of three men. But with a routine that never varied, every Friday afternoon at the end of his shift, he would head for his favourite watering hole, where he would proceed to indulge himself as it were, and enter into the spirit of things with much enthusiasm. Later, towards the early evening he would appear at the end of our street, and as he moved forever onward with a decidedly unsteady gait, the air in the immediate vicinity would be punctuated by a series of English and Swiss profanities, that threatened to turn the air about six shades of blue.

However, in keeping with this Friday event, all of the children who were aware of his arrival, and that usually included all of us, because due to the strength of his voice, if you failed to acknowledge his presence, it meant you were domiciled somewhere in the neighbouring suburb. So as we gathered before him with expectation displayed on all faces, one by one he'd pick us up, give us a bear like hug accompanied by a kiss on the forehead, which I always felt was just as well, because I was convinced one on the lips would have left us in a severe state of intoxication for the next couple of hours, then he would proceed to pop into our mouths with varying degrees of accuracy, one of his seemingly never ending supply of snow white peppermints. Although all of the horrors associated with the Second World War were now fortunately in the past, many essentials still remained in short supply, and with confectionary being something we only dreamt about, acting on advice from our parents, asking where he obtained them from was discreetly avoided.

Solely because of the old man's extremely colourful language, my mother made a series of devious attempts that were designed to have me miss this Friday ritual. But no matter what distraction she tried to place in my path, without fail I always found a way around it, because as far as I was concerned, his language meant absolutely nothing, but as with the rest of the children, those peppermints were the highlight of my week.

But back to the Gossini boys; with my relationship with the two younger brothers ranging from the closest of friendship, to mortal arguments that on rare occasions ended in full on brawls.

With no brothers or sisters to advise me on the general ups and downs pertaining to life outside the general tranquillity that usually prevailed in our home, inclusion into the mayhem and constant turmoil that passed as normality within the Gossini household, rapidly made me familiar with the age old sayings, first come, first served, and the quick and the dead. The boys also tended to function around one simple enough equation. If in doubt, thump your opponent first, and if a parent insisted, apologise later. Initially, not having much of a clue as to how to defend myself against such seasoned warriors, I often finished up on the receiving end of a series of hidings of reasonably major proportions, which resulted in Irene's nursing skills occasionally being required. But like most young boys when faced with similar circumstances, I proved to be a fairly quick learner. Slowly but surely these battles started to lengthen considerably in their duration, with the outcome not proving to be the foregone conclusion it had been, not all that long before, much I started to notice, to the old man's considerable amusement.

During those years when he played such an important part in my development, my affection for the old man never wavered, even after being on the end of a thorough hiding from him. The boys, possibly due to their family's European origin, were soccer mad fanatics. This contrasted with the average New Zealand youngsters, who were raised with the understanding the only game fit for boys to play with a ball was rugby union, and any other wasn't worth a moment's consideration.

But for all of us in the street, and a few close by, soccer it was, and once sides had been chosen, our games were played with a dedication that would have

done justice to any World Cup final. On the particular momentous day in question, as always the game was being played with our usual intensity, and lo and behold, Michael was far from happy. It was an automatic acceptance amongst us that he always captained one side, and for him, losing was simply not an option. But somehow, by defying the laws of gravity and a few others not known to mankind, I had kicked the ball in the general direction of the sticks that past as goal posts, when suddenly it bounced awkwardly, and in doing so left the goalkeeper stranded, with the result, lo and behold, Michael's side was one down and facing the prospect of defeat.

In a moment of instant annoyance, he ran up and aimed a vicious kick at the ball, with the result it smashed into the side of the house, then rebounded into the middle of the old man's prized vegetable garden. On numerous occasions we'd all been made very aware of the punishment that would result if anyone dared to place one foot on this forbidden territory, so considering where the ball was reposing, Michael took in some ways what could be termed an obvious approach to the problem, as he rather delicately suggested, 'Alright Colbert, seeing as you scored the fucking goal, you can bloody well go in and get it.'

Now I must point out I wasn't totally stupid, being only too aware of the consequences if discovered trespassing on the old man's garden, but at the same time I was also very wary of Michael's punches, especially when he was in one of his moods. Anyway, surely at this time of the day the old man was still at work, and having scored the only goal of the day, I was convinced I could get away with anything. So stepping carefully forth and wending my way amongst an assortment of healthy looking vegetables, well, my mother kept on insisting they were healthy anyway, when I reached the offending piece of leather and bent over to retrieve it, I failed to notice some diabolical form of vegetation had managed to entwine itself around my left ankle. As a result, as I turned to head back to the safety of the lawn on which we played, I tripped and fell headlong, and in the process succeeding in totally demolishing all of the old man's remaining tomato plants.

For as far back as anyone in the street could recall, Mr. Gossini's tomatoes had won first prize at the annual agricultural show. It had long been acknowledged nobody could compete with him, but this year apparently things weren't looking good. Some dastardly blight had affected most of his plants, so the few that had escaped were being treasured as never before. It took some time to extract myself and as I glanced down, even I was forced to admit the damage I'd caused was indeed a depressing thing to behold.

As I continued to stare at this scene of wanton destruction, it appeared to grow worse by the second. Squashed tomatoes I decided, had a similarity with blood. A little seemed to go a very long way. But suddenly my state of shock was compounded, because the fury that registered in the old man's voice as he appeared around the side of the house, had to be experienced to be fully appreciated. It seemed to only take a couple of seconds for him to be standing beside me, and with his huge right hand grabbing a handful of the shirt and overalls I was wearing, he marched me straight out of the garden, then headed directly for the garden shed, and nothing could have made me more aware of what lay not all that far ahead.

On a couple of occasions in the past I'd stood and watched, totally fascinated, while one of the boys would dare to stand and argue with his father, until in the end, sure enough, the old man's patience would finally expire. Then the culprit was marched into the shed, a short lapse would then ensue as the victim was made to drop his pants and the old man removed his belt, then would follow a series of sharp cracks as leather descended and connected with a pair of bare buttocks.

With my inclusion in the Gossini household now complete, I was quite aware that under the boys' guidance, as far as mischief was concerned, my innocent days were well and truly behind me, and I was now just as capable of causing mayhem as they were. Accordingly, I had accepted that my own visit to the shed was probably a foregone conclusion. This situation was enhanced by one of the rules that existed in the street relating to the nine boys who lived there. All of the parents had mutually agreed that if one of their offspring created a problem, and his father was not available to deal with him, then the punishment deemed to be in keeping with the transgression would be administered by the father on whose property said transgression occurred. On most occasions this only resulted in a thorough tongue lashing, but on extremely rare occasions a leather belt was produced, and if this happened, the use of the strap was never questioned by the parents of the offender.

So assessing the current situation as I saw it, I was in no doubt my time to feel his belt around my backside had definitely arrived. After all, logic had to prevail. What crime could possibly be worse than trespassing on Mr. Gossini's hallowed vegetable garden, especially when one considered the number of times we'd been warned of the punishment that would eventuate if said violation ever occurred. Then to compound on that, I'd demolished his remaining prized tomatoes to a point where they now resembled tomato paste.

Now we'd arrived just outside the shed door, and with one last fleeting hope of the possibility of a last minute stay of execution, I swung my eyes around searching for Michael, wondering if he would do the decent thing and offer his father a belated explanation, but strangely, Michael was nowhere to be found. Now eased firmly into the shed, the door closing with ominous finality, and any last flicker of hope evaporated during the seconds it took the old man to remove his belt. Definitely no last minute reprieve, so best get it over and done with as quickly as possible. I slipped the straps of my overalls off my shoulders so they finished up round my ankles, but suddenly a thought, I was wearing underpants. Perhaps they could stay where they were so as I could retain some resemblance of dignity, but no, something told me that was also a lost cause, so down they came as well. Finally I bent well over as the old man positioned himself behind me, then boy, did that belt hurt.

When he was finished with me I straightened painfully up and with moist eyes watched as he proceeded to thread his belt back through the loops of his pants, finally doing up the buckle in front. He moved a few paces and sat down on a battered old saw horse, from where he looked sadly up at me. He beckoned for me to come to him, so after adjusting my clothing I did, then suddenly he reached out and eased me gently to him. He held me close, and with my face pressed into his vest, I caught the trace of aromas I would never relate to my

non-smoking, non-drinking father. There was the lingering fragrance from the Mexican cigars he occasionally smoked, but only on very special occasions, so he'd previously informed me, and the taint left by a variety of alcoholic beverages, resulting I was sure, from an increasingly unsteady hand as he settled well into his Friday afternoon drinking sessions. Finally he eased me back, and I could see the pain in his eyes as clearly as he could see the tears lingering in mine, and he spoke quietly as he said, 'Boy, make sure I never have to punish you again, because I love you as if you were one of my own'.

It was at that time I became aware our affection was mutual, because I realised I loved him as well, and as he stood up I moved forward and hugged him, because I felt it was the best way of conveying to him my apology for the damage I'd caused. As I turned to head for the door, I wiped my hand quickly across my eyes. After all, if Michael saw tears, he'd make sure I'd never be allowed to forget it. As I stepped back out into the sunlit yard, I found that mysteriously the boys had reappeared, and with the old man heading back towards his garden, presumably to see if anything was salvageable from the damage, they tactfully suggested I should slip back into the shed and drop my pants so as they could compare the effect of his belt on my bottom, but I graciously declined. Michael insisted that seeing as our soccer game had been abandoned, it should be declared a draw, but I smiled to myself, because I knew in my heart we'd beaten him one nil.

Sitting with my parents during our evening meal, I briefly thought about mentioning the old man had whacked me, but with my father there, most definitely decided against it. Long before I'd already learnt to accept that when it came to anything relating to your body, he became volatile to a point of being irrational, so even daring to mention that Mr. Gossini had strapped my bare bottom didn't seem to have all that much going for it. Never did tell my mother either, but was in no doubt the old man would tell her anyway. The only lasting effect my encounter with his leather belt had, was I decided it certainly paid at all times to do as an adult said, and if ever Michael kicked our ball into the vegetable garden again, he could go in and get the bloody thing himself. Sadly, for the first time in many years, Mr. Gossini failed to win first prize with his champion tomatoes at the annual agricultural show.

Chapter 3

So where Michael and the boys played their part in my visit to the shed, previously, they had played an even more major part in my introduction to schooling. Governed by the rules and regulations that were in vogue at that time, but mainly due to a rather ill-timed dose of chickenpox , it proved impossible for me to commence my schooling at the start of the year with the other children. This happened to coincide with the fortunately short lived utterings of some moron, no doubt safely entrenched in the jungle that passed as the overbearing bureaucracy of the education system at that time, but also apparently wielding some authority, who, determined to get his name in those bright lights as it were, decreed that all children starting school that year should not be accompanied by a parent on that first all-important day.

According to his highly valued assessment, this only led to a stressful situation for parent, pupil and teacher. What in turn was created by a situation that saw five year olds attempting to come to terms with this important time in their lives without the assurance only a parent could provide, one can only assume nobody thought to ask him.

But with my mother convinced such informative utterings must surely be the way to go, the responsibility of getting me to school on that first day was entrusted to the older Gossini boys, both of whom she apparently assessed as being knowledgeable veterans of school life. This I could understand with Michael, because he was those years older, but when it came to Peter, I decided she must have considered him a quick learner, because he'd only started a few months before me. So giving these couple of devils the responsibility of one still reasonably quiet and unworldly as yours truly, could be compared with letting a couple of tomcats who'd been starved for a week, have an entertaining time with the household canary.

But with my mother's mind made up, new clothes made and schoolbag and shoes purchased, that fateful day dawned, and it took no time at all for my enthusiasm, or more specifically, lack of it, for what was fast approaching, to match the colour of a slowly darkening sky. But with my mother adamant school it had to be, reluctantly I joined the boys who were waiting impatiently on our front porch, and wandered off miserably down the road with them. Around the corner and heading down the main street, with my parent and home now out of sight, I walked up to Michael and duly informed him my foremost ambition in life was to keep my mother deliriously happy, therefore, it was imperative I spent the rest of the day with her, and preferably most of the following week as well. However, apparently this suggestion failed to please him, because he grabbed a handful of my hair, and at the same time bent me over and kicked me rather forcibly, dead centre of my brand new pants, while he informed me with considerable venom, to fucking well get on with it, or he'd punch my bloody lights out. And taking that non too subtle hint, I chose to follow along obediently, because a quick assessment suggested, surely even school had to be

better than getting my lights punched out by Michael. Recently I'd taken careful note of the ease with which he'd despatched Peter when he'd been stupid enough to try to stand up to him, and seeing as Pete's fighting ability and mine were roughly on a par, logic was clearly indicating Michael's word was unquestionably law.

We wandered along rather aimlessly until we approached an area that was thickly covered in scrub and pungent smelling fennel, and it was there that my preschool education was set to begin. After casting rather furtive glances around, the boys suddenly scampered off down a track, the existence of which was virtually undetectable to the inexperienced eye. Suddenly finding myself standing alone on the pavement, and deciding company remained preferable, I needed no urging to take off after them.

Some little distance in, I found the two boys standing in front of an old log, then entering into what was obviously a well-established routine, they hauled up the legs of their pants and proceeded to relieve themselves, making sure that the log was as thoroughly sluiced as possible. I was forced to admit this had something going for it, because I was finding first day school nerves were starting to have a rather demanding effect on my bladder. However, my inexperienced eye had failed to note the boys were wearing rather full fitting trousers, probably allowing as far as Mrs. Gossini was concerned, plenty of room for future growth.

But this happened to be in direct contrast to my mother's approach, because she possessed an all-consuming loathing of sagging, floppy pants on young boys. Accordingly, she made for me pants that were reasonably snug and fitting, so previous to this, when I'd wanted to relieve myself, I'd simply slipped my pants down and aimed accordingly. And that was all very well, but now I was a schoolboy, and this new approved approach it simply had to be. And this was fine, except for the fact I remained blissfully unaware that using this new method could well have done with a practise dry run as it were.

With the boys insisting I delay my ablutions until they'd all finished, when I was finally granted permission to proceed, to say the call of nature had become rather acute was something of an understatement. Frantically hauling up my trouser leg in what appeared to be the approved fashion, I proceeded to wet myself very thoroughly down my left leg, much to the hilarity of what was a steadily increasing audience. Mid stream corrections proved to be only moderately successful, and when I finally did get my aim right, I found I was standing too close to the log, with the resulting splashback liberally dowsing my brand new shoes. Time was to prove this was the favourite relieving ground for a large number of boys in the neighbourhood, all of whom found it preferable to hang on to the contents of their bladders, so they arrived well equipped to indulge in this morning ritual of log wetting.

But with time moving steadily on, we continued what was for me anyway, a rather damp and uncomfortable journey to school, and as we strolled along, I was made familiar with the many pitfalls associated with compulsory education. Now finally there, and with those grey school walls looking more like a prison, Michael gripped me firmly by the back of the neck and propelled me over to what was the junior building. Up some stone steps, the treads showing some

wear due to the passage of many shoes, then down what appeared to be a never ending corridor, the walls of which were lined with what appeared to be hundreds of raincoats. Contrary to many others, my mother had deemed one not to be necessary, and she was proved right, we'd arrived with the sky quite clear. But logic said sooner or later it had to be, and seeing as finding your own at the end of the day would prove to be impossible, I assumed surely one must grab any one that was handy, and make do with that.

But now we came to a sudden halt outside the last door on the right on which Michael tapped lightly, eased open, then with a violent shove, propelled me headlong into the room, then slammed the door shut behind me. The first year teacher was enthroned behind her desk, and probably due to my rather undignified entry, proceeded to run her eyes over me with about as much enthusiasm as she would greet something unpleasant, that had suddenly appeared out of a dark, damp hole in the ground. Miss Dawson was built with the contours that would have done justice to a Sherman tank, and I immediately found her bulk decidedly off putting after the slimness of my mother. Although time proved her to be gentle and patient to a fault, in other words an excellent example of a first year teacher, on that first day she failed to endear herself to me, because she tended to speak with a deep growl, that seemed to originate from somewhere beneath her shoes.

She asked me my name, and I replied I was Mathew Colbert, and after checking some paperwork on her desk, she instructed me to stand with my back to the blackboard. I stood there for quite a few minutes until music blared with an intensity that made me wince. During the years spent at Three Kings Primary, every morning we were herded into our classrooms to the sound of Souza marches. In their original form, I found them bad enough, but distorted by the school's antiquated loud speaker system, they were nothing short of diabolical. My deep and utter loathing of Souza and his marches was developed during this time, and remains just as intense to this day.

Now the sound of many footsteps and the door flung open, as the children from her class filed in, and as they settled behind their desks about twenty five pairs of eyes riveted on me with total lack of recognition or enthusiasm. This seemed to encourage some movement by Miss Dawson, because after easing me over to a central point in the room, she placed her hands on my hips and lifted so I was standing on one of the front desks, and as I scanned that sea of unfamiliar faces, her voice boomed out across the classroom, 'Do any of you know this boy?' Not a movement, not a flicker as she continued, 'Come along now, surely one of you must know Mathew.'

That did bring forth some response from a heavy set, dark haired boy, who rather delicately poked out his tongue. And it seemed at that moment, when Wallace Thompson's and my eyes clashed, war was declared. So giving him my most innocent of smiles, and at the same time making sure my new teacher wasn't watching, I delicately raised the middle finger of my right hand, then delicately jabbed it upward in his direction. As it happened, I had no idea what this action indicated, because I simply copied it after watching Michael, but when checking with Pete a little later, he assured me it was something quite rude. And there was no doubt Wallace interpreted it accurately, because his eyes

popped like he couldn't believe what he was seeing, and going by his shocked reaction, I was left in no doubt I'd come out on top of that exchange the winner.

However, finally accepting she was wasting her time, Miss Dawson placed me back on the floor, then stabbed her finger in the general direction of one of the empty desks. So reluctantly I walked over and sat down, and so began a couple of years of lonely and tormented schooling. Not that I encountered any problems with this experience called education, in fact I thoroughly enjoyed learning, it was life out of the classroom I soon came to despise. It became apparent the school grounds were controlled by the two Thompson brothers, Wallace and Nigel, and they worked their bullying around a simple enough system. They made sure you were on your own, while they had the numbers. I wondered how Wallace managed to be as consistently unpleasant as he was, but decided it was more than likely due to the fact that I'd made that sign to him in class, and he'd never fully recovered from the shock of being upstaged by a new arrival. I also felt that even allowing for his tender years, he'd already managed to form a grudge against life in general. His repertoire for abuse and torment was extensive, and I became convinced he was serving an apprenticeship for the Mafia.

Very quickly, part of my daily routine included being escorted by some of the Thompson thugs with my arms held behind my back, to a bush covered area behind the dental clinic. With my arms held up so I was forced into a bent position with my head positioned close to the rear wall, Wallace would then proceed to drive his knee with considerable force into my buttocks, with the sudden forward movement he created being terminated as my head hit the wall. The drinking fountains offered further scope for their devious minds, and I'd come away from those sessions half drowned and resembling a water logged spaniel. Before long, I suggested to some of the boys' other victims, for us there also lay safety in numbers, but this only succeeded in making my situation worse. After threatening the others with a fate worse than death if they dared to try and comply, the brothers, along with their assortment of bully boys, allotted me even more of their time.

Frustrated, I turned to Michael for advice, being convinced he could walk on water. But any hope in that direction crashed into oblivion when I discovered he'd aligned himself with the brothers, working on the theory I presumed, that if you can't beat them, you may as well join them. So I was forced to survive by living with one eye forever over my shoulder, as I did my best to avoid their tedious attention, and above all else, I longed for my own group of friends. But as my tormentors swung their attention ever more in my direction, so the other children kept their distance, frightened it may increase their own risk of involvement.

Finally, wanting nothing more than a little peace and being left alone, I started to drift away to the more deserted corners of the school, and to compensate for the dissolution I felt because of Michael's defection to the enemy, I invented my own friend, and I called him Michael in way of some vague compensation. So finally there was just Michael and I as we played together in our own special world as we plotted a never ending series of interesting things to do together. But where the brothers may have successfully

disrupted life in the school grounds, there was no way they could stop the weekends being a time of fun and friendship. The two weeks of holidays between terms was a time of absolute bliss, and the six weeks at Christmas hovered on the borderline of Heaven.

Chapter 4

Another eighteen months past, with the Thompson brothers and their assortment of hangers on, doing their best to follow me around like a series of bad smells. But one day, due to a serious miscalculation on my part, which was caused by sleeping in and not having enough time to indulge in log wetting, I fronted up in the boys' toilet, and found Wallace standing not all that far away. As was our custom, he cast a scathing glance in my direction, which I duly returned with interest, but then he quite noticeably lowered his eyes to a level somewhere between my legs. As a result, a look of contemptible horror spread slowly across his face, then he turned and bolted for the door.

Once this devastating information he now possessed was shared with his brother, conformation of this disease carrying deformity spread like wildfire amongst the rest of the boys at the school. God forbid, Heaven save us all, Mathew Colbert had, shock upon horror, a foreskin. The reaction to this dreadful discovery left me totally bewildered, because I'd never taken the remotest interest in what other boys looked like, and hard as I tried, I couldn't recall what the Gossini's had displayed while taking their turns in front of the log. So for the next little while, when circumstances discreetly allowed, I took careful note of what was being displayed, and the shock hit home with terrible force. Heaven help me, the Thompson boys were right, nobody looked like I did.

Briefly I considered suicide, but at my tender age that didn't seem like much of a sensible option, but never the less, common sense said this dreadful predicament I was in, had to be remedied with all speed possible. Arriving home from school, I charged in through the back door breathing fire and fury, well, I mean, as much fire and fury as I felt I could safely get away with anyway, and it was my mother of course, who was in the direct firing line,

'Mum, why have I got this skin on the end of my penis when the rest of the boys haven't?'

For a moment, she seemed a little lost for words, and as far as I was concerned, that slight delay spelt one thing, trouble, because it suggested she was immediately on the defensive, 'Well Mathew,' she replied, 'it simply means they've been circumcised and you haven't.'

'Why not?' I mean why waste words over a situation as urgent and serious as this.

'Well, your father and I had discussed this and decided we didn't think it was necessary.'

'That's just great, you didn't think it was necessary. Well how about coming to school and hear what the other boys are saying to me. They're treating me like I'm some diseased freak. I want it done Mum, and what's more, I want it done real quick.'

She was a mother, I guess she had to try and explain the situation and talk me around somehow. 'It's just not that simple Mathew. Boys are normally

circumcised immediately after birth. For a boy to be circumcised at your age, could prove to be very painful.'

'I don't care, I want it done, already I'm sick and tired of being different.'

It's so much easier to appear brave when you're desperate, but I knew what was coming.

'You'll just have to leave it with me Mathew. I'll have to discuss it again with your father.'

Fat lot of good that was going to do. She knew as well as I, discussing anything to do with your body, especially those sorts of bits, was asking for big trouble. So my situation at school went from bad to worse, with my uncircumcised penis giving the Thompson brothers even more fuel for their never ending torment. But what made the matter even worse was that many of the other boys joined in as well. Some weeks past, with the constant derision aimed in my uncircumcised direction seeming to increase by the day. But on the morning of that fateful day as I prepared to leave for school, my mother pressed a coin in my hand,

'This is money for your fare, we're having tea with the Donaldsons, and don't be tempted to spend it on something you shouldn't, then walk there. I'll know by the time you arrive, and if you're late, when we're back home you'll feel the strap around your bottom.'

Over the past few years, our two families had become quite friendly. Bill Donaldson ran one of the departments in the factory, and my father the other. Bill was as tough as nails, and when it came to dirty play during those midday soccer matches, according to my father, you could guarantee Bill was in the thick of it. His wife however, was just the opposite, being a fussy, dithering little hygiene and all round health freak. The oldest of the two boys took after his mother, the younger boy, Tyrone, took after his father, because he'd have a go at anything. During my previous visit, he and I had gone over the fence and cleaned out their neighbour's peach tree. Tyrone was made from the same mould as the Gossinis, and it was he who made my enforced visits to the Donaldson's something like bearable. But having tea with them, now this was something else entirely.

But as it was. Mrs. Donaldson excelled herself, then followed another surprise, apparently I was sleeping there as well. The period between the meal and bedtime passed surprisingly quickly, and the offer of a hot chocolate drink before bedding down was readily accepted. A bed had been made up on their enclosed front veranda, and as I settled down the noise from the traffic, something I wasn't used to after living at the end of our own quiet street, had me convinced sleep would prove to be an impossibility. Then I promptly woke up the following morning in my own familiar bed. But no matter, it was Saturday, which meant two days away from those Thompson pests, replaced by fun with the Gossini boys instead. So out of bed, dressed and ready for whatever fun or mischief we could devise, but as I glided past my parent's bedroom door, my mother called me back, the concern in her voice quite palpable, ' Mathew, for Heaven's sake, where on earth are you going?'

'Out to play of course.'

'Good grief,' she replied, 'surely not, I mean aren't you er, sore somewhere?'

This wasn't looking good, because there was a similarity to when she tried to stop me meeting the old man on Fridays as I replied, ' No mum, I'm not sore anywhere. Why on earth should I be?'

'Well you can't go out, you haven't had your breakfast.'

'So what, I'll have some a bit later.'

It was then my father joined in, talking ever so softly to my mother, but I heard what he said,

'Look, if the kid says he's alright, don't push it, just let him go.'

Later that day, a quick trip to the toilet necessary. Although I'd long since had this pull up your trouser leg bit perfected, bloody hell, ouch, no use kidding myself, my mother was right, I did have a sore spot after all, and no wonder, because my appendage was bandaged with a slight bit of blood showing. Hell, must have fallen out of that strange bed last night. Oh well, these things happen, and couldn't understand how I'd missed it when I got out of bed, but so what, it's not too much of a problem, so best just get on with it.

Monday and back at school, once again lined up beside a couple of boys, doing what nature insisted was necessary. And as he appeared my eyes widened because I couldn't believe what I was seeing. There he was, bandage free, and as smooth and streamlined as any young boy could ever expect to be. So with the acceptance only extreme youth can provide, how this magical transformation had come about I couldn't have cared less. All that mattered was the Thompson brothers and their insults in this area were a thing of the past. At that time, I never raised the question relating to the demise of my foreskin with my parents. Considering my father's attitude over such matters, I figured it paid not to rock the boat as it were.

Many years later my mother laughed over what had occurred during that evening at the Donaldson's. After we'd passed out due to our drug laced chocolate drinks, the three of us boys were carried out, naked as the day we were born, and placed in a row on a clean white sheet that had been spread over the dining table. From there, the doctor who'd agree to perform the procedures, moved down one by one and did the necessary. Apparently the Donaldson boys had been subjected to similar derision at their school as I'd been experiencing. Never did think to ask if the doctor had agreed to a reduced rate.

But now, absolute ecstasy, lying before me and thousands of others, six weeks of Christmas holiday bliss, and for the Colbert family, three weeks of those to be spent at a beach called Piha. Situated on the West Coast, yet within reasonable travelling time from the city, with its black iron sand, famous Lion Rock, and at times dangerous and volatile surf, our holiday promised hours of unlimited youthful enjoyment. Even the weather cooperated, as I climbed over the rocks, investigating the variety of marine life that lived in the pools created by those pounding waves, or played for hours on that black sand under the temperate, and as it turned out, abundant summer sun. And Piha still enjoys a special place in my memory, because it was there I acquired my lifelong love of swimming.

However, where that boiling surf suited my father and his surf board, it hardly provided the ideal place to introduce a child to the wonders of the world of water, so my mother would take me back beyond the sand dunes, to the lake like qualities of the large lagoons that formed there. Being determined I was going to learn to swim, because she bitterly regretted never having done so herself, she did her best to assist by providing constant encouragement. Like all learners I floundered for a while, but any coaching I received was unwittingly provided by the numerous Maori children who lived in the area, with the majority being able to swim like proverbial fish, so aided by a combination of childhood competitiveness, and the fact it proved to be one area where I was something of a natural, suddenly I took off and never looked back.

So they were days of sun, sand and salt water, but like all holidays, they finally had to end. As we moved out of our rented accommodation, two young men were waiting, ready to move in. We were to discover later, much to my mother's absolute horror, that during the course of an argument, one of these gentlemen managed to settle the issue by inserting a knife up to the hilt in the chest of the other. In a vain attempt to dispose of the evidence, he apparently placed the victim's body on the kitchen table, then after splashing around a considerable amount of an inflammable liquid, set up an elaborate, delayed ignition system, then took off with great haste for the wide, blue wonder. The resulting inferno levelled the cabin and everything in it. So our holidays at Piha were somewhat abruptly terminated, but I drew some consolation from the fact I considered myself quite famous for having been the last person not involved in this unfortunate incident, to have eaten a meal off that infamous table. The perpetrator of this dastardly deed, was captured some months later at the other end of the country.

Chapter 5

So our holiday home ended up in ignominious ashes, and to compound on my disappointment, it seemed that in no time I was back walking down the road of the tormented with the Gossini's, past Gordon's Quarry in whose bushes the fallen log rested, and through the gates into the school grounds. As I strolled past the dental clinic, I wondered how it was the dental nurse always failed to investigate the torture that went on behind her building, feeling certain the thump of my head hitting the wall must surely be audible from inside. But little did I know, fate was in the process of determining my days of torment at the hands of the Thompson brothers were fast drawing to a close.

I had found the school's sandpit an ideal place to play in. With mainly open ground around it, quick evasive action on my part meant any attempt at surprise attacks by the brothers could usually be avoided. But inevitably, there came that day when I made the mistake of becoming just a little too engrossed, and I was only aware of their stealthy arrival when my arms were grabbed from behind and forced painfully up my back. With this having the effect of forcing my head well down, I cursed myself for not being more vigilant, and at the same time assumed my carelessness would result in yet another session behind the clinic. But suddenly something very different, as Wallace picked up a handful of sand and ground it into my face.

My eyes were wide open and took the full brunt of the abrasive material, and as a result I let out a shriek of terror as I wrenched at my arms, now desperate to try and defend myself. But with my assailants realising this time they'd probably gone too far, they released me and took off leaving me kneeling where I was, unable to see, and close to a point of panic. Somewhat ironically, my saviour arrived in the form of, would you believe it, the dental nurse, she who never investigated what went on behind her clinic. But in some ways I had to accept it possibly wasn't all that surprising. There was no doubt most of us were convinced she spent an excessive amount of her time patrolling the school grounds, forever on the lookout for caries infected teeth. This time however, apparently quickly assessing she had something in the way of a major problem to deal with, she rushed over and skidded to a halt beside my inert form as she garbled, 'Mathew, what's the matter child, why are you covering your eyes with your hands like that?'

As I forced myself to remove my hands and look up at her, she let out a horrified scream, then after taking a deep breath, screamed yet again, this time requesting urgent assistance. Fortunately it turned out another of the staff was within screaming distance, and they led me back to the clinic where they attempted to wash my eyes out, but unfortunately with little success. Next stop proved to be a local doctor, who took one look and insisted I be taken to the Auckland Hospital's eye clinic, where, after a couple of hours, they were finally declared free of sand.

The recuporatory powers of a good night's sleep worked wonders, and the next morning, apart from some minor discomfort, I declared them virtually as good as new. The suggestion by my mother that a day at home wouldn't go astray was immediately brushed aside, and I set off for school with blood back in my eyes, but this time it had nothing to do with sand, it was due solely to cold, blue, calculated fury. On arrival I started roaming the school grounds, searching for just one person. I found him talking with a couple of his thugs, so I moved silently up behind him and quietly called his name, and as he turned I punched him just as hard as I could swing my fist, with the result I hit him flush in the mouth. The force behind the punch was quite considerable, but then again I'd been trained by experts. Peter was taking after his older brother, and I'd long since learnt you had to hit him with the force of a sledge hammer for him to take the hint.

But Wallace, now eager to get out of harm's way, tripped and fell heavily as he attempted to make a tactical exit, so I waited until he was half way up but still off balance, then slugged him one again. As the punch connected, I felt a warm sensation and automatically glancing down, I found blood flowing through my fingers. Using this brief distraction, Wallace leapt to his feet and bolted. I checked to see where the blood was originating from, and found I had quite a deep cut across my knuckle, but no time to be bothered worrying about that. The sound of the bell was signalling time for morning assembly, and that meant yet again striding into class to the sound of Souza and another of his bloody awful marches.

Once in class, my knuckle proceeded to bleed quite profusely, and when noticed I was instructed to go down to the main building and get it attended to. The school secretary acted as nurse and general what have you, and asked how I'd acquired such a cut. Glancing up with innocent eyes, I informed her it was a result of punching Wallace Thompson in the mouth. After a few seconds she walked away then reappeared with a large bowl which she instructed me to hold my hand over while she carefully emptied half a bottle of iodine over it. I came to the conclusion she felt anything that had originated from Wallace's mouth, could prove to be equally as poisonous as his nature. The following day I expected to be on the receiving end of violent retaliation, but it was not to be. Previous to the strident complaint about my eyes the dental nurse had registered with the headmaster, numerous complaints had been lodged by irate parents about the bruises on their offspring's heads and buttocks along with the saturated state of their clothing, and the following day Wallace was expelled. On being informed of their son's demise at the school, his parents immediately withdrew Nigel as well. In the unanimous decision of pupils, parents and teachers, it was the declared the best thing that had happened since the school was opened eighteen years previous. But for many others and myself, it was as if a dark cloud had finally been blown away, and out of the misery created by bullying emerged happy, fun filled days, and life at school became what it should be for all children, relaxed, enjoyable fun.

It seems life often decides that major changes come in pairs. The lease on our home was close to expiring, and a few days after my fight with Wallace, our landlord informed my father he was intending to sell the property, so he was

sorry, but very shortly we would have to be gone. On being informed of the news I went and sat on my bed and did my best to come to terms with the fact that before too long I wouldn't be able to slip across the street and up those stone terraces to the Gossini's, where I could always rely on a backup source of food being available.

Mrs. Gossini was a strange little woman, and any association with her had been extremely restricted, due to the fact she barely spoke one word of English. Also, at that time of my life she undoubtedly held the distinction of being the ugliest woman I had ever encountered. With the three boys being relatively handsome young lads, and Irene qualifying as being barely short of downright gorgeous, it was obvious the children's looks had arrived courtesy of their father's side of the family. My fondest memory of Mrs. Gossini consisted of peering down a long, dark, timber lined passage, which terminated in the centre of her kitchen, from where this strange little woman produced what seemed like a never ending supply of gastronomical delights, that in my opinion, had to be eaten to be fully appreciated.

But compounding on my despair that without access to these culinary masterpieces, I'd finish up starving, there was also the question of keeping a roof over our heads. An acute housing shortage was prevalent, and it was possibly fortunate only my parents were aware of how desperate our accommodation situation had suddenly become. But due to an unexplained flash of inspiration, some months previous my father had, on the spur of the moment, taken the time to fill in an application for our family to eligible for what was known in those days as a State Advance home, which were at that time, being built by the Savage Government in their hundreds, first, as a means to help lift the country out of the lingering effects of the great depression, and second, to help alleviate the misery being created by the dreadful lack of accommodation throughout the country.

And luck proved to be on our side. Only a short time after hearing the disturbing news an official letter arrived confirming our application had been successful, and we'd been allocated a home not all that far away from where we were currently residing. So life continued blissfully on, and I played with the other children in the street as if nothing was changing. But each night as I lay my head on my pillow, I offered a little prayer that our new home was in reasonable riding distance of Mrs. Gossini's magnificent pastries.

But inevitably, the day of our departure arrived, and to my parent's relief it dawned fine and clear. So after attempting to help where I could, and getting in the way more often than I should, my mother suggested perhaps the time had arrived to say my goodbyes around the street. So I trudged out of our house and made my first stop at the Mc. Kenzie's, our next door neighbours. The family had played an equally important part in my life since we'd lived in the street as the Gossini's. As our friendship with the family had strengthened, a routine had gradually been established. On the rare occasions when my parents had to spend time away, usually due to my father's tennis social events, which usually necessitated my mother's participation as well, it had been agreed I'd stay with the family, where similar to the Gossini's, I'd long been included as being virtually one of the family anyway.

Taking into consideration this convenient and pleasant arrangement, the only advantage I could see from moving away, was that it would put some distance between myself and that dreadfully repulsive concoction Mrs. Mc. Kenzie held so much faith in. There were also three boys in the family, but that was where any comparison ended. In contrast to the Gossini's healthy young specimens, the Mc. Kenzie brothers tended to be slight, almost frail youngsters, and there seemed to be rarely a time when one of them wasn't suffering some sort of usually mild ailment. So when I started to stay overnight with them, much to my absolute horror, I found myself included in what was a well established evening ritual. A shower was compulsory before bed, but after stepping out and drying ourselves, one after the other we were expected to stand straight, hands clasped behind our backs and with heads tilted well back and mouths wide open, while Mrs. Mc. Kenzie poured down our throats a large spoonful of this revolting abomination. She swore it could cure anything, a comment that left me totally unimpressed, because I couldn't recall suffering from anything that required curing anyway. Much later I identified the taste as that of molasses, which still rates as far as I'm concerned, on the same lowly level as Souza.

So after my goodbyes to the Mc. Kenzie's, I drifted on slowly down the street, occasionally offering my apologies for any mischief I'd been responsible for, that had ended in one of those severe tongue lashings. But finally I decided the time I dreaded most could be avoided no longer, so I bounded up the terraces until I was standing in front of that weathered old bungalow, that was perched high above the street. My goodbyes to Mrs. Gossini went quickly, because although I thanked her profusely for having fed me, I knew she couldn't understand a word I said. The boys and their sister took somewhat longer, but after suffering their firm handshakes and back patting, along with some carefully chosen insults, I slipped back outside and started searching for the old man.

Perhaps in some ways it was appropriate I found him standing beside his vegetable garden, hands clasped on the top of his hoe, with his chin resting on them, and as I moved across and stood in front of him, his eyes followed me every step of the way, As I looked up, I thought of all the things I wanted to say, which I'd carefully practised over the last few nights before I fell asleep. I wanted to thank him for patiently explaining why so many plants in his garden grew as they did. For the sound advice he'd offered on how to handle my father when he was in one of his moods. I wanted to thank him for that once a week peppermint, which had meant so much, and probably as much as anything, I wanted to thank him for telling me that Pete was a sucker for a well timed left hook. But as I stood there, I couldn't get those words past the lump that for some strange reason, had formed in my throat.

For a few moments we stood there looking at each other, then suddenly he dropped his hoe and bent down and picked me up and held me close to his chest. With my face pressed to his vest, I realised those smells were still there, like those cigars he smoked, but only on special occasions, and those from the variety of liquors he'd spilt during those Friday night drinking sessions, so giving up trying to speak, I wrapped my arms around his neck and cried on his shoulder instead. His whispered gently in my ear, saying all the right things that

such an occasion calls for, then he put me down and we walked together across the lawn where I'd played so many games of soccer with his sons, especially that one where he ended up strapping my bum. Michael may have kidded himself it had ended in a draw, but I knew only too well, we'd beaten him one nil. Finally we arrived at the top of the path that led down to the street, then he placed his hands on my shoulders, then looked me straight in the eyes as he said, 'Boy, promise you'll always behave and grow up straight and strong, because I have always cared for you, just as if you were one of my own, you understand what I'm saying?' So I assured him I'd do my best, even allowing for the looming reduction in my food supply, but I didn't go overboard with that behave bit, because after the training I'd received from his sons, I figured there was only so much one could expect from an expertly indoctrinated eight year old kid. Then with one last special hug, I took off down the path and across the street.

Less than an hour later the removal truck was packed and now moving slowly down the street, with my having been granted the honour of sitting in the cab with the driver, while my parents followed in our car. I looked across and there the old man was, like some solid, indestructible old tree stump, standing out clearly against the backdrop of a crystal clear blue morning sky. I leant across and waved, and deliberately he slowly waved back, then we turned the corner where I'd run to meet him to get my peppermints, and in that instant he was gone. So, one stage of my life complete, another, similar in some ways, appallingly different in another, about to start.

Slowly but surely the excitement of moving into a brand new house managed to dull the pain of those goodbyes. Our allotted home proved to be a neat, brick and tile structure, with two bedrooms facing the street, and a large open veranda at the rear, at one end of which was another small room, that in dire circumstances my mother insisted could act as a third bedroom, but in reality, finished up as her sewing room, from where she continued to make for me those trim fitting shorts. The rest of the rooms were set out in predictable but sensible order, and my parents agreed our new abode passed all our requirements with flying colours.

From my eight year old point of view, I found this change that had occurred in my life was assisted by the fact that some small but important things don't change at all. One of those was the clock that had reposed on my bedroom cabinet for as long as I could recall. It was special, because it possessed a tick that was louder than any clock I'd ever heard, and why this was so was something I never found out for sure. So having given this mystery some detailed thought, I decided it was either the German mechanism it used, or it was something to do with the metal body in which it was housed. But over the years, on the rare occasions when I woke during the night, there it would be, ticking away, the sound so loud it seemed to reverberate off the walls.

So this time of change moved steadily on. New home, new school, new friends and neighbours. To our left, the Levers, with the Burnsides beside them. To our right, the Williamson family, and right again the Bradford's, all of whom where to play varying roles in this saga of my life. And my concern as to who would replace my previous friends lasted all of two days. The suburb in which we were now domiciled consisted of street after street of brand new Government

built houses, and as far as our own street was concerned, every day saw at least another six arrivals, and this trend continued until all the homes were occupied.

Included in this local population explosion were many children, with the only minor problem in that direction appearing in the form of one Arnold Burnside. This ten year old consisted of a pair of pale blue eyes, a head of thin, sandy coloured hair, that hung in every direction but where it was meant to, shirts that needed to be two sizes larger around the waist, so as to disguise the bulge that existed there, and a very, very big mouth. Arnold was an expert on all subjects, and as far as all the other children were concerned, we found his loud mouth rather tedious. Fortunately, compensation arrived in the form of Colin Bradford. Within a couple of months of the same age, and of somewhat similar build and the same coloured hair, our friendship was virtually instantaneous. In no time at all we were rarely seen apart, and it didn't take long for the new arrivals to assume we were brothers, something we found highly amusing, and which leant itself to a certain amount of devilish behaviour on our part. My apprenticeship under the Gossinis soon saw to that.

With a number of families having moved into the street before us, it meant their children had investigated the various attractions our new suburb offered, but as far as Colin and I were concerned, heading the list was the crystal clear waters of the local council swimming pool. And it was there I found one major difference between my new friend and myself, and that was he swum with the buoyancy that related to that of an extremely large rock. This situation I decided, must be rectified with all speed possible, so using my formidable persuasive powers, I convinced his mother nobody could teach her oldest son to swim better than I. Seeing as it was a council pool, she assumed there must be adequate supervision at all times, so in her innocence, allowed our visits to continue, and in doing so remained blissfully unaware that anything relating to supervision was totally non-existent. Accordingly, some of the disputes that inevitably erupted, were settled in the form of full on fist fights, all of which were settled, one way or the other, in a small area behind the filtration building.

The competence I'd acquired in this direction, due entirely to my association with the Gossinis, had definitely been noted. However, I was left wondering about Colin's chances of survival in this gladiatorial cesspit, but no problem, because it quickly became apparent he knew how to look after himself alright. And as far as his swimming lessons were concerned, he proved to be a quick learner, and while they progressed I managed to acquire a sun tan to rival those I'd acquired at Piha. And it must have been pretty good, because my mother claimed the only way she could pick me out amongst the Maori boys I played with, was by my mop of blond hair.

As the summer drifted pleasantly on, at the pool I started to move in a slightly elite circle. I'd joined the swimming club, and before too long was acknowledged as the leading swimmer in my age group. Accordingly, the coach took me firmly under his control, and as the training he insisted on started to enhance the broad set of shoulders I'd inherited from my father, gradually I started to become aware that my improvement , both in the water and physically, was starting to attract the occasional admiring glance from some of the younger female patrons. This was something that made me slightly uneasy, because it

was a situation I was far from familiar with. But my tutor in this direction appeared in the form of a new arrival in the country.

Arnie van de Meure was a recent addition from South Africa, and the moment our eyes clashed, our relationship, or to be more explicit, lack of it, immediately headed in the same direction as I'd experienced with the Thompson brothers, in other words, instant loathing. Within days he'd picked a fight which did nothing more than cause a few minor bruises, and set in stone our mutual dislike for each other. I accepted he was well built, and could probably be classed by those with poor eyesight as being relatively good looking, but as far as I was concerned, I found him arrogant and generally much too full of himself. And to rub salt into an already open wound, I simply couldn't tolerate his guttural South African accent. But there was one area where I couldn't compete with Arnie. He could wrap those female hearts around his little finger in a matter of minutes.

But as it happened, Arnie's appearance managed to coincide with the arrival of the new, daringly brief style of boys swimwear, and as he stepped forth, displaying this revealing wonder garment, it seemed the world the girls at the pool lived in, momentarily stood still, and the only sound emitting from the pool enclosure, was that of numerous throbbing female hearts. But as I stood back while the boy strutted up and down, logic said surely the less you were wearing meant the quicker you could move through the water, and for that reason alone, decided I couldn't get my hands on a pair quick enough.

Rushing home, and after giving my mother a detailed description, I begged her to purchase me a pair. So after giving my urgent request careful parental consideration, the following day she took me into the city and excelled herself by choosing a pair, and much to my delight, allowed me to select another. Later she told me she'd worked on the theory that revealing though they may be, she didn't have all that much to worry about, because I wasn't blessed with all that much to reveal anyway.

But secretly I knew her comment was open to question. Due to some sleight of hand on my part, she never did get a good look at the pair I'd chosen, and I'd noticed the small amount of material that existed between thigh and waist, had been reduced close to extinction, because a series of diamond shaped sections had been cut out, thereby leaving what was left of the garment covering a boy's essentials in the barest possible way that decency would allow. So when I finally plucked up the courage to step forth wearing this ultra brief version, going by the attention my appearance created, I knew I'd finally managed to upstage that South African upstart as no one around our age had ever managed before.

Chapter 6

That summer proved to be something of a milestone for our family. My father finally decided to act on what he'd been contemplating for some time, that being leaving the financial security his well paid position provided, and starting his own business. It seemed almost overnight, twelve hour working days and seven day working weeks became the normal thing, as he poured his intense dedication into his business, being determined above all else to ensure its success, and what turned out to be many years of decided prosperity.

The trivial penalty I paid for his working those excessive hours, was he became even more stressful to be around, with the result he was slightly more inclined to settle any minor differences we had with a swift clip around the ear. Maybe his conscience pricked him, I was never to find out, but a few days after our most recent minor disagreement, I walked into my bedroom, letting off a bit of steam as usual, when I noticed an envelope on my pillow. On opening it, I found it contained, much to my enthusiastic delight, a season ticket to the pool. As I stood in my bedroom, staring at that ticket in my hand, I was convinced it was even better than having all my birthdays arrive at once. So after homework and other trivial items such as mowing the lawns and other maintenance around the house had been completed to my mother's satisfaction, I virtually lived in those crystal clear waters, conveniently leaving my mother to deal with my father's variety of moods at home, thoughtful son that I was.

But as always, those summer months seemed to fly past, and finally the closing of the pool arrived as almost welcome relief from those frigid, late autumn waters, and this meant the time of the year had arrived when life had to evolve more closely around the local neighbourhood. I was wandering a bit aimlessly around our backyard, a bit fed up because of my best mate's unavailability. It was a typical Autumn day, a clear sky, a cool, gentle breeze, absolutely nothing to warn me of the catastrophe that lay waiting, not all that far ahead.

It was a Saturday, and with my chores complete, the day was mine to fill in as I pleased, then I happened to glance across to the Burnside's, whose property was two doors further down the street. Two boys were in their backyard, and they appeared to be fighting, so with my interest activated, I walked over to our fence, and from the closer scrutiny this offered, was able to confirm it was the Stoddard twins. This suggested nothing really had changed.

They lived right up the far end of our street, so I hadn't played with them all that much, but during the occasions when I had, I'd become convinced the brothers fought so much, I figured there was a good chance they'd been born fighting. But as I continued to stand at the fence and watch, I realised this time there was a difference, because a more accurate description would be sparring, and standing alongside and instructing was Albie Burnside.

Arnold's father was a slightly built, gently spoken and rather nondescript man, with darting grey eyes and movements to match. Time was to prove that

the seemingly benign personality that he displayed on the surface, expertly disguised the true temperament that thrived just underneath. Not long after we first met, Arnold had boldly informed me that his father, in his younger years, had been an amateur National Lightweight boxing champion, and at the time I'd brushed his comment aside, convinced it was yet another example of Arnold's vivid imagination and determination at all costs to impress.

Sensing my disbelief, a couple of days later he'd risked his father's annoyance by spiriting me inside where I was able to view the array of trophies that stood discreetly out of sight in a cabinet in their study. The display was so intensive, it effectively brushed any dubiousness on my part aside, leaving me in no doubt of Albie's ability with his fists. However, this acquired knowledge of Albie's past left me more mystified than ever as to how he'd managed to marry a woman so completely opposite in all ways to himself, conveniently forgetting something similar existed as far as my own parents were concerned, but with the personalities between husband and wife reversed.

Compared to Albie's slight frame and quietness, Enid was a large, heavily set woman, with a voice that could shatter windows at twenty paces. And compared to her husband's speed of foot, she moved with a ponderous, determined gait, that suggested woe betide any unfortunate who dared to cross her path as she wended her way through life. From the day she arrived, it was obvious she intended to rule the street, and after barely surviving a couple of confrontations with her, I'd been left in no doubt which of his parent's personalities Arnold had been blessed with. As far as my clashes with his mother were concerned, my upbringing had taught me the child always gives way to the adult, but as far as the other families in the street were concerned, many hushed words of sympathy were uttered behind Albie's back.

But as I draped myself over the fence and watched as the sparring session continued, it was obvious Albie was in his element, so with my interest now fully activated, I turned and took off down the side of our house, across the front lawns and around to the rear of the Burnside's. A make shift boxing ring had been rather crudely erected, and as I settled down on the grass and watched, it became apparent this tuition had been going on quite some time, while I'd been almost permanently domiciled at the pool. During the next hour, a steady stream of boys arrived from around the neighbourhood, and after being carefully paired off, they'd enter the ring for their lesson. I became so engrossed, I failed to notice that Arnold had come and settled down behind me, and when he spoke, he did so with his head close to mine,

'Well, what do you make of all of this Colbert?'

His question caught me slightly unaware, but not for long as I carefully replied, 'What do I make of it Arnold? Well from what I can see, there's no doubt your father's been putting in quite a bit of time with these kids, because some of them look like they can handle themselves pretty well as far as I can see.'

I should have been wary, his voice was soft and flowing like molten honey.

'And tell me, just how good do you think you are Colbert?'

Strange he should ask, I mean how good was I? Let's face it, if the truth be known, I considered myself more than just a little competent when it came to

this boxing thing. After all, that time I slugged Wallace was worth a mention, then there were those left hooks I'd flattened Pete with, well alright, I admit, hardly flattened, but thanks to his father, at least I'd caught him with a couple of beauties. So yes, now you come to mention it Arnold, I'm pretty confident I can find my way around a ring. His next question was so casual, honey was almost dripping on the grass.

'Do you think you'd be prepared to get in the ring and go a few rounds with me Colbert?'

Now would you believe it, there he goes again. He must have gone to university to have reached that degree of optimism. Sure, I was aware he was those couple of years older, and he definitely weighed more than I did, that bulge around his middle guaranteed that. But the fact was he couldn't jog between the lampposts in our street without running out of breath, so if the bout managed to last a full three rounds, it would only be because I'd held him up for the last one and a half.

And my thoughts flicked back to the humiliation I'd suffered at his hands up in Parran's Bush. Twelve of us, with my having been chosen on the side opposing his. Deviously tricked into being taken prisoner, made to walk for ages deep into the bush with my hands tied behind my back, while those on his side walked along making crude jokes at my expense. Finally tied to a small tree, and what happened after that was something I preferred not to think about. And what had made my humiliation all the worse, was that Colin had been chosen on his side. Straight after I'd been released, the boys had decided to head back, satisfied with the fun they'd had at my expense, leaving me sulking well behind.

Now at our house and straight into my bedroom, convinced I could never look any of them in the eyes again. My decision was made, I'd become a hermit, and as far as future food was concerned, my mother could pass it through a hole I'd cut in the centre panel of my door. But a short time later she'd called out, time to wash my hands, our evening meal was on the table. The tantalizing smell of a roast dinner had wafted into my room, just about my favourite, and after a few seconds of thought I'd decided it best I leave becoming a hermit until tomorrow, or on the other hand, maybe it would be sensible to leave it until sometime next week.

I'd just finished my meal when Colin appeared, football under his arm, ready as usual for our evening routine, kicking his ball to each other over the power lines in the street. Location changes meant soccer was forgotten, rugby was in. It seemed things were back to normal, at least as far as he was concerned anyway. So now here was Arnold in all his innocence, offering me a golden opportunity to get even. I thought about it for all of a split second, then I couldn't get those gloves on quick enough. We climbed into the ring, butter boxes acting as stools in the opposing corners. I held up my hands as one of the twins laced up my gloves. Had no idea which one it was because they were so identical, I still couldn't pick them apart.

The lacing complete, leaving the gloves feeling slightly cumbersome and awkward. No Albie, he'd been called inside, so one of the older boys had appointed himself referee. An old paint tin, hit with a lump of metal acted as a bell, both of which the twins had absconded with from their father's workshop.

The improvised bell rang, well sought of rang, so I moved out of my corner and looked up to find Arnold bearing down on me like some rampant gorilla. A punch smashed through my hastily prepared guard, even though I'd copied it directly from Joe Louis. It terminated with considerable force somewhere in the region of my left cheek and I staggered back, only to find myself trapped in my corner. Punches flooded in from every direction, including some I'd never known existed. I was desperate, I had to do something, so I tried swinging one of Mr. Gossini's lefts. It missed by the proverbial country mile, so Arnold retaliated with a right that landed flush on my right ear, and immediately it started ringing.

By weaving and ducking, just like Peter Gossini had taught me, somehow I managed to extract myself from the slaughter taking place in the corner. But it didn't change things all that much, because Arnold simply chased me around the ring, throwing every punch in the boxing manual at me, which I valiantly attempted to avoid with notable lack of success. That unpleasant, dull sound of metal on metal finally heralded the end of the round. I decided someone should check on the time keeper. The rounds were supposed to last for three minutes, I was sure that one lasted more than ten. As I collapsed on my butterbox, I realised someone had materialized beside me. One of the twins had appointed himself my second. He bent down, offering what I presumed were urgent words of advice, but it was no use, because my ear was ringing so loudly, I couldn't hear a word he was saying.

I was certain no more than thirty seconds past before some sadist hit the tin again. I just managed to hear that, then immediately wished I hadn't. As I dragged myself to my feet, the butterbox was immediately whisked away, with what appeared to me to be indecent haste. Once again Arnold was lumbering towards me, so I decided to surprise him and actually throw a punch somewhere in his general direction. A right cross that as usual missed, and a slight loss of balance left me unable to avoid his counter. A brutal right, straight to my unprotected chin, and it was at that precise moment I swear a phenomenon occurred. To this day I'm convinced the world lurched on its axis. I swear there was no way I fell down, instead the ground just came up to meet me.

Badly dazed, I struggled back up on to one knee, wobbled a little, then attempted to elevate myself a little further. Another punch landed, equally as brutal as the last, as it exploded into the region of my left kidney. Down again, this time some variation, flat on my face, and even above the ringing in my head I could hear the booing the illegal blow created. Fortunately Arnold moved back, after all, why risk disqualification when victory is a foregone conclusion. I presumed Albie's disappearance inside meant he was on the phone, and I decided my only hope of surviving was if it was my father on the other end of the line, telling him to get his great, hulking son off me.

Somehow I found myself something like vertical again, although I wasn't all that sure where the sky was, so I failed to see Arnold closing. Another king hit, directly to the pit of my stomach. On my knees and at least I was offering the spectators some variety, because this time I was badly winded. I looked up, desperate to regain my breath, and there he was towering over me, as big as Sampson, and as far as I was concerned, equally as dangerous. He was moving

back in, all too keen to continue the slaughter, that was until one of the older boys deprived him of the pleasure, the tone of his voice clearly displaying his annoyance,

'Back off the kid Burnside you bloody bully. You know you've got him beaten, so leave him alone or I'll make sure you've got someone your own size to deal with.'

But another suggestion, offered by one of Arnold's school mates I decided, 'You're nothing but an embarrassment kid. It's obvious you can't box to save yourself. How about pissing off back home and leave this to those of us who know what we're doing.'

Yeah, so easy for him, but I wonder what his reaction would be if I suggested he get in the ring and fight him. But with my gloves unlaced I took the hint and wandered miserably off.

Some days later, and they were days that had been laced with a dire warning from my mother. She'd walked unannounced and unintentionally into the bathroom while I was drying after a shower, and had acquired a full view of the bruises Arnold had left me with. This resulted in a threat barely short of death, if I dared get into a fight of that magnitude again. I did my best to explain the bruises weren't worth worrying about, and the damage was only due to Joe Louis's bloody awful defence, which wasn't worth a tin of you know what, and once I had that mastered, there'd be no further problems. But apparently she'd seen enough. Come home with bruises like that again, and boy, would I be for it.

Sitting on our front steps a couple of days after that warning, still more than ever fed up with my situation, and nobody needed to remind me how the score sat on the board. Two for Arnold, nil for yours truly. My gaze drifted haphazardly around the street, then suddenly the serenity of that balmy afternoon was punctuated by the sound of a mower starting up, Albie was about to start cutting their front lawn. Yet again I wondered why Arnold wasn't made to mow their grass, it was a chore I'd try to avoid at risk at being grounded for over a month.

But as I sat and watched Albie start to move steadily back and forth, somehow the repetition increased my determination, and I knew there was a risk, considering what my mother had said. So taking a deep breath and trying to look as nonchalant as possible, I strolled over. With his head down while watching where he was mowing, he didn't notice my presence until he was practically on top of me, then he quickly throttled his mower back to idle, and acknowledged me in that quiet, laid back manner of his,

'Well hi Mathew, haven't seen you for a while. How are you lad, been behaving yourself, anything I can do for you?'

Don't know why, but I'd always been hopeless at this sort of thing, and here I was tongue tied as usual. Then the flood gates opened, the words burst out, just like a dam breaking,

'Albie, please, please will you teach me how to box? Please say you will because I need to learn really, really badly.'

He gazed back at me as he stood with his hands still on the handle of his mower, and as I looked up into those intelligent, blue eyes, I was certain I could see the trace of a smile lingering somewhere behind them.

Apparently sensing it was somehow appropriate, the mower gave something like a death rattle, coughed a couple of times, then stopped. As a result we were left with silence hanging heavily in the air, and for quite some moments he said nothing, he simply stood there and looked at me, not saying a word. And I squirmed slightly under that penetrating gaze, deciding he came second to my mother for possessing the ability to look deep into your soul. Then after what seemed an eternity, he said in that quiet, laid back voice of his,' So, you want to learn how to box do you Mathew, so tell me lad, why do you want to do that?'

This time, thank goodness, no stumbling, no delays, for a change the words just flowed,

'Because first of all I was bullied at school, and there've been other times when I've been made a fool of because I didn't know all that much about fighting. The truth is I hate being bullied, and I hate being made a fool of as well, so as I see it, if you're forced to fight and you don't really know how, then the situation just gets worse again. So if I'm going to be placed in a position where I'm left with no choice, then I have no alternative, I simply have to learn how to fight. The truth is, I don't really like fighting, frankly I think it's a bit stupid, but I tell you Albie, I hate having to back away even more.'

Seconds past as he appeared to stand there and digest what I'd said, and then it happened, the words I so desperately wanted to hear, 'Alright Mathew, I understand what you're saying, but nothing's possible without parental permission. If you can get that, then rest assured, I'll teach you to the best of my ability.'

I turned and charged for home, but as I approached our back door at speed, I stopped and gave the situation a little more thought. There was no doubt my mother loathed boxing like it was poison, so I didn't stand the remotest chance in getting permission from her. But with my father, it was an entirely different story. Most of the decisions regarding my life, my mother made almost to a point of entirety, that was for one small area, and that small area was sport. As far as sport was concerned, my father's word was law. So alright, he included my mother when it came to tennis, but anything other than that, she willingly stepped aside and left the decision to him, but boxing could prove to be the exception. If I asked permission while my mother was in the room, she'd dig her toes in like she'd never done before, so logic said it was imperative I caught my father on his own.

Cautiously, I sidled up to our back door, and as I peered in, sure enough, my parents were together in our dining room. Blast, foiled again, but then some luck. Whatever my parents had been discussing needed checking, and my mother clearly said she'd do it, and promptly disappeared up the hall. Hardly daring to believe my good fortune, I wandered nonchalantly in, and doing my best to look the picture of innocence, approached my father and said,

'Dad, I was just talking to Albie and he says if you'll give your permission he'll teach me how to box. Please say it's alright, because I want to learn real bad.'

He glanced up, and by the look of concentration on his face, I was convinced he was thinking more about his paper work than what he was saying

to me, because he looked back down while he spoke, ' Well Matt if Mr. Burnside's prepared to give you his time, then I can hardly say no, can I?'

There was a movement to my left, my mother was back in the room, and going by the look of abject shock that was spreading across her face, she'd heard my request and knew permission had been granted. She opened her mouth to explode, but my father beat her by a split second,

'But never forget one thing my boy. If there's anything certain about boxing, it's that sooner or later you'll come home sporting a beautiful black eye.'

My mother groped behind her, desperately seeking the support of a chair. I had no intention of hanging around until she recovered, so I turned and bolted, equally as fast as I'd arrived, back across the lawns to Albie, breathlessly giving him the good news. However circumstances dictated there was to be a short delay before my coaching began. Enid's sister had been in hospital, and was now due to go home. But she lived on her own, and the hospital deemed it would be imperative that someone else was in the house. Enid decided it was her responsibility, but seeing as she expected to be away for quite some time, she decided to take Arnold with her. My thoughts on the subject were that Arnold's manipulating mind had something to do with that. Rather than stay at home with his father, which would leave his schooling uninterrupted, he preferred to stick with his mother, so as not to be separated from her acknowledged cooking ability, his rotund waistline tended to strongly indicate that.

Also, this strange decision left me wondering how anyone recuperating from a life threatening illness, could do so successfully with those two in the house. I figured that after just one week of their combined presence, she'd be guaranteed a relapse of major proportions. But the arrangement stayed as it was, so Albie dutifully took his wife and son down South, stayed with them for a couple of days, then drove back to the city. So on the day following his return and as instructed, I presented myself, and in the soft warmth of the early morning sunshine, my introduction to the wonders of the world of boxing began.

Chapter 7

There were times, Albie explained, when boxing could be hard and brutal. And as I thought, this tended to suggest Arnold had conveniently failed to inform him of the thumping he'd handed out to me. But he also insisted it could be a thing of classical beauty, and in some ways as refined as any ballet. Yeah, well that was alright I suppose, but I didn't want to be dancing around in tights, I wanted to learn how to fight. He took the hint offered by my blank expression, we got down to business.

As my lessons started, he continually stressed the incalculable value of the straight left, and you punched using the rhythmical, balanced power from your body. I was shown how to deliver this power effectively, and he explained the priceless value of anticipation, in other words, trying to fight one step ahead of your opponent, and how this all important sense could only be developed during the course of extensive training. He also constantly stressed the value of fitness, insisting any boxer was only as good as the time he could continue to move effortlessly around the ring.

I thought about Arnold and his bulging waistline, and decided these were words that had obviously been wasted on his son. Going by the demolition he'd wrought on me, logic said he'd been a beneficiary of his father's pugalist prowess, but had decided food took preference over mobility. So in contrast I started skipping, and continued until my legs were so tired I could barely lift them, but after briefly resting the pain, I'd get back up and start all over again. In his shed there was a speed ball hanging, and I marvelled as to how Albie could make that ball sing. I'd stand there wide eyed, fascinated by the wonderful, rhythmic purr his fists created, as they beat out a magical tattoo with a speed that seemed faster than the beat of a humming bird's wings.

Then, finally it was my turn, and I struggled, because I was hopeless as that butter smooth rhythm eluded me. But as those weeks of training progressed, that sought after song of my own started, that smooth even purr, created this time by a ten year old's flashing young fists. And as that satisfied grin flashed across Albie's face, I put my head down and trained even harder. Not content to restrict myself to the time spent at Burnside's, I erected a punching bag in our shed, then proceeded to train for hours, firing at my imaginary opponent a continual barrage of rib crunching and energy sapping body blows.

Finally, Albie gave permission for me to spar with the others on the weekends, and there was the thrill that came with the realisation that I could definitely hold my own. There was no way I could rely on size like Arnold, being barely a good average for my age, but one advantage I did possess, was that of a lightning speed. Where that came from, I had absolutely no idea, and what was more, couldn't have cared less. All that mattered was that somehow and from somewhere, I'd been blessed with a natural ability to be able to punch, as Albie insisted on describing it, with a speed similar to that of a striking young rattle snake.

As those weeks of coaching and training continued, Winter reluctantly gave way to Spring, but not before resisting the onset of that delightful season with bitter winds and grey, overcast skies. On regular occasions Albie would head South to see his family, but in no time he'd be back, offering a constant flow of advice as he stood by my side.

'Always be confident lad, but never get too cocky, and always remember to rely on your speed, because some time in the future, there's a chance you'll find out what a wonderful asset it is. Keep stabbing that left of yours out so fast, they struggle to see it, but above all else, never, never lose your temper, because so often it's the one who lacks self control, who finishes up getting the hiding.'

Another Saturday morning, paired off with Errol Anderson for a sparring session. That was Errol with a shock of black, curly hair and a wide grin, who loved nothing more than mixing it with someone around his own size and age who could throw a reasonable punch; that was as long as he was prepared to accept two twice as hard in return. Not one for fooling around was Errol, and already he'd attempted connect with a couple of haymakers, that drifted around somewhere well outside the definition of sparring. And I felt just the faintest pang of irritation, because I'd been keeping my own punching to a level I considered to be more in keeping with the occasion. But yet again, as I glided under one of his bombs, in a split second the opening was there, and I must confess that as I straightened, I let him have it, a sharp, straight left.

And it was as if some magnetic force had attracted my fist to his nose, with the result it terminated on that part of his anatomy with something like reasonable velocity. His head shot back as he let out a sharp curse, at the same time lifting his glove to his face as he instinctively covered the damage. For a couple of seconds it seemed as if he'd succeeded, but then the blood appeared, running down his chin, from where it continued to drip at quite an alarming rate onto the canvas floor. Instantly I reached for his arm with the intention of assisting him to the side of the ring, but he got there first, and draping himself over the ropes, proceeded to bleed quite profusely on to the grass. Five minutes later, after ice had been applied and nature had combined to assist with rectifying the damage, the flow had been reduced to the occasional drip. I stayed alongside, prepared to accept his annoyance, but instead, as he glanced up, his grin would have more than matched Colin's, as he said,

'Jesus bloody Christ Mathew, what a flipping beauty, there was no way I saw that coming, but I reckon that signals enough for me. There's no way I'm getting back in there and risking more damage to my nose with anyone else today.'

I continued to stand there with him as we laughed about the incident together, that was until an all too familiar voice boomed out from somewhere behind us,' Think you're so good Colbert, just because you managed to give him a bit of a bloody nose. But I wonder how keen you'd be to get back in the ring with me and get another hiding.'

My day was made, unfortunately it had to happen sooner or later. His royal highness was back amongst us, and it was amazing how quickly his voice reminded me of how pleasant life had been without him spouting off.

It was a bit ridiculous really, I mean it wasn't as if I actively disliked him, in fact there was the odd occasion when he managed to be something resembling human. The trouble he caused came from the fact that ninety per cent of the time, he was nothing more than a persistent pain in the butt. And going by the tone of his voice, the sojourn down South had done absolutely nothing to change him. It gave warning he intended to reclaim the position of authority he felt he held over the children in the street as quickly as possible. So he pushed to reassert himself, with his insults relating to my constant refusal to get back in the ring with him flowing thick and fast, while I on the other hand, tried desperately to keep him at arm's length.

Different schools meant the week days didn't prove to be much of a problem, but the weekends became something I dreaded, as he kept up an incessant series of invitations to get back in the ring. And as this unrelenting combination of sarcasm and abuse continued, so my level of frustration continued to drift forever upward. I had long accepted the responsibility for the outcome of our last confrontation had been virtually all mine. So alright, he'd been the one who'd suggested we fight, and I'd agreed, being under the misguided belief I could handle him, with the result that I'd been proven so painfully wrong. Now he was spoiling for a fight again, with the obvious intention of using his victory as a stepping stone towards getting his name back into those bright lights where he felt it belonged. And what better way of doing that, than subjecting me to yet another battering.

However, nobody was more aware than I, that any improvement in my ability to hold my own in the ring with this persistent blight in my life, would be due entirely to the many hours his father had spent with me during his son's absence down South. Therefore it didn't make any sense to me, that showing my gratitude should include getting back in the ring with his son, even if said confrontation was to be hidden under the definition of sparring, because in a return fight with Arnold, there was nothing more certain, sparring it most certainly wouldn't be, with a more accurate description being a full on fight.

To further add to my discomfort, with some of his school mates now involved, the word coward started to be used more frequently. How anyone could be classed as a coward, when his opponent was about two years older and considerably heavier, was a little beyond me. But so called coward or not, the situation continued to deteriorate to a point where it became something I could certainly do without. But as it turned out, it was not I but Albie, who finished up making that final, fateful decision.

Back in Burnside's backyard again, watching Colin sparring with some kid who I thought was a hanger on from one of Arnold's mates. My best friend he may be, and there had been a number of occasions when his help had proved invaluable, during a couple of dustups we'd had with a group of kids who resided deep in one of the neighbouring suburbs, and who occasionally tried us on, mainly I was sure, to keep their hand in. But when it came to fighting in a ring, it was all too apparent, a competent boxer he most certainly wasn't.

Finally the session ended, so I moved across with the intention of speaking to him, but it seemed as always, somehow Arnold managed to get in first, 'Don't bother climbing out of the ring kid, stay in there and fight your chicken mate.

Honestly, you'd be well matched, because you're both about as useless as each other.'

I admit it, annoyance flared as I snapped back, 'And why don't you give us all a rest from your big mouth Burnside? You must go close to qualifying as the first twelve year old, who's in need of a jaw replacement, caused by excessive talking.'

He swaggered over, and on arrival thrust his face directly in front of mine as he replied, 'Yeah, you reckon Colbert, well talking about jaws, I sure got a lot of exercise punching yours the last time we met. But don't get concerned, I know it's not going to happen again, I only need to look at your face to see you're much too scared of me now.'

There wasn't a fraction of hesitation, I didn't even think about, because annoyance meant I automatically snapped straight back, 'I'm telling you Arnold, I've just about had enough of that big mouth of yours since you've been back. So alright, if you're determined to fight, be my guest, because I have been…' I held my tongue, but not quite in time, because instantly he jumped at the unintended but never the less spur of the moment invitation.

'You reckon, then come on, stop talking, pick up your chicken feathers and fight.'

Now annoyed to a point barely short of fury, I stood there looking at him, with one part of me desperate to do battle, yet another saying I shouldn't.

Some movement behind him, his father appeared, and I gained the impression he'd been standing quietly, and had heard every word that had been said. He moved closer, and as our eyes made contact, I felt there was no doubt he could read the frustration in mine. Slightly embarrassed I looked away, but as I glanced back, in a split second it was there, a barely perceptible nod. Convinced my imagination must be playing tricks with me, I looked again, but there was no mistake, because instantly that signal flashed again, and having interpreted what Albie seemed determined to confirm, suddenly my annoyance was replaced by cold, calculated determination as I turned to Arnold and smiled as I said, 'Alright, you've wanted to fight again for quite some time, so what say we get on with it.'

During the intervening months, a few improvements had eventuated. The butter boxes had been replaced by stools, one red, the other blue. The lumps of metal had disappeared also, discreetly returned to the workshop, and in their place hung a shining new bell. Stepping quickly through the ropes, I walked across and sat on the blue stool, because this was the corner I'd had the last time we'd clashed. Adding further to this repeat performance, one of the twins started to lace up my gloves, and as before, I hadn't the faintest idea which one it was. But now one major difference. With the lacing complete, they felt as if I'd been born with them on my fists. And one last improvement, this time Albie would act as referee.

But before he entered the ring, he walked around outside the ropes and spoke to me from there, 'Mathew, some of the boys have told me about your last fight with my son, and a couple were angry about the damage he inflicted. I was furious when I found out, especially considering I assured your parents that such a thing could never happen while you boys were under my care. I told Arnold

how disgusted I was, but as always I have to admit I never get very far. When situations arise where he's proved in the wrong, he heads for his mother, because she's of the misguided belief that such a situation could never occur. Now there's no need to go through with this if you don't want to. He's older than you and also weighs more, as you're already painfully aware, and it's certainly not a situation I'm happy with, as you well know, but I have to temper this with your feelings as well.'

I was aware of his good intentions, but frankly his words sailed right over my head, and I felt it only fair that he should know why, so I kept my reply short and to the point, ' Look Albie, you know what he's like. Once he gets his teeth into something, he's like a bulldog, he won't let go until he's achieved what he wants. So sooner or later we're going to have to fight again, and as I see it, it may as well be now.'

As he replied he looked back down at me, and I could see that smile of his back in his eyes,

' Over the last few months I've got to know you pretty well lad, and that's why I'm not trying to stop you now. But remember, you're a far different proposition to when you fought him last, and don't make the mistake of fighting in close. Use your speed, stay back and pick him off. Box him like that, and there's a chance we'll see a different outcome this time.'

I glanced across the ring. Arnold looked as big and dangerous as ever, and the look on his face was one of sheer delight.

Chapter 8

Somehow the news of our return bout, swept around the neighbourhood with the speed of the proverbial jungle drums. I was amazed how quickly the attendance increased with kids pouring in, keen to see what the next few minutes produced. We were called into the centre of the ring, a few words spoken, then back to our corners. A nod from Albie to the time keeper produced the clear, defining ring from the bell, which sounded louder than ever in the still, morning air. Then it was all on.

Arnold worked on the theory that had worked so well before, and must surely do so again, as he charged across the ring, but now far too ring wise to be caught like that twice, I danced away, then moved back in on perfect balance, waiting for him to throw the first punch. He moved in, but with his guard a little low, and as he swung one of his vicious rights, it dropped even further. My left snaked out, landing with a resounding smack, dead centre of his unprotected face. I danced lightly away, and infuriated, he followed. You should listen to your father Arnold, no use getting agitated after one punch and at this stage of the bout. Another right, nowhere near its mark. I said a silent thank you as I jabbed again, twice in quick succession, and each time his head snapped back with a teeth rattling jar.

Automatically he brought his guard up to protect his face, so I let him have a powerful left, well, as powerful as I could manage anyway, right into his unprotected ribs. I was sure a slightly worried look flickered across his face. Maybe something inside him was saying, 'it was so easy before, why does it seem to be so much more difficult now?' But there was no way he was backing off, in he came again, trying to get in close where he could take advantage of his weight. Oh no Arnold, this time we're fighting my kind of fight, as I slipped away, grinning at him, daring him to try again.

And try again he most certainly did. Another right that fanned past my ear, which left me remembering how last time he'd made it ring, and this time his ribs were so exposed to a point I could hardly believe. A blazing right hand, just as I'd been shown, and the shock from the impact travelled all the way up my arm. The look on his face told me Arnold was far from happy as he endeavoured to stay out of reach, so we circled each other, throwing the occasional punch, none of which did any harm, and it stayed that way until the bell signalled the end of the round.

As I sat on my blue stool, once again I glanced across the ring, and the changes were quite distinct. That look of delight was nowhere to be seen, his chest was heaving, and the right side of his face was glowing bright pink. This time it was obvious it was he who needed the break. Now the sound of the bell, we stood and moved to the centre of the ring. This time no charging in, he moved slower and much more warily, we circled, then in he came, and this time I let him. He tried a combination, a left, then a right, both of which I countered with comparative ease, then another beautiful right that almost made me wince.

Immediately I could hear Albie's voice, as if he were in the ring with me, 'be confident, but don't get cocky'. Sound advice, so I stepped back, then retaliated with two left jabs. The first he blocked most efficiently, the second caught him flush on the mouth. For a split second it reminded me of that time when I'd slugged Wallace, and how my knuckle had bled, and decided this time I was glad I had gloves on. Forget him, you idiot, because in a flash he'd closed right in. From somewhere came a sixth sense warning, and urgently I twisted, with the result his knee barely missed my groin. I knew there were times when you could be a bit of a low life Arnold, that time up in Parran's Bush being one of them, but I never thought you'd ever stoop as low as that. Never mind, no harm done, and anyway, there's the bell again.

The third round, a few punches flung, no undue problems, his careful approach making him a little more awkward to hit. His defence was reasonably effective, not all that surprising, after all, I wasn't the only who'd had the benefit of his father's coaching. But I remained cautious, because, knowing Arnold as I did, sooner or later his aggressive nature would once again rise to the surface and result in one of his haymakers, and if it connected, it could stop a truck. But suddenly out of nowhere, the opening I'd been waiting for appeared.

A hard left, straight to the pit of his stomach, then as he'd done with me, a punch that caught him flush on the ear. The blow moved him to his right, followed by a perfect left, the punch as good as I'd ever thrown, and it landed with considerable force, flush on his predominant nose. Never saw the blood, not that I wanted to. As far as I was concerned, causing two bloody noses in one day was definitely nothing to be proud of. He brought both of his gloves up to his face, then without so much as a backward glance, slipped through the ropes, then ran across their lawn and straight inside the house.

Vaguely I wondered whether he wanted to come back out and finish the round, but apparently not, but I then accepted it was a stupid thought on my part anyway. The boys crowded around while Albie unlaced my gloves, then he placed his arm around my shoulder and gave me a brief but meaningful hug, as he said ever so quietly, 'That was a very efficient hiding you handed out Mathew, and I'm aware it's something he's needed for quite some time. It's just another lesson in life for him lad, and it won't do him any harm at all.'

Well that may be so, but out of the corner of my eye I could see another problem looming fast on the horizon. Enid had appeared on their back porch and was screaming blue bloody murder, demanding to know who'd rearranged her angelic son's countenance. It took me all of one second to decide which fence I'd bolt over. The woman was a menace at the best of times, but considering these circumstances she'd be nothing short of impossible. Fortunately, the danger passes quickly. Albie went over and spoke to her firmly, and for once taking the hint, she allowed him to ease her back inside.

Peace reigned supreme once again, but more than enough excitement for today, so as soon as the gloves were unlaced, I headed back across the front lawns to home. But part way there I could contain myself no longer, and I jumped so high it was as if I had springs in my feet, and at the same time punched my fist skywards, like I was attempting to punch a hole in the clouds, and my victory shout was so loud, I knew they could hear it in the neighbouring

suburb. And as far as that scoreboard was concerned, that fight was worth two points, and that made us well and truly even. Everyone has minor milestones in their lives, and at ten years of age, that last fight with Arnold was one of mine.

Chapter 9

Things soon settled back to normal, and life continued down a blissful, contented path, and it must have proved to be reasonably content, because Arnold was finally speaking to me again. There was nothing in the way of drama as life in the neighbourhood drifted pleasantly on, that was until Colin casually informed me, he and his family were moving. The news left me stunned, trying to contemplate life without him around seemed impossible. He had become as much a part of me as my right arm, let's face it, we did everything together, and even after all this time, many of the kids at the pool were still convinced we were brothers.

But his mother was apparently continuing what had long become a well established pattern. She would move into a house, proceed to spend a small fortune redecorating, then when finally completed to her satisfaction, gradually tire of the place and get set to start all over again. I tried thinking of various ways of disposing of her, but in the end decided none of them were practical. And what made it even more difficult, was if the truth be known, I really liked her, so was forced to give that away as another lost cause. There was no getting away from it, not having Colin around was going to create a void I was convinced no one else could ever fill.

During the time we had left, that dreaded day, by mutual agreement, became an absolutely forbidden topic. But as the saying goes, nothing's more inevitable than the inevitable, and as I woke on that black day with the haze of sleep slowly lifting, it was replaced by a morbid premonition, something was terribly wrong. Then the reality finally registered, by midday my best friend would be gone, and that meant all I would be left with would be memories of endless amounts of fun, that had resulted from a wonderful friendship.

Briefly I thought about going over and helping, but decided against it, not wishing to see the cartons and suitcases and carefully stacked furniture, then once the truck arrived and it had all been loaded, there would be nothing but forlorn emptiness. A few minutes later, sure enough the truck appeared, and the procession from house to vehicle started, but still I stayed away, still preferring to watch from afar. More minutes slipped miserably past, then the goodbyes started around the street, followed by the finality of Colin's father backing their car out onto the street.

But Colin wasn't with them, similar to myself those years back, he'd been granted the privilege of riding in the cab of the truck. Finally I rode over and stopped and looked up, and he looked back down at me from the height of the huge vehicle. He wound down the window and spoke to me, but the driver had started the motor, so I didn't hear a word he said. He beckoned to me, urging me to move closer, at the same time hanging precariously out of the window, making it obvious his words were intended for my ears only. What words I thought, could ever prove adequate for a sad time such as this, but Colin managed to excel himself, as it seemed only Colin could, 'I just want to say

Mathew', and his perfectly timed pause cut deep into my heart, 'you remember that time up in Parran's Bush, when we took you prisoner and tied you to that tree?'

As if I'll ever bloody forget I thought, as he continued,' Well not that I've had all that much experience in that sort of thing, but after Arnold pulled your pants down, and we all lined up to take our turn, I just want to let you know that you've got by far, the smoothest balls I've ever felt.'

For some reason my sadness instantly departed, 'You smart bastard Bradford. Why don't you try hanging out of that window a bit further still, then hopefully there's a chance you'll fall out and break your skinny neck.'

Now the truck was easing slowly away, and even above the noise of the engine I could still hear him laughing as it moved off down the street. He continued to wave furiously back, and leaning against my bike I laughed and waved just as hard back at him. The truck paused briefly at the corner, then as the traffic cleared, swung right and disappeared, and as it did, my best friend disappeared along with it.

I stayed where I was for quite some time, sitting on my bike, one foot on the ground for support, accepting it was more than likely I'd never see him again. One thing though, I hope he knew I was only joking, because there was no way I'd ever want him to break his neck. Arnold on rare occasions, like when he was in one of his know all moods, and Wallace and Nigel, any time they liked, but never, never Colin.

A small consolation, but not all that much. At least the weather was doing its best to offer something in the way of sympathy for my friend's departure, as I woke to seemingly never ending mornings of constant, clear blue skies. Having been informed there was to be no holiday away, something I'd become used to, after the sad demise of our holiday cottage at Piha, I compensated by continuing to live at the pool, revelling in that crystal clear water, constantly improving my tan as I soaked up that endless supply of Summer sun, with the only hurtful reminder occurring when one of the kids would innocently ask where Colin was. The truth was, I was missing him, more than I could ever have thought possible.

Just before Christmas I rode back to our old street to mix with my friends, something I'd done on the odd occasion since we'd shifted. It was always good to talk of times past, and if I got a chance to insult Pete, that usually resulted in a bit of a dustup, I mean, after all, a kid needs to keep his hand in, by having a good, old fashioned wrestle. But it was while I was chatting with the Mc. Kenzie boys when their mother casually asked, 'And are you going away for the holidays this year Mathew?'

Actually, if the truth were known, I'd become quite an expert as this, and if I handled her question with my usual deviousness, one never knew what might eventuate. So with a suitably sad voice, although not so sad to be blatantly obvious, and with downcast eyes that I hoped helped with the atmosphere I was trying desperately to create, I replied, 'Not this year Mrs. Mac. Mum says we can't afford it, and Dad won't leave his business. I reckon he'd sleep there if he could.'

Then I held my breath, literally hanging on her reply,

'Oh, sweetheart, that's a shame. Tell you what, why don't you check with your parents? See if they'll allow you to spend a few days with us down at the beach.'

Was she kidding? They'd be only too happy to get rid of me and give themselves a break. Whoopee, let the bells ring. Past experience had proved those two days usually extended into something more like two weeks.

The source of their annual migration was a superb private beach North of the city, that consisted of a mile long sweeping arc of golden sand, on to which the sparkling waters of the Hauraki Gulf tumbled. These ranged in intensity from soft, lazy waves with their accompanying lullaby, that possessed the unmatched ability to send me straight to sleep, to beautiful, white capped rolling surf, that on occasions more than matched Piha. My opinion of the beach was quite simple. To me, it was the closest thing to paradise, this side of Heaven.

So with a ritual that went as far back as anyone could recall, they'd load their family car and trailer to the legal limit, and then somewhere considerably beyond, and take off for six weeks of total holiday bliss. Constant attempts on my part to try and persuade my parents to apply for permission to camp there, had been met with something considerably less than enthusiasm, with their excuse being they weren't attracted to camping. Well, that was always my father's answer anyway, whether my mother agreed with him was open to question. But with my stay with the family having been duly approved, as always, I was immediately welcomed into the gang of boys, whose families, similar to the Mc. Kenzie's, religiously returned there year after year.

So we swam and surfed, went spearing flatties at the Northern end of the beach, with the companionship of two metre long eels, who insisted on swimming between our legs. We'd hunt for rabbits on the rolling paddocks at the top of the cliffs, with notable lack of success, and would water ski as often as we could persuade one of the fathers to take his boat out. Yet on a couple of occasions amidst all this non-stop activity, I'd taken the time to lie back on the golden sand and think about the changes that were fast approaching. With my years at Primary School now complete, two years at Intermediate were looming, as a prelude to High School.

But as I'd hopefully predicted, those two days had extended to the usual two weeks, so the belated enrolment at my new school had become something of a priority. Therefore on the day following my reluctant return to the city, as I walked into that new school's grounds, I paid particular attention to the other boys, with those problems I'd encountered with the Thompson brothers firmly fixed in my mind. So, some of them might be a bit bigger than me, but the fact was most of them looked, as I no doubt did to them, just typical youngsters becoming increasingly more nervous, as the first day of the new term and school moved closer. But as I sat back as my mother provided the necessary information at enrolment, I made a solemn promise to myself. There was no way I'd ever go looking for trouble, that sort of stupidity left me totally unimpressed, but if any trouble appeared similar to what I'd experienced with those brothers, then stand by, because I'd fight bordering on death for the right to be left alone. So with absolutely no room left for compromise, that promise was once again as if it had been cast in stone, there was no way I was going suffer any bullying.

When I set off on that first day, in my new uniform and my compulsory cap on my head, my confidence was boosted by the knowledge that fifty per cent of the children attending the school that day, were in exactly the same position as myself. And by the end of the day I accepted things couldn't have gone better. I was friendly with most of the boys in the class, and amazing for me, a few of the girls as well. But as the first week pleasantly slipped by, I knew it was still too early to relax. Logic said somewhere bullies had to exist, but I was wrong to be thinking in the plural, as only one of any consequence emerged, and his name was Ivan Jameson.

Ivan Jameson, a name as European as my own, but somewhere along the path of life one of the Jameson family had trod, there'd been a mixed marriage, because Ivan was only once removed from that of a full blooded Maori. Not that this worried me in the slightest, as similar to most youngsters growing up in New Zealand, I'd encountered my share of the race, with Piha being a good example of that. I'd willingly accepted them as I found them, invariably characters, fun loving and at times a bit mischievous, and also frustratingly unreliable, and often a bit too laid back when it came to concentrating on their education, like for instance, homework was nothing but a pest, and something to be ignored. For this reason, they always seemed to be hovering around the bottom of their class.

The boys were often well put together youngsters, many of whom had a tendency to settle any disputes that arose, be they minor or otherwise, in a similar fashion to the Gossini's, in other words they tended to hit first and ask questions later. This also caused me no particular concern, after all, I'd served my apprenticeship in that direction as well. But after a few days of watching Ivan as he strode around the school, invariably leaving chaos in his wake, I came to the decision I wasn't interested in platitudes, because it had taken no time at all to place him in the category of being nothing more than a big, aggressive, foul mouthed slob.

Being by far the oldest and largest boy at the school, blood curdling stories abounded relating to his pugilistic exploits during the previous year, and accordingly, I immediately assessed Ivan as being someone to definitely avoid. However, fate has an annoying tendency to ignore such decisions, and I have no doubt that some higher being had already determined our paths were destined to cross.

This somewhat momentous happening occurred about three weeks into the year. The wind had acquired an unpleasant sharpness, that encouraged many of us to eat our lunches in an area adjacent to the main entrance of the school. Sheltered as it was, it was popular at all times, but especially so now. With my lunch finished, I stood up, ready to head for the playing field and a game of cricket, a sport that had recently shot up close to the top of my sporting preferences, much to my father's disgust, because he thought I should be concentrating on tennis. But the movement caught the attention of one of the teachers who'd appeared at the top of the steps at the entrance to the school's main building,

'Hey lad, just a moment will you,' he bleated, 'you're in Miss Hall's class aren't you?'

I acknowledged the guilt associated with this terrible sin.

'Take this note down to her for me will you? It's just been phoned in, so make it snappy.'

I'll give him snappy. Surely he realised this inconvenience is eating into my cricket time.

So I took off, running down to her room as fast as I could. Then with her thanks ringing in my ears I headed back at speed. Flat out past the line of children still sitting and eating, flashing by as I attempted to increase my speed even further. Now literally running so fast my feet barely seemed to be touching the ground, then suddenly they were taken out from under me, and I proceeded to give an excellent impersonation of the proverbial flying object. My airborne momentum was abruptly terminated as I struck some poor unfortunate in full flight as it were, and as a result the child's head was slammed back, in the process making violent contact with the concrete wall behind.

I in turn, finished up sprawling full length on the path on which I'd been running, badly grazing my shin on the edge of the seat on the way down, then removing a considerable amount of skin off my right knee on arrival. Sitting back up, my first thought was for my unintended victim, but two of her friends had immediately sprung to her assistance, and assured she was being cared for, I ran my eyes over my own damage. Sure, there was blood, and what's more, plenty of it, but overall there was nothing that a combination of some healing balm, sticking plaster and time wouldn't take care of. So I swung my gaze back up the path, looking for whatever had caused me to trip. And it didn't take long to find. There was Ivan, sitting there in all his solitary glory, with the leg he'd used to upend me still stuck out arrogantly across the path.

There was no denying it, for the first time in many months I felt the burning flame of deep resentment starting to ignite. For a few seconds our eyes locked, then casually he bent down and made a point of carefully examining his right shoe, then those eyes as black as coal swung back up and once again locked onto mine as he said, 'Look at the mark you've put on my new shoe, you clumsy little bastard. Why don't you look where you're going? Come over here right now and get on your knees and wipe it off you dormant idiot, and hurry up about it, that's if you want to keep on living.'

I took a deep breath, according to my mother, it was imperative I stayed cool, calm and collected, and above all else, excruciatingly polite, so it's imperative I choose my reply carefully, 'Well sure Ivan, I'm only too happy to come and wipe your shoe for you. The only trouble being that when I've finished, you could find you're at risk of choking.'

Now he was looking vaguely at me, convinced I'd taken leave of my senses as he replied,

'What the hell are you talking about, you pathetic little moron?'

Looked like the time had arrived to explain myself, 'The problem we have Ivan, is that when I've finished wiping your shoe, I intend to rip it off your foot and ram it down your throat, you ignorant, brain dead, dangerous bastard.'

My mother will not be pleased. I've decided not to be polite after all.

The rather blank expression that appeared on his face, indicated it was taking a few seconds for what I'd said to register. And I could understand that,

after all, Ivan's intellect couldn't be classed as being on an overly high level, but now he was slowly getting to his feet, and I did the same. The children in the immediate vicinity vacated at speed, being well aware, nobody spoke to Ivan like that unless they'd booked a seat for an early departure from this life, so this meant one thing, a fight. But at the same time, I felt I could read him like an open book. Half the children still needed to be shown what a big, bad proposition he was. What better way of displaying this than slaughtering some first year upstart. His fear rating would climb through the roof, and he'd cruise through the rest of the year unchallenged, doing whatever he liked in the playground. It all seemed so familiar.

I watched him carefully as he eased closer, then as I'd anticipated, came with a rush. Shades of Arnold, but much more dangerous, no bulge around his middle, instead muscles rippled. But as he launched himself forward, so did I, and we clashed like two raging young bulls. Locked together as we were, we hit the ground very hard. More skin off my knee I reckoned. I opened my eyes and couldn't believe it, had no idea how, but he was the one who'd finished up underneath. In an instant a voice seemed to say, 'Don't just lie there, why look at a gift like this and do nothing about it', so deciding that was fair enough, I let him have it, a powerful, bare fisted slug.

I aimed for his nose, trying to lift my tally in that direction to three, but at the last split second he managed to roll his head which left his right cheek taking the impact. The pain it induced must have been considerable, so before he could gather his wits, I belted him one again. One for my shin and one for my knee Ivan. Didn't want to hurt him unduly, I just wanted to hit him so hard, that his skull left a permanent indentation in the tar seal path on which we were fighting. Now wrestling on the ground, and it was no use trying to kid myself. There was no way I could survive like this, he was much too strong, so taking the opportunity he unintentionally offered, I sprang to my feet and so did he, equally as quickly. He lunged straight in, no defence, maybe he thought he didn't need it, but he did. My left flashed out, and his forward momentum turned what was no more than an average jab into something reasonably lethal, and as a result he staggered back, slightly hurt again.

In an instant he was back, round house swings, vicious enough that if one connected it would take my head off, but telegraphed as if he was swinging in slow motion. Easily avoiding them, I moved left, then right and struck again. More jabs, very fast, Albie would have approved, Ivan got even more furious. Briefly he stepped back and wiped the back of his hand across his face. I didn't see a thing, but what he saw didn't appear to please him. Maybe my tally was up to three after all. No time to dwell on that, he was coming at me again. A beautiful left caught him full in the stomach. In theory it should have stopped a train, but for all the effect it had on him, I may as well have hit the concrete wall. He replied with a punch to my ribs. The pain had me convinced he must have broken about three of them. Stay away from him you moron, keep jabbing and moving, just as you've been taught.

We battled on, with Ivan now working on the theory, if he threw enough punches, logic said some of them had to get through, and they did and they hurt like hell, but I knew I'd landed a few real beauties as well. But there was no use

kidding myself. I was starting to tire, this was a fight that in the end I had no chance of winning. Although I'd kept up my fitness with skipping and plenty of work on the punching bag, in the end I knew his superior power would wear me down. There was a chance they'd take what was left of me home in a box, or I'd walk into our kitchen, that was if I was still capable of walking, and say, 'thhhhhhthory mummth,' the slurring due to the fact I didn't have any teeth left. There must have been over a hundred kids watching, all of them screaming encouragement, but the din was so loud, I couldn't tell who they were encouraging, me or Ivan.

My saviour appeared in the form of one of the senior teachers. Mr. Smith was a slight little man, with a physique that was a carbon copy of Albie. His grey hair matched the grey suits he always wore, and I figured he must have had five of them, because there seemed to be a different pattern for each day of the school week. He was the most popular teacher at the school, and during the lunch breaks he would roam the school grounds, constantly encouraging us with our cricket or any other sports the kids indulged in, where the rest of the staff would secrete themselves in the teacher's common room, never to be seen until classes resumed. Military service had left him with a badly damaged knee, and on good days he'd endeavour to get around unaided, but on bad days, and unfortunately most were, he required the use of a heavily carved walking stick. As I looked over Ivan's shoulder as we continued to fight, I could tell Mr. Smith was having a problem manipulating the front steps, but once down he pushed his way through the crowd, and as he arrived, that's when the fight ended.

He apparently dismissed Ivan with a few well chosen words. I didn't hear what he said, but one of the girls standing close by obviously did, because I heard her say to her friend, 'Oooooh, I heard Mr. Smith say bloooody.' But whatever he said to Ivan definitely worked, because after one last withering scowl at me, he turned and slunk away. Then Mr. Smith turned those blue eyes of his on me as he quietly said, 'Young man, as you're no doubt aware, the school rules stipulate you should both be punished for fighting. But this time it's not going to happen, that is to you, anyway,' and as he continued, I couldn't help wondering what it was he'd said to Ivan, 'and the reason for this is I was standing at the window in my classroom, and I clearly saw why the fight started.'

I glanced quickly across. Yes, no doubt about it, from there he'd have had a perfect view, but then suddenly he asked,' Now tell me lad, where the hell did a kid of your size learn to box like that?' but then just as quickly added, 'Never mind, it doesn't matter, because it appears no serious harm's been done. But I suggest you make a point of thanking whoever taught you, because today he went close to saving your life. Now off you go, but remember one thing, no, on the other hand, make that two things. First, take my advice and try to avoid getting into fights with boys a head taller than you are, and second, if you have to get into any more fights, and I certainly hope you don't, then pick a more deserted part of the school, rather than the main entrance.'

I grinned back my thanks and took off for what was left of my cricket.

But I was still concerned about the girl who'd hit her head on the wall. She was from my own class, and when I returned there after the lunch break, there

she was in our classroom. Kay was a real little sweetheart, and I hated the thought of her being hurt, but she assured me she was quite alright. The only lasting damage was a minor headache, and something one of the staff had given her was well on the way to taking care of that. Definitely relieved, I turned to walk away, but as I did she called me back.

'Mathew,' she coyly said, 'as far as that fight with Ivan is concerned, I want you to know I thought you were just marvellous.'

Then she spoilt it all by quickly leaning forward and giving me a kiss on the cheek. Oh God, girls, honestly you never know what they're going to do next. I glanced around, there were only a few kids in the room, and fortunately it appeared none of them had noticed. Just as well. Any notoriety I may have achieved by standing up to Ivan would disappear in a second, if that had been broadcast around the school community.

Briefly I wondered whether Ivan would follow Mr. Smith's advice, by grabbing and dragging me to a deserted part of the grounds, where he'd proceed to beat me unconscious, but he didn't. A couple of months after our fight he went missing, and the police were informed, because one of the girls went missing with him. They were discovered living in a holiday home that Ivan had broken into. Beverly, or whatever her name was, returned to school, where she was immediately treated with a status normally reserved for royalty by all of the girls. Ivan on the other hand, was instantly expelled, and that sounded familiar as well.

But that living on an island bit had me guessing, so what does one do when something needs explaining? You ask your mother of course, everyone knows that, after all, what are mothers for. So on arrival home I confronted her with my question, 'Muum, why would anyone want to live on an island for ten days with a creep like Ivan Jameson, I mean it's almost Winter, and it's so cold, it's not as if they could even go swimming?'

My mother looked at me with those brown eyes of hers, and with a face as straight as a poker replied, 'Mathew, sweetheart, I'm sorry, but I haven't the faintest idea.'

Oh well, a kid can't win all the time, and top of my list now was to make sure she didn't see my bruised ribs. And that set me thinking. Just as well Albie got my Joe Louis defence worked out. If I'd have arrived home sporting similar bruises on my face, I've been grounded until the other side of Christmas.

And at least one good thing emerged from that fight, and I was sure it was those jungle drums that spread the message. If I could get involved with a fight of that magnitude with Ivan, and emerge still capable of standing, then it suggested I was one to leave alone and not attempt to bully. The rest of the year flowed on without any major occurrences, and possibly that's why the Christmas holidays seemed to be appearing on the horizon.

Even I was aware that my father's long hours and total dedication to his business was paying dividends, because obviously the business was thriving. It crossed my mind that with our family finances improving along with it, perhaps this meant there was a chance of a holiday away. But yet again I was told it just wasn't going to happen. I thought about it, and came to the decision that it simply didn't matter. In some ways I'd rather fill in a lot of my time at the pool,

especially considering Arnie seemed to have suddenly evaporated as quickly as he'd arrived, and let's face it, spending a couple of weeks with the Mc. Kenzie's had become something of a foregone conclusion.

So the months continued to flow by, mainly because no matter what, that's what months seem to have a habit of doing anyway. My second year at Intermediate was proving to be even better than the first, because I finished up with Mr. Smith as my teacher. In reaching eleven years of age, I'd come to a firm conclusion. As I saw it, most teachers are taught to teach, but there are a select few who are born to it, and he was one of them. Under his firm but fair guidance, it was impossible not to move forward, so with my parents happy with my scholastic achievements, there was the same in the sporting area as well, because I represented the school at both swimming and cricket.

However, half way through the year I made the decision I'd like to consider scouting, but my introduction hadn't gone smoothly. On my father's insistence I'd trialled at a troupe South of where we lived, but the boys as a group were rather raucous, and as a result the hall always seemed to be in a minor state of bedlam. My thoughts were I wasn't going to scouts to learn how to misbehave, because when in the mood, I knew I was proficient at that already, so accordingly, my attendance became rather spasmodic. Around the same time, those who camped at the beach would arrange a weekend to assist with any maintenance, and due to the Mc. Kenzie's continuing kindness, as with the other boys from the families, I felt I should also offer my services.

The Saturday and early Sunday morning saw the necessary maintenance completed, leaving the rest of the day for us to do as we pleased. But it was during the Saturday that I noticed a new face had appeared amongst us. Adrian Fulton was a boy about my own age and height, but in build he was decidedly lighter. His rather angular but not unattractive face was dominated by a pair of large, dark brown eyes, over which a head of dark hair resided to a point where he'd developed an unconscious habit of flicking it away, only for it to fall back to its original position. His faintly olive complexion gave the impression he was sporting a permanent sun tan, but hinted as far as I was concerned, at some long lost mid European ancestry. I noticed him doing his best to help, but glancing back a few minutes later, found he was gone. With this will of the wisp pattern repeated for the rest of the day, finally my curiosity got the better of me, and I asked the others for an explanation. And it was provided in an abrupt manner that only young boys seem so expert at, 'Oh him, he was down here a couple of times last year. He's got something wrong with him, and some days are worse than others, and he was to go and lie down. We think he has trouble breathing or something.'

So in other words, with the callousness of youth, he was left with a simple enough option. Keep up with us, or tough luck.

Seeing as we had part of the morning and all of the afternoon to ourselves, and with it still being too cold for swimming, we decided to explore the picturesque farmland that lay beyond the towering cliffs at the Northern end of the beach. We took our time as we wandered along, our feet partially buried in the thick, golden sand. But now aware of the boy's problem, I noticed he chose

to walk on his own further down towards the water, where the sand was firmer and made for easier walking.

Finally we arrived at the base, and anyone not familiar with those almost vertical, rock clad and scrub covered cliffs, would consider them an almost impossible challenge. But as fit as young buck rabbits, the distance to the top was normally conquered in a matter of minutes, so one by one we started to climb, the other boys ahead of me, Adrian following on behind. Just over half way up, and I glanced back. The boy had stopped climbing, and with one hand was holding onto a small shrub. I continued on a little further, then once again looked back, and the look of fear on the boy's face was all the warning I needed.

I yelled to the others, telling them I was going back, then started on down towards him. There was no doubt about it, going down was infinitely harder than climbing up. By the time I reached him I'd collected a couple of bruises and scrapes, and it was obvious he was struggling to breathe at all. So wrapping one arm firmly around his waist, and using the other to hang onto anything that offered something in the way of support, I began to edge ever so slowly and carefully down towards the safety of the sand below. Part way there, so I looked down again and immediately wished I hadn't. Progress was proving to be tediously slow and those rocks managed to look more dangerous than I'd ever thought. But patience was the essence, because even with the worst of the descent behind us, a slip could still see us crashing down to those rocks below, which could cause serious damage, and at worst, possibly one of us his life. Finally, after what seemed an eternity, first the feel of the rocks on my feet, then at last, thank heavens, the sand.

But now it was obvious the boy's condition was frightening, so I suggested he sit quietly while I ran back to the camp for help, but he held onto my arm while silently indicating he didn't want me to leave him. And there were mixed emotions because I felt scared and helpless and so sorry for him, but all I could do was place my arm around his shoulders and offer what encouragement I could, while his dreadful affliction took its toll. Around twenty minutes, some slight improvement, although he was trembling and I assumed he was feeling cold, due to the shadow cast by the cliffs. I suggested we move around past the headland to a small inlet, into which I knew the sun would be pouring.

It took us a little while, due to his shortness of breath, but instantly we knew the move was worth it as we settled down on a cushion of thick grass that was thriving under some Pohutakawa trees. Lying side by side in that welcome comfort, we gazed up through a mantle of leaves and scarlet blossom. As his condition continued to improve, we chatted away together, well on into the afternoon, and during that time, the basis of a new friendship was formed. We parted later that day, with my having received his grandparent's gratitude, but early in the New Year there was a knock on our door and there he stood. As a result, my mother insisted she'd been right, someone had come along to replace Colin, but I didn't completely agree with that, as I replied, ' Come off it Mum, Colin lived two doors away, for this kid it's two suburbs, but I guess when we do see each other, we get along pretty good.'

Chapter 10

For once it was my assessment that proved closer to fact. Adrian and I didn't see all that much of each other, due to the distance between our homes. But during our latest sojourn he made an interesting statement. He was attending scouts, and this caught me by surprise. I'd been friendly with him long enough, to become accustomed to the parental cloak of protection his mother constantly attempted to smother him with. And in some ways it was understandable, due to his somewhat delicate health, but the fact was he was a twelve year old boy who was desperate to be left to enjoy, as much as his health would permit, the life a twelve year old normally indulged in. The fact he was prepared to tackle that difficult cliff was evidence of that.

The fact his mother allowed him to join the organization, told me the troupe he'd joined would have been thoroughly investigated. So as casually as possible, I asked him about the general standard of behaviour, hinting I'd previously trialled with a troupe, and the lack of sensible discipline hadn't impressed me at all, and his reply reactivated my interest,

'You can forget that sort of thing where I go Matt. Our scoutmaster won't tolerate anything like that, not for a second. All the boys are well behaved, so why don't I ask if it's alright for you to come along for a couple of weeks and see what you think? Let's face it; wouldn't it be great if we could attend the same troupe?'

So the enquiry was made and my attendance approved, but one problem remained, that of persuading my father. Suitably encouraged, I started pestering, constantly stressing it made more sense for me to be attending a troupe I was happy with, that was as long as it passed my scrutiny, even if it was much further to travel. Finally, under the weight of my non-stop harassment, he agreed. So with much personal satisfaction, due to the fact I'd managed to manipulate my father, something that didn't happen all that often I might add, I prepared to walk down this bright new path that had rather unexpectedly appeared in my life. But with clouds of doom hovering not far above, I remained blissfully unaware I was about to take the first step down a road that led to purgatory and then somewhere beyond.

That first day, and after meeting Adrian at his home, we walked the relatively short distance to the hall. It proved to be an old, weatherboard building, needing a coat of paint more urgently than the Gossini bungalow, and boy, that was saying something. It reposed in the corner of a large car park, the surface of which was about four metres below the road. It was there mainly to service the congregation of a church, which was situated on the right hand side of a driveway that provided access from the road above. As we wandered past, I couldn't resist the temptation to slip across and peer inside, but it was not worth the trivial energy expended. What appeared grand and imposing on the outside, proved to be rather morbid and forbidding inside, so I rejoined my friend and we strolled on down to the hall.

Immediately we stepped inside, Adrian pointed out the scoutmaster, who appeared to be deep in conversation with two boys on the opposite side of the room, but immediately they parted, Adrian moved across and made the introduction, 'Mr. Bergman, I want to introduce Mathew Colbert. Do you remember? He's the boy I was telling you about, the one who's been trialling at a troupe he's not all that happy about, and would like to check us out with the idea of attending here in the New Year instead.'

Phillip Bergman was a man of no more than average height, who glanced down at me with piercing blue eyes, through a pair of rimless glasses. His smooth, bordering on handsome face, was crowned by a head of thick, black hair, which he brushed back in a style slightly similar to that of my father. What appeared to be a perfectly proportioned, well muscled body, was further complimented by powerful arms and legs, with the latter covered by a pair of white socks that sat at exactly regulation height. Both his shirt and shorts fitted to perfection, and gave the impression the source he obtained them from, outfitted only those who tended to move in a rather elite social circle. His skin had an even tan to a point not far below my own, and this, combined with his physique tended to suggest he was a man who was actively engaged outdoors.

The only slightly disconcerting thing, was I found his gaze seemed to linger on me quite a few seconds longer than I felt was necessary, but when he finally deigned to speak, his voice was resonant, relaxed and pleasantly friendly, 'Well Mathew, obviously there's no problem with you attending here. After all, the Christmas break is not all that far away, so that still gives you a couple of weeks to make up your mind. Adrian certainly told me you weren't overly happy with your original trial, and I must say it's unusual to hear of a troupe that's not properly controlled. But rest assured, you'll find that doesn't happen here. The boys are aware of the standard I expect, and accordingly are well behaved. One thing I must point out though. My position here is only temporary, and once a permanent replacement is found I'll be stepping aside. But I'm in no doubt my replacement will continue with the standard I've tried to set.'

Well maybe, I thought, only time will prove that, but all in all, decided to give it a try. As I settled in, I found most of the boys extremely friendly, with only one possible exception, and his name was Paul Cunningham. He was reasonably tall for his age, which I decided was probably three years older than myself, had a head of thin fair hair, and got around with what I was convinced was a permanent scowl. As a senior scout, it soon became obvious he enjoyed the authority he held over us younger boys, so I made the decision to do my best to ignore him. But it quickly became apparent that he literally detested Adrian, and as far as Adrian was concerned, the feeling was undoubtedly mutual. The situation between them was so volatile, I was certain that sooner or later it had to ignite, and as it turned out, the explosion wasn't long in arriving.

It was during my third day of attending, and the moment Adrian walked in, Paul was after him. But I thought it best to keep my distance, hoping common sense would prevail. I didn't hear the argument, but I was alerted by the noise, caused by Adrian crashing into a couple of chairs as a result of the heavy shove he'd received, and there was Paul bearing down on him. I shot across, placing myself between them, and his rather colourful language indicated he didn't

appreciate my intervention, so I retaliated, unfortunately somewhat in kind, 'Piss off Paul, you've made your point, so bloody well back off and leave him alone, or he won't be the only one you have to deal with.'

He turned away, appearing to take the hint, and I assumed the brief confrontation was over. Bending down to assist Adrian, it was his warning cry that alerted me. As I turned back, I was just in time to encounter a swinging fist, as it connected flush with my left eye. I knew straight away, I didn't have to be told, that black eye my father predicted, had well and truly arrived. It took half a second to dwell on my mother's warning about fighting, and another to recall Bergman's insistence on good behaviour at all times, then reacted as any red blooded kid would do under similar circumstances, and proceeded to bury my fist with all the power I could muster, dead centre of his unprotected stomach.

I must confess the result was rather dramatic. He dropped as if he'd been hit with a shovel, then lay with his arms clasped tightly around his stomach, at the same time emitting strange gurgling noises, which I assumed resulted from him desperately trying to get some air back into his lungs. I looked down at him while he continued to writhe around on the floor, and strongly considering the possibility of kicking him firmly in the teeth. But having been brought up to be the honourable sportsman I was, reluctantly decided against it, but for a while I don't deny I was tempted, the devious, underhand bastard. And that was the end of the confrontation, Bergman appeared breathing fire and fury, and once we'd waited for his highness to be able to stand upright unaided, gave us a thorough tongue lashing for fighting.

My penalty, four evenings of sweeping out the hall, and I expressed my annoyance that my opponent only got two. I tried the age old excuse, 'but he started it,' and didn't get past first base, because Bergman's reply was, 'No Mathew, the penalties stay as they are. You chose to get involved with something that was none of your business.'

Yeh, well, that's his opinion, not mine, but decided it was best to let things settle. I had no idea what Adrian had said to him, and knowing the boy as I now did, I admit there are times when his vocabulary can be described as being rather volatile, to say the least. So the quicker the incident's forgotten the better, but Heaven help me when my mother sees this black eye, because I looked at it in the mirror in the wash room, and I have to admit it sure is a beauty. Never mind, first time ever, so I may as well have made a job of it.

Sure enough, my mother ranted and raved and threatened dire consequences, but on the other hand my father couldn't stop laughing. Hard to fathom parents sometimes. Happily the year finished without any more major occurrences, so the holidays were a combination of the pool and the beach with the Mc. Kenzie's, and while lying back and soaking up that wonderful Summer sun, I contemplated with some trepidation, my introduction to High School.

And with my first day concluded, I accepted I doubted whether it could have gone better.

But the second day, a major surprise, because I ran into Bergman in the grounds, and it was this that started me thinking there was definitely something strange about him. On one of the last days before scouts broke up for the year, he appeared beside me and casually stated,

'Well Mathew, I daresay in the New Year you'll be going back to complete your last year at Intermediate.'

And I corrected him by saying, 'No Sir, I'll be starting my first year at High School.'

Then he'd looked at me and briefly said, 'I'm surprised lad, that means you're a little older than you look. So which school will you be attending?'

And when I told him, he'd completed the conversation by saying, 'That's wonderful, in fact perfect, and I know you'll find it an excellent school.'

So my question was, why initiate a conversation like that, yet not mention he taught at the school? All it did, was add to another incident I'd experienced with him. The late afternoon sun had been beating down, and similar to most of the others who I'd been instructed to help, I'd removed my shirt while we cleaned up some rubbish that had accumulated around the hall, then decided I needed to quench a raging thirst. But as I stood with the glass in my hand, I realised I was standing in front of a series of glass panels that had been stacked against the adjacent wall, and probably due to a combination of the reflection and the angle they were stacked at, it was almost as good as looking in a mirror, and that's when I noticed Bergman, with his eyes riveted on my back.

His gaze was so intense, I found it decidedly disturbing, so purposely I moved to one side, and his eyes followed with every step I took. Now definitely uncomfortable, I moved again, with exactly the same result. Finally, I swung around and stared straight back, and for a few moments he held my gaze, then what I felt was almost reluctantly, he looked away, and that's when I took the opportunity to walk back outside.

Ten days of High School, everything going well, except for science, something I'd already decided I despised. The door to the classroom flung open as Mr. Walcott stormed in. We were used to it, he gave the impression there was only one way between A and B, and that was in a straight line. If one was standing at a point where a deviation was required, then movement was essential, or he'd walk right over you. Our science teacher immediately took evasive action by making sure his desk was between himself and this latest intrusion, as Walcott took up a position in front of the class and bellowed, ' I need eight boys to assist with the preparations that are required on the two main fields. Who's prepared to volunteer?'

Was he kidding? With around thirty of us sitting mournfully in class, immediately about twenty eight hands shot skyward. The two that didn't we'd already assessed as being a bit thick in some directions anyway. Never mind them, I was one of the eight chosen. Felt sure he'd recognised me from cricket practise. Due to a vacancy that had occurred, I'd been chosen to play for the fourth eleven, not overly auspicious, but at least it was a start. Anyway, anything was better than sitting on your butt like so many of the kids seemed content to be doing.

After gathering up our gear, down to the playing fields, where Walcott continued to bawl,

'Right, four of you work carefully across the field, picking up anything in the form of rubbish, and I mean everything, you hear? I want the field left looking like it's been vacuumed, absolutely spotless. The rest of you, over to the

heavy roller. Bring it here and slowly roll the wicket, and keep rolling until I tell you to stop.'

With the main field meeting with his approval, it was over to number two ground, where the cleaning and rolling was repeated. The boys from Kings College were playing our first and second elevens this coming weekend. Their school was like something out of a picture book, with which we had no hope of competing, but Walcott was doing the best he could.

But a small problem was appearing. Dark clouds had been ominously hovering, but now it was starting to rain. Walcott's response was to move up another gear, 'Come on boys, that's enough, get the roller off the field, and hurry, don't want you all getting soaked. Now who of you choose to go back to class?'

It's definite, he's lost the plot. Who in hell would want to go back to science class?

Walcott displayed a flash of humour. There was a smile behind what he said, 'Can't say I blame you. Detested the bloody subject myself, that's why I teach history. So all of you over to the gymnasium, you can shelter there instead. But if I hear of any of you attempting to leave the school before three thirty, you'll answer to me, and you know what that means.'

We certainly did. At the school, punishment was delivered in the form of the cane. Already, I'd watched a boy receive two strokes, and it looked pretty brutal. With my knack of getting into trouble, I figured sooner or later it was a foregone conclusion, but common sense said, later was preferable to sooner. And sending us to the gymnasium made common sense as well. The complex stood on its own away from the main school buildings, and from where we were standing, it offered much closer protection.

So we took off, running as fast as we could, bursting through the main doors, but screeching to a halt just inside the entrance, where we sat down and removed our shoes and socks. None of us were certain, but we suspected shoes on the floor of the gymnasium could be considered a transgression, so better sure than sorry. Although we'd headed for shelter as fast as we could, by the time we'd reached the gym our shirts were quite damp. Moving further on into the dressing room, we found some heaters had been installed. So all of us took of our shirts and hung them on clothes hooks on the walls, then turned on a couple of the heaters on the hope of drying our shirts before we took off for home.

However, with eight young and rather vocal boys, sitting in the room without any supervision, needless to say the noise created was fairly substantial, and as a result a door at the end of the room was flung open and Bergman appeared, looking decidedly put out as he thundered,

'What's all this noise, what are you boys doing here, why aren't you in class?'

One of our group offered a quick explanation, and Walcott's name acted as an instant pacifier. All the masters seemed a bit wary of him, and Bergman didn't prove to be an exception, because in a far more laid back tone he said, 'Well alright, seeing as you've been granted permission, that's fine, but keep the noise down, I'm trying to do bookwork in here.'

He turned, then strode back into what turned out to be his office, closing the door firmly behind him. But as he disappeared, once again my thoughts swung in his direction. There was something about the man that left me feeling decidedly uneasy. I had confirmed his position at the school was the senior master in charge of physical education. This went part of the way in explaining two things. First, that his seniority supplied him with his own office, and second, that his qualifications in the area of youth physical development was such, that no one in the country could approach the qualifications he possessed.

These apparently included a doctorate from a world renowned source in the United States, that was considered the pinnacle of achievement in this area. It was also common knowledge amongst the staff, that he'd recently been approached by some bureaucrat, possibly the Minister of Education himself, to draw up a physical exercise curriculum, that was to include a day by day programme extending over a three year period, which when completed, would become compulsory throughout all the High Schools in the country. It was accepted this would be a major undertaking, and it was rumoured that during the course of the discussions, he'd finished up on a first name basis with the Minister himself.

This apparently left the staff more than slightly wary of him. And a brief conversation I had with one of the seniors down at the cricket nets, left me very wary as well, when he warned me, 'Don't ever get caught on your own in the gymnasium with Bergman. There's nothing surer than that blond head of hair combined with that body of yours will attract him. So he's sure to try to do with you as he's done to some other kids at the school, and that is he'll try to get you into his office and get you to take your clothes off. Don't say you haven't been warned, understand what I mean?'

And as I thought back to those couple of incidents at scouts, I realised I understood all too well. It confirmed my unease had been validated, but then as if on cue, once more his door opened, and leaning nonchalantly against the doorway, he spoke to us again, 'Tell me boys, with all of you here like this, have you all been medically examined?'

The noise in the room stopped in an instant, as eight pairs of eyes flashed worried looks at each other, then the silence was broken as one boy enquired, 'What medical examinations Sir? None of us have ever been told about having to be medically examined.'

He continued, but now I was certain I detected a slight nervous waver in his voice, 'Oh, I'm surprised you haven't been informed. Someone in authority has decreed all boys entering High School this year, must be medically examined, and at this school it's turned out to be my responsibility. However, there's no need for any concern. It's not as if any of you have to remove your clothes, or anything like that. Seeing as none of you are wearing your shirts, all that's required is for you to undo your belts and the flies to your pants, but the strict regulations that apply, state that you only undo them half way down, so as your pants still stay sitting on your hips.'

Remaining where he was, he demonstrated what was required by doing so with his own clothing. Then after making us stand in single file in front of his door, he walked slowly down, carefully checking, making sure each boy had

done as he required. As far as the line was concerned, I'd finished up around the centre, but as he approached me he looked up, then taking me by the arm, eased me back to the rear of the line. As a result, one of the boys who'd been behind me, but due to this adjustment, was now in front, turned around and asked,

'What do you reckon his reason was for him doing that?'

And quite truthfully I replied, 'I haven't the faintest idea.'

Now another decision. Apparently the rules and regulations relating to these so called medical examinations, stipulated one other boy must be in the room while these 'examinations' were carried out. He chose a boy named Stephen King, and Stephen and I were well on the way to becoming good mates. But no time to think about that. The examinations are underway, because the first boy had entered his office, closing the door quietly behind him as instructed. A couple of minutes, now he's reappeared, but rather than stopping and answering the questions levelled at him by those of us who were still waiting, he ignored us as he ran over, grabbed his shirt, then after casting in our direction a look that reeked of humiliation personified, proceeded to bolt out of the room.

His reaction didn't instil a lot of confidence in those of us who were still waiting. But as each boy, one after the other, disappeared inside his room, only to emerge those couple of minutes later, the expressions on their faces displayed a combination of shock, humiliation and resentment. So as the ritual continued as each came out, followed what had become an established pattern of claiming his shirt, then departed at speed, I decided what I was witnessing didn't instil in me any desire to experience what was happening behind that closed door of his room. But finally, as the last one standing and nervously waiting, his never varying instruction of 'next please' rang out. So taking a deep breath and hoping for the best, I stepped inside and closed the door behind me as was expected.

I swung my eyes around the room. Stephen was sitting behind a beautifully mellowed old Kauri table, that was positioned over to the right hand side, and he was writing in a small notebook, that didn't look very official to me, with Bergman standing behind, carefully scrutinising. Directly in front of where I was standing was his desk, then behind that a sink bench, with a water heater fixed to the wall above. But that was where my appraisal ended. Bergman slowly straightened and his eyes swung up, then he stopped, and it was if he appeared to look again, as if at first glance his eyes had deceived him, but it was when he spoke that I sensed I was in big trouble. It wasn't what he said, after all, he only spoke three words, it was the anticipation in his voice that gave me cause for concern, as he very quietly murmured, 'Ah... Yes... Colbert.'

And as far as I was concerned, he may as well have added, 'and I've been waiting especially for you.'

The way he was gazing at me, reminded me of that unsettling episode at scouts, and I knew there was a similarity, because same as then, I was only wearing shorts. So I stood there, decidedly unsure, becoming more uneasy by the second as I wondered what was expected of me, that was until he issued some instructions, 'Walk over and stand in front of my desk boy, then turn around and face the door, standing with your legs apart, and your hands clasped behind your back.'

As I took up the position he spoke once again to Stephen, then he walked towards me, holding his right arm straight out, but at the same time twisting his hand back so his fingers were pointing to the floor. The reason for this unusual position soon became clear. He smiled at me, then placing his palm flat on my stomach, he slipped his hand down inside my pants, then further down between my legs, from where he proceeded to fondle my testicles. Now I understood the reason behind the other boys' varying reactions, and my own warning bells were ringing loud and clear, and that warning got louder still as he suddenly took my penis in his hand and started to rather forcibly masturbate me. Enough was enough, it was time for this gross intrusion to end, but be it as it may, he was still a master at the school. No matter how humiliating the circumstances were, care was still needed in the manner in which I spoke to him, yet at the same time was desperate to make my resentment perfectly clear. So after giving my position a couple more seconds of thought, I said, 'Sir, I'd appreciate it very much if you'd stop doing that to me.'

And the result of my request, absolutely nothing, as the violation continued unabated. So with my resentment running at full steam, I looked up, staring directly into his eyes, and that explained why there'd been no response. His eyes were blank, there was nothing there, it was obvious he hadn't heard one word I'd said. He was breathing hard, and as far as I could tell, off in some sort of weird world of his own. This left me at a loss as to know what to do, so decided my only option was to repeat very firmly what I'd said. But it proved not to be necessary, because he removed his hand, spun around and strode back to the table. He spoke to Stephen, and the boy wrote something in that stupid notebook, then he turned and said,

'Well, all that remains is for me to have a brief word with Colbert, and your presence isn't required for that King, so you can depart.'

As he stood up and headed for the door, Stephen cast me a worried glance, which clearly showed he wasn't happy leaving me alone with this man, but I glanced back, trying to reassure him, because I was aware there was nothing more he could do. And as the door closed behind him, Bergman immediately turned his attention back to me. 'Colbert,' he said,' I'm afraid I must go back on what I said earlier. My examination indicates you could be developing a problem. It's essential this is followed through, after all, that's what these examinations are intended for, so I'm afraid you're going to have to take off your pants.'

And immediately those words from that boy down at the nets rang loud and clear, and so my immediate response was, 'Sir, I really don't think I should be doing that.'

Straight away his reaction was that of frustration personified, 'Good grief, there are times when I find it hard to understand some of you boys', he muttered, ' surely you all have enough sense to accept these examinations are designed to ensure you encounter no unnecessary problems in your adult life', and then as he added just a little more pressure, 'and I would also point out I have an appointment straight after school, and I'll be most unhappy if your foolish reluctance makes me late.'

I knew pressure was being applied, but some doubt had also appeared in my own mind. During the previous year I'd suffered a hernia. Had no idea where it had come from. All I knew was I got up and was preparing to dress for school, and realised I had a lump in my groin that shouldn't have been there. I recall thinking to myself, 'I know there's a name for this, but right now can't think what it is.' No panic, simply continued on dressing, then strolled on down to the dining room. The table was laid out with my mother's usual fastidiousness, and my father was still finishing his breakfast. Knowing better than to mention anything like that around him, I waited until he departed, then promptly forgot to mention it for some time after that. Finally the penny dropped, which resulted in something like, 'Hey Mum, meant to tell you, I've got this lump in my groin, I'm sure it wasn't there yesterday.' Some embarrassment as the problem was checked, resulting in, 'Right my boy, no school for you. Your first stop is our doctor.'

Great, day off school, but in no time lying on an examination table, the doctor carefully probing as he turned to my mother and said, ' Obviously a hernia we have here Mrs. Colbert,' and I'm thinking, ' that's right, that's what they call it', but then he continued, ' but before we do anything dramatic, let's give it forty eight hours. Sometimes when nature springs things like this upon us, it fixes them just as quickly. If nothing changes during that time, we'll have to take the other option, and we both know what that is.'

Oh boy, surely that means two days off school. I'm certain adults read kid's minds, because my mother immediately asked, 'Am I to keep him home from school?' and the doctor replied, 'No, let him go, it won't do him any harm.'

Blast, foiled again. But our doctor anticipated correctly, the problem did disappear, but as I was lying once again on his table for a final all clear, he looked down at me and said, 'Remember boy, if this happens again, you'll be straight into hospital, understand?'

At the time I'd grinned back at him, but now his words were going around in my head. What if Bergman has discovered something, then odds on it means an operation, so I'd rather know, one way or the other. Slowly I undid my belt and let my pants fall to the floor. He held out his hand to take them, then placed them on the chair Stephen had been using.

Highly embarrassed, due to my nakedness, I looked at the floor and waited for him to do what he had to. But I waited and waited, and then waited some more, until finally I lifted my head to see what was happening. And the answer, absolutely nothing. He was standing at the table with one hand resting on it, with his gaze riveted on my body, and there was that blank look on his face I'd seen before, which said he was off in that special world of his own again.

Finally, my penetrating gaze got through, and he started, as if he'd been interrupted while deep in thought, then came over, placed his hand between my legs and repeated at length what he'd done before, and the fact was I still found it offensive. Apparently satisfied, he turned away and glanced at his watch, suggesting he wanted this all over and done with. Then casually he asked, as if it was an afterthought and not all that important, 'One last check Colbert. I'd like you to bend well over for me, and that should see the end to it.'

I did so without hesitation, convinced he wanted me to place some pressure on my groin. He moved across until he was standing behind me. Placing his left hand gently enough on the back of my neck, then with his right hand, suddenly inserted his forefinger straight up my rectum. Letting out a yelp of protest, I endeavoured to lunge away from him, but his strong hand tightened the grip around my neck, and at the same time spreading his fingers across my buttocks, he effectively held me in a vicelike grip, then expertly eased me off balance, making it virtually impossible for me to resist, while at the same time saying, 'Hold still boy, stop trying to fight me, this internal examination is absolutely essential.'

Almost beside myself with a combination of humiliation and frustration, all I could do was stay in the position he had me in, while he continued his crude violation. After quite some time, he finally withdrew his finger and at the same time released me, and as he did I spun away, literally beside myself with fury, then when I'd managed to put a safe distance between us and turned to face him, I literally exploded, 'Sir, you had no right to do what you just did to me, and I intend to lodge a complaint about it.'

'Oh, for Heaven's sake boy,' he countered, 'I can't understand what all the fuss is about. Anyway, I've some good news. My examination has indicated there probably isn't a problem after all, so surely that's a relief, especially seeing as you seem so upset about it.'

'Yeh, isn't that just great,' I snapped back at him,' so does that mean I can clear out of here?'

'I daresay it does', he replied, 'but why not consider staying here with me for just a little longer. There are a number of interesting things we could do together yet.'

I stood there looking at him, barely believing what I was hearing. Another adult who's lost the plot I thought. Why would I want to stay down here with him after what he's just done? Sometimes, I decided, actions speak louder than words, so I shot across, scooped up my clothes and bolted for the door. Seeing as I was naked, I wondered if any of the others were still around, but it seemed they were all as keen to get away from him as I, because the changing room and gym were deserted. I didn't stop running until I reached the point where we'd left our shoes, so I paused just long enough to get dressed and put my shoes on, then three thirty or not, took off and headed for home.

Still seething when I arrived, I was determined to tell my mother what had occurred, after all, mentioning such a thing around my father would put me at risk of my life. Purposely I stayed close to home, determined to catch her the moment she arrived, but incredibly, for the first time ever, it was my father who got home first. Another first, he'd come down with some potent bug, so my mother insisted I spend all of my time over the weekend at the pool, and as little time as possible inside the house, and somehow that put paid to telling her as well.

Back at school on Monday, heading across the quadrangle to join a group of my friends, when I hear someone calling my name. It was Roger Hammond, and I was surprised, he and I weren't what one would politely describe as being overly compatible, something he appeared to be ignoring, for the time being

anyway, ' Hey Colbert, you were down in Bergman's office on Friday. He's not allowed to do what he did to us, and one of the boys told me he had you in his room twice as long as the rest of us. Would you back me up if I reported what he did to the Principal?'

My chance of getting revenge after all, 'I wouldn't just back you up Hammond', I replied, 'I'd be more than prepared to come along with you,'

The Principal listened carefully to our very vocal complaints, then placed us in an empty classroom, with instructions to write down everything that had occurred. Although new to the school, he was already a man I'd trust with my life, and accordingly felt certain our reports were passed on to the proper authority. But Bergman remained at the school, and I was left with the knowledge of how easy it would have been for someone to have placed a barrier across that road to purgatory.

Chapter 11

After that disastrous episode, I made a golden rule. Stay as far away from Bergman as possible. This however, proved to be easier said than done. He finished up as our form's PE instructor. Not happy with the situation, I did my best to keep in the background, thereby trying to have as little to do with him as the circumstances dictated. But with my New Year routine now firmly established, to add to my disquiet, scouts was due to start again, and because of my dislike of the man, I gave some thought to not attending. But it reminded me of Arnold, aware that the scoreboard wouldn't make for overly encouraging reading. Two troupes attended, none completed, making a failure rate of two nil.

So encouraged by Adrian's persistence, I continued, all be it, with considerable caution. I was also encouraged by the fact that persistent rumours suggested Bergman's replacement had been approved, and with the new Scoutmaster's arrival, once he'd settled in, Bergman would be history, a situation I eagerly looked forward to. However, some weeks before the holidays, it had been announced there was to be a meeting of all teaching personnel on a Friday in the new year, thereby giving all parents ample warning there'd be no school on that day.

'Bloody sight different to the wharfies', so my father had thundered, 'they just strike at any old time, so as to cause as much chaos and general disruption as possible.'

This meant there was an unscheduled three day weekend looming, and according to our new scoutmaster, whose appointment had apparently been approved, a camp had been arranged at short notice, at a superb private property, that only on extremely rare occasions, the owners allowed access to. He also stressed the camp had not been officially approved by the scouting hierarchy, but had been organised by the father of a boy from one of the other troupes, who happened to be friendly with the property's owners. This meant that only the scouts from no more than a couple of local troupes would be included, so it was an opportunity that shouldn't be missed, and Bergman stressed, 'I know you're not officially a scout Mathew, but if you decided to join, and Adrian insists you will, then this camp would offer a great start, because I know you'll be keen to get that first patch sewn on your sleeve.'

And it seemed to make sense. Adrian was right, I did intend to join, even though I'd be in the same troupe as that moron Cunningham. But since our fight he'd kept his distance, and I felt there was a good chance the situation would remain like that, which suited me just fine.

And as far as that first patch on my sleeve was concerned, Bergman was dead right. I wanted to start as soon as I could, because some of the boys had so many, they seemed to go up their sleeves and down again. Also, as far as the weekend away and my parents were concerned, I knew they'd be happy knowing I was somewhere being supervised. Well, I mean who could blame a kid, it was fruit season, and the fences around the neighbourhood were a piece of

cake. You could be over one, grab a couple of whatever was available, and be back again in seconds. So as far as getting approval, from my point of view, it was a foregone conclusion. My parents were forever encouraging me to 'get involved' as they tended to put it. But we both knew that wasn't the case with Adrian.

I'd found his mother's moods varied almost as much as the weather. So was there any day when she was in a better mood than the others? Tuesday, definitely a Tuesday, apparently she always went shopping with her sister in the city on a Tuesday. So after school I turned up, cap sitting straight for once, socks at the right height for the first time ever, shirt even tucked in neatly, an example of trustworthiness personified.

Sure enough, she huffed and puffed and sighed and generally carried on, as it seemed only she could, then came the punch line, ' Mathew, you're aware of Adrian's health problems as much as anyone outside our immediate family, so I'll allow him to go on one condition. You must give me your most solemn promise that you won't let him out of your sight, and that you'll look after him, no matter what.'

Brilliant, even if things were a little back to front. Much to my surprise, I'd found Adrian was seven months older than I was. But who cares, the main thing is permission's been granted.

To make the most of the full weekend, we were to be transported to the camp, early on the Thursday evening. Our departure point was our own car park, and with Adrian's father having agreed to provide the transport from their house to the hall, as we approached the top of the driveway, that's as far as we got, because we were greeted by a scene of unmitigated chaos. There were scouts and packs and whatever in abundant confusion, but with some resemblance of order finally insisted on, and subsequently achieved, the first of the two buses hired to transport us finally appeared.

The company's name, that originally had been painted on the side, had faded to a point bordering on oblivion, and as I ran my eyes over the state of the dilapidated vehicle, I decided that as far as beneficial advertising was concerned, it was probably just as well. With our packs stored in the rear compartment, as we filed on board I noticed the interior was on a par with the exterior. The driver, who appeared to be older than the bus itself, sat on a thick cushion, apparently placed there so he could peer over the top of the steering wheel, and hopefully I decided, partially out of the windscreen as well. Whether this position allowed him to reach the brake pedal, I felt was anyone's guess, and once underway, the roar from the antiquated engine made any attempt at conversation impossible. So we sat back in enforced verbal silence, content to enjoy the scenery, such as it was, as we lumbered our way across the city, and on and up into what I assumed were the ranges.

Up in the hills the scenery was worth viewing, but not for long. With the red of the setting sun heralding the end of another perfect, late Summer day, before long darkness descended , and as the bus continued to rumble along on what was fast seeming to be the proverbial never ending journey, a bit of boredom accompanied by the inevitable restlessness set in. But finally the bus swung sharply left off the tarsealed ribbon, and on down a bumpy, pot holed and metal

covered track, until it shuddered to a halt on an expansive and newly mown grass area.

We scrambled out, not sorry the noisy confinement was over, then were directed to a small shed. I wasn't sure whether the man inside was a scoutmaster or parent who'd offered to help out. If he was a parent, then I felt, Heaven help his children, because he couldn't have looked less approachable if he tried. He was a small, overweight little man, with a paunch that hung well over his belt, who'd been given the responsibility of allocating the sleeping arrangements. As Adrian and I eased up in front, after giving us no more than a perfunctory glance, snapped out in a rather abrupt and decidedly unpleasant voice, ' Right, you're in number one shed,' and as he ran his eyes briefly over me, 'and you're in number two kid.'

Deciding nothing ventured, nothing gained, I felt I took my life in my hands as I dared to say, 'Any chance of being in the same shed Sir? He's got a bit of a health problem, and I've promised his parents I'll keep an eye on him.'

Now his eyes did flick up, and as they bored into mine they said it all. Instantly he'd assessed us as another couple of mates, who'd try to be able to stick together. In a desperate move to combat this, I steeled myself to look straight back, eyes wide with that well practised look that reeked innocence personified. And apparently this, combined with the truth behind my request proved to be enough to win the day as he growled, ' Alright, I'll wear it this time, so move, both of you in two,' then added as we turned our backs, ' Christ, some of you kids are the limit. You'll try any bloody thing to get what you want.'

And move we did, purposely putting distance between us before he could change his mind. So we detoured slightly and picked up our packs, then walked across to the shed. The door creaked as it swung in, and I felt that in a past life, it may have been an army shed, but lately had been used for storage, because there was the faintest smell of what I assessed as being fertilizer in the air. But it had been hosed out and thoroughly scrubbed, and resting on the spotless floor were around twelve or fourteen stretchers on which we'd be sleeping. However, with only two sheds being available, there was no doubt the overflow would be sleeping in the couple of tents I'd noticed. Looking at the sturdy walls surrounding us, I wondered if my parents were right about camping after all.

But as far as our shed was concerned, more boys from the bus strolled in, and this resulted in plenty of laughter and general playful nonsense, as to who was sleeping on which stretcher was decided. Next, it was down to the main camp area, where two barbeques were cooking what was going to satisfy some healthy young appetites. Finally done with our meal, we wandered further down to a clearing where a log fire was burning. The charred timber was glowing like molten metal, and periodically throwing up showers of sparks that were floating lazily upward, only to be consumed by the blackness of the night. Some of the boys had arrived before us, having been transported by car, and a group had started singing, so we joined them, and the serene evening drifted pleasantly on, as the clear, perfect sound of young voices drifted up and away, following those sparks into the deep mystery of the sky.

Perfect as it was, in the end tiredness won out, so we wandered back to the shed, and the way I slept had a lot in common with those logs. The new morning dawned fresh and clear, so I lay uncovered, allowing the slight coolness to disperse those last, lingering remnants of sleep, and also I allowed my eyes to drift over the others in the shed, tousled heads on pillows, all still dead to the world. Gradually the sun appeared, heading upward on yet another of its easterly journeys, at the same time painting the sky in a golden blaze of glory. Slipping out of my sleeping bag, I crept silently down and sat on the steps, enchanted by the outstanding beauty unfolding in front of me, content in a magical world of my own.

With the property situated in a valley, there were two encircling hills that seemed to climb to the sky, the tops of both bathed in the early morning sunlight, and all of them covered in luxurious native bush, over which wispy clouds of early morning mist floated, soon destined to disappear with the warmth of the approaching day. But behind me some of the others were stirring, so reluctantly I walked back inside, and playfully we took turns at waking those who were showing an inclination to want to sleep on.

Now the start of the semi official day. First callisthenics, then breakfast, and following that, the rules relating to the camp were explained. The use of the property was due entirely to the generosity of the family concerned. All the boundaries were marked, and it was made clear, it was imperative we didn't wander beyond those points, and woe betide anyone who did. However, for those who were interested in the bush and plants in general, a couple of excursions had been planned. These would leave the camp next morning, and the boys involved would sleep out overnight. The lengths of these treks had been carefully calculated, so as to arrive back at the camp on the Sunday, leaving plenty of time to coincide with the buses that would be taking most of us back to the city. It was stressed, the treks were in no way compulsory, but for those involved, there was a possibility they could earn a patch for their sleeves on completion, and that alone made them worth considering.

It was doubtful if the strong recommendation was really required, because immediately the talk ended, there was a rush of boys lining up outside that small shed to register, the chance of another patch on their sleeves obviously being a major attraction. But after looking at the queue that had gathered, Adrian and I decided to come back a little later when the rush had subsided. So instead we wandered off, content to let curiosity take care of the next twenty minutes or so. We strolled along, occasionally stopping and chatting with many of the boys we knew. A little further, and up ahead a fence post adorned with a yellow ribbon, the obvious sign we'd reached the outer limits of the area we'd been assigned for the camp.

So we turned left, and almost immediately heard the sound of laughter. There was a far from clear path leading into a bush-clad area that reminded me of the infamous fallen log. But deciding that direction was as good as any, we took off down the track, now interested to investigate. We emerged into a reasonably sized grass covered clearing, and to my delight, there in front of us lay a shimmering waterhole. The supply of water, that logic said had to be fairly cold, was arriving courtesy of a minute waterfall, that was tumbling down the

face of a large rock at a point adjacent to where we were standing. And it wasn't small, because I calculated the surface area being at least three quarters the size of the Council pool.

The laughter was originating from four boys who were treading water, and was aimed at one other who was standing naked and apprehensive on a rock. But after another burst of youthful encouragement, he started to ease himself down, at the same time emitting shrieks and gasps of horror, as the water continued to envelope him. My immediate thought was for my favourite pair of swimming briefs, but that didn't last long. If the boys could swim naked, then so could I. We were at a boys' camp, not a girl guide convention, and at the same time Adrian seemed to read my thoughts. 'Go on Matt,' he said, 'I know you and water. You're like a fish, you can't seem to be able to live long without it. Hop in and have some fun, and I'll go back and get your towel.'

As the morning drifted pleasantly on, a number of boys came down to investigate the source of our enjoyment, but for most, the water was much too cold. But for the few of us who did enjoy it, we established a set routine. When we reached a point where the water was starting to chill us, we'd climb out, rub ourselves vigorously dry, then spread our towels on the grass and lie in the heat of the sun until we were toasting-ly warm, then it would be shrieks of horror as we dived back in again. As far as I was concerned, lunch became a forgotten meal, as we continued to enjoy ourselves, well into the late afternoon.

Inevitably however, the sun started to sink lower in the sky to a point where it was starting to be obscured by the tops of the trees, and with the lack of warmth slowly becoming too much, even for us, we dressed and headed back up to the main camp. At various times during the afternoon, I thought about registering for our trek. There was no doubt about it, starting scouts and the chance of getting a patch on my sleeve would be great, yeh, fair enough, but swimming was even better. Now time for our evening meal, and no lunch meant I'd worked up a healthy appetite. But even after stacking away a rather prodigious amount of food, as I sat talking with some others, I silently had to admit to the occasional shiver persistently running through my body. So alright, maybe I had stayed in that cold water a bit too long. Glad my mother isn't here, she'd really be getting stuck in.

Talk about timed to perfection. An announcement, courtesy of the camps temporarily installed loud speaker system. For those who'd like a shower before bed, there was a limited supply of hot water available, so it was a case of first come, first served. No doubt about it, under the circumstances, a warm shower had a lot going for it. With Adrian not interested, I bolted for the shed, scooped up a dry towel, then headed at speed for the showers, the position of which I'd noted earlier. Quick as I was, a number of boys had beaten me to it, so a short wait until a shower unit became available. Once inside, I felt it was anyone's guess what the shed was used for under normal circumstances, and it was apparent, going by the number of leaking joints, that the showers had been hastily and rather crudely contrived, by the use of an assortment of galvanised fittings. Never the less, crude or not, they were proving to be quite adequate, going by the number of boys who were showering. And as I stepped into a vacant cubicle and that warm water cascaded down, I found it absolutely

delightful, with my shivers seeming to depart for good in seconds. But in contrast to this pleasantness, little did I realise I was in for an unpleasant surprise.

A senior scout had been despatched to supervise, his responsibility being to make sure the boys got in and out of the showers in reasonable time, thereby ensuring the restricted supply of hot water would last as long as possible. The only trouble was that from my point of view, their choice couldn't have been more unfortunate, because that scout turned out to be Paul Cunningham, and immediately I knew I had a problem. As I continued to shower, he came over and stood directly in front, then his childish and stupid comments started to flow.

Long before, I'd accepted I hadn't been born with a smart mouth, and at various times I'd envied boys who possessed this handy ability. During past situations that had occurred at one time or another, when I'd been on the receiving end of a quick tongue, if I'd ever thought of a reply that was appropriate for the occasion, it had always arrived at least half an hour too late. But this time, with my lack of pubic hair having already placed me in a similar position at High School, with one of Hammond's favourite utterances being, 'Come on Colbert, strip right off, show us what colour the nappies are you're wearing today,' for what felt like the first time ever, I'd had the time to formulate a few verbal responses of my own.

And there was no doubt they were proving highly effective. With the boys in close proximity having stopped showering while they listened to this verbal exchange, in no time at all they started laughing. But much to Cunningham's embarrassment, rather than laughing at me as he'd intended, he found them laughing at him instead. Accordingly, the renowned Cunningham aggression surfaced rather quickly, and as he took a threatening step forward, I was pleased with my reaction, or more specifically, lack of it, because I didn't even stop washing as I replied, 'Look Paul,' I quietly stated, 'I don't want to fight with you, in fact, if the truth be known, I don't even want to talk to you. However, I will say one thing. If you attempt to throw a punch at me, then rest assured, I'll do my level best to let you know you've been in a fight, so back off, alright?'

He stood there, still oozing aggression, but something about his eyes suggested some small seeds of doubt had effectively been sown, and I accepted that in some ways, it was probably just as well. He was those years older, and even allowing for his slight frame, I was sure he still weighed more than I did, and that fight with Ivan still acted as a warning. Never the less, he did appear more than just a little wary, as his reply tended to indicate,

'Think you're such a smart little bastard. I've heard the stories about you being pretty slick with your fists. Obviously think you're a great boxer, don't you?'

His comment caught me by surprise, it had no validity what so ever. Ever since that fight with Ivan, I'd gone out of my way to avoid any similar trouble, and none had appeared. Well, that was except for that set to he and I'd had, which I'd come out on the wrong end of, as it happened. He'd received a punch in the stomach, which he'd got over in minutes, I'd collected a black eye, and it lasted for days. Things however, were improving. My reply rolled off my tongue

like I didn't have to even think about it, 'No Paul, I don't, in fact nothing could be further from the truth. But I'll tell you one thing though, and that is there's a chance I'm at least good enough to give you quite a run for your money.'

A few more seconds as he stood his ground and glared, but now a bit of a commotion down the far end of the shed. Nothing much, a couple of the lads letting off a bit of relatively playful steam, but it provided him with an opportunity to back off and move away. He turned to do so, then suddenly turned back, firing one last shot before he left, 'That's alright, my smart, blond headed young friend. What's happened here today, means I'm going to enjoy all the more what I'm going to do to you tomorrow.'

After quickly drying and dressing, I headed for the shed. Wanted to have a bit of a moan about Cunningham with Adrian, but as I glanced over to where he was lying, his eyes had that distant look, indicating sleep was in the close vicinity of his intentions. I'll leave it until tomorrow. Right now, the last thing I need is another punch-up with that unpleasant slob. Hopefully during the night he'll cool off, and by the morning everything would be forgotten. All I could do, was try and stay out of his road. Sleep came as if I'd been drugged.

The morning, and consciousness hovering, experiencing a little difficulty in breaking through the fog. Somewhere amongst the vagueness, something was telling me things weren't quite right. Gradually the problem registered. Something to do with that meal last night, wasn't sitting all that comfortably, and the slight pain was hinting a trip to the toilet block was fast becoming an urgent necessity. While I was sitting there I thought about Cunningham. Hell, the way I was feeling told me the last thing I needed, was even more trouble with him. It was like he was starting to haunt me. While walking back, I decided I was feeling much better, but still not quite one hundred per cent. Something else was needed, and then it hit me, what could prove better than the therapy offered by cold water.

Grabbing my towel, and checking that Adrian was still sleeping, it was down to the pool. If the water was classed as cold yesterday, today would see it as freezing, but still, I dived in, and it took quite a few seconds to recover from the shock, but after ten minutes or so of fairly vigorous swimming, I was feeling more like my old self. After half an hour on my own, gradually other boys started appearing, invariably familiar faces from yesterday. We played around, enjoyed ourselves, until one of them climbed out and explained why he was leaving,

'Time for me to go you guys. The group I'm trekking with is leaving shortly, and I need some time to check my gear.'

This resulted in a twinge of guilt. Never did get around to putting our names down, mainly because I'd become too engrossed in my swimming. Adrian had plenty of opportunity, but often he wouldn't do anything, unless we could do it together. It crossed my mind. Maybe I should try and check and see if he wants to try and put our names down now. On the other hand, it was more than likely much too late. Only one way to find out, so I dressed and headed back to the camp. A glance in the shed, not a sign of anyone, the place looking so tidy it was downright indecent, barely fit for a group of boys to survive in. At the same time

it set alarm bells ringing, because it screamed of Bergman and his insistence on absolute tidiness.

Hadn't laid eyes on him since we'd been here, and let's face it, since the appointment of the new scoutmaster, there was no need for him to be here anyway. Never mind, no use thinking about something there's no need to think about, so I shut the door and went searching. Wandered vaguely around, asking the occasional boy if they'd seen Adrian. Next I found myself not far away from the so called administration shed. Then it registered, someone was calling my name. And what a turn up for the books, it's Eric Holland of all people, our most senior scout. I'd already assessed him as being so full of himself, it was as much as he could do to bring himself to acknowledge us younger kids even existed, and that included talk to us, but now talk he did, his voice laced with impatience, 'Jesus Christ Colbert, where the hell have you been', he snapped, 'I've had kids out looking for you everywhere. It's been noticed you haven't put your name down for trekking and camping out overnight, and they say it's something you can't afford to miss. But as it happens, you're in luck, I'm taking a small group out, so you can come with us.'

It had clearly been stated, trekking wasn't compulsory, yet here he was literally demanding instant obedience, and as I saw it, there was just little more to it than that as I hit back, 'Just a moment Holland,' I countered, 'I don't mind coming except I promised Adrian Fulton's parents I'd keep an eye on him, so unless he's prepared to come, you can forget it.'

But he immediately came back with, 'I've checked Colbert, and he's waiting round the back because he's said he wants to come. Now get your gear and get back as soon as possible. I don't want to be any later than I can help leaving, after all, we've got a fair distance to walk.'

Conveniently Adrian appeared around the side of the shed, and confirmed everything Holland had said. He'd rather experience the variety trekking and camping out offered, rather than staying here at the camp. It appeared the decision had been made, whether I approved or not, and still slightly reluctant, but at the same time not really knowing why, I went back and collected my pack and sleeping bag. When I returned, Holland was in the office, such as it was, being briefed again on the route we were to take. So taking the opportunity his absence offered, I sat down with Adrian on the grass, and studied the others who'd be with us. And I was surprised. We'd previously mixed with the scouts from the couple of other troupes who were also attending the camp, and if I didn't know them by name, I knew them by sight, the number we'd met during the previous day confirmed that. But the six who were sitting together on the grass, talking amongst themselves, and who appeared to be about three or four years older than us, I was certain I'd never seen before in my life, so somehow I suspected, and once again I didn't know why, but something was telling me they weren't even scouts. There had to be an explanation, and the only one I could think of, was the possibility they were trialling, similar to myself, but on the other hand, if this was the case, they seemed to have left it a bit late, because they appeared a bit old to be doing that, but the seventh I knew all too well, it was the charming Paul Cunningham.

I thought about it, and admitted to myself I wasn't all that surprised. It was common knowledge at the troupe, that he and Holland were the best of mates, and what's more, had been for quite some time. In some ways, I decided, they're no different to Adrian and myself, just a couple of friends determined to stick together. However, so much for trying to stay away from Cunningham and his unpleasantness. For the better part of the next two days, we were literally going to be living on top of each other. The thought of it left me feeling totally uninspired, but too late to do anything about it now, because Holland's already appeared back out of the shed and issuing instructions, something he's quite good at, so along with the rest of the boys, I take the hint and after slipping the straps of my pack over my shoulders I join the others and walking in single file, we head for the road above the camp.

Chapter 12

We walked for some little distance down the tar sealed road, until we came to a sign post, on which written instructions clearly indicated the track we had to take, which wound its way down into yet another valley. Fortunately, the weather was behaving, almost perfect, blue skies above, with only the occasional cloud to be seen. But before too long, they started to disappear, as a thick canopy of trees and shrubs started to close in almost ominously around us. During the previous few days, before we took off for the camp, there's been a reasonable amount of rain, and as we pressed on the atmosphere became increasingly more heavy, as heat from the sun continued to interact with moisture contained in the valley floor. And the plants appeared to be thriving in this hot house environment, with the recent profusion of growth, constantly keeping me fascinated.

I was aware many people spent untold hours studying this sort of thing, and as we continued on through this green wonderland, that hinted at an existence all of its own, I imagined Mr. Gossini being in his element. Apart from the chirping and twittering of the birds, and occasionally the sound of rippling water, nothing else seemed capable of intruding on this rarely experienced serenity. Well, being born and bred in the city, it was rare for me, anyway. As we kept up a fairly steady pace, gradually, one after the other, we were forced to surrender to the heavy humidity by removing our shirts and stuffing them unceremoniously in our packs. The track we were walking on proved to be in excellent condition, due to a recent and liberal coating of gravel. The sports shoes I was wearing were my pride and joy, and I disliked the thought of getting them muddy and unsightly. A friend of my father had brought them back with him from Europe, intending them to be a surprise gift for his son. They'd proved to be at least a size too small, so guess who finished up being the lucky one. They fitted me as if they'd been tailor made.

Another twenty minutes of walking, and I knew the time was accurate, because I could tell by my Mondia watch, another pride and joy, a gift from my parents for my eleventh birthday. Now Eric, who was leading up front, swung left and started climbing up a somewhat overgrown track, which proved to be nowhere near as well maintained as the one we'd been walking on. It entered my mind, perhaps I was going to get my shoes muddy after all. We continued on and steadily upward, with the result that the blue sky gradually started reappearing, with the scenery changing from heavy, dense bush, to the open, rangy feeling of lush green paddocks, that reminded me of those that reposed at the top of the cliffs at the beach.

Now across a road, through a fence, then trudging on down to the expansive farmland below. Through a gate, that Eric checked to make sure we'd shut and secured correctly, then we started to follow tracks, obviously made by some reasonably heavy vehicle, because the tyre marks were deeply imbedded in the grass and gravel covered ground. We followed these indentations for some little

distance, then after using some large rocks as stepping stones as we crossed a charming, but reasonably substantial stream, we swung left, walked a little further, then looped around to the right as we skirted a large group of trees, then walked on into what was a fairly substantial clearing. The relatively even height of the grass, suggested it had been mown not all that long back, and to the rear, settling comfortably enough into a backdrop of more trees and scrub, stood an old, weather beaten shed.

And it wasn't small, with the front being quite wide across. The walls consisted of what looked like handmade concrete blocks, the standard of which indicated they'd been poured and formed onsite, and in keeping, the ability, or lack of it, of the person or persons who'd laid them, gave a strong hint they'd been doing so for the very first time. The surface of the corrugated iron roof had long before started to succumb to the elements, leaving it in places a rusty coloured red, and a number of the fixing nails had departed as well, with the result that a couple of the sheets were moving slightly in the barely perceptible breeze.

The hip roof was serviced by guttering, most of which had deteriorated to a point of being useless, the one exception being a section on the right hand side. This one length was still in moderate condition, and spasmodically was helping to fill a water tank that was reposing on what was still a sturdily constructed stand. Apparently in sympathy with the guttering, the upper portion of the tank had disintegrated, but as we moved up and stood beside it, I couldn't resist climbing up and peering inside. As I suspected, the bottom half contained a reasonable depth of crystal, clear water, and indications were it would continue to do so for some time yet.

Immediately to the left of the tank, the supporting frame of which had been built about two metres from the shed, was a battered, tongue and grooved door, sagging slightly on well worn hinges, with these attached to an equally battered doorframe. At the other end, and on the front of the shed, stood a pair of double doors, the condition of which was in keeping with the single door, and in front of which those tracks we'd followed terminated, indicating that whatever had been responsible, could well be housed inside. Around the base of the building the grass was growing unhindered, having constantly evaded the blade of the mower. Apparently suitably inspired, it gave the impression of being determined to grow high enough, so as to block out a large percentage of the sunlight, that was endeavouring to filter through the years of accumulated grime and cobwebs that covered the windows. These were of a colonial design, and if they'd ever been painted, they certainly weren't any more.

But with Eric now standing in front of that single door, he reached out, grasped the badly dented brass handle, and with one flowing movement, turned it and stepped straight inside. And it instantly registered, he must have been here before. Maybe my form of logic had deserted me, but as I saw it, surely if you intended to open a door you were unfamiliar with, you gently turned the handle first, testing if the door was locked or not. But not a moment's hesitation, he knew the door would open, because he'd just stepped straight inside without so much as a moment's hesitation.

For some reason, my inner warning bell rang loud and clear, and it also flashed through my mind, why were we here anyway? After all, even I knew we had quite some distance to travel yet, before we reached the campsite where we were to spend the night. However, equally as quickly I realised my warning bell had switched off. More than likely Eric simply intended to use the shed as a brief rest stop, before we continued on. Also, not long after I'd taken my shirt off, the left strap on my pack had started to chaff my shoulder, and stopping here gave me the opportunity of trying to adjust it, and if that didn't work, I'd just have to put my shirt back on, whether I got hot or not.

One by one the others filed into the shed, with Adrian and I bringing up the rear. It took a few moments for my eyes to adjust to the semi gloom, after the time spent outside in the bright sunlight. And sure enough, down the far end with its nose pointing at the back of those double doors, stood what appeared to be a relatively new Ferguson tractor. I wandered further in, and immediately to the rear of the tractor and neatly stacked in a corner was a collection of gardening tools, a glance at which confirmed they'd been carefully oiled and kept in top working condition. Now walking back in the direction where I'd entered, the rear wall taken up with a strongly constructed full length work bench, the top of which I noticed was heavily discoloured, due to years of saturation in a combination of oil and grease. Pushed to the rear were numerous jars and tins containing an extensive collection of washers and screws, nuts and bolts, used spark plugs, and an extensive supply of other nondescript items.

But what mainly caught my eye, was that in front of those jars and tins and scattered around haphazardly on top, was a conglomeration of mechanical and wood working tools, that going by what I'd learnt from my father, must have been worth a small fortune. Various items of larger proportions had been stacked underneath, with the variety and size of this collection suggesting it had taken many years to accumulate. Once inside, I'd immediately noticed the building included another large area at the rear. The concrete floor was on a lower level to a point, where the difference in the two floor levels provided an ideal place to sit.

As I stepped down, I noticed in the far right hand corner a collection of timber boxes, and beside those, a carefully stacked pile of sacks. And in the centre of the floor stood a solid, timber frame, and it had been there for quite some time, because the four posts that formed the basis of the unit, had been concreted into the floor, and these stood up at each corner at around my waist height. More timber had been cut between those, forming a square on top, and the strength of the construction suggested that sometime in the past, it had supported a heavy piece of machinery, possibly a generator, which I felt was as good a guess as any.

However, recently it appeared additions had been added in the form of two lengths of very thick bamboo, one of which had been lashed to the front top edge, and the other on the opposite side, but this time a small distance up from the floor. The structure had been completed by nailing four short lengths of timber on top, completing what could be described as a platform. But as I sat down, I gave the structure nothing more than a cursory glance, because dealing with this strap on my pack was what held top priority. As the other boys

concluded their own inspections, they chose to toss their packs up on the workbench, while Adrian came and sat on the step beside me.

A couple of minutes, no luck with the strap, I glanced across, the others were grouped together and were obviously engaged in deep conversation, and noticing the occasional furtive glances being cast in our direction, felt it wasn't out of the way to assume, we were the topic of their discussion. Now some movement, Eric had extracted himself and was making his way over. There was something about the way he was walking I couldn't quite fathom, because outwardly, he seemed to be trying to appear nonchalant, as if he had all the time in the world, but I, on the other hand, gained the impression he couldn't get here quick enough. On arrival however, he dispelled the possibility of both of us being included, because completely excluding Adrian, he aimed his words solely at me, 'I think you should know kid, I've spent a lot of time around here, and I've known about this shed for years.'

Well good for you I thought, and frankly, couldn't care less, but ignoring my indifference, he carried on regardless, ' So the reason we've come here is with it being so secluded, and knowing the workers don't come anywhere near it at this time of the year, I know there's absolutely no chance of anyone disturbing us. Now given these ideal circumstances, there's nothing more that all of us want, than to have some fun with you. Now you're not stupid, you know what I'm talking about, so make it easy on yourself and provide us with what we want.'

And it all sounded fine, as far as I was concerned. After all, having fun came high on my list of priorities in life, but there appeared to be one small problem. Contrary to what he apparently thought, I didn't have the faintest idea of what he was talking about. And this definitely registered, because as I continued to gaze blankly up at him, his tone suddenly changed to one of underlying aggression, 'I warn you kid, don't try playing young and innocent with me. You know bloody well what we expect from you, so take my advice and accept it kid, because it's going to happen, one way or the other.'

He turned and pointed in the general direction of the timber frame standing on the lower section of floor as he continued, ' So take your pants off, then go over there and wait for me, because it was decided some time back, that I was the one who got first turn with you.'

Alright, I may be a bit clueless in some directions, but that didn't mean to say I was stupid, and the fact he'd told me to remove my clothing was all the warning I needed. I glanced across at Adrian, assuming he'd be as worried as I was, but he returned my gaze, giving the impression he was comparatively unconcerned. In an instant my eyes flicked around the shed, taking less time than it took to blink to assess our position.

I was convinced our only chance of a quick exit lay solely with the door through which we'd entered, but the odds were still far from in our favour. The other boys had eased away from the workbench and spread out while they watched our reaction, and in doing so, either inadvertently or on purpose, two of them were standing slightly closer to the door than we were. At the same time while speaking to Eric, I'd eased closer to Adrian, trying to give the impression I was unconcerned, where in reality, I was becoming more so by the second.

Typical of most sports minded twelve year olds, I could run like a young gazelle, and when his health allowed, Adrian was just about as quick. In here I accepted our position was hopeless, outside I decided, at least we stood a chance.

Time for an attempt to make Eric see reason, 'Look, we don't want any trouble, so let us go. I couldn't care less what you guys get up to, so let us go and I'll tell them at the camp that Adrian wasn't feeling all that good, and I thought it best we should make our way back.'

But all that created was a burst of raucous laughter as Eric continued. 'Good try kid, but not a chance. Look, the fact is if we wanted to do it with him, we sure as hell wouldn't let his health stop us. It's not an issue kid, we've been discussing and planning this for quite some time. It's you we all want, so for the last time, strip off and show us what you've got, and most of all cooperate, or you'll leave us no alternative, we'll do it to you the hard way, and I warn you kid, I know what I'm talking about. We came up here yesterday and practised, you know, height off the floor and all that, so I've been in the position we'll put you in, and I can tell you now, it'll suit us, but you certainly won't find it too comfortable.'

Something was telling me it was now or never. I flung a quick glance at Adrian, at the same time rolling my eyes towards the door. As always, I knew the communication was there, he knew exactly what I intended. I tried again, but it was really no more than an attempt to try and catch them off guard, 'You lot must be crazy if you think you can get away with something like this. You won't even start to believe the trouble you'll make for yourselves, and it will see you…' I stopped and bolted for the door. Always thought that going by my mental calculations, we had reasonable hope of success. Never was all that good at mental arithmetic, and this proved it, I never stood a chance, because two of them had me before I was half way there. As I fought them, a third joined in, and as his arms forced my own up my back, I glanced across to find Adrian hadn't even moved.

A combination of fear and fury meant I cut loose, using some of the language I'd learnt from the Gossini's, but it was completely ignored as they dragged me back and made me stand in front of Eric, and he smiled arrogantly as he said, 'Don't ever say you weren't warned kid, and what happens from now on, will have been your own stubborn fault.'

By increasing the pressure on my arms, they dragged me over towards that timber frame, but part way there, one of them stumbled and released his grip which allowed me to get an arm free, and for a few seconds some of them really collected some bruises. But my arm was grabbed again and forced brutally up my back until I thought it was going to break. Then suddenly it was relaxed, and as I straightened up, Eric's fist smashed with sickening force, directly into the pit of my stomach. Badly winded, I collapsed forward, determined not to make those gurgling sounds like Paul, and while almost on my knees, Eric snapped out terse instructions, ' Hurry up, come on, get on with it, you all know what to do, exactly as we practised yesterday. Make it quick, because it won't take him long to get his breath back.'

Now dragged those last few paces, held face down over that timber frame with my arms forced out and securely held, then as I struggled to draw that first shuddering breath, I realised one of them was starting to tie my left wrist to that forward piece of bamboo. At the same time some of them held my legs as my shoes and socks were wrenched off, and that allowed them to pull my pants down and cast them aside. Now a warning was registering loud and clear, if they managed to complete tying my wrists, I was finished, from then on I didn't stand a chance. A quick decision, another lungful of air, then somehow managing to get my right leg free, I lashed out with a vicious kick, and I felt it connect, and it hurt, that's if the language that eventuated was any indication. But it was nowhere near enough, that lashing around my wrists secured, and a knee pressing painfully into the small of my back was successfully restricting any chance I had of fighting back. Then they were forcing my legs apart, and that's when I heard Eric call out, 'Get his legs spread further than that. I told you, I want good access to that part of his body.'

As instructed, they forced them further apart again, then lashed them to that lower piece of bamboo. Finally they stepped back, leaving me naked, spread-eagled and utterly helpless.

I glanced around, desperately trying to come to terms with what was happening. Most of the boys had gathered in a group, talking and some openly gloating over what they'd achieved, while a couple looked decidedly unsure and slightly nervous. It was Eric who came over and stood beside me, 'It's time we had a chat kid,' but before he could go any further I interrupted, 'Yeah, well I don't want to talk to you, you bastard. I mean it, you'd better let me go. You'll all be in so much trouble over this, especially when I tell my parents what you've done, and they'll contact the police, and you won't be so smart when that happens.'

But it seemed my threats just rolled off him, as apparently undeterred, he squatted down and said, 'Just listen kid, I'll tell you a story, and I swear it's true. Quite a few months back, Paul and I had our eyes on a kid, he was a little older than you, and dark haired, but similar to you, had quite a body on him. We waited for a day when my parents were out, then got him into my bedroom on the understanding he could look at my model plane collection. But finally we explained what we really wanted from him. Well, you know, at first he blustered and carried on, then finally finished up blubbering, but in the end he undressed and allowed us to have him, and it lasted quite a while. Made him stand facing a wall in between, because yet again like you kid, he had a cute bum, and we both did him three times. Just over a month back I saw him again, and asked if he'd told what happened, and when he said no, I asked him why, and he said he was ashamed to tell his parents that two boys used him for sex six times. Back then there were two of us, here there's eight. So you're in for a busy time kid.'

I thought about telling my father, and felt more desperate than ever.

Surely there was something I could do. I studied the frame, and realised the bamboo had been lashed to it using strips of flax, that broad leafed plant, so common in New Zealand's native bush. To secure my wrists and ankles, they'd used three very thin strips, plaited together, making a lashing as strong as any rope. Carefully I tested my wrists, but there was virtually no movement possible.

With my concern escalating rapidly upward, it didn't help to have to accept the only way I'd be free, was when one of them either cut me loose or untied me. Eric stood and strolled over to Adrian. The conversation lasted a couple of minutes, and obviously doing as he'd been told, the boy moved over and stood with his back to the side wall, then leant back against it, apparently obeying Eric's instructions to the letter.

Eric wandered back and squatted as before, and when he spoke, he did so with a menacing softness, 'The position you're in gives a clear enough indication of what we'll mainly be doing with you. But later, there'll be a few other things we'll be wanting, and for them to be successful, I'll require your complete cooperation, so you're going to have to agree to do everything I tell you kid.'

My reply wasn't tactful, but at least it got straight to the point, 'Go to bloody hell Holland,' and as an afterthought, 'and you can stop calling me kid.'

'Well alright,' he replied, 'but don't forget, you brought this on yourself.' He turned to walk away, but suddenly stopped, his eyes riveted on my wrist, then he exploded, 'Hey you guys, what did I tell you yesterday? I made it clear I wanted him naked. Do you need that interpreted, it means naked, you know, nothing on, and that includes his fucking watch.'

He stalked back, and after removing my precious Swiss Mondia watch from my wrist, held it up briefly while he admired it, then casually tossed it in the direction where my pants were lying, with the result it landed with a resounding clatter on the concrete floor. Next he walked over and picked up one of my shoes, then held that up and studied it also, probably because he'd never seen one quite like it before. He wasn't on his own there, because when I'd been given them, I hadn't seen anything like them either. But having satisfied his curiosity, he proceeded with exaggerated casualness, to strip out the lace.

He wandered back, holding the lace out in front, as he crossed it and formed a loop, then stepping behind, he squatted between my legs, and slipped the loop around my testicles. Drawing it reasonably tight, he passed it around once more, pulled it a little tighter, then tied it firmly in place. As a result, the skin normally pliable and loose, was pulled drum tight. He placed his hand there, rolling my testicles in it, checking the effect he desired had been achieved, then taking his knife, cut off the excess lace. He bent forward, placing his mouth close to my ear, then spoke in a lethally threatening voice, 'Be warned, I'm running out of patience kid, now will you agree to instantly do what I tell you?'

The lace was tight, but not overly painful. Unpleasant, yes, humiliating, definitely, but even allowing for that, I decided I was still prepared to try and fight on, 'As I said before Eric, go to bloody hell, you disgusting, perverted, bullying bastard.'

Acts of bravado can be fine, but can also lead to distressing results. Back to squatting behind me, he brought the blade of his hand up, swinging from the floor in a vicious, upward arc as the blow thudded in, directly between my legs. The explosion of searing, excruciating agony that followed, arrived with an intensity I'd have never thought possible. It exploded up into my groin, seared like a blast of white hot metal on into my stomach, then radiated out to my

extremities, as if only to be content when it had destroyed every shrieking nerve in my body.

I let out an involuntary scream of agony, convinced nothing could create more pain, but as if to prove me wrong, he hit me again, if anything harder still, and at that point one of the boys rushed over and shouting loudly, admonishing Eric for what he was doing, 'For Christ's sake Eric, do you have to hit the kid like that. Surely there's some other way we can make him do what we want. For God's sake, don't hit the kid like that again.'

And the reply he received was brutally to the point, as Eric snarled back, 'Shut the fuck up. If you don't agree with what I'm doing to him, then piss off outside. We agreed this would be done my way. Well, this is my fucking way. My father told me if you hurt someone bad enough, you can make them do and say anything you want. So take it from me, when I'm finished with this stubborn little prick, he'll perform for us like a trained little monkey, just you wait and see, you'll find I'm right.'

And already I knew he was, because I'd do anything to avoid more pain like this. I'd been in plenty of rough and tumbles, and would never forget that time when Colin caught me with an unintentional knee in the groin. Back then I'd been able to curl up with my hands clasped around my stomach, and stay like that with my knees drawn up, until the terrible pain dispersed. But here, tied down like this, there was no option other than to accept every wave of this dreadful pain he'd caused. Now his voice was in my ear again, equally as soft and lethal as before, 'Tell me kid, after what you've just experienced, now will you agree to do everything I tell you? And don't forget, this can carry on until I decide it's time to stop.'

I thought about it for all of two seconds, then decided my answer was yes, excruciating agony had seen to that. I opened my mouth to surrender, and not a sound, my vocal chords paralysed from the shock, and I panicked, certain he'd take my silence as a sign of more resistance. I tried again, desperate to tell him I'd do anything, as long as he didn't hit me like that again. Too late, another blow, then another for good measure, and they left me convinced my groin, stomach and heart were about to burst, and to add to my misery, I was on the verge of being physically sick. He bent over and asked again, so I nodded my submission instead.

Perspiration was streaming down my face, mingling with my tears as they combined to hang briefly on my chin, before falling to the floor. I looked down, a damp spot was spreading rapidly under me. It was much too big to have been created by tears, and it took some seconds to realise the pain had caused me to lose control of my bladder. Bright lights were flashing and dancing before my eyes, and they also scared me, because I sensed they were there because I was teetering on the edge of what my system could tolerate.

Now Eric's there again, asking that same question, making sure my submission was complete, so I nod. No matter what they intend to do with me, and no doubt what they intend to make me do as well, I know I'll finish up doing it, because nothing could be worse than the pain I'm still experiencing. Yet again, Eric's voice manages to penetrate through the mist of my semi consciousness, ' That's good kid, seems we're finally on the same wave length,

but don't forget, hesitate for even a few seconds when I tell you to do something, and you'll get three more, so I hope for your sake, you fully understand how things are between us.'

Once again I nod, still not prepared to risk trying to speak. Apparently satisfied his dominance was complete, he stepped up onto the upper level, then turned right and out of sight, where I could hear him laughing and talking with the others. Now I realise I'm trembling, goes on for about ten minutes, then gradually eases and stops. Probably due to shock, and I immediately think of Adrian after I got him down from those cliffs. That was probably shock as well, but never mind, shock or whatever, shifting around to that inlet took care of that. Eric's reappeared, jumps down to the lower level and comes over and squats, this time in front of me, ' You know kid, you were stupid to try and stand up to me. All you achieved was to cause yourself a lot of pain, and having suffered through that, you have to accept what a mistake it was, because nothing's changed. We're still all going to take turns at having sex with you, it's just we'll be doing it in a slightly different position, that's all. Actually, it's suits me just fine, because past experience has taught me that if we raise your buttocks just a little higher, it will place you in a position where we're guaranteed maximum penetration. And another thing that hasn't changed kid, is I still have the privilege of doing it to you first, and I don't deny I sure am looking forward to it kid. I made up my mind I was determined to have sex with you, right from that very first time you turned up at scouts. Up until then I'd had my eye on one of the other young kids who'd joined, but when you arrived with that combination of those looks and that body of yours, I soon forgot about him, because you went straight up to the top of my list. You know, in some ways I can hardly believe it's all worked out, and you lying here all spread out and ready and waiting for me. Guess it just goes to show what a bit of careful planning and following a bit of advice from a mutual acquaintance of ours can achieve, doesn't it?'

One of the others called, so he stood and once again disappeared from sight. I was still in dreadful pain, but couldn't help wondering about what he'd said, 'following advice from a mutual acquaintance.' What mutual acquaintance? We moved in different circles, thank God, and the only mutual acquaintance I could think of was Mr. bloody Bergman, and surely he, considering the high esteem in which he's apparently held, surely he wouldn't be so stupid as to get involved in something as dangerously sordid as this. But now Eric was back, as persistent and lethal as ever, ' Guess everything comes to those who wait kid, so seeing as you're ready and waiting for us, it's time to make that final adjustment I was talking about, and get on with what we're here for.' He called across to the others, who were lounging around the workbench, 'Hey you guys,' he called out, 'we need something to put under the kid's bum to raise him a little higher. Anyone got any suggestions?'

'I know', said one boy, 'why don't we roll up some of those sacks.' But the next suggestion proved to be far more popular, 'Tell you what', another of them said, 'his sleeping bag is one of those expensive thin ones. Why don't we roll that up as tight as we can, and put that under him instead?'

Apparently, problem solved, so while two of the boys unstrapped my sleeping bag from my pack, spread it out on the floor, then started rolling it up as tight as possible, two others came and stood either side of me, and when the sleeping bag appeared, lifted my buttocks well up, while it was slipped in under my lower stomach. And from the moment they moved away, instinctively I knew I didn't stand a chance. I was a lost soul, and badly needed help, and immediately, thought back to my brief involvement with Bible Class.

It occurred during one of those brain storms my mother occasionally had. 'I fear there's not enough religion in your life Mathew', she'd warbled at the time, 'it's something we need to rectify, so I've arranged it, this Sunday you're going to Bible Class.'

I, on the other hand, remained suitably unimpressed, 'Why do I need to go to Bible Class?' I protested, 'you don't go to church'.

'That's different', she replied, 'my church is here in this house'.

'Buggered if I can see it', I snapped back, accepting there was a chance I'd get my mouth washed out with soap for swearing.

'Adults see things differently to children,' she countered, 'anyway, there's to be no more argument, my mind's made up, you're going to Bible Class, whether you like it or not'.

The room at the back of the church was damp and dismal, and the woman who took the class, even more dismal still. I was convinced she would make an excellent scarecrow, because she was thin, had a large nose, her face seemed to have more crevasses than the moon, and her grey, thin hair hung down untidily from under a strange little bonnet type hat, that she perched precariously on the top of her head. She wore a coat that was about three sizes too big, a greyish, mousy coloured thing, and as she strode up and down in front of the class, she constantly assured us we were the children of Satan, and we'd spend eternity confined in the fires of Hell, unless we changed our heathen ways.

And as she paced up and down while she preached what I assessed as being this biblical drivel, each time she turned, ready to pace back on her never ending religious crusade, she'd make sure she turned sharply, and as a result her coat, which finished up almost touching the floor, would swirl out like some medieval cloak, with the effect created apparently helping to drive home the message she was preaching, although what that message was, I realised I never really found out. But just occasionally, during her bursts of rationality, which in my youthful opinion had proven to be few and far between, she'd stress that if we'd be prepared to change our ungodly ways and attempt to live according to the Ten Commandments, then there was a faint possibility we could be saved from the fires of Hell.

This was the only part I felt made any sense. I mean, if you put aside all her rantings, I figured it all added up to simply doing your best to behave yourself, and as far as my life was concerned, I felt I hadn't wandered all that far off that road that was considered as being acceptable, well, apart from the usual, like the occasional fight, broken window, and fruit mysteriously missing. And so, as I tried to make some sense out of her so called Biblical wisdom, I still felt if there was a chance I ever needed help, Jesus would save me.

Mind you, I was prepared to accept I could have, 'put my foot in it' as it were, on that final day. I was sitting at the rear of the class, doing my best to ignore the sound of her unpleasant voice as she droned on regardless, that was until I noticed whatever nonsense she'd been spouting, had caused a couple of the younger kids to start crying. That's it, I decided, enough is enough, so I stood up quietly and headed for the door, and I was very close to making it, when suddenly her shrill voice rang out across the room, 'May I ask where you think you're going boy?', she'd said, and I answered very politely, just like Jesus would expect me to, 'I've had enough of your preaching lady, and I'm going home'.

I was staggered how quickly she appeared beside me, in fact I reckoned she'd give Mr. Gossini a run for his money. But that was where any similarity ended. She proceeded to dig the nails of two of her fingers into the lobe of my left ear, and with yours truly stumbling along beside her, was unceremoniously dragged back to the front of the class. Apparently, I was to be made an example of, but that didn't sit well with me at all, so I gave her a strong warning, 'Lady, I'm telling you, you'd better let go of my ear'.

She replied by digging her nails in harder still, but while attempting to ease the pressure on my ear, I noticed her shoes had soft leather uppers, with age helping to make them even softer still. On the other hand, I was wearing fairly new shoes, and the soles were so hard I needed heel and toe plates to stop me skidding everywhere. So I thought, right, one more warning, then that's it. So it was, 'Lady, I'm giving you fair warning, so for the last time, I'd strongly advise you to let go of my ear.'

Still no response, so I lifted my right leg well up off the floor, then brought my heel down with all the weight I could muster, right square on her toes. The response on her part was immediate and rather dramatic as she let out a shriek of Biblical proportions, then started hopping around in ever increasing circles. There was no doubt she let go of my ear, and while she continued on her circular journey around the front of the room, on my second attempt I experienced no trouble at all in getting out the door.

But now, as I lay across the frame, naked and tied hand and foot, and with my buttocks raised to a point where Eric's experience in such matters deemed as being appropriate, I decided that if there was ever a time when I needed help from Jesus, it was never more than now. But as my eyes swung around the shed, taking in every dusty and dirty corner, I looked in vain, because Jesus was just nowhere to be found.

Chapter 13

Eric came over and positioned himself in front, with a look of eager anticipation spreading across his face, as he smiled and said, 'Alright kid, the time we've been waiting has finally arrived', then seemingly as an afterthought added, 'and take it from me, in a few minutes from now, your life will never be quite the same, ever again'.

He started to slowly remove his clothing, first his pants, then his briefs, and for a moment I thought he was going to keep his shirt on, but after some slight deliberation, removed that as well. He was already erect as he moved around behind me, then he eased my buttocks apart and positioned himself. I felt his penis, so I gritted my teeth and waited for him to thrust into me, but instead he turned to Adrian, and beckoned to him to come over, 'Kneel down kid', and then added, 'no closer than that, close enough you can almost feel what's happening to your mate, and while you're watching, don't forget what I said earlier. Behave yourself and you won't be touched, but any nonsense, and you'll get what I'm about to give him.'

A few more moments, then I let out an involuntary gasp as he penetrated me. Quite some time past while he fully inserted himself, then he bent over and said, ' You know what this means kid?' and when I made no attempt to answer, he said, ' it means that as far as male to male is concerned, you're no longer a virgin, that part of your life has gone forever'.

While he remained stationary inside me, the full feeling it created was vaguely similar to when I needed to sit on the toilet, but when his rhythmic movement started, all I felt was total humiliation. What he was doing was bad enough, but was compounded by the knowledge Adrian was kneeling within touching distance, watching the sex act being performed.

In total despair, I gazed around the shed, hoping to find something that would help distract me from what he was doing, but I finished up closing my eyes instead. His thrusts were so brutal, everything was lurching, the movement caused by my head jolting every time he thrust into me. One of the boys came over and stood in front watching, but after a while squatted and grinned, and with his face almost touching mine said, 'Well, how are you enjoying yourself kid? Watching from where I am, he sure is doing a job on you, isn't he?' At twelve years of age, I'd been subjected to my share of crudeness, but nothing even remotely approaching that. I was tempted to respond in kind, but humiliation meant I finished up not uttering a word. The sex act seemed to be going on and on, and I found myself silently pleading, willing him to stop, but he didn't. So I continued to lie on that timber frame, while I was very deliberately, quite methodically, and very, very thoroughly raped.

It seemed as if he intended it to go on forever, but suddenly his thrusts became even stronger, and subsequently more brutal still, which did result in a brief cry of pain, then his movement stopped, and due to the deathly silence that was prevailing, I could hear his heavy breathing quite clearly. A couple more

thrusts, then a faint moan signalled the end, and seconds later, he withdrew. He was panting slightly, as once again he leant forward and said, 'You've just taken my first load kid, and I always knew you'd be good, but not even I thought you'd be as sensational as that, so get used to it kid, while you're here with us, we're sure going to make the most of what that cute, tight little arsehole of yours has to offer.'

For the next thirty seconds, it was as if you could hear a pin drop, as if the boys who'd gathered round to watch, had been mesmerized by the sex act they'd been viewing. Then it started. Like a voice from the wilderness, one of them said, 'Right, that settles it, I'm next.'

Then it was, 'No you're not, I am.' Then this was followed by, 'What gives you guys the right to go before me?' And finally, 'What about me, where do I fit in?' Arguments continued for a couple of minutes, that was until Eric shouted to make himself heard above the steadily increasing din, ' Come on you guys, shut up, just shut up you hear me. Christ you've all got bloody short memories. You know this was all sorted out yesterday. I told you, seeing as I was mainly responsible for setting this up, I got to have first turn with the kid.'

He stared at them, as if openly daring anyone to defy him. No one did, so he continued, 'Then due to a promise I'd made to him weeks ago, Paul gets to have the kid next.' Yet again no dissent, so he carried on, 'After that I made it quite clear that after Paul's finished with him, I'd sort out the order in which you boys did him, and there's one thing I forgot. From the time one finishes with him, until the next, there's to be fifteen minutes in between.'

This resulted in murmurs of protest, but one voice was raised above the rest, 'For Pete's sake Eric, I mean there's eight of us, so that means two hours mucking around waiting, then add to that, the time it takes for each of us to play with the kid, and it means some will still be using him well into the afternoon.'

And Eric's reply snapped straight back, 'So what, we agreed we'd play with the kid until early tomorrow afternoon, surely that gives us enough time to use him in any way we want.'

He stood there, literally daring any of them to challenge him, and they didn't, so he offered something in the way of a crude explanation, 'Look, trust me, take it from one who knows. If there's anything experience in this sort of thing has taught me, it's that no matter how good any kid is, and take it from me, this kid is good, it's even better again, when you make them wait for it.'

I thought about what he'd just said, and felt certain they'd find it imbedded in my brain when I was dead. So with the issue apparently settled, while most of the boys wandered off, Paul strolled over, stopped briefly, then wandered on past, and it took a few seconds for me to realise he'd turned while standing behind, and was looking back at me from there. He stayed there for quite some moments, then casually wandered back, but as he passed alongside, he spoke in a very quiet voice, almost as if he was talking to himself, but just loud enough so he knew I could hear, 'You know, I'm sure I recognise that cute, smooth, little bum from somewhere', and as he squatted down in front of me, he added, 'so let's see if I'm right'. With that, he grabbed a handful of my hair and wrenched my head back, so I was forced to look him full in the face, then he said, 'Well,

what do you know, I am right, it does belong to that cheeky little bastard, who made me look a fool in the shower room last night.'

And even allowing for the pain and position I was in, coupled with the knowledge of what he wasn't far off doing to me, I still wasn't prepared to let him get away with that, so I continued to look straight back at him as I said, 'What do you mean, I made you look a fool? You started it Paul, you made yourself look a fool, you sure didn't need any help from me.'

His eyes narrowed and his lips tightened, and I tensed, thinking I was about to get a slap or a punch in the face. But as quickly as his annoyance flared, just as quickly it departed, in fact when he answered, if anything his voice was quite conciliatory, 'Maybe you're right kid, maybe you're right, but tell me, out of the two of us, who is it who looks the fool now?'

When I didn't utter a sound, he added, 'Who is it who's been stripped naked and tied face down with his legs wide apart, so he's displaying everything he's got? And talking about displaying everything he's got, who is it who's had his balls laced, so as they stand out like a puppy dog's. And tell me kid, who is it who's already had his cute little arse fucked, and can't do anything but lie there and wait for more. Well as you've heard, I'm next, and by the time I've finished with you, I'll guarantee you'll know what pain up there is all about.'

After giving my hair another painful wrench, he moved away, over to where he joined in a discussion with his equally repulsive mates. Although he stood there laughing and joking, it registered, there was something cruel about his eyes, and Eric was exactly the same. No wonder they were close friends, because it was obvious, they were one of a kind, they both obtained pleasure from inflicting humiliation and pain. Just after Eric had finished with me, I noticed a thin ray of sunlight, shining in through the still partly open door. It struck the floor just to the left of the head of a rusty nail, that for some obscure reason, had been driven into the concrete floor. Eric had insisted, fifteen minutes in between, and a quick mental calculation suggested when the time had expired, that ray of sunlight would strike directly on the head of that nail. It was part way there already. My stomach tightened in a knot.

At school, I was always uncomfortable when the other boys talked about sex, but I laughed along with them, mainly because I felt it gave the impression I knew more about the subject than I did, but the truth was, I barely knew anything, and what's more, couldn't have cared less. But now this was happening, and I couldn't understand why. Up until now, as far as I could tell, my life had been little different to that of my friends, and their lives were carrying on as normal, so why had I been singled out for abuse like this? I tested my wrists, nothing had changed, other than the fact that after they'd forced my sleeping bag under me so as to raise my buttocks, if anything they were tighter still.

Hell, now a few tears were flowing. I blinked, but too late, now they're slipping down my cheeks. Hope the others don't notice. Now I know what an animal feels like while it's waiting to be slaughtered, the only trouble being that as far as I was concerned, the slaughter had already started. I glanced across, the beam of sunlight was striking the head of that nail. If my calculations proved to be correct, then it meant the fifteen minutes was up. And it seemed they were,

because I realised Paul was strolling over, with the others wandering along behind as they prepared to watch. Standing in front of me, he grinned as he slowly undid his belt, and slower still he allowed his pants to fall to the floor. What he exposed certainly didn't help, because it made what I knew was to come even more frightening still.

Being raped, as I'd found out, was a shattering, humiliating and painful experience. During the act, Eric had hurt me quite severely. He was a strong, well put together youth, and physically he'd make two of Paul, but when it came to that particular part of their maleness, if anything, the situation was reversed. So logic said when Paul inserted himself, the pain he'd cause would be nothing short of extreme. Fear lanced through me, but it was totally irrelevant, because going by the look of anticipation on his face, raped again I was going to be. The truth was the thought of more pain scared me, it was something I felt I didn't handle all that well, and I loathed that part of myself that I felt was a weakness. Eric's reappeared, positioning himself so he can watch, so I attempted to plead with him, 'Eric, please, stop what you're doing and let me loose. I'm so sore being tied down like this.'

But his reply shatters any vestige of hope I felt I might have had, 'Not a chance kid, and I'll tell you why. Remember what I said about that kid we had in my bedroom, and how he carried on when we told him what we wanted from him, but then finished up cooperating for us anyway. Well the only comparison between him and you is you're both from the cat family, but where he was just a mild little pussy, you're more like a young tiger. When I told you what we wanted, so alright, you tried to make a break for it, under the circumstances, it was understandable, but after that, you fought back like some wild cat with everything you possessed. So imagine us trying to have sex with you, Christ, while one of us tried, the other seven would have to attempt to hold you down. But this way, tied in the position you're in, none of that, no fuss, no problems, we just have you whenever we want, I mean, let's face it kid, it's perfect, so as far as letting you lose is concerned, take it from me, you can forget it.'

I didn't tell him that as a wild cat, I'd shed a few tears. Now Paul was inside me, the pain even worse than I'd anticipated, and when he'd finally finished, a couple more tears for good measure. But he didn't notice, instead he started dressing, then when finished he added,

'Remember I told you yesterday, after what eventuated between us in the shower block, it meant I was going to enjoy all the more what I did to you today. Now you know what I was talking about. Bet you and that cute little arsehole of yours don't feel so clever now, you cheeky little bastard.'

As he dressed, I'd noticed a smear of blood on his penis.

Through the tears and pain I realised some of them were grumbling again, wanting to know when their turn was happening, and once again Eric displayed his authority, 'Slow down, there's something that needs sorting out first. Yesterday, a couple of you weren't all that sure you wanted to have the kid,' he said, 'you claimed you were happy to watch, but were undecided whether you wanted to take it any further. So what's the story now? You were one of those Bruce, and you also Ian, where do you stand on this today? You want to go ahead, fine, that's all I need to know. Now all of you remember,' he glanced at

his watch, then continued, 'nobody touches the kid for the next twelve minutes. I'm going outside, I won't be long, and I warn you, nobody is to even touch the kid while I'm gone.'

He disappeared, but returned minutes later holding some stalks of paspalum grass. Moving over to the workbench, he cut them into lengths varying from fifteen to twenty centimetres, then beckoned to Paul, 'Stretch the kid's buttocks, while I insert these up him.' He did so, leaving them all protruding the same length out of my body. 'Alright, he's ready, so make your selections. The one who draws the longest straw does the kid next, then moving on down to the shortest. This is the fairest way of deciding.'

The carnage went on, the third and fourth boys indulged in the sex they desired, but as the fifth moved forward, ready to position himself, Eric stopped him. I wondered why, only to glance up and find one of them holding a camera, and it was then Eric explained what was required, 'I'm going to untie your wrists kid, but you're to hold your position until this guy's fully inserted himself. Then you're to rest your elbows in front of you, cup your hands under your chin, and look straight at the camera and smile.'

I did as he said, knowing I'd feel the blade of his hand if I didn't. The abuse continued as others took their turns, with numerous photos being taken from different positions, my face always fully in view, theirs turned well away or obscured. Finally it was over, my wrists retied in their original position, and once again I checked them. The flax was strong, but also slightly abrasive, and due to the movement of my body the boys were causing, an angry band of chaffing was evident, and I suspected my ankles were almost as bad. Vaguely I wondered what the time was. I strained my head upwards, the sun was obscured by some trees, but the brightness still flickered, even through the filth on the window. I guessed around three thirty.

Another minor problem, my neck was aching, so I turned my head, mainly to help ease the pain, and instantly it registered. The boys had drifted down the far end of the shed, with some of them fooling around on the tractor. Although I couldn't see him, I was certain Adrian was still standing close behind. And it proved to be so, because I spoke in barely more than a whisper, and he still managed to hear me, 'Adrian, quick, look where they are, if ever there's a chance, it's now. You could make it to the door, and the way you can run, with the length of the shed start, there's no way they'd get anywhere near you, so take off, see if you can find someone who can help.'

He took a few steps forward, and for the first time since I'd been tied down appeared in front of me. Warily, he glanced up the shed, slowly shook his head, then retreated to his original position as he said, 'Eric promised me if I didn't do anything foolish, he'd guarantee none of them would touch me. So there's no way I'm taking the risk of them doing to me as they're doing to you. Let's face it Matt, I'd have to be bloody stupid, and anyway, where the hell am I going to find anyone way out here?'

Movement meant his refusal was of little consequence. Eric had parted from the group and was strolling back towards us, with the others wandering along haphazardly behind.

He squatted in front, and informed me of what I was to be introduced to next. I gazed blankly back, and informed him I didn't know what oral sex was. He explained in graphic detail, and my stomach went close to rebelling. The thought of taking another boy's penis in my mouth, filled me with revulsion, and the other oral acts he wanted to watch were equally as atrocious. If Jesus had ever started, he must have got lost trying to find me. Surely that was the only explanation as to why he was leaving me to this. More minutes past, and I thought about home. My mother always changed the sheets on my bed on a Saturday, and how I loved the smell of their sweet freshness. God, how I wished I was at home.

No use trying to persuade Eric to let me go. After all this time I'd accepted it wasn't going to happen, so maybe it was worth trying something else, 'What about letting me up? I've been tied like this for so long, so please let me up for a while.'

With his right hand supporting his chin, he stood there while he gave my request serious thought, and when he answered, he agreed, but not for the reason I'd requested, ' Alright kid, I'll let you up, but only because you can perform better for us on your knees.'

My wrists untied, a couple of minutes of bliss as I stretched my arms and examined the chaffing, but all too soon his voice rang out again,' Right, that's enough kid, now cross your wrists behind your back. As they were retied I decided it certainly didn't help the chaffing. Now my ankles released, the pleasure of standing upright, the delight of being able to stretch, even if I was naked. Eric pointed to the pile of sacks as he said, 'One of you bring some of them over here for the kid to kneel on. He's going to be in that position for quite some time. So to make sure he lasts the distance, its best we make him as comfortable as possible'.

The sacks arrived and I was forced to kneel on them. Considering what I'd experienced over the last few hours, and knowing what lay ahead, I kept reminding myself it was imperative I kept on fighting, because I was determined there was no way I was going to let them defeat me. Yet again my mind drifted as I thought about home, then I snapped back to reality. Eric was standing in front of me, his penis erect, which made his intentions clearly evident, ' Come on kid, you've had enough time to yourself,' then he added, 'so let's proceed with the next part of your sex education. I've explained what you have to do, so open your mouth and get on with it.'

I stayed just as I was, and due to my reluctance, Eric's fuse instantly ignited, 'I won't tell you again kid, open your mouth and get on with it, or do you want to experience more of that agony between your legs?'

Instantly fear conquered all, so reluctantly I opened my mouth, but apparently not wide enough, ' Come on kid, wider than that, good, that's much better, now drop your head back slightly, right, that's perfect, now remember what I told you earlier. You suck when I tell you, and stop when I say. That way I can make it last as long as possible, and where that might not suit you, it sure as hell will guarantee my satisfaction.'

Thoughts of retaliation entered my head. Once he'd inserted himself, just one firm clench of my teeth was all it would take, and he wouldn't be raping or

demanding oral sex for quite some time to come, but he appeared to read my mind, ' Don't be tempted to do anything stupid kid. I'd make you suffer like you would never believe, and then I'd turn around and do exactly the same with your mate. I know you're not looking forward to this, so it's best you imagine you're sucking a lolly pop, then suddenly you're rewarded with a burst of flavour.' I wondered why the others laughed so hard. The head of his penis felt firm and smooth in my mouth, then after a couple of minutes, I found out. The revulsion associated with the fluid made me instantly want to retch, but he placed his hand on the back of my head, forced himself even further into my mouth and mentioned two words, ' Now swallow'.

I was still retching when Paul positioned himself. The sex was completed to his satisfaction, with exactly the same result. The third boy was moving towards me when Eric spoke again, 'You're doing well kid, but for the next I'm going to tie your ankles and release your wrists. Once he's in your mouth, you're to place your hands on his buttocks, so as to make it appear you can't get enough of him, then you're to hold that position while we get more photos. When he's finished with you, there'll be quite a few more interesting shots we'll want to take while you're performing for the others while they bend over in front of you.'

The vile abomination continued well into the late afternoon. The last of them finished with me, then similar to the others, wandered off outside. From somewhere, one of them had produced a football, and the constant thump as they kicked it to each other across the clearing, was clearly audible from inside. It reminded me of the fun Col and I used to have, as we kicked his ball to each other over the power-lines in our street, and vaguely I wondered where he was living, and I hoped it was nice, because with that mother of his, if she wasn't satisfied, they could well have moved again by now, so I wondered what school he was attending and if there was a Council pool handy. But most of all, I hoped he was feeling better than I was.

The lingering, taste of sex in my mouth made me feel sick, and to compound on my misery, Eric strolled back in, calling back to the others as he approached, 'I want the kid back over the frame, and any who want him before we start our meal can have him.'

A rush of enthusiasm as some of them indulged in anal sex again, and as the last of them disappeared out the door, still adjusting his pants as he went, I raised my head and looked towards the window. The branches of a tree stood out stark and gaunt against the backdrop of a slowly darkening sky. I was convinced they resembled gnarled, twisted fingers, eager to reach out and take hold of me, so the boys could do more repulsive things.

Suddenly, why I'd been left here became so obvious, of course, the Devil had beaten Jesus to me, they'd both been looking, but the Devil had found me first. The pain from my wrists seemed to mingle with all of the pain deep inside. Now, the sweet, fresh smell of burning wood was wafting in, combining with the aroma of cooking food. Their evening meal was underway, and so I was missing another meal, and due to the sickness in my stomach, I couldn't care less. One of the boys walked in, and the sound of his voice gave me a fright, but he wasn't talking to me, he was talking to Adrian, 'Hey kid, Eric says it's alright if you want come out and prepare yourself some food.'

Engrossed in my misery as I was, I'd forgotten he was still in the shed, silently standing behind me, watching everything they did and were making me do. Purposely avoiding my gaze, Adrian walked on past and out of the shed. A few more minutes, then Eric appeared in the doorway, 'Listen kid, its fine by me if your mate brings you some food'.

Yeah, great, tied like this it would mean he'd have to feed me. I didn't even bother to acknowledge his presence. There was no way I was accepting anything even remotely like a favour from him. After a few moments of indecision, he turned on his heel and strutted away, and I watched him until he disappeared, then once again lowered my head to ease the strain on my neck. And that's when I saw him.

Peering closely, I convinced myself there was a little figure of an elf, etched in oil that had obviously been spilt long before on the concrete floor. He had a sharply pointed hat, that sagged to one side, exactly as I believed all respectable elves hats should, then below that, a large crooked nose jutted out from a time weary face, that clearly displayed the ravages of what I suspected had been a hard, dreary life. All of this was complimented by a thin, emancipated body, one of the legs of which was in the process of taking a huge exaggerated step, that left his bent knee suspended high in the air, giving the impression he'd been frozen in time. So I made a solemn promise to myself. When my elf was allowed to complete that step and walk away from this terrible place, then we'd do so together, because I was convinced only walking away with him, would make this misery end.

Quite some time passed before Eric reappeared, 'I'm going to tie your wrists behind your back again kid, then when I untie your ankles, you're to walk over and lie down on the sacks.' After I'd complied with what he'd said, he retied my ankles and departed. Another fifteen minutes or so, and the temperature was noticeably dropping, not so bad now, but later it could prove to be a problem. Also, the sacks offered little in the way of protection from the hardness of the concrete floor, but anything was better than the humiliation of being spread over that frame.

The sound of footsteps, and Paul appeared, talking as he moved towards me, 'Well, if it isn't my little blond headed mate with the cute little bum, still all tied up with nowhere to go.' And utter loathing guaranteed I snapped straight back, 'Think you're so bloody smart Cunningham, but some time you're going to have to let me go, then it'll be my turn'.

But he immediately came back, as vulgar and arrogant as ever, 'What are you talking about kid, your turn? I've fucked three times already, and you've had my dick in your mouth, and you've also had to lick and suck my bum, and I don't recall you getting a turn yet, so you're sure missing out somewhere. But enough of this small talk, we've far more important things to discuss, so where are you going to take it this time, in the mouth, or down the bottom end?'

Of all of the boys in the shed, he was the lowest of them all, so I let him know what I thought of him in no uncertain terms, 'You're just a filthy, obscene pig Paul', then finished with, 'so why don't you do us all a favour, and jump off

a very high cliff. You'll need all of your filthy mates to hold me down, before I'll let you do anything else to me.'

But his reply immediately had me back on the defensive, 'Suit yourself kid, I couldn't care less. Eric told me he'd come to some sort of loose arrangement with your mate. He knows it's you I want, but he said that if you turn in any way uncooperative, then he'll agree to letting me have some fun with your mate instead. So no matter which way the coin falls, I still get what I want, with the possibility of a little variety thrown in as well.'

This talk of an 'arrangement ' had me wondering, but if they decided to do to him as they were currently doing with me, I assumed the position would be reversed, while they made me watch what they made him do. Then I'd have to live with the knowledge it had happened, because I'd refused to cooperate with this youth standing beside me. Could I happily manage to live with that on my conscience, especially considering the delicate state of his health? The answer was no, I could not, so once again I accepted I was effectively trapped.

'Alright, you win, stay away from him Paul, so do what you want with me, but on the understanding you must promise to leave him alone.'

And his reply was straight to the point, 'You've got a deal kid, and be prepared for something a bit different. I can tell you now you won't enjoy it, but to make sure you carry out your side of the bargain, I'm going to bring your friend in. He's watched everything else, so he may as well watch this, and don't make the mistake of forgetting it means he's real handy, if you even think about backing out of our agreement'.

He knelt down and untied my ankles, then continued, 'When we get back, I'll expect to find you on your knees with your legs wide apart, and your forehead touching the floor, and accept it kid, we're going to have a session you won't forget in a hurry.'

He took off to get Adrian, and briefly I thought about it. For the first time I'd been left on my own with my ankles untied, perhaps I should attempt to make a run for it. Was I kidding? I'd be lucky to get out the door, and with my wrists tied behind my back, what hope would I have in trying to out run them. So reluctantly and slightly awkwardly, I got on my knees, spread my legs, then using a sack to soften it, placed my forehead on the floor and waited. No more than a minute, and the two boys walked in, and as they approached, Paul spoke to Adrian, 'There you are kid, I told you he'd be ready and waiting for me. What do you think of that view of your mate? Gets better all the time, doesn't it. Jesus that lace makes them stand out, guess that's why Eric likes to do it. Go on, bend right down, have a good look, bet you've never seen that view of your mate before, and it certainly leaves nothing to the imagination, does it'. Then he turned to me as yet again I knelt in gross humiliation, 'And seeing as you're perfectly positioned and ready, it's a case of here we go again, only this time it's something different'.

He undressed and knelt down behind me, and as he placed his hands on my hips, I clenched my teeth as he thrust up violently into me. The rhythm of anal sex started, quite some time passed, and due to the position I was in, I looked back through my legs. No wonder he caused so much pain, so I closed my eyes and stayed like that until he'd finished. Now a repeat performance as he moved

in front of me and bent well over, then turned his head and told me what he wanted, 'Your mate can hold me open while you lean forward and lick me', then he turned to Adrian as he added, 'then when I tell you too, you're to place your hand on the back of his head, and hold him there while he sucks me. I enjoyed it so much before, I want more again now.' I protested, pleading with him not to make me do such vile things again, but he insisted, ' Face up to it kid, the rules haven't changed, you do it, or your mate has to, and if it's him, I'll bring one of the others in to make sure he does it properly'.

Finally complying with his demands, he made Adrian hold my head, but it hadn't finished there, and a shock, as Adrian's hand held my head, his other hand slipped down as he fondled my penis and testicles. I couldn't understand it. I'd never heard Paul tell him he had to do that. But now, with my vile time at his anus once again complete, Paul stood and positioned himself in front, ' You've done well kid, but there's one last thing. You're to take my penis in your mouth, and stay like that while I piss, and the rule is you have to swallow six times'.

And my fury at Adrian's indiscretion passed in a heartbeat, I couldn't believe what I was hearing. As far as I was concerned, there was only one place for urine, so I adamantly refused to cooperate, desperate to avoid such an abomination, after just having been made to perform the others. As before, he spoke calmly as he drove his threats home, making it apparent he'd have no hesitation in activating them as he said, ' Suit yourself kid, but I warn you, your mate's going to have to do it instead. One way or the other it's going to happen. I've waited a long time for this, and an opportunity like this won't happen again. It's just too good to miss'.

He stood there and raised his eyebrows, indicating he was demanding my decision. I thought of Adrian's mother and the promise I'd made, and even allowing for what her son had just done, once again indicated my surrender with a brief nod. So it started as I opened my mouth, and it was as if those degrading minutes would never end. But finally it proved too much, and I was forced to ease my head back and remove his penis from my mouth as I pleaded, 'Please Paul, say I can stop. I just can't do it anymore, because along with those other vile things you've made me do, I can feel it, I know I'm going to be sick.'

And that certainly produced a reaction. Hauled to my feet, out the door and around to the rear of the shed. On down a slight slope, at the bottom of which there was some longer grass, which I knelt in front of and proceeded to be violently ill. Finally down to retching and nothing else, a few more minutes, then made to stand and walk back to the shed, but on the way we stopped at that old water tank. As Paul turned on the brass tap, a chance to thoroughly rinse my mouth, then drink some of that crystal clear water, and it was a long time since I could recall anything tasting so good. But my problems hadn't ended there. During the strain associated with being so ill, I realised fluid was seeping from my anus and running down the inside of my right leg.

But the boy named Ian, who'd proved on a couple of occasions, to be the most reasonable of the group, suddenly appeared and instantly demanded an explanation, 'What's the kid doing out here Paul, what have you been doing to him?'

'Nothing much', Paul replied, 'he was a bit sick, that's all'.

Ian wasn't going to back off that easily, 'So alright, what made him sick? I know you and that weird mind of yours, and oh, Christ, look at him, the poor little bastard. I tell you Paul, I'm starting to get a really bad feeling over what we've been doing to this kid. Now don't you move, I'm going to get something to clean you up with.' He returned and did as he said.

Back on the sacks, my ankles retied, and that was good, it indicated Paul had taken the none too subtle hint, and for the time being at least, was finished with me. My mother had a saying she believed in. Everything comes to those who wait. I'm prepared to wait Paul, then when we meet, whether you're bigger or not, things could get interesting. The lingering smell of that burning wood, combined with that delightful drink of cold water, helped my stomach to partially settle. Now some of the boys were starting to lay out their sleeping bags, preparing for the night ahead. Eric came over, 'You can have your sleeping bag draped over you kid, but you're not getting in it. Most of us will want to use you during the night, so that arrangement will leave you readily available'.

He's another I hope I run into sometime in the future in a dark alley somewhere.

And as the darkness added another chapter to this saga of sexual depravity, while I was left alone, my mind refused to rest. I knew they were checking on those who were camping out, and logic said whoever had been assigned to check on us, knew we wouldn't be there. The other option was someone finding an empty site, and a search would have been well underway by now, so there was no way they could have risked lighting a fire? The smoke would have acted like a magnet in attracting those who were searching. Surely that meant the boys were aware they weren't at risk of being checked on. Many questions, no firm answers, and at this point the boys were leaving me alone, so somehow, I drifted off to sleep instead.

At varying intervals during that black, forbidding night, I was dragged across to the frame and draped over it, so yet again, they could indulge in the sex it seemed they craved for. But on this occasion, as I woke, for the first time I found I could see reasonably clearly.

Moonlight was flooding the shed, bathing everything in its haunting, mystic beauty. Surely it meant only one thing, it had to be a sign from Heaven. Jesus hadn't given up searching, and had found me after all. The message as I saw it was clear. With the arrival of the new morning, this nightmare was destined to end, so I drifted off again into a troubled, restless sleep. The new morning dawned exactly as I'd anticipated. Although my wrists and ankles hadn't been tied excessively tightly, various attempts to free my wrists had only resulted in more chaffing. During the periods when I was being left alone, I'd spent most of the night alternating between lying on one side or the other, or flat on my stomach, definitely not my preferred option, and I'd been so cold, so very cold. With the sleeping bag on top of me, it had offered nothing like the warmth of being in it. And now, as a result, my neck was aching like I couldn't believe. Also, what had started out as being slight discomfort caused by the shoelace, was extending well beyond that, suggesting it would be prudent if it was

removed as soon as possible, but I knew I'd be wasting my time asking Eric to do that.

Now the others were waking, noisily stretching and yawning, their conversations waxing and waning, as one by one they wandered outside. The sound of a fire cracking, the aroma of more coffee brewing, and that, combined with the smell of toast, reminded me of how empty my stomach was. Eric strolled over to where I was lying. With a steaming mug of coffee in one hand, with the other he bent down and whipped the sleeping bag away, then ran his insatiable gaze over my nakedness. 'Well you guys', he said, 'and what games are we going to play with this one this morning? Remember, time is starting to run out, so we better make the most of it while we've still got him. Someone try and think of something a bit different'.

Didn't they know I'd received that message during the night? They weren't supposed to be playing at anything, they were supposed to be letting me go. But Eric's next movement dashed any hopes I may have had in that direction. He gripped me by the arm and wrenched, with the result I was flipped over onto my stomach. He placed his forefinger at the base of my neck, then using his other hand to hold my wrist up from my body, he gradually eased his finger down my spine, then further down between my buttocks, until finally inserting it up my rectum. The stupid, mindless act apparently intended to convey just how much in control of my body he was. My opinion of him sunk even lower, then realised that was impossible, because it couldn't get any lower than it already was. The boy Ian spoke up, his voice displaying more than a hint of the unease he'd displayed earlier, and had been evident the previous evening as well, 'Honest you guys, I'm starting to get a really bad feeling about all of this. Considering what we've already done to this poor little bastard, if he promises not to tell, I vote we let him loose'.

He needn't have bothered to open his mouth, because he was studiously ignored. Eric spoke up, 'Alright, seeing as none of you can think of something different, I suggest we play triples, that always guarantees a bit of fun. So we'll need him back over the frame'.

Once again lying across, my legs spread well apart as usual, but this time a small variation. With my wrists left tied behind my back, one of the pieces of flax was tied loosely around my neck, then down to the rail below, with this providing the necessary restriction. But one thing hadn't changed, with the sleeping bag once again rolled up and placed in position, I was then informed what triples entailed. Three of them using me at once, anal and oral sex, combined with masturbation.

Once again, more straws inserted, confirming their rotation for the morning. Now the first three started, the sex acts continuing until they satisfied themselves in the position of their choice, the taste in my mouth as unpleasant as ever. Because three were involved, Eric insisted on a thirty minute interval. But now another dreadful addition. One of them produced a screwdriver from the workbench, and during the time that lapsed between their game, a few of them entertained themselves by inserting it up my rectum, until only the shaft protruded, then gripping the shaft, they'd viciously wrench the handle out, and the pain they created was nothing short of atrocious. But each time the handle

was reinserted, I shut my eyes and clenched my teeth, determined not to utter a sound.

Now three of them were there again, and with Eric having agreed to let others go before him, as he worked his loins in front, he said to one of the others, 'Make sure you get photos of everything, I told him we'd get a record of anything we did to the kid.'

With the second trio having finished about half an hour back, and with the last two in the process of undressing, Eric raised his hand to delay them, while his eyes locked on Adrian, 'What about you kid? You've been standing around watching, why don't you make up the third?'

As the shock of what he'd suggested fully registered, I waited for his adamant refusal to become involved in such a thing, but it didn't eventuate. Without any hesitation he walked over and started to remove his clothing. As he moved around and positioned himself, and I felt his hands on my buttocks as he eased them open, I shouted at him, 'For God's sake Adrian, what are you doing? You're my friend, please don't do it'.

But he ignored me, and as I felt him insert himself, then thrust up as far as he could inside me, a few tears flowed as I lay there helpless and humiliated, while I was raped by one of my best friends. But not content with that, he insisted the oral act be performed also, but distress had been replaced by blind, seething fury, as I clenched my teeth and refused to cooperate.

There was no warning as those three blows thudded in, with the pain once again rendering me submissive, but once Adrian was finished, I turned my fury on Eric, 'You planned this, you set me up, you pig, and when I get home I'll tell my parents what you've all done, and then they'll contact the police, and see what happens then, you bastard'.

He turned away, arrogant as ever, then came back and squatted, just as he'd done in the past, 'Look kid,' he snarled, 'I'm not as stupid as you apparently think. I was always aware of the risk, so go right ahead, say what you want, I won't try to deny we had sex with you, and why? Because I'll tell them you wanted it as much as we did. There's eight of us to back up our story, if it should prove to be necessary, and there's only one of you, and I wouldn't be counting on your mate. The photos we've got of him doing it with you will take care of that.'

That was all very well, I thought, but after I'd given my version, I felt they'd still have trouble explaining these abrasions on my wrist and ankles. But it continued, with late morning blending into early afternoon. Another refusal to cooperate had resulted in another vicious beating from Paul, and those lights were back, flashing and dancing in my eyes. Through the fog of pain I could hear his voice, convinced he was well away, only to find he was standing right beside me, 'I reckon we can play with the kid for just a little longer, but before too long we'll have to think about tidying up. I want the shed left like we've never been here, and we need reasonable time for getting back to the camp. Now do you agree we've done everything to the kid I promised we would?'

The silence suggested they did agree, that was until Paul spoke up, 'I'm one up on you guys, because I made the kid do something late yesterday that none of you have'.

At their prompting he described in detail the oral act that finished up making me so ill, but noticing the sudden anticipation that registered on their faces, I chose to get in first,

'Do what you like, but I'm telling you I'll never do that again as long as I live. So if any of you are thinking about trying to make me do it, I swear, I'll bite you just as hard as I can. So give that some thought, you scum'.

Immediately most of them backed off, not being prepared to place themselves at risk, but it seemed, as always, that cold look of determination appeared on Eric's face, as he snapped at me, 'That's where you're wrong kid, I'm determined to watch you do this one last thing', then as he turned to Adrian, he added, 'Take your pants off and stand in front of him kid. You can be the one who supplies it, after all, I couldn't care fucking less if he bites you.'

It was at that moment, ridiculously late though it was, I decided enough was enough. I knew my refusal would result in more agony, but this time I was determined not to give in, and sure enough, his threats weren't long in arriving, 'Don't be stupid kid, especially after what you've been through. I won't make your mate give you too much, and once you've done it, that'll be the end and we'll both go our separate ways.'

My mouth stayed clamped shut, and I could recognise his rising fury by the tone of his voice, 'Open your mouth and get on with it kid, or I'm warning you, I'll beat those balls of yours to pulp. This is something I'm determined to watch, so bloody well get on with it, or else'.

The first blow created so much pain, for a few seconds I found it impossible to breathe. More of his demands, no response on my part, so his beatings increased, spurred on by a frenzy of determined and frustrated fury.

The pain he was inflicting was so bad I knew it was blurring my senses, but somehow in the midst of my tears I managed to turn my head, determined to see if my elf was still there. And I couldn't believe it, because before my eyes he managed to take some steps, and he smiled back at me as he balanced precariously on the edge of what appeared to be a bottomless pit. Occasionally I'd be forced to look away as I writhed in agony, but always I managed to drag my eyes back as I sought the sympathy I knew that little man was offering. But as eyes blurred with tears swung back yet again, this time I realised he was gradually slipping away, as he started to spiral down and down into that vast, black void, with one arm raised as he beckoned to me to follow.

Many years before, I'd dreamt I was flying, and it was the most beautiful sensation I'd ever experienced. For many nights after I couldn't wait to go to bed, hoping and praying for that dream to be repeated, but it was not to be. But as I watched my elf as he floated down and down into that black abyss, I decided surely it had to be the next best thing. After all, we'd made a pact, that little man and I, that when we left this terrible place, we'd do so together. So I got up off that frame and walked over and stepped out into that huge, dark hole after him, and as I did, the blackness closed around me as if it was the end of time.

Chapter 15

Never was sure how long the darkness lasted, but one thing I felt was certain, it wasn't all that long at all. Consciousness returned gradually, as I slowly recognised the sounds of the birds twittering away in the trees, the soft rustling of the leaves in the breeze, even the faintest of clatter from the loose iron on the roof. But unfortunately, I realised the pain in my groin and stomach was still there, once again bad enough to make me want to retch. My eyes felt as if they'd been weighed down with lead, and for a while it didn't seem to be worth the effort required to try and open them, however, what finally encouraged me to do so, was the thought of my little elf. If anything was worth the effort, he was, so gradually, I eased my eyes open, eager to confirm his presence. But instead of looking down, as I'd done for so long, I found myself peering straight along the surface of the concrete floor.

Completely disorientated, it took some seconds to adjust to the fact I was no longer spread over the frame, but was instead sprawled face down on the concrete. I attempted to look down the shed, but found my left arm obscuring my vision, so I moved it, and instantly wished I hadn't. It seemed as if every muscle in my body screamed out its own form of protest, so briefly I thought about it, and decided, I couldn't find a part of me that didn't hurt. I lay where I was for a few more minutes, and it seemed to be working, the pain appeared to have eased slightly, but as it did, concern took over. I convinced myself the others must still be here, standing back in the shadows, waiting patiently, watching while I recovered, so as it could start all over again.

Now scared, with an involuntary movement I jerked my head up, as I attempted to see further down the shed, and yet again, immediately wished I hadn't. The shed gave a sickening lurch, and my stomach lurched with it, so I moved my arm carefully closer, and using it to rest my head on, I waited for the unpleasant sensation to stop. The world finally stood still, so I tried again, this time much slower, but the shadows hid nothing, there was no doubt I was alone. Gradually it registered, and for a few moments I couldn't determine what it was. Then I realised that lying naked on the concrete floor, the coolness of the concrete on my body was feeling like bliss, especially considering my face was hot and burning. So I eased my arm away and carefully lowered my head, first resting then rolling my cheek on the floor, then after a minute or so, repeated the process on the other side.

But above all else, where were my clothes? Nothing has a higher priority than putting on my clothes. Problem quickly solved, they were still lying over by the wall where Adrian had spent most of his time standing and watching what they'd been doing to me, that was until he'd accepted Eric's invitation to get involved as well. Now there's a thought, where's Adrian, my ex friend? Truth was I couldn't care less, in fact hopefully thoroughly lost to a point where it takes a search party three or four bitterly cold and rainy days to find him.

But enough of him, now for my clothes, no more than five metres or so away, but somehow it managed to look more like fifty. Cautiously I eased onto my knees, then similar to an infant testing himself, I set off crawling across the floor. Barely half way, and already my heart's pounding, and again, every muscle screaming abuse. I paused long enough for things to settle down, then tried again. Finally success, but as I turned and sat on my buttocks, the pain the position caused was nothing short of atrocious, but never the less I brought my knees up, and with my elbows resting on them and my hands supporting my head, once again I waited for the unpleasant pounding to stop.

But I was also painfully aware that the beatings I'd taken, especially that last one, had caused some swelling, and this was telling me the shoelace should be removed as soon as possible. With trembling fingers I attempted to untie it, but it proved hopeless, because fluid had welded the knot into an immovable thing. I wondered why he'd tied it there in the first place, but decided Paul was probably right, when he assumed it was something visual, but I was convinced the pain he'd inflicted would have been just as bad, if it had been there or not.

Suddenly a shadow appeared in the doorway, and it gave me a fright. In the condition I was in, I'd be doing well to stand up, let alone fight. But the shadow had a familiar but unwelcome voice, 'Mathew, it's me, Adrian, are you alright?'

Considering the circumstances, I wondered why he'd bothered to ask, 'You must be joking, you filthy, double crossing little creep. Of course I'm not bloody alright. You stood there, you watched what they did to me, then turned around and did it to me as well. Yet through all of that, you've got the nerve to stand there and ask me if I'm alright', then added as he started to move into the shed, 'And don't come in here, unless you want to get killed, stay outside. I can't stand you anywhere near me, and you ever so much as even try to touch me again, and so help me I'll take you apart, and what's more you rotten bastard, I'll enjoy doing it'.

And his reply left me feeling even more vicious still, 'Oh, come on Mathew, you can't blame me, I mean, what was Eric going to do to me if I didn't do what he said?'

I couldn't believe what I was hearing, and did I let him know it, 'What the hell are you talking about Adrian. Do you think I've lost the ability to understand English? He asked you whether you wanted to make up the third, it was a question Adrian, not a threat, and after that, we both know what you did. I think back at what Paul made me do late yesterday, and why did I do those filthy things? One reason Adrian, because I promised your mother I'd look after you, and look what I got in the way of thanks in return. You had one hand on the back of my head, forcing me into him, and you played with me with the other one as well. Anyway, I don't want to talk about it anymore, so shut up, and keep right out of my road, or mother and promises or not, you'll be taking a very big risk.'

He took the none too subtle hint and stayed outside, so I started getting dressed, but when it came to my shoes, with one of them without a lace, I found I had a problem. When I'd first wandered into the shed, as I passed the workbench I'd noticed a small roll of thin copper wire, but that meant the next test, I'd have to try and walk. Fortunately, no problem, because the stiffness and

pain in my legs, caused by them being tied for so long overnight and during the morning had well and truly departed. At the bench, I cut four short lengths of the copper wire, then slipped them through the eyelets and twisted them until the shoe felt fairly secure and as comfortable as the arrangement proved was possible.

Now there was the question of my watch, and I dreaded the thought of having to pick it up. It was still lying over where Eric had tossed it, and as I bent down to retrieve it, I was thrilled to find the seconds hand still ticking merrily away, and a close examination showed that somehow, it hadn't even been scratched. Next, my pack and sleeping bag, the latter still in its place across the frame, and as I rested my pack while I strapped my sleeping bag on top, I looked down at the floor, searching for my elf. Sure, the oil mark was there, but no way did it look like an elf to me. And as far as the bottomless pit was concerned, I decided the only explanation was that a combination of stress and pain could do weird things to your imagination, so after one last glance around, I headed for the door.

As I stepped outside, once again the fresh air offered a welcome relief after the mustiness of the shed, but before commencing the long walk back to the camp, I stopped at the water tank and thoroughly drenched my face, then had a long drink of the beautiful, clear water. But now I was back on my feet, I was forced to accept the pain I was experiencing was considerable, sending a clear message it was imperative I get back to the camp and then home as soon as possible. Although he certainly hadn't been invited to do so, Adrian stayed close, as he entered into as far as I was concerned, a flow of nervous and unnecessary conversation,

'Believe me Mathew, you sure scared the hell out of them. That fair haired boy kept yelling at Eric, telling him he was a cruel, dangerous bastard, and he was sorry he'd ever been so stupid as to have had anything to do with him. And I could tell, Holland was frightened also, because I know he was worried how badly he'd hurt you, so he kept shouting at the others, telling them to make sure they collected every bit of their gear while he cut you loose. He cut all the flax away and made a couple of them help him lift you off that frame and onto the floor, then he cut the bamboo away and collected it all and flung it in a ditch well back in the bush, and then boy, did they take off '.

The truth was I wished he'd taken off with them, but no matter, the damage was done, but as far as getting back to the camp was concerned, I knew there could be problems. In theory, we were lost, because I was convinced when Eric moved off that original gravel path, he'd swung around so we finished up somewhere to the rear and a long way South of the camp, and due to this, I felt there was no chance the shed was anywhere near the property. But if my instincts proved to be correct, they were telling me there was something vaguely familiar about those two hills I could just make out in the distance. They looked like those I'd admired as I sat on the steps of the hut, early on that first morning, and whether my assessment was correct or not, they were the only guide I had to go by, so it was a case of heading for them, or nothing. But before we moved off, I cast that shed one last, lingering look. If I'd suspected in any way what

they had planned, rather than walk on through that doorway, I'd have bolted, and wouldn't have stopped running until I dropped.

We passed through that gate that Eric had checked, to make sure we'd closed it properly, then followed the fence line of a number of paddocks, but as we walked into yet another, it became obvious it was the lowest point for some distance around. During the Winter the rain had come, along with a herd of cattle, with the combination turning the area into a pock marked bog. Then the Summer heat had arrived, setting the ground as hard as rock, leaving it resembling a lunar landscape, but no matter how hard I tried, it seemed there was no way I could stop stumbling. Encouraged by the constant jarring, the pain in my stomach and groin increased, until finally I was forced to drop to my knees and once again be quite ill, but this time obscured by a convenient bush. And much to my despair, the other problem reasserted itself as well, as more fluid was seeping out and running down my leg. The bush's leaves turned out to be large and as soft as velvet, so I was able to reasonably discreetly clean myself up with those, and in a way I found my embarrassment slightly amusing. Considering some of the positions Adrian had seen me placed in, let's face it, this was nothing compared to those.

Fortunately my stomach settled fairly quickly, so we pressed on, forcing our way through a large section of scrub, following more fences, walked yet again through another series of paddocks, clambered up a substantial rock covered bank, then after another thirty minutes or so of reasonably easy walking, there in front was a fence post with a yellow ribbon fluttering gently on top, proving my instincts about those hills had proved to be correct. With more than just a little bit of convenient luck, we were back at the camp.

Directly across from that so called administration office, there was a small group of trees, with their graceful, drooping habit suggesting they were probably Rimu. I settled down under one of them, resting my head against its reasonably substantial trunk. I gazed up through the foliage, and thought about the time I'd helped Adrian down from that cliff. That had resulted in the start of our friendship, what had occurred today, heralded the end. Many vile things had happened, too many damaging things done. In the past there had been so much fun, but now there was too much pain, too many memories of things done, I'd never forgive or forget. I found it incomprehensible he'd done the things he had, and as a result had destroyed a friendship I felt had been destined to last for years.

Time to snap out of my thoughts. Boys were steadily arriving back at the camp, and I scanned their faces. A part of me urged Eric and Paul to appear, but common sense said it best they didn't. If a fight started, I was aware there could only be one outcome, and I was feeling bad enough, without going out of my way to make things worse again. Instead, something resembling officialdom appeared, that man with the huge stomach being one of them, and they insisted on something resembling order. Another twenty minutes, many of the boys milling around impatiently, with the camp finished, now eager to be heading for home.

A few more minutes, and the sound of an engine drifting down from the road above, the tone changing as the driver slips into a lower gear, as he

prepares for the descent down to the camp. A few more, the second and last bus arrives, different to the one that brought us, both it and the driver much more recent models. As I get to my feet, the pain is there, as stubborn as ever. Our packs stored, followed by the rush for seating, but I hold back, all I need is an accidental shove in the stomach or groin. As we move away, with no sign of Eric and Paul, or the others, I automatically reach up for a strap for support, and the jolting as we traverse the track back up to the road, does absolutely nothing for me at all. Casually I glance up, and let the strap go as if it's red hot, because the sleeve of my shirt has dropped back, exposing the abrasion around my wrist. I glance around, concerned someone may have noticed, but no problem, everyone's eyes are on everything but me.

Adrian is sitting up forward near the driver. Just once our eyes meet, and his instantly fall away. Now nearing the end of our journey, some of the boys already dropped off, and a seat appears beside me, so I sit, and then immediately accept I'm better off standing. Finally back at the hall, and due to the fact my pack was one of the last on, it proves to be one of the first off, so I swing it over my shoulder, then head for the road above. Half way up I glance down, and Adrian is standing with his hands on his hips, as he thrust them crudely towards me. How I'd love to go back and smash him one in the face, but who cares, nothing matters except I'm on my way home.

The walk from the main road to our house, the longest I can ever recall, the slight slope up our front path, more like climbing a mountain. Now inside, with faint voices coming from our lounge. I dump my pack on my bedroom floor, then cross over the hall and ease open the lounge door, just wide enough to poke my head through. And I couldn't believe my luck. Jean Levers our neighbour is sitting there with my parents, and it was the first time I could remember her ever setting foot in our house. Her husband was a merchant seaman, who fortunately spent most of his time away, but on the rare occasions when he blessed his family with his unwelcome presence, chaos reigned supreme in the Levers household.

If Eddie didn't qualify as an alcoholic, then he was currently intent on rectifying the situation with all speed possible. He'd finally departed for distant pastures a couple of months previous, and it was hoped by all who knew the family, that his departure should prove to be permanent. Due entirely to the embarrassment Eddie had caused her, Jean had stayed friendly, but independent to a fault. However, as far as this visit was concerned, for my sake, she couldn't have timed it better, and I blessed her presence in our lounge like she would never have understood.

My mother glanced up as the door moved, and as always, the warmth of her smile seemed to flood the room, ' So you're back Mathew', then added as if she didn't really need to ask, 'and how did you enjoy the camp?'

If only I dared to tell the truth, but instead replied, 'Oh, it was OK, but I'm absolutely bushed, so is it alright if I have a bath and go straight to bed?'

'Sure, that's fine,' she replied, 'but don't forget your meal, it's in the oven waiting for you'.

I thanked her, nodded with a smile to Mrs. Levers, then closed the door and headed for the kitchen. The meal was there, one of my favourites, prepared as a

home coming treat, but empty as my stomach was, I managed to eat a little, then the rest finished up in the rubbish.

Next stop the bathroom, and after turning on the bath, while it was filling, I cleaned my teeth, but only after the third attempt did my mouth start to feel anything remotely like clean. Stripping off my clothes I dropped them on the floor, but it was as my underpants joined the pile that the shock struck. The crotch had been saturated in what I assumed was a combination of body fluid and blood, and just the thought of my mother finding them in this condition was quite enough. I knew there was a sharp pair of scissors in the drawer in the vanity, so I cut them into pieces and flushed them down the toilet, even if it did take quite a few attempts to succeed, working on the theory it would be far easier to make up a story to explain their disappearance, than the actual reason behind their condition.

And next on my list of priorities had to be that shoelace, because the pain it was now causing was making me desperate to remove it. Once again I sat down with my legs wide apart while I tried to untie it, but it seemed more hopeless that it had back in the shed, so I searched for something that would help, but the scissors proved useless, the drawers yielded nothing, so close to a point of panic, I could imagine having to say,' Mum, please come and cut this lace a boy tied around my testicles' but as I opened the door of the shaving cabinet on the wall and peered inside, perhaps I decided, my saviour might just have arrived. There, beside a bottle of pills on one of the lower shelves, sat an open packet of Gillette blades.

Couldn't even remember the last time I'd seen my father using a safety razor, but there they were, and at this time of strife, that was all that mattered. Gingerly easing one out of the packet, and just as carefully removing it's greased paper wrapping, once again I sat down with my legs well apart, and holding my privates to the side so as to expose the lace as much as possible, ever so carefully, one fibre at a time, I started to cut the lace. What saved me was that when Eric had tied it in position, he'd passed it around my testicles twice, and this meant I was left with one strip between the one I was so gradually cutting, and bare skin. Finally, after much patience and perseverance, the last fibre gave way, and dropping the blade as if it was red hot, I clamped my hands between my legs, and somehow managing not to utter a sound, rocked from side to side until the excruciating pain associated with the circulation returning to that delicate part of my body had abated, then flushed the lace away as well.

Now into that warm bath, and after washing non-stop for half an hour, I topped up with hot water and started all over again. It still didn't work, I still felt soiled and filthy, but a clean pair of pyjamas helped, and that newly changed bed felt even better than I'd imagined. Lying in that blissful warmth, my thoughts drifted back to that previous evening with Paul. That brutal rape, and those other obscene acts he'd made me perform, and I'd cooperated, mainly to protect Adrian from being subjected to the same thing. And what thanks and help had I received in return, absolutely nothing. Humiliation was fast turning into resentment and fury.

A brief flash of light whipped across my room, the headlights from a car as it sped away into the night. Instinctively I winced as it reminded me all too well

of what those other flashing lights in my eyes had meant, frightful agony, the likes of which I never wanted to experience again. Maybe others would feel I could be forgiven for not being able to stand the pain and cooperating for them, but I wasn't sure how long it was going to take for me to be able to forgive myself. I turned my head to my pillow and a few tears flowed, but exhaustion finally defeated despair, and I drifted off into another troubled, restless sleep.

Now deep in the night, and I woke with a start, momentarily convinced my wrists and ankles were still tied, while the boys continued to do disgusting things. Barely awake, I thrashed and twisted, my blurred instincts telling me I was desperate to be free, finishing up lying on my stomach, soaked in perspiration. So I rolled over and wrenched at my bedding, making sure there was no restriction left. The only noise was from a vehicle as it passed in the distance on the highway, and it registered, my room was unnaturally quiet, there wasn't the faintest sound of ticking from my clock. It seemed that fate had decreed that after all these years, tonight of all nights, it had apparently decided its time was up, and considering what had happened over the last two days, I wondered if part of me had died along with it.

With the unusual silence keeping me awake, my mind slipped into an unwelcome cycle of thought. I knew my parents should be made aware of what had happened in that shed. Due to the severity of the beatings I'd been subjected to, coupled with having had that screwdriver handle forced into and then wrenched out of my rectum, which I was fairly certain was the cause of most of the blood, when combined with those beatings, common sense alone said I should be medically examined. But a series of past experiences had left me wary of that, with the prime cause of my reluctance having occurred about eighteen months previous. On arriving home from school, I'd been informed I'd be spending the evening on my own, due to my parents being committed to attending a meeting, which, my mother had stressed, was of some considerable importance to all of the people living in our street.

Slightly put out by being left with the washing up, I stood at the sink and watched as my parents joined some of our neighbours, then continued on out of sight. No more than ten minutes later, a knock on our door, and there stood Justine Williamson, accompanied by her cousin. Over time, Justine and I had become good mates, but as far as her cousin was concerned, I remained slightly wary. Joanne's father managed a dairy company, whose factory was buried deep in the country, and with nothing more than some housing for those employed and a general store, this left Joanne about as far away as possible from the bright lights of the city she craved. So whenever the opportunity presented itself, she couldn't come and stay with her cousin quick enough, and due to her fast emerging sexuality, I'd continued to give her a slightly wide berth. But now here she was, dressed in all her finery, panting on our back doorstep, and sure enough, it happened, 'Mathew,' she coyly asked, 'seeing as we're all on our own, why don't you come over and spend the evening with us?'

With Justine there providing protection, the suggested arrangement seemed to make sense, so I locked up and went over. The evening passed pleasantly enough, and when Justine's younger brother passed out cold while playing with his toys, I duly helped the girls to get him into bed. Following that we enjoyed a

supper the girls had prepared, but not all that long after, found my eyes getting heavy as well, so I informed the girls I also was heading home to bed. But after saying my goodbyes, as I walked down the hall, heading for their back door, Joanne blocked my access, and at the same time playfully asked,' Seeing as we prepared a nice super Mathew, don't you think we deserve a goodnight kiss?'

Wasn't all that sure what they deserved, mainly because I'd never purposely kissed a girl in my life. But seeing as it appeared to be the only way I was going to be granted a means to escape, after some slight hesitation, I leaned forward and kissed her lightly on the lips. And with my innocence when it came to kissing girls, now a thing of the past, due to the youthful but innocent attraction that already existed, I admit, Justine's lasted just a few moments longer, then it was straight home to bed.

The next morning saw Colin and I indulging in our usual early Saturday morning routine, punting his football to one and other, over the powerlines in the street, when our front door was flung open, leaving my father standing there, breathing fire and absolute fury, 'Get inside boy, it's obviously time I had more than a few words with you.'

As I walked down the side of the house, I thought about where I may have been a little indiscreet, but there was nothing, all our neighbour's windows were intact, and I hadn't had my mouth washed out with soap in weeks. Now inside, and the look of annoyance on his face gave ample warning that trouble lay not all that far ahead, and the fact he'd called me 'boy' confirmed something really unpleasant was brewing as he grunted, 'I want some answers, and you're to reply either yes or no, understand?'

I understood alright, he seemed so infuriated; he appeared to be having trouble breathing,

'Tell me boy, is it correct you spent most of last evening with those girls next door?'

I now knew without doubt I was in big trouble, but I was still prepared to stand up for the girls, 'So what's so wrong with that dad, they're a couple of really nice well behaved kids'. Not a wise decision under the circumstances, with his face changing from a light shade of pink to purple as he exploded, ' Don't you dare talk back to me, and tell me boy, am I correct in understanding you kissed both of those girls?'

I thought about a lie, but decided on the truth, mainly because it was obvious he knew I had, 'Well yes Sir, I did, but only because…'

That was as far as I got, he was not interested in any form of an explanation as he thundered, 'Right, then get into your bedroom and get your gear off. I'll be in to deal with you shortly.'

I considered bolting, but realised it would only delay the inevitable. As I walked down to my bedroom, I knew I was in for a thrashing. 'Get your gear off', he'd said. Hell, I was only wearing shorts, so it seemed it was like Mr. Gossini all over again, because that was the last time I'd had a bare bottom hiding. I was wrong, there was no resemblance, it was like trying to compare a picnic to a banquet. As he stormed into my room, I saw what he had in his hand, a razor strop, and from where I was standing, it looked pretty lethal. Over the years he'd been through the gambit with his shaving, first a cut throat, then a

safety, and now he was into electric, and that meant the strop was quite aged, the leather cracked and open. After making me remove my briefs, and as once again my dignity departed with them, I was instructed to lie across my bed, and that's when the thrashing started. The sharp cracks of leather descending on my bare buttocks resounded around the room, and that, unfortunately, was when my mother returned from next door.

Rushing in, she threw herself at him, pleading with him to stop. Never had I seen my father lay a solitary finger on my mother in anger, he just wasn't that sort of man, but now he literally flung her aside, determined above all else to continue the thrashing. Back she came, and it was then I realised the situation was becoming quite serious, so I called to her,

'Mum, don't worry, I'll be alright, stay out of it, you're only making things worse'.

Reluctantly she understood, but after wringing her hands while she watched, finally it became too much, and she rushed out of the room. But whether I'd be alright, was fast becoming open to question. The pain the strop was inflicting was diabolical, because due to the cracked leather surface, it felt as if the skin was gradually being peeled off my buttocks. I bit hard on my bedspread, with perspiration running down my face, then thankfully, finally, it stopped.

My mother came back in, and on viewing the damage, headed straight for the bathroom where she soaked a towel in cold water, then came back and placed it over the damaged area. As always, time quickly took care of the loss of dignity and the pain, with a little longer required to repair the damage. My mother had another saying, 'no hiding is as bad as the one you know you didn't deserve'. I decided I'd remember that one for the rest of my life. But as the years slipped past, I had to admit it was deep inside the lasting damage had been done. For the first time ever, I became wary of him, and it stayed that way until I knew I was strong enough and more than capable of fending for myself. And it was regrettable, because from that day on he reverted to the father I'd always known, and never laid a hand on me again.

How he found out about those kisses was simple. The following morning, the girls couldn't wait to inform Mrs. Williamson of their amorous conquest, and she in turn came over and laughed over the incident with my mother. But unbeknown to them, my father had been sitting quietly in the adjoining room doing some paperwork for his business, and had heard every word they said. The two women looked on it as being nothing more than an innocent, childish experiment, but as far as my father was concerned; to him it was an unforgivable sin.

But as I continued to lie in my bed, listening to the occasional sound of the highway traffic, gradually I started to realise that for a few seconds it would be there, then would start drifting away. Sleep was in the process of claiming me again, but before it inevitably won the battle, it was essential one last decision was made. It seemed so ironical I could speak so openly with my parents about what happened in my life, yet circumstances appeared to make it impossible to tell them about what had occurred in that shed. So with the turmoil of indecision going around in my head, which included thinking about that boy who the two boys had abused in Eric's bedroom, yet who had been too ashamed to tell his

parents, I decided he and I had something in common. My father's reaction when it came to do with anything relating to my body, was that any incident, no matter how trivial, was blown out of proportion, and manipulated to a point where I was always in the wrong. So the loudest voice of all was telling me the risk was too great, the possible ramifications too distressing to even think about, so for the sake of guaranteeing my life would carry on into the future, exactly as it had in the past, I accepted those boys were going to get away with what they'd done. In the end, my decision turned out to be relatively simple, there was no way I could risk my father finding out what had happened in that shed.

Then to compound on what had turned out to be a dreadful three days, on the way home in the bus, I'd found out the camp had never been sanctioned by the Scouting Association, but had been hastily organised by a couple of the boys' fathers, one of whom had been friendly with the owners of the property, and feeling that such a golden opportunity was too good to be missed, that was the sole reason why the camp had been hastily organised. How I wished they'd never bothered.

When I woke the following morning, in seconds I knew things were still far from right. That stubborn, devastating pain in my groin seemed almost as bad as ever, and that alone was enough to give me cause for considerable concern. Noises indicated my parents were already up, preparing for the work day ahead, and seeing as I could recognise my mother's footsteps from anywhere in the house, I waited until she was passing directly outside my door before I called to her, ' Mum, could you come in here for a second? I sure don't feel too good.'

She placed a hand on my forehead, with her immediate response being I was to stay in bed, 'You're running a temperature Mathew, probably due to something you've eaten at the camp', she said, then added, ' Do you feel so ill that I should be taking you to our doctor?'

Fortunately I soon talked her out of that. The last thing I needed was a doctor poking around and asking all sorts of dumb questions, and I was also able to talk her out of staying home with me as well. She'd started working again, and after being with the company for a relatively short time, I knew she'd be uneasy about having to ask for time away, so fortunately an acceptable compromise was reached. As long as I promised to phone her if I felt things were deteriorating in any way at all, then compared to just over the hour required using public transport, a taxi would have her home in no more than fifteen minutes. Although still slightly uneasy, that arrangement she reluctantly deemed as being acceptable.

A large amount of time was spent on catching up on lost sleep, but it also left plenty of time for thought. As I saw it, one of the personnel at the camp had to have been involved, otherwise, the boys couldn't have possibly taken the risk they did, and as always my suspicions centred around Bergman. In keeping with what I'd been subjected too in his office, there'd been one other incident that had disturbed me as well. There'd been no physical contact, not a word had passed between us, but yet again it had increased my wariness of him.

Down at the pool, where one of the members of the school's swimming team playfully challenged me to a race, and I finished up highly amused at the surprised look on his face when the distance I'd beaten him by registered. But as

it turned out, the school's other physical education master had been watching, and on his insistence, I competed in a number of trials, with the end result being that a few days later, it was announced at assembly, I was now officially a member of the school's swimming team. It also became apparent, that whether I wanted to swim for the school or not, was totally irrelevant. If you'd been granted the honour of being included in this hallowed group, then it simply wasn't worth your life to refuse.

And considering Hull was the master involved, I readily accepted a refusal would be most unwise, even though I was already heavily involved with swimming for the club. He was a tall, dark skinned and extremely powerful man, and it was well known around the school, that lurking not far below that sullen exterior, lay a violent temper, that left him as an example of someone not to get on the wrong side of. On the morning of the day in question, I'd left home with nothing more than a slight sniffle, by midday I was fighting a full on roaring head cold. Just the thought of training after school left me totally unimpressed, and after managing a few unenthusiastic lengths, I fronted up to Hull, shivering and miserable,

'Like to be excused training today Sir, got a shocking cold.'

And I must have looked like hell, because he granted permission without hesitation, 'Alright Colbert, you can take off', but then added, 'but remember, back to it as soon as you can'.

With a casual wave to the others, I jogged off with my towel around my neck, keen to get back to the gymnasium and out of the cool breeze as quickly as possible. But as I stepped on into the changing room, it was like I'd walked into an oven. With the sun beating down on the iron roof for most of the day, the building had retained the warmth, and as a result was beautifully warm. So I slipped off my swimming briefs and stood there naked, luxuriating as I slowly towelled myself dry, purposely taking my time, allowing my mind to drift to other things, like how I could somehow avoid mathematics homework, when through my daydream it registered, I was not alone, and what was more, probably hadn't been for quite some time.

Now wary, I glanced around, and there he was, standing by his office door, and he gave me the impression he'd been watching me for quite a little while. Purposely I stared straight back, but refusing to show any sign of embarrassment that he'd been caught out, he continued to keep running his eyes blatantly over my body, until finally his eyes looked straight into mine, smiled in a most disconcerting way, then turned and casually strode back into his office. So with his demeanour proving once again to be decidedly unsettling, I proceeded to dress as quickly as I could, and beat a hasty retreat outside and then home.

However, waking on the Thursday morning, school I decided it had better be. Sure, I was still in quite some pain, but generally, the combination of rest and nature had worked reasonably well. The only lasting problem had been that angry chaffing around my wrists, but fortunately the long sleeves on my pyjama top had effectively hidden those from astute eyes as well. Purposely I left home about twenty minutes earlier than I normally would, which left me plenty of time to walk, as I pushed my bike up the few hills, that under normal circumstances, I'd handle with ease. On arrival, I strolled rather apprehensively

into the school grounds. It was as if something was telling me what I'd experienced had left a visual mark of some kind. But apart from those grazes on my wrists, which had reached a point of being virtually undetectable, there was nothing, those cheerful greetings were there as usual.

Our period of physical education was straight after the lunch break, and with my suspicions dictating my attitude, I kept in the background as much as possible. And this approach seemed to work, because the days continued to slip by without incident, with Bergman rarely giving me a second glance. As a result, that barrier of self protection I'd attempted to erect around myself started to fall away. I knew there was a chance my suspicions could be wrong, the only time his presence had been mentioned at the camp was I'd been told he'd organised the callisthenics, and that he was keen for me to go out on that trek, but there was no proof he'd had anything to do with the abuse as well.

And as far as the school was concerned, I knew my situation was no different to any of the other boys. His dubious reputation was well known, after all, the 'nick name' the boys used for him behind his back was obvious proof of that. So the advice that was constantly passed around from boy to boy, just as it had been with me, was, avoid getting caught with him on your own, and you didn't have too much to worry about. Apart from that, as far as a comparison with the rest of the masters at the school was concerned, he was reasonably popular, due to his well known distaste for the use of the cane.

And taking my life into consideration, the only change was Adrian's continuing non appearance, along with my refusal to even discuss the matter. My mother conveniently put it down to nothing more than a temporary falling out, 'all boys have them at some stage' I heard her mentioning to my father. Then there was his initial annoyance at my refusal to continue on at scouts, but this was quickly overwhelmed by the pressures involved in running a thriving business. So life in the Colbert household managed to flow along, and the steadily increasing nip in the early morning air, hinted that Autumn was drifting forever closer, and although it meant the closing of the pool was also getting closer as well, I still didn't look on this as being overly detrimental. The reason for this was because it was a season I had come to adore, with its frequent soft showers and picturesque colour, however it did mean that our swimming programme was virtually complete, except for one last meet, at which I was determined to swim well.

But out of nowhere, suddenly there was the prospect that I may not be able to swim at all. During a rather enthusiastic game of touch rugby, I'd received something considerably more than a touch. Fortunately the damage that resulted from the fall, turned out to be a badly torn muscle, rather than a broken collar bone, as had been first feared. Now most of the therapy and healing was behind me, so it was back to those repetitive lengths of training, as I fought to regain fitness in time. So yet again, as our last class for the day concluded, it was straight down to the pool. Sitting at the far end while having a much needed breather, some slight apprehension as Bergman appeared, but similar to how it had been in class, he ignored me as he disappeared inside the filtration shed.

A few more brisk lengths completed, then he reappeared and stood, chin in hand, while he watched me surge up the pool towards him. But as I flipped into

another tumble turn, a slight tap on the head indicated he wanted me for something, so I stopped and glanced inquiringly back, 'Hold back on those turns a split second longer lad', then he added as an explanation,' you'll find it increases the power of your thrust off the pool wall.'

So for the next fifteen minutes or so I continued to train, with Bergman offering further words of advice, then he stood, at the same time, cut my training short, 'You're going to have to make that do for today Colbert, it's time for me to lock up,' then added, 'anyway, thoughtless of me to keep you here like this, your parents will be wondering where you are.'

Felt I should put his mind at rest, after all, he had been doing his best to help, so I replied,

'No problem there Sir, my mother's working, and doesn't get home to close on six, and my father a bit later. So it makes no difference, because I just go home to an empty house.'

Apparently satisfied, he turned and strode back inside the filtration shed, and with my training having been suddenly terminated, I sprung out of the pool, and headed for the gym to change.

On reaching the entrance, I glanced back, and having locked the gate to the pool enclosure, he was starting to jog up the path, and with his even, golden tan and smoothly muscled build, he seemed to glide with the fluid motion of some jungle cat. Due to the fact he'd moved as quickly as he had, by the time I'd walked into the gymnasium and on into the changing room, he was right behind me, but whereas I moved across to my clothing, he carried on straight into his office. I'd dried myself, and was pulling on my briefs, when suddenly the door opened and he stood there and spoke to me, 'Colbert, step in here for a few moments lad', he said, 'there's something we need to discuss', then as his eyes dropped to my underpants he added, 'You may as well come in as you are, because what we have to discuss shouldn't take overly long at all.'

The man must have lost his mind. Did he really expect me to front up to him like this, especially considering what had occurred the last time I'd been in there? Anyway, the fact was I didn't want to go in there at all. However, similar to a couple of other boys in our form, I'd found out what a bit of fooling around in class had resulted in. The welt and bruising the stroke of the cane caused, had only just disappeared, and I was of the opinion that risking another because of disobedience, could wait for a while yet. And although the injuries I'd received in the shed were nothing more than a past, unpleasant memory, another stroke of the cane in that area was something I wasn't prepared to risk. But going in there as I was, simply wasn't going to happen, so I pulled on my pants, plus my shirt for good measure, then stepped apprehensively into his room, leaving the door wide open behind me.

And I found that my recollection was reasonably vague, probably due to what had occurred. The Kauri table was the main point that registered, with his desk well behind that, and the bench with the water heater on the wall, I certainly remembered all of that. But just to my left there was a door that appeared to provide access to a small storeroom, then closer still, a row of clothes hooks, screwed to the wall at just above my shoulder height. The only other item on display of any note, was a large picture that I noted was hanging

slightly askew, of some obscure sportsman, apparently victorious in some equally obscure sporting event.

It was also apparent that one of his predecessors had been a smoker, which he certainly wasn't, with the result being the ceiling was badly discoloured, and this was accentuated by a series of hairline cracks, which convinced me the ceiling had been protesting about the unpleasant pollution for quite a number of years. Altogether, an immediate impression of bland austerity, that I decided did absolutely nothing for me at all. But enough of that, because he'd finished writing, this confirmed by him scrawling with a certain amount of flourish his signature, then placing his pen carefully in a holder on his desk, where it joined a number of others, including some coloured pencils. He eased his chair back, which enabled him to open a centre drawer, from which he extracted a large, white envelope. He stood and carefully placed his chair back under the desk, then strolled over to the table, at the same time indicating he wanted me to follow. Then, with deliberate precision, he removed from the envelope, from where I was standing, appeared to be a collection of photos, which he started to slowly place one below the other on the table, and when he'd completed the first row of five, he started another alongside. And it was then that the warning bells started ringing.

At twelve years of age, I knew I could hardly be classed as being overly perceptive, but even I was aware the atmosphere in the room had suddenly changed. Within seconds, the air seemed to have been charged with some form of almost electric anticipation, and it increased again, as for the second time, he beckoned impatiently for me to come over and stand beside him. Somehow I didn't need to be told what those photos proved, other than the fact he'd been involved with the boys at the camp, just as I'd originally suspected. And as I glanced down, the shock of what I was viewing struck with terrible force, as I froze, seemingly almost paralysed by a combination of fright and embarrassment.

Nobody more than I knew that the sex acts I'd been forced to perform had been shocking, sickening and grossly humiliating. But now, as I stood beside him, they seemed a thousand times worse, possibly due to the photographer's meticulous attention to every repulsive and offensive detail, with the result that all I wanted to do, was bolt headlong out of the room. But I didn't, because fear like I'd never felt before, kept my feet glued to the floor. Finally he spoke, effectively breaking the silence that seemed to be permeating the room,

'Well now Colbert, and what have you been getting up to? Must admit, I'd assessed you as a lad who knew how to behave himself, but I daresay this proves one can never tell, especially when sex is involved.'

I didn't say a word, because shock had rendered me silent, so after waiting for my response, or lack of it, for a short time, he carried on, 'You know lad, it's a strange coincidence, but at one of the last schools I was teaching at, one of the boys got involved in something similar to this, and somehow photos of him finished up in my possession as well. Naturally, when I showed them to him and demanded an explanation, first he was shocked, then insisted I give them back. It took me quite some time to assure him that as long as I had, shall we say, his cooperation, he had my promise he had nothing to fear. And considering the

circumstances, he did cooperate, at least for quite some time, but one day when we were together in my room, he foolishly decided the time had come to rebel, and stormed out. Not a wise decision on his part I'm afraid, because some days later, a selection of those photos started appearing around the school'.

I knew that I could be slow in some areas of life, but I wasn't a fool, I knew what he was hinting at, because what he was saying sunk in the subtlety of a razor sharp knife. But I remained silent, so he continued, 'Of course, once that happened he became quite notorious, but certainly not in a way he enjoyed. In trying to extract himself from the position he'd placed himself in, at one point he tried to include me as being the major source of his problems by making a series of rather rash statements, which, I might add, I had no problem what so ever in proving to be entirely false. Then to compound on his already unenviable situation, it seems that somehow a number of copies were made, that in turn were made available to boys from other nearby schools, who it seems, paid surprisingly large sums of money to get their grubby little hands on them. Unfortunately, the non-stop torment and ridicule he was subjected to, finally forced his parents to remove him from the school, but even that didn't prove to be enough. In the end I understand they had to move well away from the area. I also heard it rumoured that all kinds of trouble erupted within his family. A great pity, wouldn't you agree lad?'

The fact was, I couldn't have agreed more. My parents and the stability they provided meant everything to me. Well alright, so my father could be a bit strange at times, but generally speaking, we got on reasonably well. Also, there weren't any brothers or sisters, grandparents or uncles and aunts to turn to, if I needed consoling, or a little bit of sound advice. The fact was, one of my main necessities in life was to be able to go home each day and receive the care, affection and understanding, that similar to most children, I'd long since taken for granted. Any disruption, or worse still, destruction of this pattern, I feared more than death itself. The truth was, that he could speak so casually of such problems in a family, scared me as much as the knowledge that he had those photos in his possession.

So if he was telling the truth, and instinct was telling me he was, then exposure of the boy's involvement had devastated his family, and from where I was standing, that was probably the greatest tragedy to emerge from the whole sordid and unsavoury mess. A slight hesitation, then with impeccable timing, his next question seemed to explode in my brain,

'Tell me, what would your parents' reaction be, if they happened to be shown these photos?' Instantly, an image of my father's face literally contorted in diabolical fury, flashed before my eyes, 'Sir, please, my mother would die, and my father, after half killing me, would ban me from the house. Honest, I swear, I couldn't help what happened.'

He continued to stand where he was, one hand resting on the table, while his eyes bored into mine, 'What do you mean when you say you couldn't help what happened?'

I knew my situation was deteriorating, and I had to try something in the way of an explanation, 'Sir, one of them punched me in the stomach, then while I

couldn't fight back, they stripped off my pants and tied me down, so I couldn't stop them doing those things.'

His eyes flicked from mine to the photos and back again, 'I can't understand what you're getting at lad. These photos offer no evidence of you being restrained in any way at all. And as far as these acts of oral sex are concerned, I mean, good grief boy, actually kneeling and licking another boy's anus, and possibly worse again, sucking on it as well. Then to compound on that, there's these other acts of oral sex, with at least four of them showing you with their penis' in your mouth as you place your hands on their buttocks and hold them to you. And what about these? They clearly show you lying across some sort of frame, with your chin cupped in your hands while you smile, as a number of boys use you for anal sex. What sought of excuse can you possibly dream up for that?'

And it scared me that I could offer nothing tangible. Only I knew that after Eric had untied my wrists, and each of them had taken his turn while I lay over the frame, nothing showed Eric standing just out of camera range, threatening me with the blade of his hand, making sure I did what he said as I placed my hands on their upper legs or buttocks and held them too me while I performed oral sex, or when they bent well over and faced the other way and held themselves open, while I performed those other filthy oral acts as well.

I'd felt there'd been no option, I'd done exactly as I'd been told, and now I knew there was no way I could make anyone understand my fear of the dreadful pain he'd inflicted, if I didn't do as he'd demanded. It was for that reason, and that reason alone, I'd done the things I had. Maybe some would say I'd been weak, but I knew different, because I failed to see how anyone could stand up to that level of cruelty. But I was all too aware now, that at this time, what I knew and what I thought was completely irrelevant.

Also, I was very aware that even if circumstances were such that I was made to try and explain the existence of those photos, as far as the boys at the school were concerned, my attempts wouldn't even rate a moments consideration. Only one thing was certain, the howling pack would descend, thirsting for my blood, and the majority of boys would experience the greatest delight in grinding me into the dirt with their ridicule, having already conveniently convinced themselves, that was where I belonged. From there, I knew only one thing could happen. Life at school would plunge into that of a never ending purgatory, from where there'd be no escape. But little did I realise, that more than one road leads to purgatory, and no matter which one I chose, that was where I was going to finish up anyway.

As I continued to stand and face him, I could feel the web he was so expertly weaving, slowly tightening around my neck. And as his eyes studied mine as he tried to assess my reaction, suddenly he spoke so very softly, 'Well lad, as I see this situation, the time has arrived for you to make a very important decision and for me to also make my position very clear as well. I confess to being one of a certain section of adults, who fully appreciate the pleasures on offer by the young, male juvenile body, and I've long been of the opinion that in your obvious innocence, you happen to possess one of the most perfectly proportioned bodies of any boy at the school. So it's best you understand your

position, then make your decision accordingly. Are you prepared to cooperate for me, and after what you experienced with those boys in that shed, I'm sure you know what I'm talking about, or do your parents and the school have to find out about the existence of these photos?'

And I shuddered, because the fact was I couldn't think of anything worse as I replied,

'No Sir, please, please don't ever do that. I'm desperate to make sure no one else sees them.'

And as he replied, the domination that was there in his voice, made me shudder again,

'Then I'm sure your obvious intelligence is such, you'll know what I'll expect from you.'

It was like a never ending nightmare, but I nodded, and there was no doubt it pleased him,

'Good, you're showing some sense. Now clasp your hands behind your back and face me.'

Briefly, rebellion flared, but as fear quickly dominated, I turned and stood as he'd demanded. He undid my belt, and as my pants fell to the floor, he squatted and eased my briefs down as well. Then he stood, and placing his hand gently enough on the back of my neck, eased me across until I was standing about a body length away from his desk. But after turning around, suddenly I realised that due to my caution at having to enter his room, I'd purposely not closed the door, and it was almost still wide open, and here I was standing naked from the waist down. But at that same moment, so apparently did he. Striding out quickly into the changing room, he returned in a matter of seconds carrying my school bag and shoes. He dropped them on the floor, just inside the room, then he closed and carefully locked the door.

He smiled at me, as he gathered up the photos, and after placing them back in the envelope, and putting them in and locking the drawer, he settled back comfortably in his chair, then said quietly, 'Take off your shirt boy, collect your pants, and place them over with your other gear, then come back and stand as you are, facing me, but with your legs well apart and your hands behind your head, and don't move from that position until I give my permission to do so.'

I glared straight back, refusing to move, and instantly his voice took on an edge that would have cut steel, 'I'll warn you just once lad, don't make the mistake of playing your stubborn games with me. Do as you're told, when you're told, or you have my promise, you'll regret it like you'll never believe.'

There was a boy at my last school, who'd get that identical look in his eyes. Kyle would willingly do virtually anything, as long as it guaranteed he'd get his own way, and if it proved to be necessary, he wouldn't hesitate to take you down with him. I was convinced this man was an adult version, blessed with the same disturbing mentality, with my problem compounded by the fact he was wrapped and presented as an infinitely more dangerous package. Reluctantly I surrendered, so after slipping out of my shirt and placing it on my bag along with my pants, I returned and placed myself in the position he'd demanded, wary of what could eventuate if I didn't.

After sitting and watching me for a few more minutes, he stood and moved around and placed himself in front of me. He reached out, enclosing my testicles and penis in his hand, then after fondling me for a number of minutes, suddenly said, 'The last time I did this to you in this room, I could feel resentment literally coursing through you. But from now on, accept things have changed, because I intend to use you in any way it pleases me, understand?'

Once again, although I knew it was a risk, I glared straight back at him, not saying a word, and this annoyed him, because he quickly added, 'If you've got any sense, and I'm sure you have, you'll accept your position', and as I still remained silent, he snapped at me again,

'Well speak up lad, do you fully realise where we're at?'

Finally, 'Yes Sir,' I replied.

'Good' he said, 'and for the sake of your continuing survival at this school, make sure it remains like that. Now stay as you are and bend well over. From past experience I'm sure you know what's coming next.'

He inserted his finger, and I stayed perfectly still while the nauseating act continued, and when he bent low and spoke to me, I decided it was just like Eric, all over again, ' Yes, no doubt about it boy, it appears we're destined to have some interesting and very satisfying times together.'

After that, it ended fairly quickly. He washed his hands and returned to his chair, and as instructed, I resumed the position I'd been in. He leaned back, and the chair creaked, due the pressure he imparted on it. Then after studying me for a little longer, he bent down and picked a briefcase that was standing beside his desk and extracted some papers, and on transferring his attention to those, proceeded to ignore me as if I no longer existed.

Chapter 17

And I was becoming increasingly more scared by the second. I felt I'd suffered enough abuse at the hands of those boys in the shed, to last me a couple of life times. However, there was no avoiding the fact this man was determined to do similar things. Surely, there was a way out of this, but I couldn't think what it could possibly be. That was it, I needed more time to think, but logic said how could I do so with any clarity, while standing here looking at him. There was a mark on the wall, just above his head, so I concentrated on that instead.

Common sense said the best thing to do was scoop up my clothes and bolt, but deep down I knew the possible consequences terrified me. I was convinced that without my so called 'cooperation' some of those photos were destined to appear around the school, after all, I had to admit, I was powerless to stop him. All he had to do was arrive early one morning, and leave an envelope on one of the seats in the quadrangle. Sooner or later a boy would sit down, and as curiosity got the better of him, there was nothing surer than he was bound to open it, and once that happened, I knew my fate at the school was sealed. And as the bedlam continued to intensify, finally, my parents would find out why the hopeless situation at school existed as well.

My mother would be devastated, but I was sure she'd stand by me through thick and thin, but my father was a different proposition entirely. He was a good man, of that I had no doubt, and he'd forfeit his life for my mother without a second thought, and in most circumstances, would do the same for me, that was until the word sex was mentioned. Then, in a flash, a stranger took his place, and a highly volatile stranger at that. There'd been other incidents before that almighty thrashing, and now I wasn't prepared to risk his unwarranted fury again. But if he was to ever view any of those photos, never again would it be a question of whether he'd die for me, on the contrary, he'd take pleasure in slaughtering me instead.

As with the boys at the school, right or wrong, innocent or guilty, it wouldn't make one scrap difference. All that would register is that I'd been soiled by eight boys, nine if they included Adrian. Worse still, as the whole sordid performance was gradually exposed, he'd find out I'd been raped on many occasions by all of them, and that wasn't even taking into account the numerous acts of oral sex I'd been made to perform. As I glanced down at that man, calmly sitting and writing at his desk, trying to comprehend my father's reaction was beyond me. But standing alone, naked and scared in that office, with the threat of unfair and untrue exposure frightening me in a way I'd never experienced before, I transferred my thoughts to the reaction I could expect at school instead.

The fact was my introduction to High School, had gone better than I could ever have dared to hope. However, the 'cultural' shock had been reasonably severe. It had rapidly become apparent that the relatively carefree days of the previous two years were now a thing of the past, and in no way had provided an

effective baptism for what lay ahead. Not that the school was in a state of turmoil, the military style of discipline, combined with the fairly constant use of the cane, guaranteed that. But certain situations that did exist, presented a clear enough picture of what secondary school life held in store.

By far the majority of the boys presented little in the way of problems, but languishing just below the point of what was considered as being acceptable behaviour, lay a hard core of individuals, who it seemed, preferred to live their lives according to the laws of the jungle. This on occasions, tended to create a somewhat volatile situation within the natural social structure that existed. Unfortunately, there were times when this situation was also not improved by the emphasis that was placed in the direction of the school's sporting teams, who were encouraged to excel at all costs. So in keeping with this policy, any boy who displayed even a hint of ability in any of the sports the school's name was associated with, was immediately allotted much time and encouragement.

Therefore this situation continued to flourish, whether the majority approved or not. And there was no doubt many of the masters didn't, apparently being of the misguided opinion that boys were at the school to be taught, not to be side tracked along the way, so that an excessive amount of their time was taken up with sport. But as far as the majority of the boys were concerned, they were all for it, as it were, because any success that was achieved within this echelon of sporting ability, guaranteed a status that ranged somewhere between minor recognition, to something approaching that of hero worship.

But before too long I was forced to admit that above all else, it provided first year students like myself, with one of the few opportunities to place one foot on that ladder of social acceptance, that every boy's existence at the school tended to be controlled by. And standing on a pedestal all on its own on the top rung of that ladder, stood the school's annual boxing championships. Those who managed to battle their way to success in this most hallowed of sporting events, were assured of accolades that immediately placed them on a level of some divine being. So be it as it may, since my first day at the school, it was as if some helping hand was hovering, never all that far away. Accordingly, I found my rather unexpected inclusion in the swimming team had been well documented by most of the boys, and I have to confess, the recognition resulting from this, hadn't proved all that hard to digest. Then, following on from that, the question of my ability on the cricket field had also surfaced.

With a set of broad shoulders, resulting from constant swimming, working in conjunction with a lithe, flexible young body, so common in boys my age, quite by accident I'd discovered this combination, mixed with just the right amount of youthful exuberance, was starting to enable me to bowl a cricket ball at opposing batsmen, with a decided amount of velocity, especially considering my somewhat tender years. So with my enthusiasm now well and truly activated, I started to spend many hours practising. But there was no doubt the most beneficial coaching I ever received, arrived via a most unexpected quarter, and it was during the six months leading up to High School, that those invaluable lessons took place.

On the afternoon in question, I'd settled into what had become quite a regular routine, bowling at a single stump down the side of our house, behind

which my father had erected a hessian net, so as to stop me constantly shattering the pickets on the fence behind. Then from seemingly out of nowhere, Eddie Levers appeared and wandered over, and after watching for a few minutes, during which he made some reasonably complementary comments, he started to offer what I interpreted as being very sound advice. And this surprised me, because I'd always assessed Eddie's sporting ability, as extending no further than an enthusiastic game of marbles. But over the next few months, I found his knowledge and guidance invaluable, as he proceeded to equip me with additional ammunition to add to my existing firepower.

Much later, at an appropriate time, considering the unfortunate situation that existed within the family, I tentatively raised the question of his obvious ability with Jean. She explained that when they met, it was common knowledge amongst the local cricketing fraternity, that it was only a matter of time before he was offered a contract with one of the leading English County sides. But rather than wait for this to eventuate, instead they married and set off for a new life on the other side of the world. But as alcohol started to claim an increasingly important place in his life, it was all downhill from there, and resulted in the waste, it would appear, of yet another outstanding talent.

But now at High School, and chosen to fill a vacancy that had appeared in one of the lower grades. Nothing in the way of earth shattering results, but never the less, a reasonable enough number of victims, that was until that Saturday morning, when once again that guiding hand appeared at just the right time. The day had dawned sultry and overcast, with a mantle of ominous, heavy cloud hanging low over the city. At any time I expected the Heavens to open up, but arrived to find the ground still dry and the teams preparing to do battle. Our opponents were leading the competition, with ourselves close on their heels, and our captain, normally a fairly laid back type of boy, went out of his way to stress the importance of the game.

The opposition won the toss, but put us in to bat, and I could understand their decision, but our top order batsmen responded, even though it was a decidedly difficult pitch, and by the time it was my turn to stride out to the crease, a reasonably formidable total had been amassed. And I was to become aware that the reason for this was their bowlers lacked that extra bit of pace to make the most of the conditions. As I stood at that crease and eyed that wicket, I could visualise Eddie literally drooling with anticipation. With its green covering of grass, combined with that heavy, humid atmosphere, I knew from experience he'd have had that ball swinging and bouncing like a magician. And as things turned out, I didn't do too badly myself. With five wickets in their first innings, and another four when they were forced to follow on, it meant that as far as my cricketing successes at the school were concerned, I realised it was one I wouldn't forget in a hurry.

I was also unaware that our esteemed coach of the first and second elevens had been watching, and as far as cricket at the school was concerned, his word was on about a par with that of God. So after the game, when he wandered over and suggested he'd be most appreciative if I could spare the time to present myself at the practise nets after school concluded on the approaching Monday, I took the invitation as it was intended, being nothing short of a cold blooded

demand, and to be treated accordingly. So I bowled at some length to a variety of the members of the school's first and second elevens, and as a result, two days later, it was announced at morning assembly, that I was now a member of the latter. Although elated at my sudden elevation, I was all too aware of the standard that already existed in the team. Accordingly, I realised my participation on the field would probably be fairly limited, and I'd see more cricket by staying where I was, but on the other hand, as far as that all important social structure was concerned, there was no doubt I had unquestionably arrived.

Doors that previously I'd been unaware even existed, suddenly opened wide, and once again the notoriety and acceptance that went with my new position, meant it became very easy to live with, and very hard to even think of doing without. Gradually a voice started to penetrate my thoughts, but it still took a couple of seconds to realise Bergman was speaking to me, 'Come on Colbert, snap out of it and do what I'm telling you. Turn your back to me, then resume the position you're in.'

So with the threat of exposure now scaring me to a point of panic, I didn't hesitate. Anyway, I found it was a definite improvement, because now it meant I couldn't see him, and once settled in my new position, it didn't take long for my thoughts to wander again.

For some reason, Eddie slipped into my mind, along with the sad termination of my coaching. On the day of his demise, I was sitting at my bedroom window, vaguely gazing out at the street in general when he appeared, staggering around the corner. Normally, I could estimate Eddie's level of alcoholic saturation, by the amount of pavement he was requiring, as he lurched from one side to the other. But on that occasion, even the width of the pavement wasn't enough, because he was constantly finishing up in the gutter. I decided this was about as bad as I'd ever seen him, but somehow, due to admirable perseverance, he got as far as the foot of the path, leading to their house. The slope up the front, could at best, be described as being barely minimal, then the path levelled out as it carried on to their back door.

Eddie stood on the public pavement and eyed that slope, then making his decision, took a run at it. He got half way up, then stopped, and then completed this exhibition by staggering back to the point where he'd started. After the fourth unsuccessful attempt, I wondered whether I should go out and help, but using what must have been some telepathic ability, he must have sensed my good intentions, because finally he made it without any assistance. Fronting up to their back door, which was wide open, he announced his arrival by pulling a large clump of grass out of the ground, then roots and all, tossed it into the middle of Jean's spotless kitchen, where the soil exploded in every direction. And no doubt anyone unfamiliar with the area would wonder why the long grass was there at all.

With the Government having supplied all the tenants with brand new houses, it was deemed the grounds were the responsibility of those now residing on the premises. Accordingly, in no time at all, newly sewn lawns were sprouting forth, up and down the street, but for one exception, that being the Levers. With Eddie not having the slightest inclination of expending the energy required in organising a new front lawn, months later, the front of their property

still resembled a jungle, happily thriving in the middle of a carefully manicured oasis. With some of the men finally deciding something had to be done about this continuing blot on the landscape, they finished up preparing the lawn themselves. But the Levers' backyard stayed as it was, hence the existence of metre high grass.

With my interest in proceedings now entering somewhere in the stratosphere, from my new vantage point, that being a side window in my parent's bedroom, I noticed Jean had put in an appearance, though still partly obscured by Eddie, as they argued in the doorway. But suddenly, in what seemed to be no more than a second, he gave a perfect imitation of the proverbial flying object, with his airborne momentum being abruptly terminated as he landed flat on his back on the path below. With his sudden removal now leaving Jean in full view, so was the large saucepan she was holding, with which she'd obviously hit him with. The intent in Jean's eyes was unmistakable, as she moved threateningly forward, obviously determined to finish once and for all, what Eddie had started.

I was staggered how quickly, sheer, unmitigated terror rendered an inebriated man instantly sober. Although he'd just suffered a blow that should have felled a bullock, he leapt up, grabbed the saucepan out of Jean's hand, and threw it as far as he could, out into the long grass, then headed at amazing speed, directly for their back fence. But unfortunately, Eddie had one more obstacle to overcome. All the houses had been equipped with standard issue clothes lines, which consisted of two posts with cross members on top, with two wires stretched taunt between. However, their eldest son had used the forward line to swing on, with the result I'd had to acquire a forked branch from Parran's Bush to act as a prop.

Considering the extenuating circumstances, which included the fact that Jean had retrieved her saucepan, and also that the prop wasn't in use, it was understandable that Eddie failed to notice that lethal, low hanging wire. It caught him under the chin, with the result his head shot back, his feet flew up, and yet again he landed flat on his back. However with his wife almost upon him, still armed with her saucepan, terror ensured Eddie was able to clamber to his feet and take off, somehow still managing to keep Jean at a reduced but safe distance behind him. I wondered how he'd get on negotiating the back fence. But displaying admirable ability, he cleared it without too much of a problem, the only trouble being, Jean displayed the same level of fence clearing ability. The last I heard, Eddie was sighted careering down the main highway as he headed at breakneck speed in the direction of the city, with Jean still in hot pursuit, not all that far behind. Briefly I thought about it, but was forced to come to the conclusion, my cricket coaching lessons were confined to the annals of history.

So where Eddie had helped bring changes into my sporting life that had proved to be beneficial, I was astutely aware this man sitting behind me, wanted to change my life also, but in an entirely different direction. But as I stood naked and alone with my thoughts in his office, I continued to try and assess my position. The changes at school had proved to be little short of miraculous, and following on from those had been the start of my friendship with Christopher

Martin, because there'd never been any doubt about it, from the first moment we spoke to each other, we clicked, and the basis of our friendship was formed.

He hailed from the depths of the Waikato, an area deemed amongst the best farming land in the country, and he was the ideal example of a boy, born and bred to work on the land. During his junior years, he'd been schooled locally, but his parents had made the decision he'd attend High School in Auckland, so boarding had been arranged with a couple who lived within reasonable proximity to the school, but it was a situation Chris decided he detested with a deep and utter loathing. But as far as I was concerned, looking on from the sidelines as it were, the problem was obvious, he was terribly, hopelessly homesick.

Just trying to imagine myself in similar circumstances, had proven to be quite enough, so whenever it became necessary to offer words of consolation, they came very easily indeed. We were down on one of the lower fields, sitting and chatting quietly together, when all that pent up emotion became just too much, and finally the tears had flowed. He wept for his parents, and his young sister who he adored, his horse and his dog, and those green, open fields, that to him could only be home. And I was surprised to find a couple of tears in my eyes as well as we sat there together. He wept for the family and home he missed so much, and I shed a few for a new found friend, who was feeling so much pain. But those tears managed to provide the healing lotion that was needed, because from that time on, he never mentioned an unhappy word again, and at the same time, a new friendship was firmly bonded into place.

As the pain of separation gave way to the anticipated joy of reunion at the end of term, Chris turned his attention back to his main infatuation, that being his love of boxing. Nothing showed me how deeply our friendship had been cemented, than when he took me aside and discreetly showed me his two most treasured possessions, these turning out to be the gold medals he'd won in consecutive years, at his local provincial boxing championships. And it was duly noted by yours truly, that it was obvious Chris really knew how to use his fists. However, as far as the school's annual boxing championships were concerned, there was now some serious doubt whether they would proceed. In accordance with a well established custom, the finals were always held in June, with this date going back as far as anyone could recall, and due to its extreme popularity, it had long been fashionable to acquire the services of some leading boxing identity to act as referee.

This year the invitation had already been accepted, only for the gentleman concerned to find out a short time later, that due to changing business commitments, he was now required to be somewhere in Europe at that time of the year. So, no problem, logic said to get someone else to take his place, but things turned out to be not quite that simple. The appointed referee turned out to be a close friend of the headmaster, who himself was a new arrival, who'd taken up his appointment at the start of the year. But in direct contrast to his predecessor, who'd proven to be a boxing mad fanatic, it was discovered the new arrival had something in common with my mother, that being an all consuming loathing of boxing.

Apparently allowing his distaste for the sport, to overrule his rationality, he decided that seeing as his friend wasn't going to be available, he'd prefer the tournament didn't proceed at all. Now shocked to a point of disbelief at hearing what he'd so foolishly suggested, boxing stalwarts amongst the staff, rushed to inform him of the cold, hard facts of life, and in doing so, they stressed they couldn't guarantee his safety as he strolled in the school grounds, unless said tournament went ahead. Fortunately, along with much relief by all involved, they managed to convince him of the dastardly predicament he faced, by coming to such an untimely and hasty decision. So with much confusion to the school's already saturated sporting calendar, the event was brought forward to an earlier part of the year. This meant that said referee could still officiate, but most important of all, it meant a face saving decision had been devised for one and all.

So it was duly announced that all boys wishing to compete, were to submit their names as quickly as possible, and for those wishing to train for the event, two rings would immediately be erected in the gymnasium. On hearing the news, and letting out a yelp of delight, Chis promptly moved his preparations into top gear. Down to the gym in search of a sparring partners he went, but after searching and pleading for quite some time without success, in desperation he finally turned to me, 'Christ, this is frustrating Matt, you'd think at least someone would be available. How the hell can I prepare properly and be at my best, if I can't find at least one bloody sparring partner?' Then from somewhere the light dawned, 'Hey, hang on, can you help me out Matt, have you ever done any boxing?'

Somehow, don't ask me how, but somehow I could feel trouble looming as I replied,

'Well, not really all that much Chris.'

Our conversation was abruptly terminated as he found some gloves and hauled me into the ring, presumably before I had a chance to have second thoughts, and attempt to change my mind. And as we started to spar, I became quickly aware of the slight awkwardness that was there. Although I'd still kept up my fitness with sessions on the punching bag, and skipping, there was no denying, my reactions were a bit slow, my timing just that little bit off, that edge of speed I'd relied on; just that little bit lacking. But as our sessions continued, the necessity to protect myself soon guaranteed that my old skills, such as they were, quickly returned, if only due to the fact that they were needed to guarantee any chance of survival.

Mixing it with Chris, soon proved he was nothing short of a young, fighting machine. He moved around the ring with a silken grace, and delivered his punches with devastating power. Early on, he could have destroyed me, but as time wore on, slowly but surely the improvement on my part was there, and our sessions started to attract some attention, but mainly from the daydreamers and non participating experts, 'Jesus, that kid Martin can box.'

'Ah, I reckon I could take him.'

'Well, what about that kid Colbert? He doesn't look all that bad either?'

'Nah, he'd pose no problem, I know I could take him.'

But with Christopher's entry having been long before submitted, he started to suggest I should be doing the same, 'Come on Mathew, you know you can bloody box alright. Go on, get your name in and have a go.'

And I admit the temptation was there, but I knew it wouldn't be wise, 'No way Chris, can't risk it. If my mother found out I'd entered a boxing contest, she'd ground me for six months, and that would be after skinning me alive first. Honest, it just wouldn't be worth it.'

However, as our regular sessions in the gym continued, it was becoming increasingly apparent there was one other whose dedication was equal to ours. There was no question that Lindsay Hull had a hard road to travel. His father's popularity was hovering around the pits, and if anything, was still rapidly falling. So life at school wasn't easy for Lindsay, and I found this grossly unfair. From my point of view, I'd always found him extremely pleasant, clearly indicating that as far as his nature was concerned, he was an example of a boy who'd taken after his mother. But there was no doubt future years would see him as a physical image of his father, long, lean and powerful. Already, some of the height was there, but that sinewy, seething power was still some little way from developing, leaving him tall for his age, but just a little light in the body.

There was however, no question that heading the list of his father's current priorities, was making sure his son won his weight division at the championships, and occasional glances in their direction, confirmed that parental pressure was constantly being applied. Occasionally we'd stop and talk with Lindsay, as he hung over the ropes in the adjacent ring, but as far as his father was concerned, we were nothing but pests, as he waited impatiently to press on with his son's meticulously planned preparation. The drawer for the tournament was completed in record time, and while we were standing around in the quadrangle, waiting for the bell to announce morning assembly, I suggested to Chris, 'Come on, why waste time standing around here? Let's slip over and see who your first opponent is'.

And he was more than happy to comply as he replied, 'Yeah, good idea, and at the same time we can find out who you're fighting as well.'

I stopped dead in my tracks as I flung him a look, 'What the hell are you talking about, stupid? You know I didn't enter, I told you what my mother thinks about boxing'.

To which he replied, 'You sure did Matt, so guess what? I entered your name instead.'

I stood there gazing at him, tongue tied, well, that was until I exploded, 'For Pete's sake Martin, do you realise what you've done? What's my mother going to say when she finds out, and how in hell am I going to be able to pull out now, with my name already on the board. It would look like I panicked and pulled out because I was too scared to go any further.'

No doubt about the amount of sympathy I got, it was like he could hardly talk for laughing, 'Just tell your mother the truth you moron. After all, she can hardly ground me for six months, can she? And as far as pulling out's concerned, it wouldn't just look bad Matt, frankly, it would look bloody awful, so the fact is it looks like you're competing Mathew, whether your mother agrees with it or not'.

For a while I kept on blazing at him, insisting it was a stupid thing to have done, and all the effect it had was he just grinned all the wider still. In the end, to hell with it, we purposely missed morning assembly, risking a detention if we got caught, and it was around then I started to see the funny side of things, and as we headed off to our first class, we did so as two friends laughing together.

There was no doubt about it, the atmosphere the event created, was like nothing I'd experienced before. The constant build-up of tension around the school was such, it was a relief when the preliminary's got underway. As I slipped through the ropes, ready to face my first opponent, I sensed he probably shouldn't have been there at all. He was visibly shaking, and it turned out he had something in common with Lindsay, another boy fighting due to his father's insistence. So reluctant and slightly scared, his eyes seemed to plead with me not to hurt him, and as it turned out, this was understandable, because this time, unlike Lindsay, he couldn't box to save himself. At the conclusion of the bout, with my name having been announced as the winner, he came over, vigorously shook my hand, murmured his thanks for my not having hurt him unduly, then promptly scuttled away, relieved he was mainly intact, and his duty apparently done.

My second opponent couldn't have been more of a contrast. A rough, tough and extremely dirty little street brawler, fighting came as naturally to him as breathing. He bustled me a little in the first round, due to his underhand and nasty little tactics, I started to get his measure in the second, and confess to a certain amount of pleasure as I methodically took him apart in the third. The remaining bouts proved to be rather mundane affairs, and as Chris and I stood together, studying the names of those, who, similar to ourselves, had fought their way into the various finals, the name above mine and registering as my last opponent, was that of Lindsay Hull.

Seeing as the finals were fought in the evening, the fact I was fighting couldn't be hidden from my mother any longer, but as it turned out, it didn't create too much of a problem. Once again, my father found the whole thing highly amusing, and the shock associated with my apologetic confession rendered my mother speechless, so she didn't get around to saying much at all. I was in my bedroom packing my gear when my father walked in. He looked at me for a couple of seconds, then said, 'Mathew, I just want to wish you all the best for tonight. I would have liked to have been able to come and watch you fight, but I'm working the factory overtime, so obviously I must be there. I hope you understand?'

I glanced up at him and simply said, 'Sure, don't worry about it, there's no problem'.

But suddenly I sensed there was concern lying just below the surface in his voice, 'Well promise me you'll be careful, for both your mother's and my sake, because in a situation like this, I worry about you as much as she does, so don't go getting yourself knocked around.'

I looked straight back at him as I replied, 'Dad, don't worry about it, I can look after myself, he'll hardly lay a glove on me.'

Suddenly, much to my amazement, he moved forward and gave me a quick hug, then he was gone. As I heard our back door close behind him, I was still

standing there, because I couldn't recall him doing anything like that before. Now the sound of his car as he drove away, and minutes later I followed on my bike. And as I rode into the school grounds, the assembly hall stood out like a beacon of blazing light. The noise emitting from the open doors and windows, seemed to have the walls pulsating under the strain. There was no doubt the place was packed, and after depositing my bike in one of the racks, then moving closer, I noticed in the centre of the hall stood a professional boxing ring, most likely supplied courtesy of our esteemed referee. Although I knew virtually nothing about professional boxing, one thing I did know, and that was that he possessed much influence amongst the local boxing hierarchy.

We'd been informed that all contestants were to report on arrival, to one of the classrooms, and this was where I'd agreed to meet Chris. But with many boys milling around, some who were meant to be there, and it seemed, many who weren't, we did what we had to, then quickly returned to the hall, where we sat down in an area reserved for those who were competing. Quite a few minutes past as we sat and chatted, but now a decided increase in the noise, if it was possible. The Headmaster appeared as he climbed up to, then into the ring, and finally, with much waving of arms, something resembling silence was achieved.

His speech was very much to the point, possibly indicating his disapproval of what lay not all that far ahead. My fight was scheduled for around the middle of the programme, and although Chris was heavier, he was destined to appear a couple before. The time passed quickly, and it seemed that in no time at all, his name was being called. As he stood and went to pass in front of me, I couldn't resist offering some last minute advice, 'Go get him Chris, but don't forget to watch his right. He'd hurt a couple of boys with it, on his way to getting this far, so make sure you don't add to his tally.'

No problem, as I watched my friend demolish him with a superb display of precision boxing.

And I was still savouring his comprehensive victory, when finally the loud words registered,

'Come on Colbert, what are you doing sitting there as if you've got all day? You're due in the ring in twenty minutes, so what the hell are you doing still buggering around in here?'

The nerves started to flutter as I walked back to the improvised dressing room. All very well for him to talk, but what was I doing here anyway? Training and sparring in Albie's backyard, a couple of fights in the school grounds, well alright, maybe a few more than a couple, the occasional attempt at bullying still needed to be dealt with, but let's face it, that was one thing, fighting in front of this ranting, raving mob was something else entirely.

A couple of men were moving around in the dressing room, neither of whom I knew. Their confident movements suggested they'd done this sort of thing, all too often before, and it was obvious they couldn't care less if I was nervous or not. 'Just get on with it kid' their actions seemed to say. 'The sooner this is over, the sooner we can all go home to bed.'

Lindsay wandered in, looking cool, calm and collected. I decided it was an act he was putting on, just to impress me. Probably been told to do so by his father. The boxing trunks were supplied by the school. Lindsay and I stood side

by side as the coin was tossed. It clattered loudly when it hit the timber floor. The result, he'd fight in blue, I in gold, and it turned out there were only two pair of gold trunks anywhere near my size. The first, perhaps the merest fraction small, so I tried on the others, they finished up well South of my knees. I reverted back into the others, and could almost feel my mother nodding her approval.

One of the prefects stuck his head in the room and bawled, 'Right you two, you're on, no more mucking around. Get out there and get on with it.'

The walk through the centre of that massive crowd seemed to take an eternity. I figured it was a toss-up as to who made the most noise, the boys, or the fathers and general hangers on they'd brought with them. I climbed through the ropes, and from my corner, peered out over the hall. The brightness from the overhead lighting gave the impression of melting that sea of faces into a mass of indefinable vagueness, and it did nothing for me or the noise at all.

Another prefect was standing in my corner, presumably to act as my second. I glanced at him and gave him a bit of a grin, but the bored expression I received in return suggested he was another of those who'd done it all before. We'd always had him classed as being full of himself around the school; he was living up to his reputation here. Vaguely I wished one of the Stoddard twins was here instead. They both might be bits of characters, but at least they'd be an improvement on him. Lindsay was over in the opposing corner, holding the ropes, bending and stretching; giving the impression he'd done this sort of thing numerous times before. His father was beside him, leaning over, his mouth close to his son's ear, talking constantly, no doubt driving home those last minute instructions.

Our time was near, the referee beckoning, indicating for us to join him in the centre of the ring. We stood face to face as he reeled off those pre fight instructions, and bloody waste of time I thought, nobody listens to them anyway. Lindsay gives me a cheeky grin, and I give him one equally as big back. No stupid hype or nonsense with him, just a really nice kid who was about to do his best to knock my block off. We touch gloves and step back, then the referee gestures to us to close on each other. This is it, it's all on, the roar from the crowd seems even more deafening still. No doubt about it, from now on it's him or me.

I danced on my toes, searching for an opening, Lindsay finds one first. His glove smacks into my face, a stinging, point scoring left. Didn't he know I was supposed to be the one with fast hands? Apparently not, because in a flash he's there again, almost before I can blink. I dance back out of range, and at the same time decide something didn't seem quite right. How could anyone be standing that far away, yet still score with his left? Now I understood why he stretched his arms, they seemed to be about two metres long. The pattern continued, things were starting to get a bit one sided, most of the round was behind us, and I hardly seemed to have touched him. What was it I'd said to my father? If this was an example of him barely laying a glove on me, then it was going to get bloody uncomfortable when he started. Now I found myself being forced to fight defensively, constantly wary of that long left hand. The bell signals the end of the round and I walk back to my corner, glad of the break.

It seemed to take all of the energy my second could muster, to lift my stool into the ring. Lindsay sat over there breathing in deeply, his father beside him and speaking into his ear. I could imagine the tone the conversation was taking, 'Keep boxing just as you are, don't change a thing. Keep using your reach advantage, and the fight's as good as yours.'

Not much of a chance for any advice from my side of the ring. It was obvious the idiot standing behind me was struggling to keep his eyes open. Then I heard it, through the noise, someone was shouting my name. I looked around, carefully scanning the crowd, and finally I saw him. Somehow Chis had battled his way through until he was almost beside the ring. But even from there, he was having to shout at the top of his voice, so as to make himself heard above the incessant din, ' Mathew, Mathew, you've got to go in after him, get in close and nail him, because if you don't, he's just going to stay back and keep on picking you off. So get in close and nail him.'

I nodded, showing that I understood, but it was just a case of two minds thinking alike, because the fact was, the decision had already been made. The bell sounds, I stand up, the stool removed, I'm ready for the second round, but as we close on each other again, I hold back, effectively blocking everything that he throws. And my patience pays off as he suddenly chances a rare right hand, and sure enough the opening appears. I glided in fast and low, his ribs so exposed it reminded me of Arnold. My punch lands so solidly it moves him sideways, and clearly I hear a sharp, gasp of pain. He moves back, suddenly overcome with the desire to get back out of range as quickly as possible. Probably needed to catch his breath, but as he moved back, I went with him, keeping him slightly flustered, and due to that, another of my punches lands in exactly the same spot. His gloves drop a little, now my turn for a left, and what a beauty, plenty of venom, punching from the shoulder with all of my weight behind it, just as I'd been shown so often in Albie's backyard., and he staggers slightly as I punch again, this time my right glove connecting with the other side of his face.

That's another of those I owe you Lindsay. Early on he'd had the better of me, but now I knew I could do something about it. I keep on crowding him, snapping out punches, and yet again as he backs away, I notice he stumbles slightly. Could I sense his timing and balance aren't quite up to the standard they had been earlier? He may possess a beautiful left, but his father should have insisted on more work with the punching bag, because in close there's no doubt he's definitely floundering. Another rip to his ribs, and although not scoring as well as a punch to the head, it still wouldn't do my points tally any harm either. The bell sounds, it's the end of the second, and as I return to my corner, would you believe it, this time my second seemed much more enthusiastic, 'Hell, that wasn't half too bad, much better than the first.' At least it proved he could speak. Across the ring Hull was hammering away as usual. Lindsay's head was bobbing as he acknowledged what his father was saying. I was prepared to put money on the fact it was slightly different to what he'd been telling him earlier.

I knew he'd got away from me in the first, however, I was fairly certain the second was mine. But whether I'd made up the points difference was anyone's guess. So to be sure of winning, I had to take this final round by a decisive

margin, and as the roar from the crowd continued to drum in my ears, I suddenly realised, winning was all I was interested in. There's the bell again, so the fact is one way or another, we'll soon know. The round progresses, his turn to change tactics, now it was he who was fighting defensively. Sure, his left still shoots out, but a fraction slower, allowing me that split second more time, and I knew it was that split second that made all the difference. My pride had been dented, no doubt about that. I was supposed to have fast hands, but there'd been times when he'd proven to be faster. But instinct was telling me that was no longer the case. It was my turn to feel him ill at ease. Another opening, and I made the most of it, with my left terminating on his right cheek. We fight on, and as I keep crowding him, I'm sure I can almost feel his frustration.

And I'm proved right. He closes on me, swinging a long, looping right hand, and one thing was certain, after all that tuition he'd received from his father, he should have known better. He'd been so badly off balance, when in frustration he'd attempted the punch, and as a result, was considerably more so now. As the punch fans harmlessly by, his chin is so exposed I can hardly believe it, as I automatically retaliate. My punch is straight and clean, and in contrast to Lindsay, has all of my body weight behind it as it lands flush on the side of his jaw. Then, it was as if everything changed to slow motion. For a split second Lindsay seemed to hang in mid-air, as if momentarily suspended by some invisible support, then I watched in amazement as he crashed to the floor. It took a second or so to collect my thoughts. I was convinced there was no way it could have been solely due to my punch, after all, it was rare for boys of our age to knock each other off their feet. That boy that Chris had fought had belted some his opponents with that right fist of his, and they hadn't gone down, badly hurt maybe, but they'd still managed to remain upright. The only theory that seemed to make any sense, was that he'd gone down because he'd been so off balance when I hit him. The hall erupts in an explosion of noise, but above it all the referee's voice rings out so clearly, 'Stop fighting, step back and away from him boy, that's it, the fight's over.'

And it was only then that the realisation hit. During those few, probably very lucky seconds, the fact that Lindsay had gone down meant that as far as the school's rules were concerned, victory was mine. It took but seconds for him to regain his feet, obviously a long way from being seriously hurt. As he walked back to his corner, I found myself wanting to go over there with him, to be able to take the time to tell him that I liked him, and I hoped the future would see us become the best of friends. But I knew at this time it couldn't happen. I had to stay in my corner, until summoned to the centre of the ring, where I'd have my arm raised as I was declared the winner. So I stayed where I was and looked across at him instead, and as he looked back, that grin of his flashed, and as before, I gave him one just as big in return, but at the same time I felt his was dulled slightly by the disappointment of defeat. So we met in the centre of the ring, where I was duly declared the winner, and this time I did walk back to his corner with him. His father was standing there, and after chatting briefly with Lindsay, I turned to his father, wondering if I should say something, although what, I admit I wasn't quite sure. But after the look he threw me, promptly decided not to bother. Never before had I seen such undisguised fury registering

on anyone's face, and the sheer venom the man was exuding was so unpleasant, I decided it was best to just leave him too it.

The following morning, after hearing my news, my father congratulated me, and my mother breathed a huge sigh of relief that I still inhabited the land of the living. And as I entered the school grounds, the congratulations and general back patting that had started the previous evening, carried on as the accolades kept flooding in. There was no doubt my victory was being received with much satisfaction, but I was all too aware it was due mainly to one thing, that being my opponent had been burdened with the loathed name of Hull. Much later, fed up and frustrated, I told Chris what I thought of the whole, stupid, senseless business,

'Why they all have to stick their back stabbing knives into Lindsay because of his father is beyond me', then added as an afterthought, 'but I tell you what, I sure as hell made an enemy of his old man last night. I tell you Chris, if looks could kill, I'd have dropped dead right in front of him'.

But he passed it off, something Chris was quite good at, 'My heart bleeds for the bastard. You won, so his son or not, you were too good, and that's the end of the story'.

And not all that much later, how I was to wish the story, such as it was, had ended there.

Chapter 18

Not more than a week after the finals, there was an announcement. Bergman would be away from the school for a few weeks, apparently on 'Government' business, as it was described, so Hull would be taking all classes of PE. Since the end of the fight, and due to my increased wariness of him, I'd successfully managed to keep at what I felt was a safe distance, but I was aware this latest development would see an end to that. During the first few classes that I participated in under him, I did so with extreme caution, but as a few more passed without any undue problems, I relaxed just a little, and the brief episode of minor misbehaviour that followed, gave him the opening I remain convinced he was so patiently waiting for.

Over the preceding few months, the game of golf had been taking up a steadily increasing amount of time I dedicated to sport. I'd started caddying at the golf club where my father played, the situation activated by the fact it offered a means of financial remuneration that helped supplement my pocket money, that for reasons too numerous to mention, never seemed to get close to stretching anywhere near as far as my financial commitments required. From there, it was inevitable that swinging a club had to follow, and from the moment I made my first, futile attempts to hit that frustrating and elusive little white ball, the spell was cast, and like countless numbers before me, I was well and truly hooked.

Keith Benson was another friend in class who'd succumbed to the disease much earlier. So with both of us discovering we were blessed with this mutual sporting interest, every Monday morning I'd sit, totally engrossed, while he described stroke by stroke, his weekend rounds, where his constant improvement was allowing him to take the municipal course apart, or so he would have me believe, anyway. As far as my own progress was concerned, I'd at least reached the point where I was getting the ball consistently airborne, but unfortunately, accompanied by a horrendous slice. With this fault causing me much frustration, not to mention loss of sleep at night, I'd lie there visualising myself hitting the ball so straight, it was as if it had been fired out of a rifle.

A variety of suggestions from my father hadn't helped, so Keith, with his bottomless pit of wisdom when it came to curing such technicalities, loomed large as my only hope of curing this blight that had appeared in my sporting life. It was late morning on a Wednesday, a day I was destined to never forget. We were out on the field, with Keith and I sitting well to the rear of the class, so those in front presumably offered something in the way of a distraction to Hull's wandering gaze, and he rambled on and on, somewhere in the background. Deeply immersed in our usual topic, the first hint we had a problem arrived when I glanced up to find we were sitting on our own, with Hull standing and towering above us, and when he spoke, his voice was laced with sarcasm, 'And may I ask what you two think you're up to?'

With it taking a couple of moments of getting over the shock we'd been nabbed, hastily we both replied in unison, 'Ah, nothing really Sir.'

By this time, making the most of the moment, his sarcasm was literally dripping down his chin, 'Well, surprise, surprise, and for managing to be doing nothing, you can jog around the field three times, then, when you finally condescend to join us, perhaps you can grant me the courtesy of your attention'.

As we set off, I breathed a short sigh of relief that I was escaping what could have proved to be a rather nasty situation as easily as I was. Past experience still had me convinced that as far as his list of favourite people was concerned, my name definitely didn't appear on it.

Circuits completed, we joined the rest of the boys, who Hull was in the process of dividing into groups, so we could all practise various forms of athletics and field events, and accordingly his voice rang out as he bellowed, 'Right, this group can practise some sprinting, you lot over to the long jump pit, you people can do some hurdling, you people try out the discus and shot put', and as he turned to the group in which I'd been included, he added,

'And all of you can go over and practise the hop, step and jump'.

Silently I cursed, then for good measure, swore again. Of all of the options available, I had to be landed with the bloody hop, step and jump. All of the others I could handle, and in a couple of cases, excel at with ease, but for some reason I could never fathom, the hop, step and jump I never even come close to mastering. Constantly I stepped where I was supposed to hop, jumped where I should have stepped, then inevitably completed the disaster by hopping everywhere but where I should. Miserably I waited in line as those before me took their turn, and with most managing reasonably well, that left me feeling even more ill at ease.

Never the less, when my turn arrived, I took a deep breath and charged for the line, determined to prove to all and sundry, finally, this time I was going to prevail. But I didn't fool anyone, including myself, as yet again I messed up the whole thing as only it seemed I could. Hull, who'd been standing and watching close by, snapped at the bait that had been so innocently offered like the proverbial shark as he thundered, 'What an absolute mess boy. Get straight back and do it again, only this time properly'.

But with my second attempt even worse than the first, his abuse, if possible, got louder still,

'You stupid, uncoordinated, useless idiot, get back where you were, start over, do it again'.

So sure enough, I tried again, with exactly the same result, so he responded with, 'I can see through you boy, you're purposely having me on. Nobody, even you, you moron, can possibly be that stupid, so you're to carry on until you do it properly'.

So once again, and I could hardly believe it, a ray of hope, a reasonable attempt that left me feeling quite proud of myself, but Hull's enthusiasm seemed to linger well below mine,

'I can't believe the constant mess I'm seeing boy. Absolutely hopeless, do it again you fool'.

Something was telling me I was in for quite a session, and I was right, it dragged on and on, with some of the others coming over to watch, with by far the majority offering quiet words of encouragement, 'Go on Matt, show the ignorant son of a bitch you can do it.'

But Vernon Waldon was the exception. He'd always possessed a knack of getting on my nerves, and he placed himself where he could mouth his own special brand of insults,

'Christ you're useless Colbert,' and as I failed again he added, 'A five year old could do it.'

And as I tried yet again, with another failure, he sarcastically commented, 'Try doing it backwards, you bloody moron, surely even that couldn't be worse than that bloody attempt'.

I admit it, my patience finally expired as I rose to the bait and snapped at him, 'Shut your loud mouth Waldon, or I'll come over and do a special job of shutting it for you.'

I knew the smart arse all too well. He headed the list of those non participating experts. He'd made it known around the school that after I'd defeated Lindsay, he reckoned he could take me. Quite a number responded by asking why didn't he enter on the night of the fights and prove it, and his explanation had been, because he'd forgotten to put his entry in. Where had I heard that excuse before? But now it seemed, he felt his time had arrived, as he thrust his face belligerently into mine,

'Oh, you think you can do it do you Colbert, well just you come on and try and prove it.'

Had to admit it, the offer was just too tempting to resist, so I placed my hands on his chest, and shoved, with the result he finished flat on his back on the ground. The roar that Hull let out, blazed out across the field, 'That's enough you two, get apart', and seeing as I'd grabbed Waldon by the front of his shirt, with my right fist drawn back as I prepared to settle the issue, he hastily added, 'Come on, back off him Colbert, do as I say, let go of his shirt, don't you dare hit him, step back, and don't have to be told again.'

As I reluctantly stepped back, he hurried over, and outwardly there was a look of annoyance, but masked behind that, one I was sure of sheer delight. Doing his best to give the impression of a much wronged school master, he ranted, ' Waldon, two circuits round the field if you please,' then as he turned his attention to me , he added, 'And I feel I've put up with enough from you for one morning Colbert, so get up to the gym, I'll deal with you up there.'

And as we all knew, that could only mean one thing; the cane.

As I turned and headed for the building, I could feel the sympathetic looks from the rest of the class, boring into my back. The last time I'd been caned, was two strokes for another prank in class. That I accepted as being deserved, this I felt wasn't. What made the situation even worse, was Hull's reputation for caning was nothing short of frightening. Consistent rumours indicated that at some time during the previous year, he'd been briefly banned from administering it, but after a short period of self control, it was generally accepted he was wasting no time in returning to his former, brutal best. Most of the boys were convinced he was a sadist, and accordingly, obtained considerable

satisfaction from inflicting pain. The walk up to the gymnasium complex was one of the longest I could ever recall.

Standing inside, I glanced around, and the vast emptiness created an atmosphere that was morbid and forbidding. The minutes dragged on, but finally I could hear his footsteps on the path as he approached, and at least it meant the strain associated with waiting was almost over. He strode in, but purposely ignored me as he carried on through into the changing room, then further again into the office. He reappeared a few moments later, cane in hand, but once again ignored me as he walked past until he stopped beside one of the large, timber vaulting horses, that were scattered haphazardly around the building. Finally he acknowledged my presence by pointing to a position directly in front of the one he'd selected, then as he glanced back over his shoulder, finally dawned to speak, 'Right, my trouble causing young friend, get over here and stand there.'

As I moved over and stood where instructed, he swung his eyes deliberately around, as if confirming we were definitely alone. Apparently assured, he rested the cane on the end of the vaulting horse, then positioning himself directly behind me, placed both of his hands on my hips and lifted, so as I finished up draped over the horse, which left my feet hanging well up from the floor. The units were heavy, and to assist in moving them, they'd been fitted with two thick rope handles on either side. So as I lay across, with my position leaving me looking down at the floor, he walked around and spoke to me from there. 'Take one of those handles in each hand boy, and I suggest it wouldn't be wise to release them until I've finished with you, and you've received my permission.'

Reaching down, I found the ropes were still out of reach, and as I eased myself further over so I could grasp them, I felt my gym shorts ride up and tighten like a second skin across my buttocks, until it seemed as if they were half exposed. Now draped in the position he apparently found satisfactory, I clenched my teeth and waited for the inevitable.

And it was not long in arriving. With him being almost two metres tall, and similar to his son, possessing long arms, he swung the cane in a huge, vicious, sweeping arc. As the first stroke smashed into my buttocks, that searing, screaming agony was like nothing I'd previously experienced. The resounding crack as the cane connected seemed to fill the building, and as it did, those appalling waves of excruciating agony just kept on coming. It felt as if my buttocks were on the verge of igniting, and I gripped that rope so tight, I knew my knuckles must have turned white, but I couldn't see them through the tears of pain in my eyes. But as I bit my lip and waited, that dreadful pain just kept on coming.

It seemed like an eternity passed before the warning whistle the cane produced was there again, and as it connected, the result was another explosion of frightening horror. I sure as hell wasn't crying, there was no way I'd give a sign of any kind that he'd hurt me as badly as he had, but those uncontrollable tears of pain still ran down my cheeks. And that was only after two strokes, and I already had the impression he'd singled me out for more than that, so I lay there in dreadful pain, waiting for the third. But nothing, and while the seconds ticked painfully on, all I could do was bite my lip and wait. The fact I could taste blood told me I'd bitten my lip to a point where it was bleeding, but I didn't

care, all that mattered was there was no way I was going to let this cruel man defeat me. I knew it would suit him fine, if I was lying here begging for mercy.

But what I couldn't understand was why there was so long between each stroke. When I'd received those two strokes previously, it had been over in a few painful seconds, but this time, it was as if the pain was never going to stop. Then the reason became brutally clear, he was doing it on purpose, making me wait, and in doing so, making me suffer as long as possible. And at the same time, something else became abundantly clear. I wasn't being caned for my indiscretion with Keith, or for that matter, fighting with Vernon. I was being thrashed for beating his son at boxing. As the third stroke was delivered, and now fully aware of the game he was playing, I started to count, and reached twenty five before the fourth smashed into my buttocks. The agony it produced was almost beyond description, possibly because the cane had connected higher than where the others had landed. The next count reached twenty two, before another sharp crack echoed around the building, and at this rate the punishment was going to last well over two minutes, rather than seconds. Twenty five, twenty six, twenty seven, then the sixth delivered with such terrible force, the vaulting horse, heavy as it was, shook from the concussion the last stroke produced.

I sensed Hull still standing behind me, and it gave me the impression he was reluctant to move, leaving me wondering whether he was going to risk hitting me again. It was like he was regretting the punishment had to stop. As I waited for his decision, perspiration continued to run down my face, but following that forth stroke of the cane, the agony seemed to have reached a point where nothing seemed capable of making it any worse. But it appeared that after some deep deliberation, he'd decided that risking another, no matter how tempting, wasn't worth the trouble it could possibly cause him, so reluctantly he moved away, snapping back at me as he went, 'Right boy, that should teach you not to mess with me. Now get down, get dressed and get out.'

But the truth was, I was reluctant to move. The pain I was suffering was so bad, there seemed to be a lot going for staying exactly where I was. However, the thought of the others coming in and finding me draped over the vaulting horse like this, finally provided incentive enough, so down I decided, it better be. Letting go of the rope handles, I pressed my palms on the side of the horse, with the intention of easing my feet slowly and carefully down to the floor, having previously made the decision that jarring my body was the last thing I needed, the only trouble being, it appeared a hole had materialised from somewhere, because I simply continued on down, finishing up in a heap on the floor. So much for carefully devised plans. As I lay there, I tried to comprehend what could have happened, but it didn't take all that long to work out, because there was this strange lack of feeling in my legs. Briefly a flash of panic, as I wondered what harm he'd caused, but within seconds a distinct tingling sensation started, that tended to indicate normal feeling was in the process of returning.

Hull had reached the doorway to the dressing room, but attracted by the noise as I hit the floor, he turned back and stared. Going by his eyes, he knew something was badly wrong, and the look of fear that spread over his face went

some way towards compensating for what I'd experienced. I hope I scared you half to death, you ignorant, cruel, sadistic bastard. But torn between coming back, as he knew he should, or preferring to gather himself and give the impression he was unconcerned, he chose the latter, and continued on through the doorway and out of sight. For a little longer, I stayed where I was and thought about my legs. But the only explanation I could come up with that seemed anything like plausible, was that somehow that fourth, higher stroke of the cane had been responsible for that strange and slightly scary brief numbness.

But enough of that, there were other things to be done. My school clothes were on a seat some distance away, and I decided it might be a good idea to get changed as quickly as possible. I knew the damage he'd caused was extensive, and there was a good chance the shorter length of my gym pants could well be struggling to cover the welts and bruising. So getting carefully to my knees, then equally as carefully to my feet, I set off walking slowly across the floor. Getting dressed proved to be painful and even slower, and I'd just completed tying my laces when the rest of the class suddenly pounded in. A couple threw me the usual mindless comments that schoolboys come to expect, but the majority left me alone, and in the end it was Chris who came over and made the discreet inquiry, 'How many did you get?'

'Six,' I replied. There was a distinct pause, then he added, 'Six, bloody hell, you'd have to burn the bloody school down to warrant that. The rotten bastard, are you alright?'

And I answered him quite truthfully, 'Frankly, I'm still in agony, but I'll get there.'

We flung our bags over our shoulders and strolled out of the building together. Somehow I expected the sky to be dull and overcast, which seemed in keeping with the tone of the morning, but it proved me wrong by being perfectly clear. Not that it mattered one way or the other, but what did matter was it was good to be outside and away from that man. Later that day I arrived home, the pain once again reactivated from riding my bike. As I was changing into casual clothes, I backed up to my bedroom mirror and slipped my underpants down, and the kaleidoscope of colour on display went close to giving me a fright. Never could I have envisaged such damage was possible, and the welts he'd raised stood up as high as my little finger, and I found the effect of what he'd done so devastating, I quickly finished dressing and walked outside. The best approach, I decided, was to try to forget about it as quickly as possible, at the same time hoping the damage healed as quickly as possible also.

The following morning, another class under Hull, where fortunately, he reverted to his preference for ignoring my presence. Back in the changing room, where I was playfully but firmly grabbed, and I knew I should have known better, after all, it was a standard practise that the buttocks of boys who'd been caned were examined by all those present. But as I waited for the usual variety of colourful comments, the silence that ensued as my pants were wrenched down and my buttocks placed on display, seemed to hang in the air like some ominous cloud. Finally, after quite some seconds had passed, one of them spoke, 'Jesus bloody Christ, what a fucking mess.'

Then someone else added, 'That ignorant, rotten, dangerous bastard. Someone should be told about this, it's beyond a fucking joke, he ought to be banned from the bloody school.'

So after many consoling pats on the back and shoulders, accompanied by numerous words of sympathy, they drifted slightly self consciously away, except for one, it was Vernon,

'I just want to say how sorry I am Colbert. Honest, I'd never have annoyed you if I'd known it was going to lead to something like that. I really am terribly sorry.' This was something new, Vernon actually apologising, but never the less, I appreciated it,

'It's alright Vernon, you weren't to know, and I shouldn't have reacted like I did. I looked at the damage yesterday, and decided to forget all about it, now you do the same, alright?'

Two days later, back with Hull again, and just to round off what had proved to be a couple of painful days, I'd twisted my ankle during a game of rugby. As usual, Hull had the class doing some circuits around the field, and I was struggling to keep up. With the instincts of some animal stalking its wounded prey, once again he pounced, 'Stop lagging behind boy. Try to exert yourself, make a supreme effort, get back up there, keep up with the others.'

I wondered how he'd accept my explanation. Guess there's only one way to find out, 'Hurt my ankle yesterday Sir, it's proving to be a bit of a problem when it comes to jogging.'

Considering the situation between us, his reply was something like I should have expected,

'Stop trying to have me on boy. I know your kind, you're nothing but a trouble maker, so stop purposely trying to irritate me or we'll be spending another session in the gym, with me standing behind you with the cane, and you bending over and looking down at the floor.'

The warning signs were there, loud and clear. He was after me, and something had to be done. There was no way I was prepared to risk another unwarranted caning from him.

Decision made, I stopped dead, spun around and looked back at him as I replied,' Ah, after giving what you've said a bit of thought Sir, I don't think it's going to happen'.

This time it was his turn to stop, and he did so, as if he'd suddenly run into some invisible object. For a moment he stood there, mouth open, as if he simply couldn't believe what he was hearing, then he took a deep breath and exploded, 'What did you dare to say to me boy?'

I decided that from here on in, it was shaping up as definitely being all or nothing,

'I said, I don't think it's going to happen', and as he continued to stand there gaping at me, I carried on before he had a chance to collect his wits and his fumes ignited once again, 'And I'll tell you why. My father said you just so much as touch me again, and he'll bring assault charges so fast, you'll hardly realise it's happened.'

Now I was warming to the task, surprising the effect a bare faced lie can have. Hadn't even told my father I'd been caned, so with my survival balanced

precariously in my hands, it was my turn to take a deep breath and carry on, 'You talk about going back to the gym, well I'll go back with you alright, and while we're there, I'll show you the mess you made of me.'

Going by the look on his face, it appeared my manipulation of the truth was having the desired effect, so without wanting to appear greedy, I was prepared to risk another,' Also, my father took photos of what you did, and the other boys in the class are prepared to confirm the extent of the damage as well. And do you know why? It's because they think you're as big a menace at the school as I do. And you're also prepared to stand there and call me a trouble maker. Well how about checking with some of the other masters, who've had a lot more to do with me than you, and you'll find I don't have a reputation for causing trouble, so unless you want to find out what trouble really is, I suggest you just back off and leave me alone.'

I turned and limped off after the others, and I wondered, once he'd recovered, whether he'd call me back, but he didn't, and to my knowledge, he never used the cane on another boy at the school again. Possibly he finally accepted the danger to his position the combination of his violent temper and lack of control created. On Bergman's return to the school, we were immediately transferred back under him, and this was received with considerable relief by all the other boys in my form. But as far as I was concerned, it heralded the beginning of a slow but sure descent into a world dominated by pornography and both sexual and at times physical abuse, that as a twelve year old, I had been totally oblivious to the fact that such a repulsive section of the community, who indulged in such things, even existed.

Chapter 19

So my problems with that sullen, brutal man appeared to be over, but as I stood in that somewhat austere room, I was aware my problems with this manipulative man sitting behind me, were just beginning. I couldn't help thinking, the school sure missed out badly with its allocated physical education instructors. The sounds from the voices of a few of the boys who'd tended to linger around the grounds, had long since started to fade, and now had disappeared altogether. The only intrusion on the silence in the room was from the occasional rustle of papers as he moved them across his desk, and the fleeting hum from a vehicle, as it passed up the road fronting the school. The knowledge we were now alone, with there being little to no chance of our being disturbed, left me feeling trapped and frightened. But I was aware that from the time I'd walked into his office, nothing had changed, because logic was saying I should still pick up my clothes and bolt, then hope and pray that by defying him, that's where he'd be prepared to let his attempt at dominance end.

But as with the treatment I'd been subjected to by those boys at the camp, the remedial action required was so simple in theory, was proving to be very different in reality. There was no use trying to deny the fact, those photos he possessed effectively supplied him with the evidence to destroy me. I felt there was no way I could successfully explain those sex acts I'd been involved with, and even if some believed me, there was no chance my father would be included amongst them. There was no doubt I'd been set up quite cleverly, and as far as the boys at the school were concerned, it would take but minutes for him to turn my life at school, great as it was now, into that of a living purgatory, from which there was no escape, and yet on the other hand, in which it would be impossible to survive. So I was convinced that unless he had my, as he so delicately put it 'cooperation' then I was convinced that streak of frightening bloody mindedness would surface, and I was all too aware of the chaos that would happen from there.

As I looked up, staring at one of those larger cracks in the ceiling, it was as if I could see those small, sniggering groups forming, as one by one the boys took their turns studying those photos. From there, the demeaning and sordid comments would start, then en masse, they'd come looking for me. My popularity and acceptance, currently running at a level I would never have thought was possible, would disintegrate within an hour, buried forever under an avalanche of scathing abuse and ridicule. I was very aware my position on the school's social ladder was admired by many, and openly envied by most. So due entirely to the fickleness of youth, nothing would suit that large majority more, than to see my recently acquired status come tumbling down. So if I refused to cooperate with him, and as a result, he carried out his threat, any attempts on my part to explain, would be smothered forever, under an unstoppable torrent of condemnation.

Deeply immersed in thought as I was, I failed to hear him move from his desk and stand directly behind me. He announced his presence by running his hand slowly and deliberately over my buttocks, then gradually around to the front, where he fondled and masturbated me, then finished, for some reason, by gently squeezing the head of my penis as he spoke to me, ' Tell me Colbert, are you starting to get tired, standing there like that?'

I decided my shoulder wouldn't exactly complain if I was told I could lower my arms, 'Yes Sir, guess I am. Recently hurt my shoulder, and it is starting to ache a bit'.

He replied very softly, mainly because standing where he was, he was practically speaking directly into my left ear,' Well we can't have that,' he replied, ' so perhaps it's time for you to take up another position, and I have one that's been specially designed, just for you.'

Resting his hand lightly on my shoulder, he started to ease me across the room, and I noticed we were heading directly for that old Kauri table. And as we approached, I realised there was an addition to the last time I'd seen it. A timber rail had been crudely checked in, quite low to the floor, between the two front legs closest to us, and I was positive it hadn't been there the last time I was in his room. All I could think of was it contributed nothing, other than to add to the demise of what had once been a fine piece of furniture. But now, standing directly in front of the table, he explained why the addition was there, 'Stand up on that rail boy, spread your legs well apart, then lie flat across, then spread your arms and hold onto the far edge. Also, accept that if there's ever a time for you to do as you're told, it's never more than now. Just do as I say, and we won't have a problem, but try to defy me, and you'll discover the magnitude of the problems you've unleashed for yourself.'

For a few moments I still resisted, my loathing so intense, it was as if it was seeping out of my skin. But my fear, that all consuming fear of the insurmountable problems I was convinced he would create if I dared to defy him, was even greater. Decisions made from a position of fear, combined with a lack of maturity, can be dangerous games to play. So as that last flickering resemblance of defiance drained away, I stepped up on that rail and placed myself in the position he'd demanded, and in doing so, surrendered my body and soul for the next two and a half years. And with that meticulously positioned rail pressing into the soles of my feet, while it raised my buttocks to the additional height he required off the floor, it instantly became apparent why he'd gone to the trouble of fixing it there. The front edge of the table top pressed into my lower stomach, at the same time forcing my buttocks outward, and with my legs angling back in, without holding onto the far edge like he'd insisted, I'd have found the position difficult to maintain.

Quite a few minutes past, the time taken up once again, with him running his hands over my body, as if to explore every last part that apparently attracted him. He started at my neck, then his hands slipped down my arms and back again as he slid them over my back. Now further down to my buttocks, easing them apart, teasing and fingering my anus, a nauseating reminder of Eric, and his filth. Next, slipping his hands between my legs, enclosing and fondling my testicles, before taking quite a few moments to once again masturbate my penis.

146

Apparently finally satisfied, he backed away and moved across to the door, making sure it was securely locked. He was naked from the waist down, and when he came back and stood behind me and placed his hands on my hips, past experience suggested only seconds remained before he penetrated me. But I was wrong, because he entered into a detailed discussion instead, as he attempted to explain how he felt the situation should be between us,

'I'm truly sorry your reluctance to cooperate has brought us to this Colbert. I would far rather it had been something like a mutual agreement, but due to your previous aggressive reaction, when I had you down here alone in my office, to reach this point, it became apparent other arrangements would be necessary. That of course, included using the boys at the camp, and believe me when I say I'm very sorry they harmed you to the extent they did, that was never my intention. All I wanted was those photos, and the way they acquired them was certainly not to my liking. But now you must accept I have them, and will use them without hesitation if you should choose at any time to defy me. Now come on lad, surely we can still come to some sort of pleasant arrangement that will guarantee your cooperation?'

Once again, my answer was straight to the point, 'No we bloody can't. And you talk of coming to some sort of pleasant arrangement that will guarantee my cooperation. The only thing I can guarantee is, you use me for sex, and I'll despise you for the rest of my life.'

During our conversation, he'd moved back, apparently hoping I'd be only too prepared to cooperate, but now, finally accepting it was futile, he returned and placed his hands back on my hips. But as I saw it, nothing had changed. In theory, I had seconds left to change my mind and willingly cooperate with what he wanted, and I knew that would never happen, so once again I was left with the choice. It was quite clear, especially considering the conversation we'd had, abuse by hundreds, or abuse by this one man. Frightened to stay, but even more frightened to defy him and move, suddenly the pain was there as he penetrated me. My humiliation had been bad enough, considering what I'd suffered in that shed, but somehow it seemed even worse again with him. Another thing he had in common with Eric, he knew how to make the abomination last, because many minutes past before it ended.

When he finally gave me permission to step down, because of my shame, I tried to avoid looking at him. But he placed a hand on my shoulder as he made me stand still, while with the other he eased my chin up, so I was forced to look him full in the face while he spoke, 'For this time it's over lad, so you may get dressed and go home, and from what you told me down at the pool, you'll still have plenty of time before your mother arrives. But above all else, heed my warning boy. If you were ever so foolish as to contemplate mentioning one word of what has gone on between us, then I suggest you think very carefully first'. He stopped briefly, while he quickly dressed, then continued, 'Naturally, I'd categorically deny any absurd accusations you may be tempted to make. Then I would make it perfectly clear, that I'd discovered, after carefully questioning some boys who'd attended a camp our troupe had participated in, that you'd been involved in a series of degrading sex acts, and after viewing the photos that

provided the evidence of this, I'd been left with no alternative other than to ban you from the troupe.'

He turned and strolled over to his desk. Opening a drawer, he casually took out a comb and ran it through his hair, before turning back and continuing,' I would also mention the problem had been compounded by the fact I'd inadvertently discovered you involved with another obscene act with a boy here at the school, when you obviously thought there was no chance of being interrupted. From there, I would stress your disturbing attempt to implicate me, was nothing more than a desperate attempt to protect yourself, due to the fact I'd told you I felt the matter should be taken up with the Headmaster. I would also make it clear, that I intended to ask him whether the problem should be mentioned to your parents, because of our responsibility to the rest of the boys at the school. If the question of these photos was ever raised, I'd say I could obtain them from one of the boys, if it should prove to be necessary. I'm aware you've already lodged one complaint, and that got you nowhere. If you should ever be so foolish as to repeat the same mistake, then I can assure you, a short time later, those photos will start appearing around the school, you can bet your young life on that'.

As I dressed, I thought about Adrian. At least he knew what happened, after all, he was there and watched it all. But even there things were stacked against me. His father was some sort of engineer, and he'd applied for a position on some large project in New South Wales. Unbeknown to me, his application had been accepted, and in a matter of a couple of weeks later, the family had departed. Not that he'd have been much use, even if he were still here, no doubt he'd adopt the same policy he had in the shed. His only priority would have been to protect himself, the last person he'd have worried about, would have been me. So it was hopeless, there was nowhere for me to turn. And where was Jesus? That woman at Bible Class had assured us that as long as we behaved ourselves, he'd step into our lives. Well I'd been behaving myself, apart from a few fruit trees and fights, I'd done nothing wrong, so if he'd ever stepped into my life, he must have stepped straight out again.

My clothes back on, my shoes tied, my bag slung over my shoulder. All that was left was to get outside and away from him. But as I unlatched and opened the door, he came over, and before I realised what he intended, he bent down and kissed me on the neck. The feel of his lips made me shudder, but for some reason, it also made me want to know how often he'd want me in his room, so I asked him, 'Sir, considering the risk, how often am I going to be expected to come down here?'

And without hesitation, he replied, 'There'll be no set times, I'll inform you on the day when I need your services. But obviously, top priority will be extreme care at all times. As no doubt you're aware, some days after school, there can still be reasonable activity in the gym, on others, there's nothing. Those days are invariably Tuesdays and Fridays, so obviously, one must assume, it should prove to be on one of those days when our sessions take place.'

I took off, up the slope, past the classroom blocks, swinging down into the massive bicycle shed, my bike standing out proudly, all alone in its rack. A

chance to catch my breath, hands on the bars, head down, breathing hard, waiting for my heart to stop pounding, and not just from the exertion of running. There'd been no excuse for what had happened, I'd positioned myself over that table, exactly as instructed, and stayed like that while he'd done what he had inside me. It was as if I was drowning in self disgust. How I wished Bridgie was still here. My grandfather had come to visit us all the way from England, while he still could, or so he'd told me, and in no time at all I found I adored him, it was as if I'd loved him all of my life. He'd shown a special understanding of what being twelve was all about. I put my face in my hands, and cried for the grandfather I needed so badly. But quickly I straightened and wiped my hand across my eyes. It was no use crying, Bridgie wasn't here, so there was no way he could help or advise me, and above all else, I knew the tears had to stop. I couldn't afford to cry, because on the very rare occasions when I did, my mother always knew, my red eyes providing her with the tell all signs. But what if they are red when I get home? The answer came in a flash. I'd have been riding my bike, so if required, I'll blame it on the wind.

Now on my bike and heading for home, and a glance at my Mondia watch confirmed, later than usual though I was, he was right, I'd still be there well before my mother. The wind in my face felt good, but I still arrived with my heart pounding. A shower was imperative, scrubbing and scrubbing, desperate to get the feel of him off me, but finally I had to accept, nothing could erase the manner in which I'd been soiled. Back in my bedroom, changing into my street clothes as was expected, now lying on my bed, doing some arithmetic in my head.

He'd said he'd be wanting me at least once a week. If the hours of darkness were eliminated, it meant there were somewhere around one hundred hours that could be spent with family, friends and whoever. If what I'd experienced today could be used as an example, that meant I'd be spending an absolute maximum of two of those hours with him. There was the comparison in black and white. The choice was mine, suffering at the most a couple of hours of humiliation with him, or the non-stop mental, physical and verbal abuse with the other. So even away from school and with time to think, nothing had changed, I was left with no alternative, I'd have to comply with what he was demanding if I wanted my life to remain unchanged, that was except for the degrading time spent in his room.

Finally my mother's footsteps on the path. I wandered out and talked with her in the kitchen while she was preparing our evening meal. Her actions were quick and assured, something that came from doing the same thing for so many years. A man came home from work, then sat and read the newspaper. Why was it that a wife and mother came home and continued working? Somehow, someone seemed to have got something wrong somewhere.

Did that mean that growing up to be a man had to be better? If that's the case, how I wish I was a man now, then what had happened, and what was apparently to happen again, would be long forgotten. But little did I realise that both were something I was never destined to forget, that such tainted memories stay like some silent, relentless cancer, occasionally reactivated, once again living and churning inside, slowly and inevitably doing their best to reach their

ultimate goal and destroy you. Suddenly I realised my mother's eyes were scanning my face,

'Mathew, are you feeling alright' she asked, 'your eyes look so tired, are you feeling unwell, is everything alright at school?'

I winced slightly, if only she knew what she'd asked. All that that question needed now, was a truthful reply, 'Seeing as you've asked Mum, things aren't alright at school, in fact I've got a major problem'. But as I looked at her, those words just wouldn't come. She spoke of tiredness in my eyes, but I was all too aware, it was there in her eyes as well. I was concerned she'd detect the evasion in my voice, 'Honest, I'm fine, and everything's just great at school.'

More concern, as once again those probing eyes scanned my face as she said, 'That's all very well, but you can't fool me Mathew. Something's not quite right, so I've made up my mind, you're having an early night. Looks to me as though you can do with it.'

If only something as simple as an early night could fix my problem.

Back at school the following day, all so familiar, all so pleasant, and I knew there was only one way I could guarantee it would stay like that. As I sat and chatted with friends, and greetings were exchanged with others as they passed, all it did was drive home how expertly I'd been backed into a corner, and the more convinced I became I was left with no alternative other than to comply with what he was demanding. That afternoon as I walked down to the gym with the rest of the class, I prayed he hadn't changed his mind, and tell me he wanted me down in his office after school. But my fear proved groundless, because it didn't eventuate.

The relief as the period ended and I walked with Chris out of the building, made me realise I was clutching at straws, desperate he leave me alone. But I was to discover, straws never stopped anyone from drowning, and accordingly, because I was too frightened of the threatened consequences to resist, at times my life was to become inundated by what seemed like an overwhelming sea of pornography, physical abuse, and untold variations of sex.

Two days later, back in the changing room after returning from the field, and as far as dressing was concerned, lagging just a little. One by one the other boys finished and strolled away and outside, and in doing so, inadvertently created the privacy he'd so patiently been waiting for. Sitting with one shoe up on the seat, tying the last of my laces as he casually wandered by, and as he passed he spoke in barely more than a whisper, 'I want you down here immediately when school ends, and be careful, for your sake, take all the time that's needed to make absolutely certain no one sees you entering my office.'

I thought about it, sure enough, it was a Tuesday, and being well away from the mainstream flow of traffic, he was right, there probably wouldn't be too much of a problem, unfortunately.

Much later that day, as I paused outside his office door, the silence lent false hope there was a chance he wasn't even there, but sure enough, I was proved wrong. He answered my light tap, and as I stepped in and closed the door behind me, he was sitting at his desk, head down, concentrating on something in front of him, and when he finally acknowledged my presence, he did so without even

bothering to glance up, ' Right Colbert, you're here at last. Now turn around and use what brains you have and go back and lock the door.'

Although more than slightly put out by his snide remark, I complied, then returned and stood in front of his desk. The fact that he continued to ignore me, didn't help my nervousness, but when he finally did acknowledge my very reluctant presence, he quietly said 'Seeing as you'll be coming down here reasonably frequently, it's essential you comply exactly with the routine I require. Never even attempt to approach my office if there's someone even in reasonable proximity. Never enter this room unless you've received my verbal permission, and when that has occurred, the first thing you do is step in and lock the door. Following that, you're to immediately remove all of your clothing. I've waited quite some time for this lad, and I want to make the most of that outstanding young body of yours. And once you've stripped, you're to place your clothing and everything else in here.'

He strode over to the small storeroom, at the same time beckoning to me to follow. Inside, there was a variety of athletic and sporting equipment, but it was apparent one of the shelves had been cleared, because there was plenty of room on it for my clothes and other belongings. From there, he moved back to his desk and sat down, then added, 'Now strip boy, then come back and stand in front of my desk in the position you were previously shown.'

As I undressed, frustration and resentment seethed, but as always, fear dominated. But as I stood with my legs apart and my hands clasped behind my head, I tried to reason with him,

'Honestly Sir, you making me do this sure scares me. Surely, sooner or later someone's bound to come down here to see you, and when they do, what's going to happen then?'

But his reply indicated he was quite unconcerned about any situation that could possibly arise,

'Naturally you're quite right lad, there will be the occasional interruption. But due to arrangements I've been able to make, I can assure you they'll be few and far between.'

He leant back and casually ran a hand through his hair, paused, and then carried on,

'When the inevitable interruption does happen, no matter at what stage of proceedings we're at, I'll automatically call out, 'Just a moment, you'll have to wait. I'm in the middle of changing', and that will be a signal for you to move over and enter the storeroom, and I'll lock the door behind you. From there I'll simply put on enough clothes to confirm my previous statement about changing, and seeing as I possess the only key, you'll remain safely in the storeroom until the intruder has departed.'

And I was forced to admit, on the rare occasions when we were interrupted by a knock on the door, the arrangements proved to be faultless. One was caused by the Headmaster, who, apparently on the spur of the moment, decided to come down and discuss arrangements for a sports day that was to be held. I wondered what his reaction would have been, if he'd been made aware there was a naked schoolboy, standing no more than a few metres away, listening to every word he said.

However, reluctant though I was, I continued to stand in front of him in the position he insisted on. I guessed about ten minutes past, and I mean guessed, because similar to what Eric had insisted on, I wasn't even allowed to keep wearing my Mondia watch, when suddenly he glanced up and informed me of an additional requirement he'd devised, 'That special time between us had almost arrived lad, but from now on, there's one extra thing I'm going to want from you first. The one thing a male requires so as to indulge in perfect sex, is an excellent erection. Now it's long been accepted that nothing achieves this better than some foreplay of oral sex. Going by what I saw in those photos, that's something you became quite proficient at, so making the most of the expertise you've acquired in that direction, from now on, that's what I'll require from you, before penetration.'

Nothing had changed from that time in the shed. Kneeling in front of him, with his hand pressing gently on the back of my head as he held me to him, his penis felt firm and smooth in my mouth.

More months slipped past, with the intermittent showers and fading warmth of late Summer and Autumn, giving way to the more persistent rain and biting cold of Winter. Never the less, my weekly visits to his room continued, although occasionally, due to various reasons, it didn't happen, and this was accepted as being a wonderful bonus, a special week to be savoured and remembered. Due to the cold, I asked to be able to keep my shirt on, but his absolute insistence at my being naked when he indulged himself never wavered, so to assist in overcoming this problem, there was an addition to the room of a small, but very efficient heater. It appeared the unwritten rules by which he functioned stipulated, although his victim was to always remain naked, that to sexually abuse a boy while he was shivering from the cold while the act took place, was not acceptable.

But as far as I was concerned, one thing did stand out. As the weeks rolled relentlessly on, any boyish innocence that had previously existed, was swept aside and destroyed forever, by an ever increasing reluctant participation in a diet of homosexual abuse. I was also to learn that similar to many paedophiles, he enjoyed obtaining a photographic record of what he subjected his victims too. When he started to explain the variety of sexually explicit poses and acts he was determined to film, I begged him not too, being all too aware of the problems those previously taken had created, but as always, a combination of his dominant position and the constant fear I was living with won out.

As a result, I found the positions he insisted I place myself in were restricted only by the extent of his warped imagination, and the seemingly never ending supply of appliances that he had at his disposal. And as his collection of pornography steadily increased, I shuddered at the thought of what he displayed to me in the privacy of his office, being made available for viewing and general display anywhere else. As a result, those flickering remnants of defiance were effectively smothered, being replaced instead, by complete compliance.

So the situation between us continued, usually only interrupted by the likes of the end of term holidays. And they proved to be times of bliss, times of the simplest of pleasures, like doing nothing more than playing around the streets

with my friends, with the memories of what happened with him towards the end of the day, temporarily being a thing of the past. They were times of going out to the golf club, practising for hours on end, finally eliminating that frustrating slice, fairly consistently hitting that ball so straight, it was as if it had been fired out of a rifle. But what still towered above all else, was the fact they were times of dressing in the morning, accompanied by the knowledge that I wouldn't have to take my clothes off again, until it was time for bed.

And when back at school, with his position more dominant than ever, my lingering hopes of something eventuating that would result in the forced terminations of those sessions in his office, slowly but surely faded into oblivion. I wasn't asking for all that much, anything would have done. For instance, the formation of gymnastic or basketball teams, whose practise sessions required the use of the gymnasium after school. Or my mother leaving the company, and finishing back in the position where she'd be at home, and able to query my later arrivals back from school. But they never happened. With the school's sporting preferences having long before been established in their current directions, and my mother continuing to thoroughly enjoy working and the remuneration it supplied her with, including the small amount of financial independence it provided her with as well, those teams never eventuated, and my mother kept on working.

So the months still managed to slip by, carrying with them the burden of weekly sex. With another session with him finished, and walking past the large shelter shed, I looked across to the main school buildings. There they stood, in my opinion, stark, grey and ugly as sin, not one attractive thing about them, and I asked myself; why did whoever designed them, seem to think it was essential that school buildings looked like prisons? Maybe, I decided, he somehow knew that for part of the time, I was going to be confined in one of them.

Now continuing on down the path to the bicycle shed, and there my bike was, alone in its rack, somehow managing to look sad, as if it felt I'd forgotten it, but on the spur of the moment, I decided it could stay where it was for a little longer, first however, going over and assuring it I hadn't forgotten it, then I turned and stood watching as the breeze drifted around the open building. This caused the leaves that had accumulated, to swirl around in a series of small whirlpools, so as they finished up in untidy heaps around the racks, where they patiently waited for the breeze to dislodge them, so as the process could start all over again.

After standing and watching this repetition for quite some time, I finally walked over to one of the more sheltered corners of the shed, and sat down comfortably enough on the tar-seal floor. Drawing up my knees, I placed my arms on them and then rested my head, and as I looked down, I noticed an indentation in the tar-seal directly in front of where I was sitting. On studying it, I decided it was just about the size Ivan's head would have made when I punched him. Brother, did I really thump that bastard. Never mind, if anyone ever deserved it, he did. It all seemed so far away now, and even allowing for that bit of major unpleasantness, the two years I'd spent at that school, were without doubt, the best school years of my life. And that reminded me, what was it Smithie had said? Something like, 'and I wish you all the best for the

wonderful years you have to come.' Was this supposed to qualify as one of those wonderful years? If it was, then sorry Smithie, but if you don't mind, I'd prefer to not have any more. I glance up, squinting slightly with the late afternoon glare, and the few clouds that were scattered around, seemed to be drifting on past without a care in the world. Where had all my carefree times gone, that's what I wanted to know? Not all that long back, I'd go to bed and sleep like a log, just as any twelve year old should. But now, when I wake in the morning, and that's after the same thing's happening at least three or four times during the night, I do so with a lump in my stomach, as I lie there wondering whether this is going to prove to be one of those days, when he wants me in his room after school.

It seems carefree days have a lot in common with the clouds. If you dare to look away for a few minutes, when you turn back, you find they're gone. Memories drift past my eyes, reminding me of those long lost innocent days. I barely knew what sex was, well, that was until I finished up in that shed. Now I sure as hell know what homosexual sex is all about. What I need is a magic wand so as to be able to cast a spell that would guarantee that after one wave, Bergman would be gone forever. One thing's for sure, as far as young boys are concerned, he'd certainly be no great loss. I brush a few tears away and stand up, I mean let's face it, there's no such thing as a magic wand. He'll still be there in his office waiting for me, making me kneel in front of him, sucking his dick, that's until he's ready for me to lie over the table, while he thrusts it up my bum. I brush a few more tears away, then walk over to my trusty bike, still waiting for me as patient as ever, so I mount it and head for home.

Sure enough, my presence wanted on Friday, but after dressing, I asked a question I wanted to for quite some time, 'Sir, why is it Mr. Hull never comes in here after school, after all, surely he's allowed to use this office as well, I mean, he's also a PE instructor, like you.' Bergman had dressed, and was sitting in his chair, and he leaned back, rocking on the legs, smiling at me in that condescending manner he seemed to purposely use in situations similar to this, 'Well, you're correct with one thing Colbert,' he said, 'but one thing only. Yes, we're both PE masters, but any similarity between us ends right there. My position in the education system is so far above his, it voids even the remotest attempt at comparison. The other thing it would be accurate to say, is that Mr. Hull and I are far removed from being on good terms. Let's just say he doesn't agree with my approach to life, and I most certainly don't agree with his. That caning you received, could be used as an excellent example of that. When I came back, some of the boys described in detail, the extent of what he'd done, and in my opinion, it was nothing short of appalling. You may recall I mentioned earlier, I'd been able to make certain arrangements as far as our situation is concerned, well, what you've just mentioned happens to be one of them. After a discussion I had with the Headmaster, Mr. Hull was informed it would be better all round, if he used the master's common room over in the main building. In fact, he's been told quite bluntly, he's not to set foot in this office after school. He's also been told that if he does, it could well result in the termination of his position.'

Bergman's explanation regarding Hull's non appearance, made me aware of the position he held at the school, and possibly beyond that as well. The fact our original complaint had been lost in what was probably a convenient bureaucratic mire, added some weight to that.

Another couple of months of the year gone, a couple of weeks of grace, but now wanted again, and after I'd completed the standard requirements and was standing in front of his desk, waiting on his instructions to kneel so as to be able to comply with what he always wanted, what he said instead, caught me by surprise, 'Today there's a change to our normal procedure. You're to place yourself over the table, but for this one time, you'll be restrained in position,' and as he saw the look of alarm that instantly appeared on my face, he quickly added, 'and don't worry, you're not going to be subjected to any form of violent abuse, I simply wouldn't allow it. We're having a visitor, and he'll be using you instead.'

I was convinced the man had lost his mind. There was no way I wanted anyone seeing me displayed over that table; I'd had more than enough of that in the shed. So I made my opinion forcibly known, but he brushed my complaints casually aside as he said, 'It's going to happen boy. I've given my word he can have you, so you may as well get used to the fact.'

And when that bloody minded look appeared in his eyes, I knew I didn't stand a chance. After all, it was nothing new, like the past repeating itself, like Eric and Paul all over again.

So I placed myself in position, and it took him no time at all to secure my wrist and ankles, but now an addition, and I watched as he took a dark coloured handkerchief out of his pocket, folded it neatly into a strip about five centimetres wide, then after placing it over my eyes, tied it in position behind my head, and as a result the world went dark, I couldn't see a thing. As I lay there nervously waiting, a disturbing thought entered my head. What if this abuser was the school caretaker, accepting payment for his cooperation in other directions? Just the thought of it turned my stomach, then finally a faint tap on the door, which, after a few indistinct murmurings was quickly opened, then just as quickly closed and locked, as whoever was there stepped in the room. A whispered conversation followed, then the familiar sounds I'd long before associated with someone undressing, then suddenly hands on my buttocks, easing them open, then a penis, obviously lubricated, thrusting up into me.

And instantly my concern evaporated. I could sense this man was quite tall as he stood, rhythmically moving behind me. A few minutes more, now some quicker, even stronger thrusts, followed by an audible moan, presumably as he gained the satisfaction he sought, and now things in reverse, as he withdrew, then next, the sound of clothes rustling, a few quiet words, then the opening and closing of the door, as whoever it was departed, and as I was being released, logic indicated it had to have been another member of the staff, surely it had to be, who else could dare to stroll so openly around the school?

The following morning at assembly, I ran my eyes carefully over the masters as they sat there on the elevated stage, all looking the picture of academic decorum in their gowns and mortar boards, and as I continued to scrutinise them, I was forced to accept there was no way I could even attempt to

155

guess who it could have been. At least seven were tall men, and not one was showing even a trace of nervousness or guilt, either of which I felt, could have caused the offender to cast the occasional uneasy glance in my direction. And the fact was, picking me out would have proved simple enough. As a first year pupil, I was sitting in the second row, and this made me easily identifiable amongst the hundreds of boys in the hall that morning.

Certain decisions create certain reactions, and the fact he'd approved such a thing as allowing another person into his room to do the things he had, caused the seeds of deep resentment, that had slowly been gaining momentum for quite some time, to rise dangerously close to the surface, and as they did, they were accompanied by another disturbing thought. Was he attempting to steer my own sexual preferences, as they started to flicker through my system, down his own perverted path? As I sat in the hall, the thought of such a thing possibly happening, struck with full, horrifying force. Later that day, kneeling in front of him, doing what I had to while he sat as his desk, immersed in his seemingly never ending paperwork, with my decision made I drew back and stood up, with the unauthorised movement instantly causing him to snap at me, 'What do you think you're doing lad? Get back down there on your knees, and don't dare to stop like that again, until you've received my permission.'

And that was the ignition that was required to light the fuse, and the explosion that burst forth was a build-up of what I'd been saving for him for quite some time, 'You can go to hell. I'm sick of what you're doing to me, and I'm even sicker still, of what you're making me do to you. So I'm leaving, and I'm not ever coming back, you filthy, blackmailing bastard.'

He continued sitting, appearing perfectly composed, but something told me, inwardly he was seething, because as his eyes latched onto me, they lanced through like some dual form of laser. And when he finally controlled himself enough to speak, the cutting edge to his voice was something I could almost feel, 'Fine, if that's your foolish decision boy, then its best you get out of here right now.'

Aware that I'd placed myself in deep trouble, I slipped across to the storeroom to get my clothes. It only took seconds for him to adjust his own, and the same again as he was standing beside me. He waited long enough for me to scoop up my belongings, then gripping me firmly by the arm, thrust me over to the door. Only moments required to unlock it, then as he shoved me out into the changing room he said, 'I warned you weeks back of the action I'd take, if you ever chose to be this foolish. I felt a touch of rebellion surfacing then. So take heed boy, only you will suffer from the shame that results from what you've just done.'

As the door slammed shut behind me, I looked around, scared some straggler may have appeared to find me standing naked here like this. But as always, I was alone, so becoming more uneasy by the second, I dressed as quickly as I could, then bolted for the safety of home.

Chapter 21

Once there, unfortunately home didn't provide the type of safety I desperately needed, because my concern over the situation steadily increased. Nobody more than I was aware of the self destructive streak that lay discreetly hidden under his well practised demeanour of total respectability. And compounding on that, much as I tried to convince myself, whether I wanted to admit it or not, the existence of those photos, and the irrevocable damage they could cause, scared me like nothing I'd ever encountered before in my life.

After our evening meal, as I lay uncomfortably twisting and turning on my bed, fear managed to turn to terror, as I constantly thought about what he'd said, as he shoved me out of his room, and his words kept drumming in my head. 'I warned you some weeks back of the action I'd take, if you ever chose to be so foolish'. Something he'd said some weeks back? Hard as I tried, it was hopeless, I couldn't think, there was nothing even close to jogging my memory. I turned my cheek to my pillow as a few tears flowed, but not enough to make my eyes red. There were times when I wished I was dead.

Time passed, I realised I'd been dozing, and it was a voice from the other end of the house that penetrated the haze that was there, my mother subtlety hinting it was time for bed. I sat up, and suddenly it was as if he was here with me, Heaven forbid, no wonder I'd forgotten them. At the time, they'd been uttered as nothing more than casual conversation, but in an instant I remembered all too clearly what he'd said, 'Thinking about it, I wouldn't leave them in the quadrangle after all, I'd pin them on the notice board instead.'

The next morning I took off for school well ahead of my usual time, and as I rode into the school grounds, it was like they were deserted, so after leaving my bike in its usual rack in the shed, I walked straight across to the main entrance, in front of which there was a low, lichen covered wall, and that's where I sat and waited. Would he be prepared to do it? Of course he would, if he was convinced it would achieve the continuing dominance he wanted. A slight noise repaying me for my patience in waiting. The doors to the entrance swing open as the short little caretaker appeared. He moved forward until he was standing at the top of the steps, where he stood, breathing in deeply, obviously enjoying the cool, morning air, then he turned and disappeared back inside the building.

Waiting long enough to make sure he'd well and truly departed, I glided up the steps and into the foyer, and the additional paces required to get down to the notice board took but seconds. And as I cautiously scanned the board, there they were, dead centre, in all their naked and obscene glory, four of the most explicit from his ever expanding collection. For a few seconds I stood there, literally immobilised with fear, then I stepped forward and ripped them down. Some ragged edges still remained, secured by the drawing pins he'd used, so after checking to make sure I was still alone, with trembling fingers I took the time required to remove those as well, and jamming the lot in my pocket, took off, in search of some normality in my life amongst my friends.

Half way through the first class of the morning, and I was still shaking. One thing was certain, I couldn't risk standing up to him again, because it proved beyond doubt what I'd always suspected. He'd risk anything, if it kept me cooperating for him. The day after, and at the end of our physical education time with him, he turned his attention so effortlessly in my direction, and as always, his voice was as smooth as silk as he casually mentioned, 'Colbert, stay back please. There's a few items to do with the swimming team I'd like to discuss,'

Miserably I hung back, all too aware what we'd be discussing, would be a world away from swimming. Anyway, we all knew the swimming team and what it entailed had nothing to do with him, it was entirely Hull's responsibility. For some reason that made me fed up as well. As I walked into his office, he was sitting on the edge of his desk, waiting for me. And he waited a little longer, making sure the gymnasium had been vacated, before he spoke to me,

'I notice those photos of you I pinned on the board have disappeared', then after pausing for maximum effect, he added, 'so am I correct in assuming they're now in your possession?'

'Yes Sir, you're right, they are.'

'So, you've mentioned the situation that exists between us to anyone, your parents perhaps?

'No Sir, I certainly haven't.'

He continued to stare at me, daring me to try and defy him as he commented, 'Strange, but somehow I doubted you would, so tell me lad, why not? Could it possibly be because they happened to frighten you?'

'Yes they did, and I promise I'll do what you want. Please don't ever do that again.'

He raised his eyes, purposely looking over my head, giving the impression he was thinking carefully before he replied, 'Colbert, you must understand, my actions over this matter are controlled entirely by yours. Behave yourself, perform for me as I expect, and we won't have a problem, but create another disturbance, and you'll have to accept the consequences, because if something similar ever happens again, then those photos will appear, and I can assure you, there'll be no hope of you stopping them. Now, do we understand each other?'

I could see it in his eyes, he meant every word he said, and so did I as I replied,

'Yes Sir, I do understand, and I'll do what you want. I don't want anything like that again.'

His eyes never left mine as once more he paused, before continuing, 'Alright, but you can't expect to create what you just have, without paying a penalty for it. During the approaching weekend I have a home at my disposal that's not all that far from the school. You're to present yourself there on Saturday morning, no later than nine o'clock. Make sure you give some thought to the excuse you use to explain your absence until mid afternoon. Is that fully understood?'

'Yes Sir, it is.'

He wrote down the address, and instantly I knew it. The street was close to a park where I'd played football a couple of years earlier. As I walked back to the bicycle shed, I wondered about the risk associated with appearing at the house,

but I knew that similar to some of the other masters, he supplemented his income by taking boys for extra studies. His educational expertise wasn't just restricted to physical education. So I assumed that anyone noticing me turning up at the house, would simply accept me as being just another of his students. Briefly it crossed my mind, I hoped he wasn't using them as he was using me, but somehow I doubted it, because it was obvious becoming involved with too many boys had danger written all over it. Anyway, it was easy to see I was the one he'd chosen as his 'boy'; his carefully contrived blackmail proved that. Nothing changed, if he ever took any risks, which was rare, everything was meticulously calculated.

There was no doubt I'd got to know him fairly well, and for that reason, at this point the only thing I failed to understand, was how he could risk having that obnoxious caretaker, who was despised by virtually every boy at the school, walk through the foyer with those photos as predominantly displayed as they were. And how was it every time I'd been told to make myself available in his room after school, that disgusting creep never appeared to do any cleaning? With Bergman as careful with his planning as he was, the obvious answer was because the caretaker had been informed of the presence of the photos, and as far as the office was concerned, he knew what was happening in there as well. Just the thought of it made me feel ill, but it all added up to being just another of his 'certain arrangements'.

The Saturday dawned with a similarity to the day Colin had left. I woke with that same unsettling feeling in my stomach. But the reason took no time at all to clarify, so I got up and dressed, preferring to be on the move, rather than lying there worrying. An early season cricket match proved to be the ideal excuse, and the ride passed all too quickly. Purposely I stopped at the park, and two boys were playing on the field, with their shouts of enjoyment cutting clearly through the still morning air. How I longed to go down and play with them, running until I could barely draw my next breath, then I'd drop to the grass, lying with my hands behind my head, gazing up, trying to catch a glimpse of that other world my mother insisted was there, somewhere beyond the clouds. But instead I had to make myself available for that man.

He'd said no later than nine o'clock, and I had no intention of presenting myself any sooner. So I continued to watch the boys, but after a few minutes a glance at my Mondia watch told me it was time, so reluctantly I mounted my bike and rode on down to the house. I leant it against a hedge that was inside the fence on the front boundary, then walked down the path. On reaching the house, I stopped, took a deep breath, said a little prayer, for all the good I thought it would do, some stupid thing that woman from Bible Class had taught us, then tapped lightly on the back door. As I waited, I hoped someone other than him would appear, and in doing so, would give me a chance to make my apologies and bolt, but as the door swung in, there he stood.

However, we didn't enter the house, because he shut the door, and taking me by the arm, guided me down the side, until he stopped outside a basement door, on which he tapped lightly, opened it, and eased me into the room. First, I saw a desk and some chairs, then a table and some cupboards, plus some posters and educational graphs on the walls, all of which I felt suggested this was indeed

where his after school tutoring took place. But as my eyes continued to travel around the room, at the same time I had this vague feeling we weren't alone. He was sitting on the floor, his back to the wall, and it gave the impression he'd chosen the position so as the open door had obscured his presence until we were well into the room.

He was reasonably young, probably not much more than early twenties, and dressed in a pair of jeans and a strongly patterned, highly colourful shirt, and his deeply tanned face set off a head of hair, that was almost as thick and blond as my own. However, what succeeded most in holding my attention, was that in his left hand he was holding a leash that was attached to a collar, that in turn was around the neck of one of the most impressive dogs I'd ever seen. It sat obediently on the floor beside him, a Great Dane of imposing proportions, although I guessed, still probably quite young. Although I struggled to take my eyes off the animal, in contrast, it paid me barely any attention at all, preferring instead to constantly swing its eyes around the room. But every so often it would stop and nudge the man so hard, he'd have to make a distinct effort to retain his balance. However, rather than admonish the animal, he took little notice other than to occasionally and gently push the animal away.

As far as the young man and I were concerned, as we continued to gaze at each other across the distance between us, on my part, a feeling of instant dislike took over. He seemed to exude a combination of arrogance and insolence, and it was Bergman's voice that finally penetrated that haze of concern, which I felt was starting to smother me, 'Now hurry up boy,' he said, ' you know the rules by now, and it's not as if we have all day. There may be an additional face and a different locality, but apart from that, nothing's changed, so strip, then place your clothes on that chair.'

And fearful though I was, I didn't hesitate. With him having displayed those photos as openly as he had, I'd accepted being controlled by this man was an unavoidable part of my life. As I moved to the chair, the young man's eyes followed me every step of the way, and as I undressed and stood naked in front of them, his grin of sheer delight got progressively wider, with lust brutally evident in his voice as he spoke, 'Hell, if this is an example of what you teach Phil, there's no doubt I should have been a school master. I just can't imagine what it would be like, having permanent access to a kid with a body like this.'

The tone in Bergman's voice when he replied, gave the distinct impression their relationship, for whatever it was, left more than a great deal to be desired, 'The boy represents the school at swimming, cricket and boxing, and I understand he's involved in other sport away from the school as well. So what you see here simply reinforces what I've always maintained. Nothing moulds the development of a young body better than a sensible mixture of exercise, although I must confess, a few of the right genes happens to help a certain amount as well.'

And as he continued to stand there gaping, it seemed the young man definitely agreed,

'Alright, don't start going on about your favourite subject. I've been told you're into this exercise thing at a very high level. Christ, I can hardly believe this kid's just standing here waiting for me. Without realising it, he's about to

provide me with something that's far better than having all the birthday presents I've still to be given, arriving all at once.'

He got up, allowing the leash to fall to the floor, and came over and stood directly in front of me, then reaching out, suddenly gripped my arms, and holding them firmly against my body, drew me to him and kissed me firmly on the mouth.

Instantly, I broke away and stepped well back, at the same time drawing the back of my hand across my lips as I roundly swore at him. But completely undaunted, he just grinned back as he said, 'Kid, that's nothing, compared to the entertainment you're going to provide.'

One hour later, very frightened and in a lot of pain, the young man virtually out of control, with Bergman doing his best to try and restrain him. Now he was after me again as he dragged me to my feet, and instinctively I attempted to push him away, nothing more than an automatic attempt at self preservation, but it literally had the effect of infuriating him. As a result, he twisted my arms behind my back and tied them, something that brought back past, frightening memories. Now another mistake on my part, as I let out an involuntary shriek of pain as he forced me over and thrust himself violently up inside me again, the act producing a resentful outburst from Bergman, 'For Heaven's sake Kevin, that sort of thing isn't necessary. There's absolutely nothing to be gained by hurting the boy, and what about the risk, just think about it, you fool, what if one of the neighbours happens to hear the poor kid?'

A problem easily solved. Totally ignoring Bergman's continuing protests, Kevin gagged me. Nothing overly sophisticated, just my hankie stuffed in my mouth, then one of his own folded into a strip and tied across to keep it in place. Frightened to a point of panic, I looked into his eyes, pleading with him, but became even more frightened still. There was something strange about them, to a point where I became convinced he was slightly unbalanced. Also, I'd noticed that the table had been fitted with those same low rails that Bergman used in his office. Sure enough, I was dragged across and forced over it. Kevin tied my ankles and neck so I couldn't move, then thrust up into me again, this apparently being the penalty that had to be paid for trying to resist him.

But with Bergman becoming increasingly more concerned by the minute, Kevin exploded,

'Just shut the fuck up will you. If you don't like what I'm doing to the kid, then fucking well take it up with Malcolm. He told me I was to find out what the kid would tolerate, so shut up, I'm a long way from finished with him yet. I won't get an opportunity like this again, so I intend to make the most of it. Anyway, you're a great fucking one to talk.'

So the abuse continued, but through my pain and fear, I tried to think. What was happening here wasn't in any way like Bergman, so no wonder he was doing his pathetic best to help. Being the selective paedophile he was, I knew he was prepared to go to any lengths to get his hands on a boy he lusted after, my example unfortunately proved that. Rather, his methods were always subtle, they never included violence. I knew how furious he was about the treatment I was subjected to in the shed, and his opinion of Hull added weight to that, so how was it he was involved in this?

And who was Malcolm, that was a name I'd never heard mentioned before. Where did he fit in as regards to this nightmare that was in the process of unfolding in this room? But now an additional problem, a corner of the hankie he'd stuffed in my mouth, was tending to want to drift down my throat, making me want to choke, and the suffocating effect was scaring the life out of me. I felt I wanted to panic, to jump up and run out of this room, and get as far away from this house and these people as I possibly could. But restricted as I was, I knew it wasn't going to happen, so yet again I asked Jesus, or whoever else happened to be available, because past experience had given me the impression, Jesus certainly wasn't, but one way or the other, why was this happening to me?

The more I thought about the whole deplorable business, the more convinced I became, that if I decided to attempt to explain to someone exactly what had been happening, they'd either laugh, claim I was lying, insist I must be mentally ill, or blessed with some sort of unhealthy imagination. But instead, as I lay over that table, with Kevin rhythmically moving behind me, all I could think of was, please, I've changed my mind, I can't bear the thought of it, I really don't want anyone to find out what's happening to me here.

Suddenly I stopped trying to think, as I concentrated on listening instead. There was a noise, and although it was still somewhere away in the distance, it was getting ever so slightly louder by the second. At first, I'd thought it sounded like a group of children, desperately crying for help, and how I wished I could join in, but as the sound moved closer, I realised it was a huge flock of seagulls, circling and swinging in low over the houses, as they prepared to land on the playing fields at the park. Maybe I was wrong, perhaps Jesus knew I was here after all, and being aware I couldn't cry out any more, he'd sent the gulls to do it for me.

Now some noise from outside, this time from a car being driven at speed up the road, and loud though the sound was, it came close to being obliterated by the screeching from the gulls. They were definitely becoming even more entrenched on the fields, a sure sign bad weather was coming, and I wasn't surprised, going by the colour of the sky as I'd walked down the path to the house. My father always insisted, a sure sign of an approaching storm was when the gulls headed inland, seeking protection from the exposure of the coast. This seemed to be proving him right, but it didn't mean I wasn't fed up with him giving the impression he knew it all. As far as I could tell, nobody was always right and never wrong, and making my frustration even worse, I knew he wasn't happy about my trialling at that troupe with Adrian. Whether I liked it or not, that made him right again.

Vaguely I wondered why it irritated me as much as it did. Maybe there was a chance I was growing up as stubborn and bloody minded as he was, but I hoped not. I'd thought about it, and had come to the decision it was a trait I could do without. More time passed, and I made an unsuccessful attempt to read Kevin's watch as he wandered past. Finally untied, standing on the floor, the soles of my feet quite painful, from having to stand on the rail for so long. Now Kevin taking me by the arm forcing me down the room towards the dog, at the same time telling me in detail what I had to do, and describing the photos he wanted of the animal doing to me.

Just the thought of what he was demanding filled me with absolute horror, so feeling a slight slackening of his grip, and encouraged by sheer, unmitigated panic, I wrenched my arm free, and charged off in the opposite direction. But it was futile, there was nowhere for me to turn, and more important still, with Bergman's apparent reluctance to get involved, no one for me to turn to. Surprisingly, it was Bergman who got to me first, doing his best to calm me with soothing words, trying to convince me it wouldn't be all that bad. But nothing worked, for the simple reason I couldn't think of anything worse, and Kevin pounded up, breathing fire and fury, 'Get the little bastard back down the room, and make him stand in front of that platform I've made. So help me, I'll make the little shit do as he's told, even if I have to half fucking kill him in the process.'

He strode over to one of the chairs, over the back of which he'd draped his jeans. He extracted a packet of cigarettes out of one of the pockets and withdrew one, then lit it, drawing in deeply, making the end glow like a crimson beacon. He held it at arm's length, directly in front of my face, close enough, so I could feel the heat on my skin, then he said,

'You see this kid? Give me any more trouble and I swear I'll bend you over and press this into the base of your balls, and that yell you let out before, will have nothing on the way you'll want to scream then. But because of the fucking gag, any noise you could manage, won't be heard outside this room. So get on and do as you're bloody told, or accept the painful consequences.'

First I looked into his eyes, then at that smouldering cigarette, and wondered if he'd dare to do what he was threatening, but long before, I learnt you could expect anything, when the lust for sex was involved. I thought of the obscenities I'd already been a victim of during the morning, and was now fearful of being made to perform one myself. But the past had taken its toll, and I lacked the courage to test whether he'd carry out his threat or not. Now just the thought of what he was insisting, made me feel sick, but it was fear and fear alone, that made me walk over and position myself behind the animal. Before the vile act started, Bergman came and untied my wrists, removed the hankie from across my mouth, and delicately removed the other one as well, at the same time whispering, saying how truly sorry he was.

During the next few, devastating minutes, the silence in the room was broken only by the click from the shutters of Kevin's camera, and the occasional instructions he issued. Then the position of the animal and myself was reversed, and as I lay over the table, with the platform for the dog to stand on behind, on Bergman's insistence, a blanket was placed across my back, so as to ensure there was no chance of it getting scratched. On Kevin's instructions, the well trained animal reared up from there, and another abomination followed.

Some years back, I'd asked my mother to explain death, and at the time she'd done the best she could. However, as time passed, the realities of life started to make it clear that death wasn't always as peaceful as she'd implied. But even allowing for all the dreadful things that I'd found could be involved, surely I felt, even death would be better than this. And it was as if those dreadful, degrading minutes would never end, but when they did, I found this abomination of a morning hadn't ended there. More threats from Kevin, this

time with the cigarette held up close between my legs, accompanied by his demands to watch another nauseating act performed, with the result that minutes later I was kneeling on the floor, retching, balancing on the verge of being physically sick. As a result, Bergman rushed over and letting out a horrified cry, grabbed my arm and bundled me over to a concrete tub that had been installed in one of the back corners, then turned his fury on Kevin, 'Damn you and damn you again. I told you under no circumstances were you to make the boy do that, and as usual, you blatantly ignore me. So now are you happy? Look what you've gone and done.'

With insolence oozing, it was obvious Bergman's display of anger didn't mean a thing,

'Fucking back off Phil. I told you before, I'm following Malcolm's instructions. He told me it was imperative we went this far to see what the kid's made of. His theory being if the kid can get through this, he'll be safe to use. So if you don't like it, take it up with fucking Malcolm', then he added, 'Now come on kid, get your head out of that tub. There's quite a few more tricks I want you to perform for me yet.'

Bergman was standing right beside me when he exploded, 'Oh no you don't. Surely anyone even as stupid as you can see the boy's had enough, he can't take any more, so this is it Kevin, get your gear on and take that animal and get out of here. You try to defy me again, and believe me, I'll certainly take it up with Malcolm,' and as he turned to me he added, 'and Mathew, you also get dressed, and after we've had a chat, you can take off as well.'

Somehow my stomach partially settled, so using water from the tub, I did my best to clean myself up, then dressed as quickly as I could, which turned out not to be all that quick at all.

Bergman insisted I walk with them up to the rear of the house, and on the way he rested his hand on my shoulder, and instantly I shrugged it off. I'd suspected for some little while, mixed up somewhere amongst the perversion he indulged in, there existed some sort of strange affection. Well if I was right, one thing was certain, it was a long, long way from being mutual. Now the men stopped at the corner of the house, peering carefully around, making sure there was no one in sight. But from what I could make out, privacy wasn't a problem, mainly because both side boundaries and most of the rear, had been planted many years before with a variety of low spreading, thickly foliaged shrubs. Now in their maturity, they were providing a mantle of almost impenetrable seclusion.

So after taking a few seconds to convince himself this was indeed so, Bergman proceeded to hiss instructions at Kevin, 'As far as I can see, this is as good a time as any, so get going.'

With the leash firmly held in his hand, Kevin strode off up the path, with the dog trotting obediently beside him. He paused briefly at the gate at the top, opened and closed it, then turned left as he started to walk up the street, and immediately became just another local taking his dog for a Saturday stroll. Obviously glad to see the back of him, Bergman's eyes swung in my direction as he said, 'Mathew, before too long, I realise I'll have to attempt to explain why I had to insist on you coming here this morning. Please believe me when I say it

164

was absolutely the last thing I wanted, and I would have done anything to try and make sure it was avoided. Now you've been forced to put in some absolutely atrocious hours, so will you be alright, considering what you've been put through, or would you like me to take you a short distance from your home in my car?'

As I looked up at him, I was surprised, because there were tears in his eyes, but not even a trace of forgiveness in mine, as I replied, 'The best thing you can do is stay right away from me. I would never have experienced the filth I've just been put through, if you'd have left me alone in the first place. So forget it, because one thing's for sure, I'll get home quite alright by myself, without any bloody help from you.'

He stood there looking at me, seemingly slightly taken back by my outburst, but never the less his tone hardened slightly as he replied, 'Alright, if that's your decision, that's fine. But if you're even remotely considering trying to take me down because of what's happened here today, remember, considering the arrangements I've made, it's you who'll crash down, not me, so stop and make sure you fully consider the possible consequences.'

I thought about the possible consequences as he'd suggested, and the whole situation in general, and came to the conclusion that sympathy could prove to be a very fleeting thing.

Chapter 22

Leaving him alone, still standing beside the house, I walked back through the immaculately planted yard, and after collecting my bike from where I'd left it, opened the gate and set off up the street. The clouds hung low, like smoke from a threatening fire, pushed along by the steadily increasing wind. It was apparent the storm was building up and moving closer, and as I approached the park, down on the fields below the gulls were still continuing to gather, standing out like so many battalions of soldiers, consolidating their positions, claiming the ground which they considered to be theirs, the stark white of their bodies, standing out clearly against the green of the grass.

But as I trudged slowly on, my legs felt like lead, and I found that before too long, I was struggling to place one foot in front of the other. Although my hands were on my handlebars, they still seemed to be shaking like leaves in the wind, and my chest was pounding with an intensity, which left me thinking that surely my heart must be about to self destruct. But worst of all, that dreadful sickening feeling was back in my stomach, lying like lead, occasionally filling my throat with its unpleasant acidity. Down in the park, I noticed a toilet block not all that far away, so I detoured across. Slipping into one of the cubicles, I did my best to clean myself up using the water from the bowl, but almost as soon as I stepped back outside, the warning was there.

Even as I swung around and dived back through the doorway, I knew there was no way I was going to make it back to the privacy of the cubicle, so in desperation I flung myself sideways, and dropping to my hands and knees, proceeded to vomit into the urinal trough. And as I knelt there, the horror of that morning took over, and never before could I recall being so ill. So I knelt on that concrete floor, retching and vomiting, being so shockingly ill that nothing else mattered, that time I was so ill behind the shed, not even approaching being as bad as this.

Time passed, I didn't know, and I didn't care how long. Now a burst of laughter, and it must have come from close by, because it was easily heard, even above the noise created by the wind and the gulls. If they came in here, I didn't care, and if they asked me why I was so ill, I'd tell them, because I could never face feeling like this again. But nobody appeared and I remained on my own. More time passed, and ever so gradually I succumbed until I was lying full length on the floor with my mouth over the trough, and still it went on. I became oblivious to all, so ill I was beyond caring, convinced it would never end, but finally and painfully it did. Back slowly onto my knees, then slower still to my feet, my stomach feeling as if it had been torn apart. During the previous day, occasional showers had combined with what had been many feet, and the combination had left the floor a mud covered mess. I glanced down, and what had started the day as a spotlessly clean shirt, was now in an appalling state, and further down, my pants were even worse. My mother would kill me when I got home, but I didn't care. Now all I wanted to do was tell her what had been

happening. It had to stop, because there was no way I could tolerate what was happening any longer.

It was imperative I tell my parents what had occurred in that shed, of the mistake I'd made by succumbing to blackmail, and as a result the things that had happened since. And if my father banned me from the house, or tried to have me institutionalised, as he'd done once, on the spur of the moment threat, which I'd felt he didn't really mean, then I didn't care, because although I could imagine living like that would be the pits, anything would be better than what I'd just experienced. So with my mind made up, and by using a combination of riding and walking, somehow I got home. Taking into consideration what had occurred earlier, I decided the journey could have been worse, but any optimism that had accumulated, immediately disintegrated, due to finding on arrival, a locked back door.

Surely, at a time like this, an empty house wasn't possible, but after using the spare key and getting inside, the reason for my parent's absence was explained in a note, propped up against the ever present vase of flowers, that reposed in the centre of our dining room table.

For many years, the last of which had not all that long passed, my father had competed very successfully in many tennis tournaments, with Cliff Hill as his doubles partner. Slightly different to Albie, our glass cabinet was in our lounge, and it displayed only the trophies accumulated from some of their more momentous victories. Inevitably, the passing years had started to take their toll, but the end had finally come when Cliff married, and moved down South to start a new business. But as the note explained, suddenly out of nowhere there'd been a phone call. He was back in the city on a brief business visit, and an evening together, catching up on old times had been suggested. It was an invitation my parents felt they couldn't refuse, and this explained the empty house.

With my plans relating to my confession temporarily halted, dejectedly I wandered down to my bedroom and took off my clothes, more wary than ever over my mother's reaction to their filthy condition, then dropped face down on my bed. Time passed, and along with it, some of my bitter resentment, so I rolled over with my eyes fixed on the ceiling. A few more minutes, now there was the intermittent chatter of rain on my window, and as always it rattled a little, each time a heavy squall struck. The storm had arrived with a vengeance, but having managed to get home dry offered nothing in the way of consolation for what had happened earlier. Much as I tried to fight them, those memories started flooding back, the variety of things that young man had done, and then there'd been that terrifying animal, along with having that hankie stuffed in my mouth, and the dreadful feeling of suffocation it had created.

Now something similar seemed to be happening, but this time, the walls of my room seemed to be closing in around me, and the overbearing silence in the house wasn't helping either. If only Bridgie were here, what I'd give to feel his strong arm around my shoulder. That feeling of resentment washed over again, making it impossible to lie still. Once again, top priority was a shower, so I wandered down to the bathroom, but before I turned on the taps, I took the time to study my face in the mirror, and even I was forced to admit I looked

167

shocking, eyes still bloodshot from crying, face drained and gaunt from having been so ill.

Almost without thinking, I opened the door of the shaving cabinet, vaguely wondering if there was anything that would help. The packet of blades was still there where I'd left them, along with that bottle of pills, and as I took them out and held them, even more vaguely again, I wondered what they'd been used for. Then in a flash, the answer was there, of course, they had to be what remained of those sleeping pills my mother had taken. She'd been ill for quite some time, and when the problem had finally been diagnosed, it had meant a lengthy stay in hospital. When she was allowed home, her recuperation had been so rapid, that things had fairly quickly dropped back into our usual family routine, except for one thing, and that was she'd been left with a distressing difficulty in sleeping.

In the end, she'd reluctantly agreed to the doctor's suggestion of sleeping pills. But not long after, she'd become convinced the drug was starting to take control of that aspect of her life. On that morning, I'd inadvertently walked in on the argument, no, hardly an argument, more like a firm discussion she was having with my father, and it had registered, because never before could I recall her being so forceful when speaking to him. And from the tone of her voice, I'd realised, for the first time I could recall, it was he who was wasting his time, there was no way she was taking any more of those pills.

However, as I stood with that bottle in my hand, they seemed to offer an answer to my problem. Why keep dwelling on those monstrosities I'd been a victim of during the morning and early afternoon, when a few pills would guarantee I'd fall into a deep, deep sleep drifting so far away, I'd finish up in that land where my mother insisted there was no such thing as misery and helplessness. So with the bottle in one hand, and a glass of water in the other, I went back and sat on my bed, where I unscrewed the cap and tipped the bottle, which allowed some to tumble out into the palm of my hand. Momentarily I hesitated, then tossed them down, then thought about it, surely those few weren't going to achieve what I wanted, so I replaced them with more and washed those down as well.

Then I thought about it again. The fact was no normal red blooded kid my age, willingly went to sleep on a Saturday afternoon, so I took some more again, just to make sure, then sat back slightly incredulous that I was staring at an empty bottle. So what, all it meant was I'd drift off all the faster. As I lay back, the wind and rain lashed against my window, and although it was only late afternoon, the sky had darkened, and there was the occasional flash of lightning, followed seconds later by the distant rumble of thunder. My eyes felt heavy, but for some reason I fought to keep them open, but then a voice seemed to be saying, don't fight, close them, and from then on, it's your choice whether you want to open them again.

Maybe I thought, maybe that's why I'd done it? Then an image slipped into my mind, an image of my parents arriving home and finding me lying naked, and flat on my back on my bed, the only real problem being, I wasn't breathing. Now definitely disturbed, I tried to fight that permeating heaviness, as I desperately attempted to keep sleep at bay. Another flash of lightning, and even at this time of day, it filled the room with its brief, vivid light. For some reason it

reminded me of the moonlight in the shed, so similar to then I relaxed as I gave up the uneven battle, and in doing so, drifted off into a deep, deep sleep.

And I woke with eyes so heavy and blurred, it was as if my room was filled with a thick, swirling fog, so I lay there, and as they so gradually cleared, I turned my head and gazed out the window. And immediately it was apparent the storm had departed, because the stars were there, twinkling like so many miniature diamonds, standing out clearly against the ebony sky. A shiver ran though me, starting at my toes, finishing through my hair, making me aware my face felt warm and flushed. And as well as that, there was a raging battle going on in my head that had me convinced some unknown assailant was attempting to demolish my skull, and in the process had created a headache of a magnitude I'd never experienced before, and for that matter, never wanted to again. My mouth was so dry, it was as if it had been lined with parchment, and to add to my discomfort, that's if it were possible, intermittent cramps were wracking my stomach. I noticed the glass was still on my bedside cabinet, so I reached across, desperate for a mouthful of water, but due to badly trembling fingers, only succeeded in knocking it to the floor, then was thankful it turned out to be dry as well.

Gradually, oh so gradually I sat up, convinced unless I was careful, my head would separate from my shoulders, then roll away, never to be seen again. I swung my legs over the side of the bed and bent down, intending to pick up the glass, but instead, barely avoided falling flat on my face on the floor. Very slowly I sat back where I'd been, glad of the support offered by my bed, from where I did my best to force my brain to penetrate through what was obviously a drug induced haze. I wondered what that drug could have possibly been, but one thing was certain, those tablets most certainly hadn't been sleeping pills.

Sitting where I was for just a little longer, the haze managed to clear enough for me to pick up the glass and stumble on down to the bathroom, more desperate than ever for that mouthful of water. As I stood at the basin, I risked peering into the mirror, expecting to look even worse than I had before. However, ironically, this time I looked fine, with the slight temperature I was running effectively replacing the colour I'd been lacking previously. But above all else, I took the time to look deep into my eyes, trying to determine I could have done anything so incredibly and selfishly stupid. Sure, I still felt some despair was warranted, considering the deviant horror I'd experienced, but as I continued to gaze into that mirror, I accepted nothing had changed from the first time he'd touched me. The remedy still lay entirely in my hands.

Barely a night would pass without my waking, frantically turning and tossing, bathed in perspiration, lying with my heart pounding. And the stillness and quietness in my room, caused by the loss of my clock, and my having declined my parent's offer of a replacement, seemed to accentuate the loathing of what he was doing with me to a point where it was burning like some seething cauldron inside me. Then from the depths of that furnace would emerge a renewed intention of summoning the courage to tell all, at the same time doing my best to convince myself I could cope with the dreadful consequences my confession would create, both at home and at school. But the problem was, come the light of day, somehow it always managed to wash that determination away,

with the result my confessions always failed to eventuate. It seemed the combination of my pride, ego and fear of my father's wrath, constantly managed to dominate over anything else.

In some small way, I felt it was possibly understandable, because those years of torment under the Thompson brothers were still firmly fixed in my mind, and just the thought of it being repeated, but this time, a thousand times worse, filled me with absolute despair. So it made me realise I was prepared to put up with just about anything, as long as it guaranteed a repeat of a similar situation was avoided. And as I lay back on my bed, gazing up at the ceiling, only this time with my pyjamas on, all indications were suggesting that this most evil of days was set to follow that all too familiar pattern. As the effects of the drug continued to dissipate, and also with my system bolstered by those hours of sleep, yet again I could feel my determination waning to a point where I accepted, deep down, I knew it wasn't going to happen. So considering the vileness that had occurred, I decided it was doubtful whether it was ever going to happen at all. Therefore, my only hope of release was that he would eventually tire of me sexually, or hopefully be transferred. Failing that, I could leave school the day I turned fifteen, but I was under no illusion, after all, I hadn't even turned thirteen, that if things continued as they are, then those remaining many months were going to prove to be very long months indeed.

Chapter 23

After the state of my filthy clothes having been accepted by my mother as being just one of those things, 'After all,' she'd said to my father, ' it can't be the first time a boy's tripped and fallen in mud while playing cricket,' it was back to school on the Monday, not having said a thing. And something of a bonus happening, with the weeks following turning out to be some of bliss, while I luxuriated in the pleasure of simply being left alone. I assumed it was so, because the events of that weekend had left him extremely wary, and the apologies that followed were accompanied by his assurances that such obscenities would never be repeated, and as always, I remained totally unconvinced. As far as I was concerned, it was only a repeat of an all too familiar theme, that being his apologies would flow, there would be no more boy sex, he had reformed, no more visits to his room after school would be required. And that was all very well, but the past had proved his insatiable lust for sex would reassert itself, and it would start again, quite often in ways he'd never used before.

But while making the most of this current period of tranquillity, I made a decision and joined the school choir. As far back as I could recall, I'd always loved to sing, and on the days I arrived home after being with him, without fail, I'd head straight for the shower, and as the water cascaded down as I attempted to wash away the abhorrence I associated with him, to help with the cleansing, I'd stand there and sing. And as the sound of my voice resounded around the empty house, I was convinced it also helped the pain that was collecting, deep in my soul. But as this routine continued, gradually I started to suspect I actually sang reasonably well, and even after having to audition with many others, something told me my place in the choir was assured, and so it turned out to be.

As the practising started, and some of the rough edges were quickly eased away, our choirmaster, being almost overcome with sheer disbelief and delight, realised he'd fortuitously gathered together a group of young voices, that with patient and proper training, possessed the capability of producing a sound of such quality, that never before had he had an array of such raw but obvious talent under his baton. For a short time he seemed incapable of believing the good fortune that some higher being had bestowed upon him, but as the light ever so gradually dawned, he grasped this opportunity very firmly with both hands.

So practise and more practise became the order of the day, and much to my delight, by the time my abuser's urge for boy sex reasserted itself, the numerous practise sessions had extended into after school hours, and accordingly, regularly clashed with the times when he'd demanded my presence in his office. To assist my situation even further, he couldn't risk placing his demands over those of the choirmaster, with the reason for this being quite simple. It had already been well documented by all of the masters at the school that our choirmaster was not averse to sending out search parties, armed with his

authority to trample down doors, should it prove necessary, as long as it guaranteed any absentee offenders were dragged bodily back to practise.

Early on, it was common for members of the choir to encounter much playground derision, but as our outstanding ability became increasingly apparent, even our most persistent of detractors were finally forced to admit the school now possessed a group of boys, whose brilliant voices had the power to enhance the school's reputation, equally as effectively as the most successful of its sporting teams. It was also being acknowledged within the educational hierarchy's upper strata of musical experts, that we were seriously starting to challenge for the honour of being nationally recognised as the finest boys' choir in the country.

And as our fame continued to spread, many requests were received for us to perform, and this also had obvious advantages as far as I was concerned, because it meant there were a number of times when I was away, which suited me just fine. However, our latest and most important commitment looming on the horizon, was a request for us to appear at a concert, to be held in the Town Hall, and our interest in this centred around the fact that another choir from the South of the country had already accepted an invitation to perform. With their reputation standing where it did, it was generally accepted that the approaching event would determine, once and for all, who would hold the undisputed honour of being acknowledged as the finest boys' choir in the land.

So with typical youthful competitiveness, our practise sessions took on an added significance, but through it all however, we remained quietly confident, because within our ranks lurked one major weapon, and his name was Andrew Keilly. Andrew's voice possessed a quality of such purity and beauty, the first time I heard him sing, it left me convinced he'd probably acquired this outstanding talent during a previous life. But not only could he sing with a brilliance that at times seemed to defy an apt description, to further complement this wonderful gift, his ice cool temperament meant he could have sung before royalty, and not so much as flickered an eyelid. Due to the fact that the songs we sung, and how often we'd sung them, meant we could warble them in our sleep, our choir master decided it was time to increase our repertoire by one more song. When he announced his choice, we were thrilled, because rather than following a similar pattern to some of the boring renditions he'd insisted on, it actually possessed something in the way of a modern rhythm, to a point where some years later, one of the popular stars at that time rediscovered it, and as a result, it remerged in the form of a smash hit.

As far as the choir was concerned, he decided it lent itself to the choir opening in full voice, Andrew following with his usual masterly performance, then as something different, another member of the choir harmonizing with him. This boy would then continue on singing solo, as he brought the song to its powerful conclusion. So after much contemplation and loss of sleep, he started his search for this new, all important soloist, and much to my amazement, chose me.

After a brief period of nervousness, I found singing in front of the other members of the choir not too much of a problem, due to the encouragement they offered, but what was probably inevitable, when the big occasion finally arrived,

the first fluttering of stage fright started to appear. Early on in the evening, we were introduced to the other choir, but they accepted our handshakes and youthful fun with a slightly stiff formality, which seemed to have been purposely designed to convey an impression of definite superiority. However, half way through the concert when they did perform, we were the first to admit they'd done so extremely well, then finally, towards the end of the programme, it was our turn.

As I took up my position in that front row and looked out over that massive audience, I couldn't believe what I was seeing. The place was packed, every seat taken, it was like the assembly hall on fight night, only a thousand times worse, and the effect it had, none, other than I was petrified, and the thought of moving forward, standing in front of a microphone and singing, turned my legs and stomach to jelly. Our first three songs were greeted with thunderous applause, but due to little help on my part, because nerves had rendered my voice to nothing more than a husky croak. And now with the choir having swung into our new rendition, and Andrew well into captivating the crowd with his awesome voice, the choirmaster suddenly gave me that barely perceptible nod, indicating it was time for me to step forward. Somehow, I managed to stagger reluctantly over to the microphone, and as I stood there in a state of deep, vocal paralysis, it was Andrew who appeared as my saviour. As his final solo notes rang out, he turned to me and grinned, then followed that with a confidence boosting wink.

Incredibly, it proved to be all that was needed, as a voice inside me seemed to say, 'If he can do it, then so can you'. As we joined in that first note together, I was elated to find not only was I singing, incredibly enough, I was also singing in tune, and as we carried on together, his confidence continued to inspire me, and the more assured I became. Now for the ultimate test, as Andrew stepped back and away, leaving me on my own, and as that first crystal clear note rang out, it was as if it almost rivalled Andrew, and I continued to sing in front of that huge crowd as I knew I'd never sung before. It was an evening destined to be never forgotten, another that ended in back patting and congratulations, while the other choir slipped as unobtrusively as possible away. I've looked back on the success at that concert, on many occasions during my life, and still remain convinced I managed to sing as I did, as something in the way of consolation for the atrocious times that lay not all that far ahead.

Chapter 24

Following our success at the concert, the only remaining commitment the choir had for the year, was a live recital over the radio station, 1YA, which meant an evening trip into the heart of the city, during which we thoroughly enjoyed ourselves, in ways that only young boys seem to be able to manage. We may like to sing, but it didn't mean we weren't capable of getting up to a bit of innocent mischief, if circumstances permitted. Then the choir was scheduled to take a welcome break, that being welcome for the other boys, but not so welcome for myself, because at that time, I felt it meant any excuses relating to my non availability in other directions, would become a thing of the past.

The truth was however, that even allowing for the intrusions created by the choir, his 'requests' for my presence in his office had fallen away quite dramatically, and on the rare occasions when I had to appear, it was noticeable his demeanour had changed, he seemed withdrawn and almost distracted, something far removed from his normal confident self. It was as I was dressing after one of his classes, that the reason behind this personality change started to become apparent. Following an all too familiar approach, he sidled up to me, and when he spoke, he did so casually, as if attempting to convey the impression he was asking for nothing unusual at all, 'Something has arisen that needs explaining Mathew, so make sure you come down here after school. No matter what the situation in the gym, as far as any other boys are concerned, you must wait for however long it proves to be necessary for the area to clear, but it's imperative I speak to you today.'

And when I finally entered his office, the look on his face broadcast one thing, trouble. The man appeared so upset, he seemed bordering on tears, and as I moved to the storeroom to start taking off my clothes, he stopped me, the tone of his voice bordering on panic, 'That's not necessary today lad, we have other things to discuss.'

And immediately I was even more wary. If he could place those 'other things' ahead of sex, then they had to be very important indeed. So I stood there and listened, and in doing so, understood immediately why he was as upset as he appeared.

He shuffled some papers around on his desk, rearranged this and that in his usual fastidious manner, then finally his story started, and along with it, the reason behind his distress gradually became abundantly clear, 'Before I became acquainted with you, I'd been involved with another couple of youngsters, who, in direct contrast to yourself, had proved to be only too willing to cooperate with what I required. Also, it was around this time I was introduced to a group, who had the same interests as myself. Once I was satisfied they were legitimate in these interests, I happened to mention to one of the group, who seemed to possess some influence amongst them, that I had a series of photos I couldn't get developed, due to their explicit content. He immediately informed me that he possessed the necessary photographic equipment and facilities required, and that

if I was prepared to release the films to him, getting the photos developed was simplicity in itself. I now accept that in agreeing to do so, I made a mistake that I'll regret for the rest of my life. As you are probably aware, some of the photos showed you performing in that shed, and you and I in various uncompromising situations, but now having viewed photos of you, he was adamant he wanted to meet you in person. Please believe me when I say I instantly refused, but he's now insisting that unless I comply, he'll release some of the photos to the appropriate authorities, and quite a number around the school as well, which proves he's developed a number of copies, and kept some for himself. I can't tell you how sorry I am Mathew, but it seems he's determined to meet you, so considering the circumstances, it's imperative you make yourself available out at the house this coming Saturday.'

I stood there, mouth open, mystified as to how he could have been so thoughtless. First, due to a lust I still struggled to understand, he blackmails me, then allows that same lust to place him in a position where he's being subjected to the identical thing himself, and the fact that it was happening, was providing little compensation as far as I was concerned. Part of me was saying it served him bloody well right, the other larger part was saying, due to his stupidity, I was obviously at risk of sinking even deeper into this dreadful mire he'd created. I thought yet again about my situation at school and with my parents, and as far as the latter were concerned, things seemed to be getting more complicated by the second.

I'd craved to do the work my father produced from as far back as I could recall. The sheer beauty of some of the work that flowed out of his factory's doors attracted me like nothing else. And now that his own business was booming to the extent it obviously was, that yearning to be involved was stronger than ever. I still had two years of schooling ahead of me, of that I was aware, but now my decision was made. When the last day of school arrived, after a short break, I would start an apprenticeship under my father. I was very aware there were times when our father and son relationship could be described as being rather volatile, but generally speaking, we got on reasonably well. The way he spoke of his business and my involvement in it, indicated he totally agreed with my future planning as far as my working life was concerned. But if this man Bergman was speaking of, ever dared to carry out his threats, it wasn't just my school and immediate family life that would be destroyed, it now included my future working life as well. I was all too aware that if any of those photos ever surfaced to a point where my father viewed them, due to his irrationality in that particular area when it came to anything remotely sexual, then the possibility of he and I working under the same roof would be destroyed forever. Previously the situation had been difficult enough. It appeared it was even worse again now.

The chaotic situation that had developed, finally hit me with brutal force, but as I opened my mouth to explode, Bergman beat me to it, 'Look, I'm truly sorry Mathew, I really am. I say once again, there's no way in the world I wanted anything like this to happen, but it has, and there's nothing I can do about it now. So I'm sure you can see that we're left with no alternative. Much as I

loathe the thought of it, you're going to have to go back to that house and meet this man.'

Well, he wanted me to go back there alright, but this time it was to save his skin as much as mine. He'd said quite enough, I knew my position was hopeless, the threats being made were familiar enough, nothing had changed, I was left with no option other than to comply.

This time the park was deserted as I rode on past and further down to the house. As I tapped on the door, I noticed my hand was shaking, but this time when Bergman opened it, he quickly eased me inside, then across the kitchen and up the hall then further on again into the lounge. The room was quite large and comfortably warm, as it spread mainly across the Northern aspect. The ceiling was off white and trimmed with an ornate cornice, below which there was a tastefully patterned frieze, with the rest of the woodwork painted off white as well. The furniture consisted of a collection of not too expensive but obviously carefully chosen antiques, and the floral carpet, normally something I couldn't tolerate, also came close to being acceptable, surprisingly enough.

He waved his hand in the general direction of a small sofa, this being where he apparently preferred me to sit, then in a manner I'd become accustomed to, he started fussing what I was convinced was unnecessarily around the room, first adjusting a pile of magazines that I felt didn't need touching, moving the positions of some cushions, that didn't need moving. His constant movement left me with the impression he was chronically nervous, and his next comment went some way to explaining why, 'By the way Mathew, I must inform you there's been a slight change of plans. Rather than my associate coming here, he'd rather I took you to him, so he's sending a car to pick us up,' and as he noticed my alarm rapidly building he quickly added, 'and you must understand there's nothing to worry about. I'll be right there with you, so do as you're told, and you'll be back here and on your way home on that bike of yours before you know it.'

So he says, I thought, and was it any wonder I remained totally unconvinced. I'd already decided my involvement with him was similar to reading some cheap, filthy paperback, and as I sat nervous and apprehensive in that room, something was telling me another chapter in that book was about to commence. So as a form of defence, I thought about that promise I'd made to myself while lying on my bed, doing my best to regain my faculties after having been so stupid in having taken those pills. And that promise was that no matter what I had to face, I'd never, ever bend again, except for one exception, and that was, if they ever tried to take me down to that room under this house again, then they'd have to kill me, before I'd walk on through that door. So after taking a deep breath to help sooth my nerves, then another for good measure, I settled back and waited for them to come for me.

At least another fifteen minutes evaporated, then the sound of a powerful engine as it purred down the road, slowing as it approached the house, then the vehicle swinging smoothly into the drive and around to the rear of the property. Now Bergman reappeared, obviously slightly flustered, caught midway while trying to climb into a brown sports coat, groping for an elusive armhole while he

spoke, 'Right Mathew, the car's here, and don't forget what I said. Just do as you're told, and everything will be fine.'

No concern about the room downstairs, straight back through to the rear of the house, the car standing directly outside, idling on the brick forecourt. A big American job, something we were starting to see a bit more of in this part of the world. But why the necessity for all of this drama? He had a car, why couldn't he have taken me to where we were going instead?

Down the back steps, the rear door of the car already open, a man sitting on the far side, a nicotine addict, who snarled at me through badly stained teeth, 'Get in kid, kneel on the floor, place your arms on the seat, then rest your head on them, and don't attempt to look up, or take it from me, you'll regret it.'

The man had to be kidding, who travels in a car like that? Apparently I did, as he repeated himself, but this time with the assistance of some really foul language, 'Are you fucking deaf or something? Get in the bloody car and do exactly as I fucking said, and don't make me have to tell you again, or by Christ you'll be bloody sorry.'

I decided Kevin and this animal would make a good pair, but taking the none too subtle hint, I did as he said, and it proved to be not all that difficult, due to the size of the vehicle. The front door opened and closed, Bergman getting in I presumed, then the driver expertly reversed the car back down the drive and onto the street, from where he accelerated smoothly away.

The vehicle powered along with almost insulting ease, and as I sat with my head on my arms, scared though I was, I realised I was at least gaining some small comfort from the fact that Bergman was here with me. So alright, I knew my opinion of the man, but in a strange and possibly dangerous situation like this, even his familiarity was providing something in the way of consolation. Some time passed, idly I wondered how long we'd been in the car, about forty five minutes was my guess. Another ten or so, and my knees were starting to feel it, the slight irritation caused by the occasional bump the vehicle's excellent suspension failed to cope with. Now my nose was starting to tickle; a sure sign I was about to sneeze, so I raised my head slightly and a hand slammed down on my neck, hard enough to make me see a few stars. The driver noticed, and seemed about as pleased as I was, 'No need to hit the kid like that Seth. Keep your hands to yourself, or I'll take the matter up with Malcolm.'

I got the feeling Seth couldn't have cared less, and how wrong I was proved to be.

The car purred contentedly, and how long had we been travelling now? I guessed about just over an hour, the assessment derived courtesy of a pair of slightly chaffed knees, and a decidedly painful neck. A few minutes more, the car definitely slowing and swinging left, at the same time the tone of the tyres changing from singing at speed over tar-seal, to the distinct sound of gravel crunching under the weight of the vehicle. It continued on at a much reduced speed, then slowed appreciably and finally stopped. The back door open, a hand lightly touching my elbow, presumably hinting I was allowed to get out. And as I complied, a house appeared before me, a huge, two storied structure, with the conventional weatherboards having recently been painted what I thought was a charming, sort of creamy off white. The roof was in keeping with the quality on

display, because it was covered in beautifully matured terracotta tiles. Colonial windows and trimmings added to the elegance, which was further enhanced by an imposing entrance that consisted of eight wide stone steps that led to a large timber door with polished brass hardware. It swung open as we approached, and closed with a resounding thud as we stepped inside, but at a point when the door was wide open, I turned and glanced back at the car. But they were way ahead of me, because the vehicle appeared to have been purposely parked at such an angle, that made it impossible for me to read the registration plates. Not that it mattered all that much. Always had been hopeless at remembering a group of numbers anyway.

And the house was proving to be just as imposing inside, as it had been out. The foyer in which we were standing was covered in plush, green carpet, and reposing in a number of appropriate locations, was a selection of beautiful furniture, with the luxurious effect being further enhanced by the use of the occasional carefully selected ornament. Rich timber panelling covered the walls up to dado height, then above, a tasteful wallpaper set off to perfection a series of six or seven what were no doubt very expensive paintings. A superbly crafted cornice trimmed the off white ceiling, from the centre of which was hanging a magnificent chandelier, and beyond that, a gracefully sweeping stairway provided access to the rooms above.

To my left, from where I was standing, a hall that seemed to go on forever, and this and the stairway were separated by a three metre section of wall, in the centre of which stood an imposing grandfather clock. And as my admiring glance washed over it, the hands tended to indicate my rough assessment of the time the journey had taken proved to be reasonably accurate, something like an hour and ten or fifteen minutes. But that was where my appraisal of the home was terminated. A heavy set woman appeared, who briefly studied me with unpleasant, arrogant eyes, then she turned and spoke quietly to Bergman, then set off down the hall, with both of us following obediently behind. After passing numerous rooms she suddenly stopped and with a nod of her head, indicated the one we were to enter, at the same time with her arm thrust out, as if daring us to attempt to proceed any further.

So doing what was obviously expected, Bergman walked in and I followed. Apparently satisfied we had no intention of intruding on hallowed ground, she turned and took a few steps down the hall, then suddenly turned and came back, and I was surprised when she spoke to me, rather than Bergman, 'With any luck kid, we'll be seeing quite a lot of each other, and if it eventuates, and I'm told there's every chance it will, then there's one thing I can assure you, and that is I'll be seeing a whole lot more of you, than you'll be seeing of me.'

Having apparently made her point, this time she did take off, laughing loudly at what had to be her own private joke, but thankfully the unpleasant noise rapidly faded, as she presumably reached the end of the hall and started to climb the stairs.

Bergman moved across and forcibly closed the door, giving the impression he was no more enchanted with her presence than I'd been, so to help ease the tension she seemed to have created, he suggested I may as well sit down, but with this being easier said than done. The sparse furnishings seemed rather lost

in what was a reasonably large room, and seeing as he'd already claimed the solitary chair, all that was left was a choice between a bed and a stool, the latter heavily upholstered and positioned under the solitary window at the far end of the room. As I hitched myself up on the bed, I notice it was slightly higher than what was usually considered as being normal, and it was covered by a single blanket, under which was a firm and well used heavily stained mattress. Directly opposite from where I was sitting, a dressing table, with the usual drawers below, and a tilting mirror above, which was showing a number of glaring imperfections.

Instead of the plush, green carpet, there was an imitation Persian rug, that was faded and well worn, and the large area of floor it failed to cover had a heavy, rather dark appearance, that I decided could only have been achieved by many applications of overly thick varnish. Similar to the entrance, a dado mould ran around the walls at around waist height, but there was no timber panelling. This time the same drab wallpaper covered them above and below, with the only relief provided by a reasonably wide paper frieze, positioned directly above the moulding, and it was this that provided the only splash of colour in what managed to be a strangely depressing room.

Unlike the immaculate entrance, a couple of large cracks were noticeable in the plaster ceiling, and just to the right of where I was sitting, another door. Already bored with doing nothing, I slipped of the bed, intending to do a little investigating instead, so I walked down and gazed out of the window, but it offered nothing more than the view of another building, with the reasonably expansive area between covered in grey, uninteresting asphalt. But as I moved back with the intention of opening the other door, that strange woman reappeared. She literally flung open the door, her actions suggesting she resented it being shut at all, then she thrust her head into the room, glanced around, then grunted at Bergman, 'He said to apologise for keeping you waiting, and would you now please come straight up.'

But as Bergman quickly stood and eased past, she turned, glared and snapped back at me, 'And while he's gone boy, don't even think about moving out of this room, understand?'

Apparently she took it for granted I did, because although I studiously ignored her in my well practised 'and to hell with you' manner, she still backed out and set off down the hall, with Bergman trailing along behind. So starting again from where I'd been interrupted, I opened the door and glanced into the room. It was a bathroom, also reasonably large, which seemed in keeping with what we'd already seen as we'd walked down the hall, with the walls and floor covered in white ceramic tiles.

The only relief from all this whiteness, was provided by a thin margin of black tile, positioned about thirty centimetres out from the walls. There were little more than the standard fitting one would expect. A vanity with a mirror above, a large, free standing bath, that was quite impressive, an expansive shower recess, with a white curtain pulled to one side, a toilet, then alongside that, what turned out to be a bidet, this being the only item I didn't recognise, mainly because it was the first I'd ever seen in my life. The overall effect I decided, was one of disinteresting cleanliness, so I went back and stood by the

bed, but as I did, that distinct feeling of unease started to reassert itself. Let's face it, I was scared, and at this point my main question hadn't been answered, that being, why was I here anyway?

What also didn't help, was I was certain Bergman wasn't any happier being here than I was, but that was as far as my worrying got. That weird woman was back, grunting at me from the doorway, as it seemed only she could, 'This is where it starts to get interesting kid. Your turn to be wanted upstairs, so do me a favour, make sure you put on a good display.'

Not bothering to check whether I was following or not, she took off, but with even her presence being preferable to being left in the room on my own, I didn't hesitate to take off after her. So back down the hall, then up that magnificent stairway, then, after a few paces down a hall at the top, she stopped at a closed door, tapped lightly, and on hearing a murmur of response, opened the door and literally shoved me into the room. The act was so rude, and annoyed me so much, I spun around, intending to shove her just as hard back, but apparently anticipating my annoyance, she stepped back, and slammed the door in my face.

Right, I thought, you'll keep. At times like this, I've a memory like an elephant.

And as I reluctantly turned back, I found myself looking at a room dominated by the richness of floor to ceiling panelling, walnut was my guess, and yet another collection of superb furniture, the predominant piece being a large, heavily carved desk, behind which a tall, well built man was sitting. Following my somewhat undignified arrival, he glanced up, gazing at me through a pair of dark, heavily framed glasses, but didn't say a thing, preferring instead to nonchalantly indicate in the general direction of where he apparently wanted me to stand, while he continued to run his eyes slowly and arrogantly over me. Quite a few seconds past, then he finally stood up, and in doing so, displayed an immaculately cut pair of tan trousers, that complimented a perfectly fitting cream shirt.

Very unsure, and still quite scared, concerned that circumstances were such that I needed to be here at all, I stood where I was, while he started to slowly circle around, left hand griping his chin, perusing me with the intensity of a horse trainer, who'd been burdened with the responsibility of making the final decision relating to the purchase of an extremely expensive colt. This unsettling examination continued for some little time, but finally he turned and spoke to Bergman who was standing a few paces away, and he did so, with a faintly familiar guttural type of accent, and while I was raking my mind, trying to determine where I'd heard someone speak like that before, as if asking for no more than the time of day, he said, 'You're to strip, take your clothes off boy, I want to see that body of yours naked.'

As a result, my fear increased, so I glanced across at Bergman, hoping he could offer some reassurance, but all he did was mouth silently back, 'Remember, just do as you're told.'

Briefly, being quite put out by his lack of response, I thought about saying something quite rude back, but in the end decided not to bother. Long before I'd accepted the fight was lost, the fact I was standing here was obvious proof of

that, so I stripped and stood naked while he resumed his inspection. And as he continued to ease around, I thought about his accent. Somewhere and at some time I'd heard someone speak like that before, then suddenly, as if out of nowhere, the light dawned. Of course, Arnie van de Meure, God's gift to the girls at the pool. He of the great physique and ego to match. Arnie had spoken using that same, unpleasant guttural tone, or so I'd found it anyway, I was convinced the man was South African.

And as it turned out, I had indeed determined his country of origin correctly. I'd never liked Arnie, there had been something about him that had consistently irritated me, and I was starting to feel this man getting to me in an identical manner, and maybe, somehow, he could sense my annoyance, and that was what acted as an incentive for him to speak again,

'Now stand with your legs apart, bend well over for me boy, and hold your buttocks open.'

Sure enough, first those boys in the shed, then this other man standing in the room, and now this piece of humanity, they all have something in common, and my reaction to their crudeness hadn't changed one little bit as I replied, 'How about considering doing me a favour and dropping dead. Maybe then you'll leave me alone?'

He continued to stand with his chin in his hand, and the tone of his voice inferred boredom, rather than the annoyance I'd expected, when he answered, 'It's obvious, following a statement like that, you need the facts of life that determine the rules that apply around this house explained to you fairly quickly boy. According to your friend here, I understand you were quite distressed at what occurred during your first visit to the house back in the city. Well, be warned, talk to me like that again, and you'll be putting on another performance of a similar nature, but it will be here in this house, with you performing especially for me. And understand one thing. You'll do it boy, because I'll be holding something considerably more than a cigarette in my hand, that'll make sure you comply with everything I want to watch. Now don't risk having to be told again. Just get on and do what I want.'

If he'd set out to scare me, he'd well and truly succeeded. I knew I'd received a very explicit warning, and as I looked back at that tall, imposing man, this time I looked past his glasses and deep into his eyes, and it took no more than a part of a second for me to believe every word he'd said. They displayed not a flicker of emotion or compassion, as they looked back down at me like two small blocks of blue ice. So I immediately bent over and did as he'd demanded, and I was surprised, because rather than being violated, similar to how I had been in the past, nothing happened other than a brief visual examination that took barely seconds. Then he moved back to the front, taking my penis and testicles in his hand, fondling and rolling them in his hand while he addressed Bergman, 'A definite advantage he's been cut Phillip, because I've always been convinced it photographs better.'

Next, he ran his hand over my pubic area, and seemed satisfied there as he commented,

'There's no doubt about it, the boy just gets better and better, not a sign of anything there yet, and I thought you said the kid is about eleven or twelve.

Christ, going by this, you'd think he was no older than eight or nine. With the boy still as clear and as smooth as this, absolutely marvellous, couldn't be better for what I want to use him for.'

And instantly my mind went into reverse. First I thought about the Thompson brothers and the unpleasantness they'd caused, because I hadn't been 'cut' and from there, why had I insisted it be done? To make me the same as all the other boys, so what was he going on about? As far as I was concerned, all boys were, but maybe it was possible where he came from, they weren't. Then next he starts prattling on about my smooth pubic area, and Cunningham had tried the same thing, and look where it got him. Looking a fool in the showers, that's what. Then he carries on about my supposedly looking younger than I was. Well what was new, I mean Bergman had bleated on about the same thing, and as far as I could tell, it hadn't changed a thing in my life, so what the hell, couldn't care bloody less.

But now he'd turned his attention to my hair, first sweeping it back from my eyes, then encouraging it to fall back across my forehead again, then after a little more fussing, finally he seemed satisfied as he turned to Bergman and said, 'Phillip, if you'll come with me please, there's a few things we need to discuss, and it's probably best it's done in private,' then he turned to me and said, ' and anything you want to add that you feel may be important kid?'

Let's face it, he was the one who'd asked, so I looked straight back at him and said, 'Yes, there bloody well is. All this rubbish about my age, well I've just turned thirteen, whether you like it or not.'

He looked at me without any expression, but I was convinced a smile flickered as he said,

'Kid, age doesn't mean all that much with the men I deal with. It's what they see being offered to them that matters, and they certainly won't be backward in appreciating what you could be supplying. But I admit, one phrase that does come up quite often is, 'the younger the better', so I guess age does matter to some extent, after all.'

They walked off into an adjoining room, but after a few moments, realised I could hear the murmur of their voices, so possessing hearing that would have done justice to a cat, I slipped across and placed my ear hard up to the door, and found I could hear some of what they were saying, especially the South African, who I picked up mid sentence... . 'and I never thought of carrying on the same business in this country, but this kid is exceptional, just too good to miss, so you're going to have to accept it, because he's got everything I want, so...'

Now Bergman, his voice rising to a strident pitch, caused by either fear or concern, but at times fading, giving the impression he was pacing up and down the room... 'and I'm absolutely appalled at what you're saying and I'll have absolutely nothing to do with it. For Heaven's sake Malcolm, leave the boy alone, There's no way...' gone again, as his voice faded, followed by a short period of silence until the South African's voice drifted in again...

'...alright, alright, stop going on about it and get it through your head, it's going to happen, if I have...' lost yet again, then I realised there'd been an overly long period of silence, so I dived back to where I'd previously been standing, and just as well, because seconds later they walked back in. Their

reappearance, along with obeying a curt instruction to get dressed, ended the first of many trips I was to make out to that detestable house.

The trip back to the city passed quickly, at least it seemed quicker than the other way around, and when back in the suburbs, Bergman offered something in the way of a pacifier,

'There Mathew, it's all over and wasn't so bad was it, now how about a cup of coffee?

Seeing as I was never allowed coffee at home, usually the occasional illicit cup was gratefully accepted, but long before I'd decided, never, never with him, as I snapped back in reply,

'No, I don't want a cup of coffee, and what's behind my having to go out to that house. I heard some of what you were talking about, so what did he mean when he said I've got everything he wants, I mean for Christ's sake, what the hell does the man want anyway?'

But his eyes refused to meet mine, clearly indicating he was resisting any possibility of being drawn into a conversation regarding that situation as he simply said, 'Look, the thing is you're back, with absolutely no harm done, so are you sure you won't have that coffee?'

As I rode home, I shuddered at the thought of what had taken place, and no harm done, he'd said. Certainly there was no physical harm, but in what category did being made to strip naked and being fondled belong? I was incredulous that I'd allowed myself to be included in what could have turned out to be such a dangerous situation. But deep down I was aware of the reason why, because without fail, there always came back came the same reply. I had to accept it, my life was now controlled by that never ending fear of untrue but lethal exposure, and if that threat was ever activated, the mindless, destructive chaos I knew would follow.

So it was obvious, absolutely nothing had changed. Accepting the taint and trauma that arrived from what he was doing to me, which also included what that other man had just demanded of me, was still far and away the lesser of the evils from the two options that existed. The alternative, and the devastation it would bring with it, was something I preferred not to even think about. However, the next few weeks past pleasantly enough, effectively and temporarily lulling me into a false sense of security. So when I went to move past him out of the gym, I wasn't expecting his hastily whispered instruction, 'I want you down here when school ends, and you're to wait as long as necessary for the gymnasium to clear, so you can enter my office without being noticed.'

Yeah, well what was new, and when I arrived, the area took no time at all to clear, but as I walked in and locked the door and headed for the storeroom, he stopped me, the strain, so evident in his voice acting as a warning, so I turned and studied him, and it was obvious the man was bordering on tears, ' Mathew, I am truly just so sorry, but Malcolm has informed me he expects you out at his house this coming Saturday. The arrangements for transporting you out there will remain the same, only this time I won't be coming. He said to allow for being out there from around ten thirty, until four, so make sure you take steps to be able to explain this time spent away with your parents, if the necessity should

arise. All I can hope is you believe me when I say I wouldn't have had this happen for the world, and I really am just so very sorry.'

By the time he'd finished, I was breathing fire, but as I looked at him, the outburst wouldn't come. The man was visibly trembling, and literally beside himself with grief, and what I assumed was self incrimination, so in the end I restrained myself and simply said,

'You realise we wouldn't be in this hopeless position, if you'd have left me alone and not set me up in the first place. But as we both know, I'm left with no alternative, but there's one thing that's certain, and that is I have a feeling I'll never forgive you for making that mistake, no matter how unintended, in getting me involved with that South African.'

On the way home, I thought about it and decided that after surviving what I already had, there was no way I was backing down now, so as I continued to pedal my way home, with the coolness from the late Summer afternoon washing across my face and through my hair, right or wrong, foolish or otherwise, I knew the approaching Saturday morning would see me making my second trip out to that house.

Chapter 25

As I stepped out of the car and was escorted inside, there was no time to admire that impressive entrance, it was straight up the stairs and into his office, and as before, he was enthroned behind his desk, giving me the impression he spent a great deal of his life there. The man named Seth, who yet again had unfortunately accompanied me on the journey from the city, spoke to him briefly, then turned and slipped silently out of the room. And the thought crossed my mind; big as he was, how he could help but be silent, on carpet that thick anyway.

The South African finished writing and acknowledged my presence with the briefest possible nod, then pulled another paper in front of him, studied it, signed it, then slowly those ice blue eyes of his lifted, travelling slowly up, stopping when they met mine, 'I intend to come straight to the point lad. I'm aware of the situation that exists between you and your schoolmaster, and can fully understand your reluctance in it ever being exposed, especially considering, as I'm also led to understand, that the situation is somewhat unique, due to the fact you happen to be a very unwilling participant. But unwilling or not, rest assured, it means absolutely nothing to me. As far as I'm concerned, the service I'm going to expect you to provide, will be no different to what you're currently providing for him, other than the fact that when you're brought out to this house, there'll be a decided increase in the extent of your participation.'

He got up, strolled over to the window, stood with his hands clasped behind his back, gazing out over the view that included a beautifully maintained garden in the foreground, with a panorama of sweeping, lush green meadows, interspersed with grazing cattle beyond, then he continued, 'I want your duties to start today, and I'm expecting you to agree and be taken downstairs and be prepared for what you must do. Following that, you'll be taken into that bedroom you were made familiar with during your last visit, and at intervals during the late morning and early afternoon, a number of men will enter the room, and you will provide them with any type of sex they demand. Never forget, any reluctance on your part to supply them with what they want, will earn my extreme displeasure. However, if it is your decision to refuse to become involved at all, you will immediately be taken back to the city, but it will also result in immediate exposure. So really lad, your position is quite clear. Provide for these men as you've been providing for that other person, and you and I won't have a problem, but defy me, and the problems my young friend, will rest entirely on your head.' He strolled back and sat down, from where he closely watched my reaction, and as far as I was concerned, I'd have rather been sealed in a tomb. All this previous mess, then on top of it, I was faced with this. So often I would lie in bed and ask myself, why me, why me of all people. As far as I could tell, I'd never come close to receiving an answer. Maybe this man could finally provide it, so I didn't hesitate to ask him, 'Why am I expected to do these things, why do these pathetic type of men want to have sex with me? I

understand there's boys out there who don't mind doing these filthy things, but I detest it, so why does it have to be me?'

When he replied, he spoke softly, obviously choosing his words carefully, 'You're quite right lad, there are boys out there who don't mind providing their bodies, but past experience has taught me that so often, they have been raised in, what shall I call it, let's just say a somewhat lower social structure. In other words, there's a constant mix of louts and rather uncouth individuals included amongst them, which has always been something I've found rather deplorable, and many of my clients are affected the same way. You must understand that the higher percentage of men I tend to do business with, who wish to engage in sex with a boy, come from a rather higher social structure, and this is so often determined by the fact they can afford the fees I charge, so they invariably prefer that the boy they use is being raised in a somewhat similar environment to what they were brought up in. In other words, they want a well cared for, clean living child made available for them.'

He turned and walked back to his chair, sat down, then carefully studied my reaction before he continued, 'So after what I've just explained, do you still fail to comprehend as to why it has to be you. Tell me lad, how old did you say you are?'

But my mind had wandered, I felt as if my head was spinning, but above all else, I was scared, and due to my lack of response, his voice took on a rasp of extreme impatience,

'Damn it boy, answer me when I ask you a question. How old did you say you are?'

I thought about it, and decided I'd better confess, 'Well, I said I'd just turned thirteen, but I'm still twelve. I'll turn thirteen fairly soon though. Guess I'm just keen to be called a teenager.'

'Alright, so you're twelve, and tell me, what do you think of girls?'

What was the man on about, I mean, why ask that sort of bloody stupid question?

'What do I think of girls? Don't know, haven't thought about it all that much. I guess some of them are alright, I mean I like our neighbour's daughter, Justine's really nice.'

'So, no great interest in that direction yet, and considering what I suspect you're about to be subjected too, there's a chance that interest may never fully appear, I guess only the future will determine that. But it's time you understood, that men like your schoolteacher, and to a lesser extent myself, tend to assess their attraction to a young boy, as others would a young woman. The shape and tone of the body is a great attraction, the smoothness and colour of the skin plays a part as well, along with the thickness and colour of the hair, and at times, the colour of the eyes. Yet after all of that, you still stand there and wonder why a certain type of man would kill to be with you. Now come with me boy, because it's high time some of the attributes you unconsciously possess, were explained to you before we proceed any further.'

Taking hold of my shirt at the collar, he eased me through the doorway at which I'd listened previously, then further on into a large bedroom, dominated by a huge, four poster bed. He stopped in front of a free standing wardrobe, on

the door of which was an exquisitely crafted mirror, and I was left gazing vaguely at my reflection, and equally as vaguely wondering why we were here, suddenly he said, 'Right, now take off all your clothes.'

And to hell with that I thought. I was fed up being made to take my clothes off to order, and that definitely included being told twice by him, but as I hesitated, a hand with a grip resembling a metal vice took hold of my neck and shook me, as if I was nothing more than a rag doll. At the same time his voice rose about ten decibels, to a shrill pitch, that I was to learn gave warning of his impending volatility, which I was also to learn, was never hovering far below the surface, and in keeping with that, he exploded, 'When I tell you to do something boy, just get on and do it, never hesitate, understand? You could place yourself at risk.'

Going by the pain in my neck, I figured I already had, and if I hadn't, then I'd better learn promptly, so I nodded, mainly because trying to speak was virtually impossible. No more resistance, I took my clothes and shoes off real quick, mainly because I'd decided I wanted to keep on living, and as I finally stepped out of my pants, he moved me closer to the mirror,

'Now let's go back over what I mentioned to you before,' he said, 'and as I do, stop and think if you feel anything I say explains things more clearly. First of all, you're a swimmer, you spend a lot of your time in the water. You wonder how I know? Because over the years experience has taught me, nothing moulds a young, developing body better than swimming.'

'Just for once boy, take the time and try and look at yourself as others see you. Look at those shoulders of yours, and that tight, firm stomach. Come on lad, just for once take the time and really look at yourself, surely under the circumstances, even you can see what I mean.'

So I stood there and looked, feeling a bit foolish while I did, but damned if I could see that I looked any different to any number of kids my age. Anyway, long before I'd decided I had far better things to do than standing in front of a mirror. That's why my mother was constantly complaining, always going on about the fact my hair was constantly in a mess. But undaunted by what was probably a rather blank expression, he carried on regardless, 'Now look at your skin, that even, golden tan, and not so much as a single blemish on your body. Can't you understand boy, similar to so many kids your age, you have a skin quality that most adults would die for.' He ran his hand over my back and buttocks, and I cringed, and was glad when he rambled on, 'Now let's assess that face of yours. The line of your jaw and cheekbone structure, tells me you have the makings of being a stubborn little bastard at times, mind you, that's something I've already found out. But allowing for all of that, the fact remains you happen to be one outstanding looking kid.'

Maybe he should have told Noelene Kidson that. The last time I ducked her in the Council Pool for giving me cheek, she came up spluttering and saying some really shocking things about my appearance. Not that I could have cared less, the cheeky little bitch. But still he waffled on, 'Then there's the question of your hair, that thick, blond, uncontrollable head of hair of yours. Believe me when I say, a high percentage of men who sexually desire young boys, have an overwhelming preference for boys with blond hair. Need I say more, taking into

consideration the circumstances that exist here?' No thank you, he needn't, that explanation was quite enough, but still he hadn't finished,

'Finally boy, there's the matter of your eyes, those superb, green eyes. Do you realise, I know some wealthy people who'd pay a small fortune, to have eyes the same colour as yours.'

Big as he was, he'd better be careful, because now he was really on to a very touchy subject. If there was one thing I'd decided I loathed in this life, it was the colour of my eyes. The first time I'd really noticed them was about eighteen months back, while cleaning my teeth before school. Suddenly there they were in the mirror, looking straight back at me, making me look like I was sick or something. Just as I was leaving, pissed off like you wouldn't believe, I'd stopped and queried their colour with my mother. Anyway, I was convinced it was her fault, I could hear her voice carrying on like a permanent recording,

'Mathew, stop arguing, you're not leaving the table until you've finished your greens.'

Let's face it, anyone could see where the trouble originated from. I was being made to eat so much of that rubbish, the inevitable was happening, and the colour was starting to seep out.

But what the hell, even though I'd discovered the source of the problem, I asked her anyway,

'Mum, why have I got green eyes, when I know they used to be brown? I hate them, they make me look stupid, like I've got some dreadful permanent illness or something.'

Talk about rubbing it in. It sure hadn't helped when she burst out laughing when she replied,

'Don't be so foolish Mathew, nobody cares about the colour of your eyes. Anyway, you've got lovely eyes, you don't know how lucky you are. They're just a little different, that's all,'

All too easy for her, she didn't have to put up with them. If she liked her kids having green eyes, she should have had a girl. For days after I'd discreetly studied the other kids. It was just as I'd figured, nobody, but nobody had eyes the colour of mine. For quite a while after I'd gone around in mortal embarrassment, eyes downcast, constantly bumping into things, and now, after all this time, he'd managed to rekindle my loathing of my eyes. But he turned me gently enough to him as he said, 'It's time for you to decide lad. You can agree to go downstairs, where Maria will prepare for what you must provide for these men, or on the other hand, you're at liberty to put your clothes back on, and be driven back to the city. I readily admit that if you decide to stay, what happens from there will bring changes to your life. But remember, they'll prove to be comparatively trivial, compared to the upheaval that'll be created, if you should choose the other alternative. Now you have an important decision to make, so take your time and choose carefully. That's all the advice I can give you.'

The last thing I needed was reminding, I'd been through all of this before, and I felt I'd done nothing to deserve the position I found myself in. I recalled what my father had said when he'd learnt I'd arrived home late, due to a class

detention, all caused by Waldon and a couple of his clueless mates, acting up in class. 'Life isn't always fair, Mathew,' he'd said,

'Sometimes it's inevitable the innocent suffer along with the guilty.' At the time it hadn't helped, I'd still arrived home pissed off anyway, but at least I now knew how true his words were. I was an innocent who was suffering again, and it appeared I had a lot more to suffer yet. The South African had moved over and was now standing by the bed, patiently waiting for my decision, so I decided to make one last, futile attempt to extract myself from the odious position I found myself in, 'Look, it won't work. I'm committed to playing cricket for the school, and I just can't not turn up, because you've decided you want me out here.'

The look on his face told me my attempt had gone down in flames, even before it had started, 'There's one thing you'd better understand very quickly boy. When I make plans, I do so meticulously, leaving nothing to chance. I'm aware you're a very junior member of the team, you don't play every weekend as you'd have me believe, in fact I doubt whether your services are required more than two weeks out of five. I'm also aware that quite often you're not even chosen as a reserve. So it simply means that on the very rare occasions when you've been included in the team, I'll simply delay the use of your services until you are available. Surely you realise I've had all of that sorted out?'

There was no doubt in my mind, Bergman, willingly or otherwise, had supplied him with the information he required, because the makeup of the teams were pinned up in the gym. Then to compound on my problem, I'd stopped playing football, which meant I'd inadvertently supplied him with access to my services, virtually all year round. With nowhere to turn, finally the inevitable question, 'How often would I be expected to come out here and do the disgusting things you want?'

He stood there, once again chin in hand, obviously giving my question serious consideration before he replied, 'Impossible to say at this stage lad. I've fairly extensive connections amongst those who'll want to use you, but for instance, a lot will depend on who can afford to pay the fee I intend to charge. However, previous experience has told me some will go without eating, if it means they can afford to be with a boy they desire. But there's one thing I can say with certainty, that is the news of your availability, will travel fairly quickly'

I was tempted to plead with him, but knew I'd be wasting my time. In his eyes I was nothing more than an object to use, and if I caused problems, he'd destroy me with as much feeling as if he was killing a fly. If the boys at the school ever saw those photos, and my father came there looking for me as well, there's a chance they'd find me in the main toilet, held down and being abused in a similar fashion to Peter Cameron. We'd met while playing tennis, and after a while had become really good friends, but for a reason I still failed to understand, he'd been singled out as being homosexual. I'd inadvertently walked in on the abuse he was being subjected to, and after having done my best to protect him, had left convinced that if ever threatened with anything similar, I'd fight to a point where they'd have to render me unconscious, before they'd succeed in doing the same shocking things to me.

Apart from what were now those very occasional visits to his room after school, life in general was still pretty good, so surely nobody could blame me if I was determined to keep it that way. So knowing those photos he possessed left me with little choice, I bent down and picked up my clothes and followed the South African back through his study and out into the hall, where my day was made, because Seth was leaning against the wall and waiting for me at the top of the stairs.

Chapter 26

As we approached, there was a total transformation. From lounging arrogantly, the moment his eyes locked on Malcolm, he stood bolt upright, and as the South African spoke to him, he radiated subservience. No more than average height, but extremely powerfully built, his broad, heavily set face was dominated by a large, spreading nose, and his coal black hair and dark eyes, hinted strongly at a liberal dose of Polynesian blood. They chatted together for a few minutes, then Malcolm turned and gestured towards me, indicating I was to join them,

'You're to go downstairs with Seth, and do as he says. Never forget, disobedience could cause you some considerable problems, so don't make the mistake of letting that stubborn streak of yours try to dictate, always be sure to keep it under control.'

Well maybe, I thought, but my problems would be nothing compared to his, when he was trying to catch me. And as Malcolm turned and walked back and disappeared inside his study, Seth stood there and pointedly ran his eyes slowly over my nakedness, 'Alright kid, get that cute little arse of yours downstairs and into the bathroom, and what's more, hurry up about it, you don't need to be shown the way,' but when I was about half way down he added,

'Hang on, don't hurry after all kid. From where I'm standing, you wouldn't believe how much I'm enjoying the movement of those smooth, young buttocks of yours. Malcolm's already informed me of the plans he has for you, and now I know why. Man, are they going to have the time of their lives, playing around with you.'

It seemed it was destined to be one of those days. As if I didn't have enough problems, now another's surfaced. I'd spent those unpleasant hours in the car with him, during which he'd constantly molested me, and now a few minutes with him in the house as well, and already I couldn't tolerate the man anywhere near me. Showing sensible restraint however, was something I still had to learn, so at the bottom of the stairs, and as it turned out, very foolishly, I decided it was my turn. So I stopped and faced him, and while displaying a perfect face that registered mild bewilderment, I asked him, 'Tell me Mister, do you ever get lost while trying to find your way around this house?'

He took the bait that had presumably been so innocently offered, like the proverbial shark,

'What the hell are you talking about, you stupid little bastard. Of course I don't get fucking lost finding my bloody way around, I mean for Christ's sake, why the bloody hell should I?'

I didn't need to be told I was taking a huge risk, but it was too tempting, I couldn't resist it,

'Well you see, I've only known you for a short while, and already I've assessed you as having a brain the size of a pea. So taking into consideration that major disability, I thought there was a good chance you could go upstairs, get

lost, then start running around from room to room, because hard though you'd tried, you couldn't find your way down again?'

You take the risk, you accept the consequences, as I was destined to find out. I was right; he was far from amused, his face changing to a strange shade of purple as he exploded,

'Why you cheeky little shit. Nobody in this house dares to talk to me like that. When I catch you, you little bastard, I'll belt you one right in your fucking mouth.'

Nobody speaks to him like that, I thought, wonder if that includes Malcolm? Somehow I doubt it, you moron, but knowing it was a stupid thing to have done, I took off and bolted, heading at speed down the hall, but he caught up with me at the bathroom door. But contrary to what I was expecting, he opened the door with one hand, and with the other, shoved me into the room.

And instantly I lurched back, at the same time holding my clothing down low as I attempted to cover myself. That weird woman was standing and waiting for me in the centre of the room, smiling, while she looked at me with those unpleasant eyes, although I had to admit she seemed to be taking my nakedness in her stride as she calmly said, 'You'll soon forget what's left of your modesty around here kid, especially considering what you'll be doing. Now place your clothes on the vanity, then get down on your hands and knees, here, right in front of me. You're about to be cleansed, so the men can enjoy that outstanding young body of yours. That's the least we can do for them, considering what they'll be paying.'

She pointed to a spot on the floor where she expected me to kneel, but I stayed exactly where I was. Surely I thought, the woman had to be joking. But I was to find out, much to my detriment, that nothing remotely like joking ever occurred around that house. Suddenly, something resembling a battering ram smashed into the side of my head. The impact sent me flying, with the result I crashed to the floor, hitting my head with another solid thump in the process, before I finished up lying on my back between the toilet and the bidet. Desperately I tried to regain my feet, deciding there seemed more than a slight chance my survival depended on being able to take something in the way of evasive action. But before I could move, a hand wrapped itself around my hair and wrenched viciously forward, so I finished up sitting on my buttocks. I peered vaguely up, and at the same time was left wondering how a large truck had somehow smashed its way into the bathroom, but as the film across my eyes slowly cleared, instead of the bonnet of a truck, I encountered the dubious pleasure of Seth's face almost touching mine. And the sourness of his breath registered as he hissed at me,

'When my wife tells you to do something kid, then get on and fucking do it. Any more hesitation and I'll have the pleasure of taking you apart, you stubborn, cheeky little bastard.'

Through the slight fog that was persisting, a voice drifted in as I sat there blinking up at him, and it was as if it was originating from quite some distance away, as Maria spoke to him,

'Seth, for Christ's sake be careful. You know as well as I the trouble Malcolm's taken to get this kid. He'll go absolutely rampant if because of you, he finishes up with marks or bruises.'

But for some reason, it seemed Seth wasn't in the mood for accepting advice as he replied,

'Shut the fuck up woman. I'll give this little shit marks or fucking bruises. You should have heard the way he spoke to me on the way here,' then he turned to me as he added, 'And you ever so much as talk to me like that again, and you'll really be sorry, you little shit. Now pick up your bloody clothes, put them on the vanity, then get on and do what you were told.'

Part of me was still tempted to resist, but a natural desire to keep on living suggested otherwise, so reluctantly I complied, finishing up kneeling where Maria had indicated. And so began what was to become an odious, and at times perilous relationship with Seth and Maria Wharatene. It rapidly became obvious they were a well matched pair, due to their delight in being involved in any perverted sexual activity. And I was to find the risk associated with Seth's participation was increased to what at times became dangerous levels, by the combination of his naturally brutal nature, and a deep seated racial hatred, that the sight of my blond hair did absolutely nothing to suppress.

There was no doubt that long before I unfortunately became involved with him, he'd accepted that being burdened with an intelligence that hovered consistently around sub zero, if he was going to survive in the adult world, it would be by the use of brawn, never brains. So he was employed on the surface, as an odd job and all round repair man. Accordingly, the gravel drive was constantly raked and kept in pristine condition, the lawns regularly mown, the gardens frequently weeded, fences and gates kept in acceptable condition, and when required, the occasional tree was felled, all of which was designed to enhance even further the already superb presentation the property offered. And as far as that occasional tree was concerned, due to Maria's insistence, a wood burning stove was still in use in the enormous kitchen, so the timber from those trees was split and stacked, so as ready to be used in that old fashioned but apparently highly efficient oven.

During the somewhat sporadic times I was to spend in that repulsive house during the next couple of years, from arrival in mid morning, to departure in early to mid afternoon, on Malcolm's absolute insistence, those hours were always spent naked. Although the ground floor was centrally heated, with heat having a habit of rising, there were times when standing beside that oven proved to be very welcome. I was also to learn that after having been employed long enough, that their loyalty to their employer had been established beyond question, Seth and Maria had been gradually introduced to the erotic world that existed within the walls of that outwardly beautiful home.

Accordingly, Seth's preference for sex with young boys was occasionally catered for, but only as much so as his lust left him all the more reliant on his employer. This effectively left him in the position where he'd do virtually anything for the South African, barely short of murder. And as far as I was concerned, after having experienced firsthand Seth and his inherent brutality, I was left feeling even this was open to question as well. Much to my misery, on

the comparatively rare occasions when Malcolm relented and allowed Seth to indulge himself, or when his employer was away, and he took upon himself to take the risk and do so anyway, the act was performed in a manner specifically designed to cause extreme pain. The physical damage he caused was bad enough, but the humiliation of having to submit to his depravity was often compounded by the fact that Maria would be in the room watching, while her husband indulged himself, while at the same time uttering the most vile, racial profanities.

The foremost mystery relating to this unpalatable couple, as far as I was concerned, was how Seth had managed to suppress his racial disharmony long enough, to be able to bring himself to marry a European woman. Not mind you, that Maria could ever have been considered as being much of a catch. She was short, plain to a point of being classed as haggard, and built with the contours normally associated with a water tank. Also, as if to top all of this off, she'd been blessed with a head of the most shocking, mousy coloured hair, and if all of this didn't add up to being handicap enough, she also had a speech impediment in the form of a distinct lisp, that took me no time at all to start imitating behind her back.

Her official title, that is if one ever existed, was that of housekeeper and cook. As far as the former was concerned, as I saw it, compared to my mother's ability, Maria's, to put it mildly, left a fair amount to be desired, but when it came to her cooking, it would be fair to say she went close to rivalling Mrs. Gossini. However, my extreme dislike of the woman, that similar to her husband, had been established within seconds of meeting her, rapidly descended to that of deep and utter loathing. Therefore, it took me virtually no time at all to become convinced that as husband and wife, it had long before been decreed they were indeed truly meant for each other.

But as I knelt on the floor in the bathroom, Maria turned away and opened one of the doors in the vanity. She extracted a piece of equipment, and the moment it appeared in full view, instantly I knew what it was. Although I'd experienced the cleansing effects of an enema quite some time back, the combination of vague interest, had rapidly turned to shock, horror and acute embarrassment when my mother informed what she intended to do with it, and it meant I most certainly hadn't forgotten what it was. After having become terribly constipated following a brief but unpleasant illness, following the doctor's advice, my mother had insisted on carrying out the distasteful procedure. Having been informed of what came next, I recalled sitting on my buttocks, absolutely refusing to move, but to no avail. Although in the end I'd been forced to admit it had indeed achieved the desired response, in my attempt to retain some portion of my shattered dignity, I'd remained embarrassed to a point where I'd refused to speak to her for two days after. No wonder I still remembered what it was.

But irrespective of the effects the previous distasteful performance had achieved, it was apparent the same thing was to be repeated. She turned on the taps, carefully adjusting until she was satisfied with the temperature, then she filled the container and as she walked around behind me and said, 'Now spread your legs slightly, and rest your forehead on the floor.'

The comment sounded disturbingly familiar, and after my last experience when told to place myself in a similar position, naturally enough, I was slow to respond, and instantly Seth was there before I could blink, towering above and coldly threatening, 'Get on with it kid, I don't like repeating myself, so cooperate, or risk another thump.'

I didn't like the thought of what was to come, but with my head still aching from his last effort, I liked the thought of what he was threatening even less. So I took up the position, and as I did, Maria knelt down and eased the tube well up into my rectum, at the same time leaning forward, so when she spoke I could hear her very clearly, 'Remember, I warned you, and it's happening. I am seeing a whole lot more of you, than you'll ever be seeing of me.'

Once again she chuckled at the crudeness of her joke, so I turned my head as far as I could back towards her and said, 'As far as I'm concerned, all I can say is thank goodness for that.' The silence in the room that followed, seemed to suggest I'd at least held my own during that exchange, but after something like a minute had passed, she said,' Right, it's finished, you've taken the lot, now over to the toilet, quickly, and if you drop any on the floor, it's you who'll be cleaning it up.'

Ten minutes later, the cleansing complete, but more embarrassment as I was carefully washed and dried. Then Seth took over, making me walk on through into the bedroom, following closely just a few menacing paces behind, at the same time issuing instructions,

'Listen carefully to what I tell you kid, because I don't expect to have to repeat myself. You're to always stand facing the window, with your hands either by your side or clasped in front. When your clients enter the room, Malcolm's adamant it's this view of your body that gets them aroused. Can't say I altogether agree, but what Malcolm wants, Malcolm gets, that's what matters around here. So make sure you do it every time kid, understand?'

And although I moved not one single fraction in response, he continued on regardless,

'Your first client will be with you shortly. He's just arrived from the city and walked into the house, so we've timed it perfectly. He'll enter the room through the hall door, and depart via the bathroom. During the allotted time he spends with you, you'll provide him with any form of sex he demands. Make sure that's clear, nothing's forbidden, no matter what he wants, that's what you give him. And be warned, any complaints, and it'll be me sorting you out.'

Standing in that dismal room, I gazed sadly out of the window, across the tar-sealed area to the building beyond. The freshly painted walls shone bright in the late morning sunlight, and the occasional shadow wandered lazily across, caused by the slow moving clouds. I thought about those hours I'd spent in that shed, convinced what was happening to me was because the devil had found me first. That strange woman at Bible Class was always talking about the devil, forever insisting unless we were careful, we'd all meet him in hell. Much as I was tempted, I never dared to argue, never dared to say a thing, because she'd always insisted she knew it all, that hell was deep in the bowels of the earth. But after all this time, I strongly suspected she was wrong, and it was my mother

who was right. She always maintained that hell was where you made it, so maybe I was making it here in this room instead.

Seeing as I'd failed to acknowledge his last instructions, I wondered if he was considering hitting me again, but I sure hoped not. That previous blow could be compared to being kicked by a mule, and it had taken me some time to realise he'd only hit me with his forearm, not even his fist. So I breathed a faint sigh of relief when he moved towards the door, but when he got there he turned and said, 'Now I'm going to leave you with your thoughts kid, and always remember, if any of them ever attempt to get rough, all you do is yell. Can't have an important money spinner like you getting hurt, can we? Make sure you supply him with some quality entertainment, and here's something else for you to think about. Sooner or later Malcolm's going to allow me to do it with you kid, and when that happy day eventuates, rest assured I'll show you a few tricks you never knew existed.'

At least one thing was certain through all of this. He sure as hell topped the list of people I wished had never existed, and even if he half killed me, I was determined to say something to the moron, 'Just do me a favour Seth, and go and get bloody lost. You think you're so clever, but the truth is you're nothing but a dormant pain in the arse.'

However, rather than take offence, he just grinned straight back, 'Look who's talking about a pain in the arse. That's your territory kid, and as far as getting lost is concerned, I guess I may as well. You're going to be much too busy doing a variety of interesting things, and placing yourself in interesting positions, to have any time left for entering into small talk with me.'

He closed the door gently behind him, and I could still hear him laughing as he walked off down the hall. 'He's just arrived from the city,' he'd said, which meant one thing. Malcolm had been so sure he had me where he wanted me, he'd booked his so called 'clients' knowing full well he'd effectively left me with no alternative. If only I possessed the courage to tell him to go to hell. Maybe if I did, that woman in Bible Class would show him where it was.

A few more agonizing minutes, then the first man stepped into the room. I could sense he'd positioned himself directly behind me, and while he remained there, I was convinced I could feel his eyes roaming over my body until he said, 'Right, I guess you can turn around kid. I'm certainly hoping the front looks as tempting as the rear.' Another thirty seconds while he fondled me, then he placed his hands on my arms and drew me to him, 'Yes, quite a bloody little looker, aren't you? Must admit I was expecting someone a bit older, but this is excellent, the younger the better as far as I'm concerned. Must admit, taking into consideration the standard they seem to be supplying, this might almost be worth the exorbitant fee they're charging. Anyway kid, we may as well get started, I'm only allowed so long with you, so go and lie on your back on the bed. First we'll spend some time getting to know all about each other, before I get you to turn over, so I can entertain myself in another particular area, and I know you don't have to guess where that is kid.'

Almost twenty minutes later, still lying face down on the bed where he'd left me. Quickly I brushed my hand across my eyes. Had to admit it, tears were lingering, but I was adamant, stay away they must. I'd made a firm promise to

myself; there was no way I was going to allow any of them to make me cry. Maria walked in, holding a small enamel dish, along with the flannel and towel she'd used earlier in the bathroom, draped over her arm, 'Right kid, stay lying as you are, but swing your legs so your feet are on the floor. Can't have the next one complaining because he's expected to do it with soiled goods, can we?'

She did what she had to, carefully wiping and drying, then departed. Another few minutes, spent nervously waiting, then the door opened as the next came into the room. The misery associated with the filth and misery of the morning, extended into the afternoon. As I lay yet again face down on the bed while another satisfied himself, I thought about the South African. How I hated that callous bastard, sitting up there in the comfort and seclusion of his study, apparently unconcerned about this disgusting business he'd devised, totally insensitive to what he knew these men were doing to me in this room.

Finally the man finished with me and left, and a few moments later Maria walked in, so I asked her, ' Please Maria, tell me how many more are there, how long before I can go home?'

Once again she carefully washed and dried my anus, penis and testicles before she replied,

'Look, just accept it kid, you're going to have to get used to it, because if what I'm led to understand is right, you're not left with much of an alternative. But one thing's certain, you just have to accept what happens to you in this room. Let's face it kid, it only stops when they've all had you, but as far as today is concerned, I'm fairly certain there's only one more, so once he's enjoyed himself, that's it.'

Cleaned and prepared as usual, then the last one sidled in. Fifteen minutes or there about, and he departed, apparently very well satisfied. I stood up from where I'd been kneeling on the Persian rug, desperate to get to the bathroom and rinse my mouth out thoroughly. One thing remained consistent. Having to perform oral sex made me nothing short of lethal. As I walked into the bathroom, heading for the basin, for no reason other than I'd been left in a foul mood, I snapped at Maria, and without hesitation she instantly snapped straight back,

'You be careful boy. Any more cheek from you, and I'll get Seth in here. After what you've just been experiencing, the last thing you need is him kicking that cute little bum of yours.' She was right, I didn't want the man anywhere near me, so I heeded her threat while she cleaned me, and cooperated when she told me to bend well over, then after she'd fussed around, jumped then yelped when she inserted something up my rectum,

'Hell Maria, what are you doing, for Pete's sake, what's that you've just put up inside me?'

'It's what's known as a tampon kid. Women use them for their period, and in a situation such as yours they're ideal as well. Saves any risk of your mother querying the soiled state of your underwear. Keep it up there until you get home, then use the string to pull it out, then flush it down the toilet, but always check the bowl is clear after. Solves any possible problems kid.'

The ride back to the city behind me, and some painful pedalling saw me at the golf club.

A couple of caddies waved, urging me to join them on the putting green, where we competed against each other for tees. But after making my excuses I slipped away, down to a special spot I'd discovered, deep back amongst some trees, while searching for lost golf balls. As I lay back on a cushion of soft grass, with the aromatic smell of pine needles hanging heavy in the air, I thought about what I'd just experienced at that house. I knew I'd been frightened by the threat of exposure before, and I knew I was literally terrified of it happening now. Lying back with my hands clasped behind my head, asking for forgiveness, thinking of carefree times that had somehow passed. A brief time to soak up the peace and fresh air, willing the combination to help with the shame and the pain, before I headed for the safety of home.

Chapter 27

Back at school on the Monday; greeted with some good news for a change. Bergman would be away for at least three weeks, on one of his so called official visits to only he knew where. Brilliant, three weeks of guaranteed peace at school, the only down side being it left Hull in an unquestioned position of control as far as physical education was concerned. In an apparent burst of enthusiasm, no doubt fuelled by Bergman's absence, he stood on the raised stage at assembly and announced to one and all, that all boys would take part in a 'cross country' run. 'There will be no exceptions' he ranted, from his elevated position of power, 'all boys will take part, other than those who already possess a sickness exemption.'

And there was no doubt that I, along with probably many others, was far from impressed at what was looming large as a decidedly daunting prospect. At around ten years of age, I'd started to suspect something wasn't quite right. In simple terms, I was starting to find I lacked the level of endurance that came naturally to other boys. So alright, I played a lot of sport successfully, and was known throughout the school because of it. But I was all too aware, that in cricket I had to bowl in short, sharp bursts, in athletics and swimming, I only competed in short, non endurance events. In tennis I'd had my fair share of success, but only if the match was over fairly quickly, if it dragged on, I knew I'd be struggling. As far as boxing was concerned, no undue problems, I could handle three, short sharp rounds as effectively as anybody, but it was at football, where my lack of endurance was exposed.

During one enthusiastic and fast paced game, greatly embarrassed, I'd had to ask the coach to take me off the field, and at home I'd complained to my mother over my regret at having been forced to do so, and her reply had been rather tense, certainly not sympathetic,

'What a stupid thing to have done Mathew. You're a perfectly healthy boy, and I've no doubt the rest of the boys were as tired as you, yet they persevered and finished the game. I'm slightly disappointed in you, so try and make sure you never make the same mistake again.'

And it hurt, but I remained convinced, no matter what she felt, something wasn't quite right.

On the morning of the so called 'cross country' I woke hoping to see a dark, forbidding sky, flashes of lightning, gale force winds and intermittent torrential downpours. Instead the sky was perfectly clear with barely a cloud to be seen, and I rode to school accompanied by a soft, cool breeze, and humidity that was virtually non-existent. In other words, perfect conditions for what lay ahead. The first boys were scheduled to start around ten in the morning, and Hull, in his infinite wisdom, had assessed the time required to complete the course at being around an hour and twenty minutes, depending of course, on the varying levels of fitness. My estimation of the time I'd require to get around the bloody course, hovered around one and a half days. Hull had stationed himself at the entrance

to the main school gates, which was where our names were ticked off, and our starting times recorded, with the time we finished to be written in alongside that. As I reluctantly fronted up in my shorts and singlet, he cast me an unpleasant, lingering sneer, a reminder that due to our last confrontation, we were never destined to be mutually compatible, which suited me just fine.

And how the definition of a 'cross country run' was devised, completely eluded me. The route we were to take ran around a local hill in the suburb, which meant the availability of any 'country' was totally non-existent, meaning we were running on concrete pavement the whole way. So reluctantly I set off, working on the theory the sooner it was over the better. The first stage of the route, consisted of a four hundred metre run up the road fronting the school to the main road at the top. The slight upward gradient was so minor it was barely perceptible, yet by the time I arrived, my heart was pounding, I was sweating profusely, and felt a strong tingling feeling in my fingers. I turned right, just as I was supposed to, and ran on towards and finally through a small shopping centre, convinced everyone was smiling sympathetically, with that pitying aloofness that adults radiate, that in reality is saying, I'm glad it's you, you poor unfortunate little bugger, and not me.

Now well past the shops with the hill clearly in view. From the school it had never appeared to be all that much at all, nothing more than an unnecessary blot on the landscape, but from my new vantage point, it looked as big as Everest, and equally as daunting. One small mercy, thank God we had to run around it, rather than over. I knew I was supposed to be jogging. In reality, I was aware I was plodding, something that was effectively proven by a group of five boys, who passed me as if I was standing still. But with that sneering look on Hull's face acting as an incentive, I pushed on, determined one way or the other that I could do it, even if I didn't arrive until nightfall. It seemed to be getting warmer by the minute, and the pavement harder by the second, each step now jarring through me like a hammer hitting an anvil.

Finally I was left without an option, I simply had to stop and take a breather. With my left arm supported by an old wooden fence, I glanced across into a property, and noticed a boy from the school sitting on some wooden steps, probably built the same time as the fence. He held what appeared to be a glass of ice cold lemonade in his hand. An old lady was standing on the verandah above him, probably his grandmother, and the source of the refreshment, I decided. He held the glass out towards me in a slightly mocking gesture, and the condensation caused by the ice cool drink was clearly visible as he upended the glass and downed the lot. I felt that at least the bastard could have saved me a mouthful.

I watched carefully, hoping he'd choke on it, but he didn't, simply grinned at me instead, so suitably put out, I pressed on. Perspiration was running down my face and back, in fact, when I thought about it, I decided there wasn't a part of me that wasn't sweating. More torturous metres covered, and as I looked up and beyond, the endless pavement appeared to be disappearing into the horizon, and with my heart pounding, I turned down into the road that led to the school, with the slight downhill gradient making the jarring even worse still.

There was a table just inside the entrance, with a prefect sitting behind it, and Hull in all his importance, standing behind him again. The prefect carefully checked my name, as if he didn't already know it, the officious pick, after all I played cricket with him; we were in the same bloody team, the idiot. He wrote in my arrival time, and with highly irritating casualness, Hull slowly leant forward and peered, then sarcastically commented, 'Good grief Colbert, what on earth have you been doing out there, having a picnic? You ought to be ashamed of that time, a child at kindergarten could have done better.'

Things hadn't changed much in that direction, frankly, I couldn't care less what he thought, because all I knew was I felt ill, and above all I needed some shade, and what was more I needed it quickly. The nearest on offer was being provided by a large, spreading tree that was growing over near the main entrance in the centre of a circular grassed area, immediately adjacent to the main school buildings. As I headed slowly across the tar-sealed drive towards it, I realised that since stopping at the table, my legs felt as if they consisted of rubber, because I was staggering.

The effort required to step up onto the grass, seemed to take the last vestige of strength I possessed, and as I dropped to my knees I looked around, and it seemed as if from somewhere a fog had descended. I couldn't understand it, it was a perfect day, yet nothing was clear, and at the same time I could hear this strange rushing sound in my ears. I knew the last time I'd heard anything like that, had been at the rugby game, and now my heart seemed to be lurching around in my chest, similar to when I'd had to ask the coach to replace me on the field. That was the last thing I remembered.

This time when consciousness returned, I wasn't lying on my stomach on a concrete floor, I was flat on my back in the soft comfort of the bed in the first aid room. Someone had placed an ice cool cloth on my forehead which felt marvellous, and as I glanced down I realised my singlet had been removed, and going by the coolness over my body, the cloth had passed over there as well. Apparently one of those tall masters had carried me up here, and now an assortment of others were hovering around with very worried looks on their faces. Hull wasn't amongst them, but one of the others came over and assured me, 'Just lie back and take it easy lad. We've contacted a doctor, he'll be here in minutes.'

Sounded alright to me, so I did just that, enjoying the coolness, and I didn't feel like doing all that much anyway. A couple of minutes and he was right, the doctor strode in, short and plump, his ample stomach and hind quarters covered by a tweed coat and a pair of tan trousers that reminded me of Malcolm's, and a mass of greying and thinning hair falling in all directions, and with a black bag and gruff but somehow friendly voice completing the picture of the experienced and no nonsense family GP as he barked out to one and all, 'Now what's been going on here? Someone said the youngster had passed out. Well kids his age don't pass out for no reason, so fill me in, what was he doing immediately before this happened?'

Deathly silence ruled for seconds, then a reply from one of them, I had no idea which one,

'He'd just finished competing in a cross country run.'

Was I imagining it, or did I notice a sudden surge of interest from the doctor's direction,

'So, a run around the suburb, you say. How long was this so called run supposed to take?'

'I understand it was supposed to take about ninety minutes, or something close to that.'

I was starting to get the feeling it was best Hull wasn't here, as the doctor thundered on,

'And I presume any of the boys who had anything like medical problems were exempt?'

'Ah, well, all boys were to take part, unless a problem had been previously identified.'

The doc seemed to take a very exaggerated and extremely long breath before he continued,

'So what you're saying is, unless the school had been previously informed of a health problem, no so called excuses would be accepted from that time on, is that correct?' He lifted his head and gazed around the room as he asked, 'Why was such a dubious decision made?'

'The master felt too many boys would try for an exemption, so as to avoid having to run.'

'Yes, well I can see the basis for a few problems forming after such a decision, but alright, speaking casually of course, if any damage has been done, it's a bit late to be worrying about it now. So let's see if we can find out what the story is with this boy.'

He poked and prodded and asked a series of stupid questions, that as far as I could make out doctors always asked anyway, then took out his stethoscope and placed it on my chest. He listened, moved it, listened again, moved it once more, listened, then suddenly exploded,

'Jesus Christ, if ever there's an example of what I've being trying to point out, it would be this boy. He has a heart murmur so severe, I could practically hear the bloody thing without even having to use this.' He held up the stethoscope and shook it while making his point,

'Who the hell is this person who made this decision? I'd certainly like a word or two with him, the bloody fool. Tell me lad, are your parents aware of this condition of yours?'

I looked up and shook my head, aware I was letting Hull off the hook. The words 'heart murmur' had never been mentioned around our house, and now I was keen to know what it was. And as he sat on the bed and explained, in some small way I was relieved, after all, it explained a lot as far as I was concerned. He insisted on meeting my parents the following day, my mother shedding a few tears as she mentioned her reaction to my coming home early after that rugby game. The next question was obvious, what could be done about it? His answer, in a word, very little. Due to the problem, I was apparently functioning with slightly elevated blood pressure, but considering the drugs that were available, the decision was made to let things rest where they were, 'Wouldn't prescribe them to a youngster his age, in fact I wouldn't be caught feeding them to my neighbour's barking dog,' was his blunt reply, 'The boy's obvious good health

202

will stand by him for quite a while, he's simply to stay away from endurance sports, and that means no more bloody stupid cross country running, and I'd prefer, no more rugby football. They're looking at it now, and I've no doubt that before too long, heart valve replacements will become quite common, and I'm sure he'll manage fine until then. But don't forget, a good night's sleep is essential to help with such a condition.'

That had an ominous sound to it. If it wasn't bad enough having my mother insisting on an excessive vegetable intake, now I was at risk of being threatened with ridiculously early bed times as well. But as far as football was concerned, I couldn't care less, I'd found other things to take its place anyway, with golf heading the list.

Chapter 28

With Malcolm remaining blissfully unaware of my 'medical situation' his prediction had proved to be correct, there was absolutely no consistency relating in his demands as to when my services were required out at his house. Quite some time back my father had gone to some lengths to explain to me what was required to make a boy a top caddie, and by following his advice to the letter, I'd rapidly become acknowledged as being one of the most sought after caddies at the club, with the result my services in this much more acceptable direction, were constantly in demand.

However, due to the erratic nature of Malcolm's requirements, I was forced to stop taking any forward bookings for my services on a Saturday. This arrangement left me flexible to a point where I could make myself available if he proved to be forthcoming with one of his obnoxious demands, or happily, if nothing eventuated from that direction, I simply rode out to the club where I never encountered any problems in getting a player to caddie for anyway. Another situation that played a major part in my deception, was my father never played golf on a Saturday, his time being spent at his factory instead, with this leaving him in a position of being unable to confirm whether I'd been out at the golf club or not.

So with this arrangement providing both flexibility and reluctant availability, another few months slipped past, but quite unexpectedly, the inevitable question of Malcolm's own sexual requirements suddenly emerged. From the time we'd parted outside his study, I hadn't come into contact with him since, as presumably, he remained alone and aloof upstairs. But on that day, after being prepared in the bathroom, as I turned to head for the bedroom, Seth appeared and called me back, 'Hey, not so fast kid, Malcolm wants you, so you're required upstairs. A surprise actually, because it doesn't happen all that often, but apparently he wants you today.'

With Seth leading the way, I trudged along dejectedly behind, and on arrival and swinging my eyes around the room, in my absence, if anything his bedroom appeared even more elegant than what I remembered, but my brief appraisal was abruptly terminated as Seth said,

'See those on the end of the bed kid? Go and put them on, and no nonsense, understand?'

I walked over, and on arrival received a shock, as 'those' turned out to be a pair of girl's panties. As I swung around and glared, anticipating my refusal to comply, Seth got in first,

'You've been warned kid, don't give me any trouble. This is what he wants, and as far as you and I are concerned, this is what he gets. Now I won't repeat myself, put the fucking things on. The fact you don't like it, doesn't come in to it, so put the bloody things on, or else.'

The warning signs had been there all morning, Seth was in one of his moods, and with his ever present lust for violence surfacing, my instincts were

telling me to do what I had to, up here and down stairs, then get back to the city as quickly as my duties here allowed. So I complied with Seth's demands, and to add to my humiliation, the garment fitted as if it had been tailor made, and as I stood facing him in my embarrassment, Seth instantly added,

'You sure as hell look cute kid, he's going to love that. Now get up on the bed and wait for him, and be warned. We both know he can be difficult at the best of times, but when it comes to this sort of thing, he's nothing short of bloody lethal. So it's a case of making sure you give him exactly what he wants, and you'll be alright, but give him any trouble because of that stubborn streak of yours, and it's me who'll have to come in and pick up the pieces. And as soon as he's finished with you, come straight back downstairs. You know what some of them are like if they're kept waiting, and with this visit being unexpected, I don't want to have to face additional problems down there.'

He turned and strolled out, shutting the door quietly behind him, so I immediately turned my attention to my unwanted piece of clothing. The material was silken smooth, and no doubt very expensive, although I doubted the cost factor would have proved a problem, because there was so little of it. So with nothing to do until Malcolm graced me with his presence, I slipped off the bed and wandered over to the mirror on the wardrobe. The high cut and general shaping of the garment, further accentuated what were already a pair of smooth, coltish legs, and as I stood there wistfully gazing at my reflection, slowly I was forced to comprehend the bisexual attraction the garment would create for a certain type of man. I had to reluctantly admit that in its own subtle way, it would cause a sexual impact that for some, would prove absolutely impossible to resist. And in addition to this, add a tanned and smoothly muscled young body, achieved by a diet of virtually non-stop sport, and I could imagine the effect on that deviant type of man, would be nothing short of devastating.

But no more time to dwell on my misfortune, a faint noise from the adjoining room made me wary, so I instantly glided over and lay back down on the bed, and just as well, because seconds later Malcolm strode into the room. He was wearing a white dressing gown, but after he'd walked over and stood at the end of the bed, from where he proceeded to run his eyes slowly over my body, suddenly he slipped it free, and in doing so exposed a strong, well put together physique, and twenty minutes later my time with him was abruptly terminated. 'I've been getting very good reports about you lad, and this little bit of personal experience has confirmed why. As far as I'm concerned, you more than met my expectations, and quite frankly, I couldn't have asked for a much better experience, but now that we're finished, you'd better get back downstairs.'

I didn't need to be told twice, so I departed at speed, but as I glanced back as I was closing the door, he was lying on his back, gazing blissfully up at the ceiling, giving the impression seconds after the act was completed, he'd forgotten anything of any consequence had occurred. Although the first of my very rare visits to his bedroom was over, I was still to discover that living with the trauma of sexual abuse was one thing, surviving the effects of severe physical abuse was entirely another. But through it all, Malcolm remained an

enigma, swinging from moods bordering on lethal insanity, to periods of kindness and compassion.

Considering his obvious intelligence, early on, I'd found it hard to understand why he was prepared to place himself in the precarious position of being involved with child sex, especially considering I'd accidently overheard him say something like…'I'm not prepared to take the slightest risk, because I'm aware this part of the world is blessed with an honest and very efficient police force' …However, as the months past, the answer became extremely simple, the remuneration he received through his various projects, far outweighed anything else, and as it turned out, additional conformation of that, was not very far away.

As always, it was a Saturday, and after a lull of a few weeks, my presence had been demanded out at the house, and on arrival, Maria had hardly dampened my spirits when she informed me only three men were expected. The last departed, and I headed for the bathroom, then following that, being allowed to get dressed for the trip back to the city. As Maria finished with me and I went to pick up my clothes, Seth stopped me, 'Hold on kid, not so fast, Malcolm wants you for something else, and you sure as hell won't be needing your clothes for that. Brother, have I been waiting to be able to watch this.'

With a hand clasped firmly around my neck, he steered me down the hall and over to a far corner of the huge house, where I'd never been even close to before. Finally he stopped, tapped lightly on a door, then on receiving muffled permission to enter, eased me on into the room. Similar to most others in the house, it was expansive, but even though it was a clear, bright day, the curtains were drawn, and compensating for the lack of natural light were a series of lamps, the illumination from which was directed at a large bed, that was covered in a spotless, white sheet. To the left, there was a chair, to the right a table, on which had been placed a series of fittings and equipment, that at that time meant absolutely nothing to me at all. But by far the most dominant item in the room was a camera, mounted on a tripod that was positioned slightly back from but directly in front of the bed. With alarm bells now loudly ringing, my eyes flashed around the rest of the room, finally stopping at another chair that was positioned well back over towards the far wall. And the reason why my eyes had come to an abrupt halt, was that slumped in it was another boy, and through my concern it registered, at least we had one thing in common. This new and unexpected arrival was as naked as I was.

Then to add even further to my concern, Malcolm suddenly appeared and calmly said,

'Well now young Mathew, the time has arrived to see what sort of an actor we can make out of you. However, I don't anticipate encountering too many problems in that direction. If you can combine those blond good looks of yours with just doing as you're told, I've no doubt you'll manage beautifully.'

So late on that Saturday morning, there was a duel introduction. The first, was to one Master James Te Kuni, and the second, to one of Malcolm's other thriving business ventures, that being the sewer level enterprise of child pornography.

And although fate had decreed I was to become acquainted with James in a highly sexual and therefore distressing manner, the fact was that through it all, a very close friendship developed. Although similar to how it had been with Adrian, with us both being within months of the same age, that was where any attempt at further comparison ended, because in every other direction, we were about as opposite as two boys could ever be. Occasionally, after we'd first met, I'd lie in bed at night and wonder how it was James and I got on as well as we did, but in the end came to the decision the reason was perfectly simple. James was the complete opposite to Ivan. Where Ivan's name had been European, but in appearance he qualified as a full blooded Maori, with James, the situation was completely reversed. With a skin tone barely more bronzed than my own, the only obvious evidence pertaining to his Polynesian origin, apart from his surname, were two huge, smouldering dark eyes. It seemed to me his outrageously handsome features had been specifically sculptured for the sole purpose of melting countless female hearts. Time however, was to prove this assumption on my part to be totally incorrect, because I was to discover that James was completely, utterly and hopelessly gay. But undaunted by his sexuality, he proceeded to breeze through life with an infectious, happy go lucky attitude that endeared him to me, mainly because it was in complete contrast to Ivan's belligerence and constant unpleasantness. Also, unlike Ivan, James moved with the grace of a young gazelle, and as far as I was concerned, his natural poise and balance should have seen him excelling at any number of sports. But rather than unduly exerting himself in such an unnecessary fashion with such trivialities, he chose to stand aloof, taking each day as it came, and approaching life with a 'to hell with it all' attitude, that no doubt provided plenty of variety, and was something I was certain he could thank his ancestors for as well.

Having beckoned to James to come over, Malcolm transferred his attention to yours truly,

'As far as what happens in this room is concerned Mathew, let's just say it will give you the opportunity to display your considerable talents to a very appreciative audience. For a number of years I've been involved in producing a series of magazines, photos and the occasional film, for the benefit of the many thousands of people out there who know how to appreciate the naked juvenile body. Now the fact is a surprisingly large percentage of these people consider the ultimate viewing spectacle is watching two boys indulging in sex, and it goes without saying, that's where you and James are about to become involved. Let's face it lad, physically you're both ideal, and when we consider your all round good looks, with one so dark, and the other blond, we find we have at our disposal what could be considered in certain circles as the perfect combination. There's no doubt about it Mathew, developing those photos of you with those other lads in that shed, has proved to be most fortunate.'

And yet again that all too familiar feeling of fear churned in my stomach, then started to move up, finishing by tightening like a knot in my throat. That may be his opinion, but for me, surely it was the beginning of the end. I glanced across, and it was as if a picture appeared on the wall in front of me, as effectively as if it had been projected there. A picture of this dark, handsome

boy and myself, locked together in a homosexual embrace, then continuing to perform a series of degrading acts, while an audience, over the years of God knows how many, sat wherever they were and watched. I thought about what I'd already endured, and accepted it had been my choice, rather than facing years of disgrace and torment, but having my face and other bodily parts placed on display through a series of pornographic publications was something else entirely. But at the precise moment I turned to Malcolm, desperate to try and make him see something like reason, the door was flung open, and another man strode into the room. Paying me not one scrap of attention in the process, he bounded over to the table on which he placed with a highly audible thump, what looked like to me to be a very expensive camera.

Rickie Tostavin was a slightly built, wisp of a man, with a broad English accent that faintly reminded me of my grandfather. With his constant, bordering on perpetual motion, Rickie was the closest I was to ever come to a hyperactive adult. I'd encountered a boy with a similar complaint at Intermediate School, and he'd just about driven the class and teacher crazy, to a point where it finally had reached a point where he'd had to be removed. But as far as Rickie was concerned, the roundness of his boyish looking face was enhanced even further by a broad forehead, from which his hair was rapidly receding.

When he spoke, which was often, and whether his opinion was required or not, he did so with a static delivery which combined perfectly with his constant movement. Accordingly, there were many times when I wished I could find that elusive button, that when pushed, would actually succeed in turning him off. But at that time I remained blissfully unaware there was to come a day after which I was prepared to forgive him for anything. During the course of the brutality that those concerned were indulging in, it was his intervention that saved me from serious injury, and taken to the extreme, could well have saved my life.

Rickie was direct to a point of rudeness, and he seemed a perfect example of someone who'd send Malcolm demented. I wondered for quite some time how the volatile South African managed to endure the situation, because the two men constantly argued like there was no tomorrow, but the reason didn't take all that long to become obvious. Rickie was an absolute master photographer, and once installed behind a camera, there were few, according to Malcolm, who could compete with him. His cameras were Rickie's life, and as time progressed, something in the way of a loose relationship developed between us, but never a close friendship. As far as I was concerned, the circumstances that had brought us together effectively eliminated any possibility of that.

A more accurate description of what existed between us, would be better described as nearer that of a mutual understanding, and on my part, a thirteen year olds' grudging respect for his so obvious talents, which was all I could muster, considering the manner in which he'd chosen to use them.

Possibly inevitably, there came a time where I was prepared to sit and chat, and as the months passed and the range of our conversations broadened as he became more relaxed in my company, after a little subtle prodding, he told me of his first meeting with Malcolm, and his surprise when confronted with the thriving business the man ran in Cape Town, where he admitted to supplying boys for sex to quite a number of the industrialists and businessmen, and to

some of the crews from the ships that berthed there. He also claimed the explanation Malcolm gave for the financial success of these unwholesome business ventures, because apparently there was more than one, was simple in the extreme. 'Prostitution never varies. It is simple for a man to acquire a woman anywhere. But what is not so often accepted is that a surprising number of men lust to have sex with a boy. Therefore my business approach to this situation has always been quite simple. When they want a boy, they come to me, and they know the boy who's provided has been carefully chosen and meticulously checked, and accordingly, I expect them to pay quite handsomely for the service I have provided.'

Following that discussion, I accepted I'd been meticulously chosen, Bergman's photos had seen to that. But as far as the carefully checked was concerned, all he'd ever done was examine my anus and hold my penis in his hand and comment that he approved of the fact I'd been 'cut'. How that qualified as having been carefully checked was well beyond my powers of comprehension. But with Rickie now in the room, Malcolm walked over and exchanged pleasantries, then entered into a detailed discussion. And as they stood and talked, the other boy in the room got up and eased closer and whispered, 'Have you ever done anything like this before? Not that it matters, if I'm going to be filmed doing it with another boy, I guess it may just as well be with you.'

I took a deep breath as I prepared to cut loose over what was apparently looming, but the blast never eventuated, not at that moment anyway. The two men moved apart, with the Englishman walking over to the table, and Malcolm striding over and talking to us as he approached, 'Now you two, it's time we got started. Get up on the bed and I'll decide what I want from you first.' But where James climbed up, I stood my ground, and in a flash his voice took on that high pitch I'd become so wary of as he snapped at me, 'Don't consider giving me any trouble boy, do as you're told and get up on that bed.'

Similar to how it had been with Hull, I decided I had little choice; it was now or never,

'Malcolm, I just won't do it. You know the only reason why I'm here, but if I agree to do what you say I must, then I may as well give up now. Honestly, literally hundreds of people know my father through his tennis, and possibly even more know him through his business, and a lot of them know me as well. How do I know what they do in the privacy of their homes? It would only take one of them to get their hands on one of your filthy books or photos, and I'd be finished. I accept the chance of it happening is fairly remote, but I'd still have to be out of my mind to take the risk.'

In an instant he was towering over me, his voice trembling with frustration as he said,

'Now you listen boy, and at risk of your life, make sure I never have to repeat myself. Do you honestly think I'd be so stupid as to release what I produce in this pathetic, narrow minded little country? Rest assured lad, I wouldn't waste my time or money. I only produce top class material, and it's released only where it's appreciated, and that's in Europe, where I've already established a grateful clientele of very wealthy people. They appreciate the

quality of what I supply for them, and as a result, what I receive in the way of payment from them, just isn't possible in this boring, pathetic part of the world.'

Must admit I was tempted. I mean, if he found this country so pathetic and boring, one had to ask one's self, why was he here anyway? Could it possibly be due to the fact he was forced to make a rather hasty exit from South Africa, perhaps due to the authorities increasing interest in his odious operations. There was also a chance he was having to be very careful here, after all, I'd heard him mention about our efficient police force. Maybe with any luck he'd consider moving again, and if that were the case, I'd be one of the first to offer to help with the packing. Alright, so maybe it was just wishful thinking, but considering what he'd said, there didn't seem to be much of a chance of any of his pornographic efforts rearing their heads around here. At least that was some consolation.

It seemed his anger subsided as quickly as it had flared, so this time obeying his instructions, I climbed up on the bed with James. Rickie carefully adjusted the lighting, interspersed with the occasional glance through his view finder, meticulously checking, then rechecking every minor little detail. Malcolm moved closer, issuing quiet instructions, in his own way, equally as fastidious as his photographer. It was apparent the pair of them were following a well established format, constantly fussing, forever adjusting, until James and I were in exactly the position they wanted. Now the intermittent flash from the camera, as Rickie started to take his photos, the loud clacks from those expensive shutters reverberating around the room, bouncing off the walls like an echo around a canyon.

Malcolm continued to stand close by, occasionally stepping in and physically moving us into the next position for the act he wanted to film. Seth also stood leaning against a wall and watching, not missing a thing, relishing what was happening in front of him. Just once our eyes met, and the look in his, coupled with the leer on his face, guaranteed I never made the same mistake again. Now time to find out what that collection of fittings and equipment on the table were used for. The restrictive feel of leather restraints on my wrist and ankles brought back unpleasant memories, as did the rubber fitting that was secured around my privates, and the large plug of some kind that was inserted up my rectum. Gagged also, but this time the leather fitting more for visual effect than anything else. With James having been trussed in a similar fashion, gradually the fittings were removed, allowing the variety of acts to commence, finally lying groin to mouth, waiting for Malcolm to indicate when the dual oral act was to start. And just before it did, James whispered, partly in humour, partly concern, 'Remember, you're not allowed to bite,' and I replied in kind, 'the deal is, I won't bite you, as long as you don't bite me.'

Riding home on my bike, a few tears flowing, mortified over what had occurred. If my eyes were still red when I arrived, and any awkward questions were asked, as always, at least I had that covered. As I lay in bed that night, I thought about what Seth had said on the way back to the bathroom, 'Hell, what you've just been through is nothing kid, compared to some of the things I've heard Malcolm talk about. So wait until the really erotic stuff starts. Going by your reaction today, you'll wonder what's struck you.'

And his comment, 'going by your reaction today' also caused me concern. Did that casual remark I'd made to James, mean I was starting to accept that form of sex as being an integral part of my life? Was what I was being subjected to, slowly but irrevocably leading me down a similar path to what these decadent men were following?

I thought about it long and hard, and decided definitely not, but there was only one certain way to find out. I'd experienced a variety of sex acts with James, I'd been subjected to every act that existed by his clients, so now as I saw it, it was essential I experienced a girl, but the big question was, which girl? Out of the comparatively few girls I knew, one stood out, and her name was Allison, and over the months, we'd become friendly at the Council Pool. In my eyes, she was what a girl around our age should be, quiet, gentle, and possessing a lithe young body, formed by hours spent in the water, and with her raven hair and lightly tanned skin making her in my eyes anyway, a junior version of my mother. But above all else, I was aware she'd previously made it tactfully known around the pool, that she and I would definitely be compatible. It took three visits before I met up with her, and another before I plucked up the courage to ask, and it happened in one of the dressing cubicles, while a couple of her friends stood guard outside. The men who came into the bedroom may be using my body to obtain the satisfaction they desired, but I was now certain where my preferences lay.

A number of weeks passed before I was summoned to appear at the house, the first to walk into the bedroom, a rather stately, broad shouldered man, probably I'd guessed in his late forties, with a thick head of silver hair, a solicitor, who'd already established himself as a regular. I knew this was so, because while browsing through the paper, I'd found him smiling back at me in the social section, his arm protectively around a woman, presumably his wife, photographed with a group, while they were attending some legal function. Idly I wondered what his lady would think, if she was aware of where he spent some of his Saturdays. Almost without thinking, and knowing my father had finished with the paper, I tore out the article and hid it in my bedroom. The next, nothing other than a nondescript will of the wisp, who glided nervously into the room, quickly satisfied himself, then even more nervously still, scuttled out again. I wondered how someone like him, who gave the impression of not mixing in paedophile circles, had found out about Malcolm's operation. Possibly the South African was right, the news relating to my 'availability' was spreading quickly and also widely.

Once again the door to the bathroom opened as Maria came in, with her usual enamel dish and towels at the ready, 'Let's check you out again kid, only one more of your clients to go, then you'll be able to take off home, or do you intend to go and caddie or play some golf?'

The woman annoyed me like nobody else, well, no other woman anyway, and how did she know I played golf? I'd certainly never mentioned it as I snapped at her, 'I've told you before, and I'll tell you again Maria, they're not my bloody clients, they're Malcolm's, so try and do me a favour and get the difference to sink into that thick head of yours. Honest, when it comes to lack of brains, you're as bad as your dormant husband.'

She tossed her head, completed her duties and strutted out. Looks like I might have offended her. My heart's bleeding all over the Persian rug. The hall door opened, the last man came in.

The aggression that came with him seemed to fill the room. No more than medium height, but very solidly built, his rather florid face complimented a head of crew cut, auburn hair, that stood straight up, like the bristles on an upturned broom, and in doing so, somehow seemed to add to the tension he'd brought with him. As he started undressing, he snapped out instructions, apparently attempting to give the impression he was no man to trifle with. But with his head turned, I failed to hear him, so when he turned back and found I hadn't responded, he took it as a defiant lack of cooperation, and accordingly, that red hair of his practically ignited as he snarled at me, 'What do you think you're doing boy? Get on and do as I said. I'm not parting with this sort of money to be defied by a little shit like you.'

On completion of this tirade, and determined to show he meant business, he lunged forward and grabbed and then twisted my arm viciously, and that was when my own fuse ignited, as I proceeded to wrench myself free as I said, 'I warn you Mister, keep your hands to yourself. I couldn't care how much you've paid, that's your stupid fault. All I care about is the fact I'm not here to be bullied by you.'

And the response was quite spectacular as he exploded, 'Why you little bastard, daring to talk back to me like that. I'll do what I fucking please with you, and apart from the obvious, it'll include teaching you some much needed manners.'

He lumbered forward, aiming an open handed slap at my face, which I avoided. But being made to look awkward and foolish inflamed him even more, so he tried again, this time wildly swinging his fist, which I also avoided with nonchalant ease, causing him to miss his mark by the proverbial country mile. But the next mistake on my part was destined to have dreadful repercussions. Born directly from those reflexes that had been instilled in me from Albie, and with the flame that had previously been flickering, now fanned by instant loathing, very foolishly I retaliated. Looping in a swinging right hand punch very hard, and I must admit, rather low, my fist literally thudded into his groin.

The effect was instantaneous as he staggered back, letting out a faint moan as he did so, then he bent well forward, arms wrapped around, obviously in a lot of pain, and needing to take the time required to recover. So quite a few seconds past while he regained his composure and slowly straightened, his face still ashen with pain as he stood there gaping.

Then suddenly he started to shuffle back, apparently intent on putting some distance between this violent thirteen year old and himself, but slight amusement on my part quickly changed to concern as he proceeded to shriek at the top of his lungs, 'Quick, someone get into this bloody room, I can't fucking believe it, this little bastard punched me, I didn't do a thing to him, didn't even touch him, and the little bastard punched me in the groin.'

It took no time at all, literally seconds for Seth to rush into the room and place himself between us as he shouted, ' For Christ's bloody sake, what's going on in here, what's with all the bloody noise?'

The toad seemed in danger of choking as he replied, 'What's going on? I'll tell you what's going on. The little shit punched me in the groin, that's what's going on. Hadn't done a thing to him, hadn't even touched him,' and although it didn't seem possible, his face managed to get redder still as he continued, 'and I want my fucking money back, so where's the guy who runs this fucking operation? It's him I demand to speak to, and unless I get my money back real quick, then stand by for some trouble. I know a few people in the right places, believe me I do. You lot won't know what trouble is until I get through with you, just you wait and see.'

There was no doubt some pacifying was needed, so Seth immediately swung into that submissive tone he was so good at, as he eased the unpleasant creature out of the room. But as they reached the door, he turned back and said, 'You've sure as hell managed to put your foot in it this time kid. Now stay where you are while I try and sort this mess out.'

He didn't get very far, because in no time he was back, bellowing at me, 'Get that bare arse of yours upstairs right this minute kid, Malcolm wants to see you in his office.'

Figured I might as well get straight up there and face the music, so it was up the stairs and into his study. It was strange, I still wasn't used to standing in front of him naked, even after what had happened between us on his bed.

As usual he was enthroned behind his huge desk, and the look of thunder on his face gave ample warning of what lay ahead, 'Have you taken leave of your bloody senses, you stupid little fool?' One half told me to keep quiet, the other said I had a right to give my side of the story. I chose the latter, 'Honest Malcolm, he told Seth he hadn't touched me, but first he tried to slap me, then he had a go at punching me in the face.'

He looked at me as if I was something unpleasant that had appeared from another planet, then replied, 'Is that a fact, he tried to punch you? The problem is boy, it appears you're more competent with your fists than he is, because there's no doubt he was the one who came off second best. And that's what I call showing a lot of sense, especially considering the times you've been told if anything like this should ever occur, the first thing you do is yell for Seth.'

And I winced, because I knew he was right. Seth had been in the room once that idiot had yelled, almost before I could blink. But Malcolm thundered on. 'Well it's too late now, the damage is done, but don't forget boy, your stupidity has mainly created this problem, and you'll have to accept what may eventuate from it. Now I've called for the car to be brought around, so get dressed and get out of here, before I'm tempted to do something I'll regret.'

So it was back to the city, then home via my bike as usual, all the way hoping and praying Malcolm could get the mess sorted out, that I'd been partly responsible for causing. But after a lengthy period of silence, during which I managed to play quite a bit of Saturday golf, finally the dreaded message was passed on, I was wanted out at the house.

As I climbed out of the car, and walked down the hall to the bathroom, I felt apprehensive, and it turned out to be warranted, because as I moved on to the bedroom, standing in the centre of the rug was a tubular metal frame. The unit appeared to be quite substantial, and a series of fittings underneath suggested it

was also highly adjustable. But what mainly attracted my attention were four black straps, two spaced about a metre apart at one end, and the same at the other, and instantly I felt the first flickering of fear, because instead of black leather, I saw flax. Those memories still haunted me, but being rendered helpless with Seth in the same vicinity, was something that scared me even more.

Instinctively I stepped back, but found the man in question had silently moved up and was standing directly behind me, as he bent slightly forward and quietly asked, 'And what do you think of our new addition kid?'

And I didn't think much of it at all, as I in turn asked, 'What is it, what's it doing in here?' The tone in his voice rang with sheer exhilaration as he replied, 'Apparently it's an ex piece of hospital equipment that Malcolm brought with him from South Africa. Seems there was a boy who was prone to giving trouble, like, couldn't keep his fists to himself.' He raised his eyes to the ceiling, at the same time placing a finger on his lower lip, giving an exaggerated version of someone deep in thought as he added, ' Now let me think, or for some reason does that sound vaguely familiar? Anyway, considering the trouble he was giving, Malcolm was all in favour of getting rid of him. But although he lived on the streets, which meant disposing of him wouldn't have proved to be much of a problem, apparently he was also quite a good looking and well put together kid, and therefore was still extremely popular with some of the more wealthy clients, so as a compromise, they hit on the idea of offering him to them strapped down on this. From what I'm told it worked like a treat, in fact it became so popular, they presented some of the other boys on it as well. Mind you, Rickie swears it was so popular, because it gave the men an additional feeling of power over the boys.'

He moved closer, then carried on, 'So here we are kid, faced with a repeat performance. Another good looking kid with a great body, who's a bit too free and easy with his fists. Malcolm was livid over the position you've put him in, and to get over the mess, he's had to agree to having that idiot back, only this time you're to be offered to him, strapped down on this. Can't see you belting him one this time kid.' His hand shot out, gripping me by the back of the neck. 'We may as well get on with it. The only way out of this room is past me, and you know that's not going to happen.' And he was right, I knew it wouldn't.

It seemed to take no time at all before he had me strapped down, and after enduring only seconds of the restriction, I found myself wanting to plead with him to let me loose. But I didn't, because there was no way I was going to give him the pleasure of refusing, so I tested my wrists instead. They were definitely very secure, but surprising for him, considering his delight in causing pain, they were not what I could call excessively tight. I knew he was standing behind me, and I squirmed as suddenly his hands started running over my body, so I shouted at him, 'Keep your filthy hands to yourself Seth. I guarantee Malcolm hasn't given you permission to touch me like that.'

It appeared he'd taken the hint, but suddenly I let out a yelp as he grabbed a handful of my hair and wrenched my head back, and during the brief instant my mouth was open, something round and firm was inserted. Next, he secured a leather strap behind my head, with the result the rubber section that was across

214

my mouth was locked firmly in place. This left the metal flange that was extending from the centre of this being forced into my mouth, so the round object on the end was left pressing into the back of my throat. Instantly I wanted to choke, yet even as I began to panic, I found it virtually impossible to make any noise.

After experiencing but seconds of this horror, all that mattered was getting the terrifying obstruction removed, but noting my desperation, Seth grabbed another handful of my hair and shook my head, although admittedly, reasonably gently, 'Listen to me kid, stop trying to struggle and listen, for Christ's sake,' he said, 'breath through your nose, listen to me will you, breath through your nose and you'll be alright.'

I would have liked to be able to tell him, apart from the fact I could barely make a sound, that I wasn't all that good at breathing through my nose, a recent attack of sinus had seen to that. However, the instincts of survival were gradually taking over, and somehow I forced myself to accept the pressure on the back of my throat and stop choking. Now with indications suggesting I was going to survive after all, Seth settled down beside me while he explained, 'Malcolm told me that thing you have in your mouth, is reputed to be the most effective gag ever developed. Now I hope you're used to it kid, because once your mate arrives, he's going to be allowed to play with you well into the afternoon.'

'Malcolm said to make sure I told you he was sorry it had to be like this, but you've only got yourself to blame. It was that fool that's coming who insisted on you being gagged, because he said that due to the money he's paying, he's already put up with enough of your cheek. And that I can understand, because you really are a cheeky little bastard at times. So taking into consideration the possible trouble he could cause, Malcolm was left with no option other than to comply with what he was demanding.' Once again he took on his exaggerated thinking pose as he added, 'And seeing as how the vehicle that's bringing him out here has been delayed a little, I wonder what you and I could do to fill in the time until he arrives?'

Maria was in the bathroom cleaning, and it seemed to me it was the only room in the house, apart from her precious kitchen, that she kept spotless. Seth walked over and spoke to her from the doorway, 'I've decided I'm going to have sex with the kid, want to watch?' Concern was evident in Maria's voice when she replied, 'My God, you'd better give some thought to the risk Seth. If Malcolm were to find out you've used the kid without his permission, God knows what might happen. You're as aware as I, he's got a lot of time for the boy, and he told me some time back, if he were ever to have a son, he'd be happy if he grew up a carbon copy of the kid. So be careful, because you're taking one hell of a risk.'

But going by his confident reply, Seth was a long way from being concerned as he replied,

'Listen woman, I'm no fool, I know what I'm doing, there's not a chance in hell Malcolm's going to find out. Now do you want to watch, because if you don't, then you can clear out.'

215

For all Maria's good intentions, lust soon won out over concern. There was a faint creak from one of the floorboards as she walked across the room, and another as she hitched herself up on the bed. Seth reappeared, and I realised I'd never seen him with his shirt off, let alone naked. No wonder the earth moved when he hit me, the man had muscles where I'd never ever known they existed. He bent down and looked me straight in the face and grinned, then moved behind and positioned himself. Seconds later, the sharp, searing pain as he entered me, five minutes or possibly a little more, the concern Maria had originally displayed, much more pronounced now, 'Look I warn you Seth, you'd better take it easy on the boy. If you keep on thrusting into him as hard as that, you'll finish up causing him some real harm. You can't keep on doing that to the boy, you're going to damage him, then, brother will you be for it.'

For the first time I could ever recall, he took her advice, so he replaced some of the physical abuse with verbal, 'Been waiting a long time to do this with you kid, in fact right from the time I watched you walk down those stairs from Malcolm's study. As you may have guessed, you're not the first kid they've had out here to use, but none of the others have even come close to your standard.'

He withdrew, and after studying the fittings, adjusted the frame, raising my buttocks fractionally higher, and after more fussing, lowering my upper body a little as well.

The rhythmic movement started again, and rather staring at the floor, I turned my head and looked across the room. The bland wallpaper offered nothing in the way of a distraction, so I concentrated on the colourful frieze instead, and this time it worked, because my imagination started to take over. The waving blue line became the sea, the straight, blue line above, the sky, and that yellow stippled pattern between could only be sand. So no longer was I in this miserable room, I was down at the beach, strolling along the shore, allowing the waves to roll in and break over my feet, enjoying the feel of the sand as it moved out from under. Now my thoughts drifted back to my friend Michael, and how we'd played together at school, away from the bullying and unpleasantness. So I made a special promise to myself, that I was never destined to forget. Away in the future, when all of this was nothing but a bad memory, I'd get married and have a son. I'd call him Michael, and I'd do my best to make sure he grew up straight and strong, and as I taught him how to swim and play cricket or tennis or golf, I'd love him as only a father can love his son. But far above all else, even if it cost me my life, I'd guarantee no man would ever do to him, as this man was doing to me.

Chapter 29

Many more minutes passed, then thankfully he finished and stepped away. Maria also departed, her lust apparently satisfied, and I could hear the rustle of Seth's clothing as he dressed. Moments later Maria reappeared with her flannel, and at the same time Seth finished dressing and moved back and stood in front, from where he proceeded to smirk over what he felt he'd achieved, 'Now I know why so many of them keep coming back for more kid, and because I enjoyed you so much, I don't intend to keep on missing out. So from now on, each time you have to come out here, you'll provide me with what I want, but with a slight difference. After all kid, I won't be paying for the pleasure, will I?'

I looked up at him, pleading with my eyes, desperate to be able to say something, and he responded, 'Something you want to tell me kid? Then I'll take that thing out of your mouth.'

And as soon as he did, I exploded, 'I warn you Seth, you'd better leave me alone. You so much as touch me again, and I'll tell Malcolm. I know he's never given you permission to do what you just did to me, so be warned and leave me alone, you pig.'

He spun around, the smirk had disappeared, his face now livid with fury as his reply and threats blasted back, 'You listen to me, you cocky little bastard. You dare to mention one word of what's gone on between us today, and as true as I stand here, you can rest assured that dog of yours is history. I've been to your house, I've strolled around the property, and I've seen where you keep him in that run behind the shed that's tucked in behind your double garage, and I also noticed the work that's being done on your back verandah. So just one word, that's all it'll take, just one bloody word kid, and you'll come home to find that animal hanging from a wire around its neck in the run.'

Having made his point, he replaced the abomination in my mouth, and as he did, I accepted that was another battle that had been fought and lost. There was no doubt he'd visited our property, his descriptions were too accurate for him to have done anything else. He was right, my father was in the process of closing in our back verandah. And similar to many boys, my dog was high on the list of things I loved in this life. We moved as one around the neighbourhood, he was always there, a virtual shadow, following at my heels. There was no way I'd risk having him hurt, let alone killed, and sensing he'd won, Seth turned to Maria,

'Get the kid cleaned up, I want him left looking like he's a virgin, like he's never been touched, because that's what this next fool will be expecting.'

Maria came in, and after making sure her husband didn't hear, offered a few words of sympathy, and slipped out again.

The overbearing silence seemed to somehow stress how helpless I was, positioned on the frame, displaying myself to anyone who came into the room. Yet again I tested my wrists and ankles, and all it did was confirm this was another lost cause. For the countless time I asked myself, how did I finish up in a mess, but really, I didn't need an answer, because I knew it had started through

a combination of blackmail and fear, and was continuing, because I felt I was in so deep, I simply didn't know how to get out.

Due to the overbearing silence, I realised I could hear a faint rustling. Briefly I wondered what it was, but it didn't take all that long to find out. Some leaves from the trees had succumbed to a period of dryness, and the light breeze that was drifting around had scooped some of them up and deposited them on the tar-seal, from where they'd worked their way down to the house. Now they were swirling and dancing in the corner directly outside the room, similar to that time I'd sat in the bicycle shed. It was as if they were playing a game, so I lay there and listened to their soft chatter, and it stayed like that until the man with the crew cut hair came into the room.

At first he ignored me, on purpose I reckoned, but finally came over and bent down so his mouth was directly beside my ear, 'You don't look quite so energetic as the last time we met boy, and I doubt you'll give me the same problems today. You know, I have a son and he'd be somewhere around your age, and if he ever dared to do as you did, I'd teach him a lesson he'd never forget, and now my young friend, that's precisely what I intend to do with you.'

He raised his hand in front of my face, and lying in it was a strip of black cloth, similar to what Bergman had used, and two small objects I recognised as ear plugs, then he explained,

'When I bind your eyes and seal your ears, you'll descend into your own special world, and when I start to do some very interesting things, you'll find the pain I intend to subject you to will be magnified to a point where you'd do anything to make it stop. But guess what kid, it won't, that is until I've decided you've learnt your lesson, and seeing as I've been told you're inclined to be a bit stubborn, it would seem that's going to take quite some time.'

During the times I'd spent in this room, I'd formed a habit of placing myself so as I could see out of the window. Not that it ever achieved all that much, because it never changed, and there was never anything to see anyway, but somehow it always seemed to offer something in the way of consolation for what I knew lay just ahead. So I gazed out of the window and made the most of those last remaining minutes until the threatened darkness descended, and when it did, I experienced pain like I'd never realised existed, with whatever implement he was using producing far more pain that that screwdriver handle in the shed. Before long I was writhing in agony, then after numerous sessions to a point where he'd finally exhausted himself, my buttocks and the soles of my feet glowed, as a result of the brutal thrashing he administered with his leather belt. Finally I wanted to scream at him, to be able to tell him I'd do anything he wanted, as long as he made the pain stop. But he was right, I couldn't, and it didn't, because for the next two hours it stayed just as it was.

But all things end, and so did what he'd been doing. Left lying on my stomach, tears streaming, my body trembling, but at least he'd stopped doing those incredibly cruel things. Still tense, fearful of it starting again, then the flooding relief arriving with the realisation it was all over, because I could feel someone undoing the straps, then more delight as that dreadful pressure was removed from the back of my throat. Now blinking as my eyes reacted to the light, and another few minutes required until the trembling stopped. Through my

blurred vision I realise Seth's there, and he leans over and speaks to me, but after mouthing off as only he can, he realises his mistake and removes the ear plugs and starts again,

'You sure didn't manage to give him any trouble this time kid, and I must say Malcolm was pleased to see him depart a very contented man. He won't give us any more trouble, because he's been warned about the photos Rickie took. Jesus, he sure got stuck into you, didn't he?'

Showing great restraint, I managed to hold my tongue. Anything was worth it, as long as it meant I could go home. Back in my bedroom, I backed up to my mirror, and considering he'd used a belt, not too bad a job, on about a par with my father, but nowhere remotely near the damage Hull had caused. I thought back to when I'd been lying on that frame, for some reason I sensed it marked the beginning of the end of my time under Malcolm. Deep down I realised the first seeds of rebellion had just been successfully sown. However, before that long awaited time finally arrived, there were a couple more traumatic events I had to survive.

Then quite unexpectedly, a decision was made in the Colbert household. As a prelude to my fast approaching fourteenth birthday, my father announced we'd be spending the Christmas period in Sydney. Fortunately the latter part of the year seemed to fly past, and in no time we were doing the same, as we winged our way across the Tasman, and in doing so, leaving that miserable part of my life behind, instead, replaced with weeks of fun under the plentiful Australian sun. The delight in being deemed old enough to take off into the city on my own, where I'd purchase my favourite lunch of king prawns and fresh bread rolls from the shop at the underground station. Then following an established routine, I'd cross to the park on the opposite side of the road, where I'd settle under a sprawling Jakaranda, and eat until I was convinced I was going to burst. The meal would be walked off by strolling into the heart of the city, where the next few hours would be spent wandering aimlessly, while I investigated the multitude of alleys and arcades, and in the process getting hopelessly lost. But this was quickly rectified, because a polite inquiry always resulted in directions to the nearest underground station, and from there, the simplicity of finding my way back home.

There were numerous trips to Cronulla with my cousins, but before the first, there was my initial amusement at their tentative but well meaning inquiry as to whether I could swim. Then came the thrill of competing against that pounding surf, followed by our arrival back at their home in Penshurst late in the afternoon, totally exhausted, of collapsing into bed in the evening and sleeping right through the night, without even a hint of those disturbing dreams. Then I'd wake to another golden morning, refreshed and ready to start all over again.

We climbed the pylon on the Harbour Bridge, and admired that magnificent city and harbour from there, then a trip on the ferry helped us cool down, as we crossed over to Taronga Park Zoo. There were trips up to the Blue Mountains and Katoomba, and others down the South Coast, but inevitably it all passed too quickly, then it was back to the misery of occasionally lying over his table, and the stress of what occurred at Malcolm's house. But it was also back to my final year at school, during which those last, defining events took place.

The first occurred on a cool Autumn morning, during which another of those pornographic photo sessions was in progress. But a slight break, as Rickie fussed over something with his camera, so I took the time to relax, flopping back in the same chair James had been in, the first time we met. With my left leg draped over the padded arm, I lounged back in relative comfort, my thoughts miles away, then gradually through my daydream it registered, someone was softly calling my name. Casually I glanced in the general direction of the voice, not all that interested in what they wanted anyway, and in doing so, looked straight into the lens of Rickie's camera as he took the photo. He grinned as he straightened and backed away, and slightly amused, I grinned straight back.

But that heralded the end of the break, because Malcolm was insisting we got underway again. As the session continued, he became increasingly more agitated, and I, increasingly more wary. I'd noticed a strong smell of liquor on his breath, and this was unusual, because although he qualified for a number of unflattering descriptions, a heavy drinker he most certainly wasn't. Due to what I assumed as being his alcohol consumption, he became increasingly more strident, until he finally shouted across the room to his photographer,

'That's it Rick, we may as well stop wasting our time. I told you it was high time we found something original, and what we're currently doing, most definitely isn't. So whether you like it or not, I've told you for some time what quite a few of them want, and we both know there's big money involved, and as far as I'm concerned, it's reached a point where we're left with no option, so it's best we just get on with it, whether you agree or not.'

As I looked across the room at him, I was convinced there was a strange expression on his face, something almost sinister, definitely something I'd never seen before. He turned to my favourite piece of Polynesian unpleasantness, ' I told you some time back that if this ever went ahead Seth, what you had to do, so go and do it, and then take the kid down to the barn,'

Then he turned to his photographer and added, 'and you get your gear down there as well Rick, and if you need any help, get a couple of the others to give you a hand.'

But there was no doubt what he intended, left Rick totally unimpressed, as he protested,

'I told you of my opinion of this before Malcolm, and as far as I'm concerned, nothing's changed. I agree, there may be large amount of money involved, but I still say the risk still isn't worth it, and what's more, the kid's done nothing to warrant being treated like that.'

And although I had no idea what they were talking about, one thing was certain, Rickie was wasting his breath. Long before I'd learnt when Malcolm was in one of his bloody minded moods, absolutely nothing or nobody stopped him, and this was confirmed by the way he spoke to his photographer, 'Listen Rick, and listen good. The time for pissing around has past. We both know what this will be worth if we give them what they want, so make your choice, get your fucking gear down there and do what you have to, or I'll take the bloody photos myself. Let's face it, I've been around and watched you long enough, so I've reached a point where I know what I'm doing with a camera as well. So you've got the bloody choice, either you take them, or I will.'

One thing was certain, Rickie may be resisting what Malcolm wanted, but Seth had no inhibitions in doing what he wanted at all. As he grabbed my arm and bundled me towards the door, something was telling me I needed help, and what was more, I needed it quickly. I was aware that if it came at all, it would only be from one direction, but as I glanced across with pleading eyes towards the little Englishman, after a few seconds, his dropped away. Seth detoured via the bedroom, and as he opened the top drawer of the dressing table, past experience told me what it contained, short lengths of pyjama cord, supplied for those who liked bondage. He extracted two of them, and wrenching me around, used one to tie my wrists firmly behind my back, while the other he stuffed in his pocket.

Now it was straight down to the barn, and as we stepped out of the house, I shivered slightly due to my nakedness, and when we arrived and stepped inside, I shivered again, but this time due to my concern. As we stood waiting, I tried to find out what it was Malcolm had planned, and most important of all, why it concerned Rick to the extent it did, so I asked, 'What's he going to do Seth, why are my wrists tied like this?'

But there was no doubt he'd been given strict instructions, and accordingly, was prepared to say barely a thing, other than, 'I've been warned not to discuss it with you kid, but there's one thing I will say. I'm bloody glad it's you they'll be doing it to, and not me.'

The minutes dragged on, still no sign of movement from the house. My eyes started to roam around the barn. It was the first time I'd ever been near it, let alone inside. It was a massive timber and iron structure, and in some ways reminded me of the gym, slightly morbid and forbidding, as if waiting for its next victim, just as the gym had done on that day. It appeared to contain a never ending assortment of those typical necessities that seem to make up an essential part of farm production, as far as I could tell anyway. The walls were draped with a multitude of obscure fittings, the majority of which meant absolutely nothing to me at all, and stacked neatly along the rear wall were a considerable number of sacks of fertilizer, and I knew that was right, because I could tell from the smell.

Over in the far right hand corner, a large pile of Maria's split Tee Tree was waiting to fuel her precious oven, and an area down by the Southern wall was taken up with the inevitable collection of useless machinery and general engine parts, that everyone managed to fall over, but nobody found the time or inclination to do anything about. And that was where my perusal ended. Malcolm and Rickie finally appeared, followed by about four others, all of carrying various pieces of equipment. For all the time I'd been coming out to the house, I could virtually guarantee some of them would be present. Their numbers ranged from just a few, to sometimes approaching fifty, and when the larger gatherings took place, the overflow of cars that couldn't be accommodated on the front drive, were parked on the tar-sealed area outside the bedroom. Persistent probing with Maria, confirmed they came out there to practise their Satanic beliefs, but mainly to obtain guidance in that direction from Malcolm, whose African origins were apparently supposed to have

endowed him with extensive knowledge on what I understood was generally considered to be an unsavoury, and at times, dangerous subject.

On the fortunately rare occasions when I'd come into contact with some of these people, and that included their children, seeing as I was always naked, and going by some of the looks that were cast in my direction, I'd decided it was definitely prudent to remain in the bedroom. And when the occasional larger meetings were in progress, rather than being prudent, I was convinced it was absolutely essential. So the fact that some of these people were coming down to the barn, apparently intent on watching what was about to happen, was in itself, definitely disturbing. But where they tended to stay well back, suggesting they'd possibly been told to do so, Rickie stepped out into the centre of the barn, and proceeded to swing his ever present light meter around, until he turned to Malcolm and commented, 'We won't be needing all that much additional lighting. With the combination of this high roof line and excellent natural light, conditions as they stand are very close to perfect.'

It appeared his quest for photographic perfection, was briefly dominating over his concern.

And Rickie's favourable comment seemed to be the catalysis to goad Malcolm into action, as he turned to Seth and said, 'right, then we may as well get things underway, so first off, get the boy standing directly under that beam Seth, then tie his ankles.'

And after Seth had complied, Malcolm offered a frightening explanation of what was intended, 'No doubt you're wondering what all this is about youngster. Well the fact is that for some considerable time, the photo we've been asked for above any other, is that of a preferably blond headed boy, hanging by the neck while he's stark naked. So now you can understand why you're here, because with the combination of that body and that head of hair of yours, it stands to reason, you were the obvious choice. I admit, it's one of the few photos Rick and I have never attempted, so that's probably the main reason why it's so sought after by so many of our clients. In theory, it shouldn't prove to be all that bad, after all, you'll only be hanging for seconds, or at least no longer than is required to get the photos we want. But accept it's going to happen lad, because the money we've been offered, is nothing short of staggering. But rest assured, we'll get it over and done with as quickly as possible.'

As the dangerous consequences of what he intended fully registered, I felt it didn't matter whether Seth had tied my ankles or not. I was so paralysed with fright, I was sure I couldn't have moved anyway. Desperately I unconsciously looked around for someone I felt could help, but similar to how it had been back in the shed, the expression of lust and anticipation on their faces said it all, compassion was a word that had been recently deleted from their vocabularies.

So after indicating to one of the men to step out from the group and come over and help, Malcolm carried on with his organising, 'Get the ladder in position Ken, then tie the rope to the beam. Also, don't forget how far above the kid's head I told you the noose had to be. Then when Rick indicated he's ready, Seth will lift the boy up, and you're to place the noose around his neck, then get down and take the ladder with you,' and then as he turned back to Seth, he added, 'and you'll continue to support the kid until Rick signals he's ready, then

all that's left is to ease the boy gently down and step aside. Now seeing as there's no way we can fake what we want, there's no alternative other than to let the kid hang. Naturally, it goes without saying the time the boy spends on the end of the rope must be kept to an absolute minimum, so the moment Rick says he's finished between each shot Seth, you must move in instantly and support him, because every second could make a difference.'

With the ladder in place and the rope tied around the beam, Seth gripped my hips and lifted, holding me well up, while the noose was slipped around my neck. I watched, wide eyed and terrified, and due to the silence that was prevailing, I could hear the heavy breathing, caused by the anticipation of those who were watching. Rickie checked and rechecked his equipment, then squatted behind his camera, then another delay as he insisted on one of the lights being shifted slightly. Finally satisfied, he squatted again, slowly raised his left hand as he said, 'Steady everyone, we're just about there,' a couple more very minor adjustments to his camera, a few more seconds, then his hand dropped, 'Right, lower the kid gently, then get the hell out of my road.'

As the noose tightened around my neck, the dreadful feeling it created made me instantly want to scream, but as it crushed into my windpipe, it proved impossible to utter a sound. Instantly, it felt as if my eyes were bursting out of their sockets, and surely my ears were reaching a point where they had to burst as well, and as the weight of my body imparted that life threatening pressure on my neck, it rippled on down my spine. I realised my legs were jerking, and there was no way I could make them stop, even though I knew the movement was tightening the noose even more. Surely this had to be the worst possible way to die, and die I must, because my lungs could only be seconds away from bursting.

But suddenly a flash from Rickie's camera, quickly followed by another, and through the haze of indescribable horror, I was certain I faintly heard him shout, 'Quick Seth, I've got what we want, hurry up and grab the poor little sod, quick, for Christ's sake, get him down.'

In a flash Seth's hands were back around my hips, lifting, removing that dreadful pressure, and at the same time shouting, 'Quick, get the ladder back in place, remove the rope so I can let the kid down.'

However, it seemed Malcolm had other ideas, 'Just a bloody minute you lot, I didn't say I was finished with the boy yet,' then added as he turned to his photographer, 'Now some shots from behind. The kid has got as good a pair of buttocks as I've ever seen, so combine that with having his wrists and ankles tied, and there's a chance they could finish up as classics.'

All of which was all very well, except Malcolm hadn't counted on Rickie's conscience flaring, 'Jesus Christ Malcolm, enough is bloody enough. I suspect the kid's already in shock, so give it away, let the kid down, I mean what are you trying to do, kill the poor little sod?'

And Malcolm literally bristled, a large percentage of which I suspected was liquor induced,

'Look I intend to carry on until I get what I want. I've waited too long for this to be cutting it short now. There's too much at stake here, so when I have what I want, that's when it stops.'

Even though a combination of shock, fear and semi strangulation had rendered me half conscious, I knew it wasn't going to stop; Malcolm always got what he wanted. And I was right, it did continue in a frightening blur of terror and pain, and to add to my fear, even during the times when the rope was loose around my neck, I was still finding it difficult to breath. Once again a voice drifted in, 'Just a few to go, so try a couple from the side Rick.'

But it seemed that was it, as far as the little Englishman was concerned as he exploded,

'No way Malcolm, enough is bloody enough. It's one thing to get what you want, but something else entirely to seriously harm or even kill the kid, so we'd better come to an understanding my friend. You'll hang that boy up there again over my dead fucking body.'

I barely recall the argument that followed, but one thing was certain, for the first time ever, it was Rickie who came out on top. The next thing I remembered clearly, the rope was gone, and someone was lowering me to the floor. As my feet touched and I attempted to support myself, my legs simply buckled under me, but as I headed on down, Rickie moved in a flash and supported me in his arms, then, did he let Malcolm have it, I remembered that alright.

'Damn you a thousand times Malcolm, why is it you'll never be fucking told? Jesus Christ, look what's happened now,' and as he held me, he whispered in my ear, 'Mathew, Mathew, it's alright kid, I've got you, and I promise nobody will touch you again. My God, what have we gone and done? Curse you Malcolm, for the cruel, dangerous, stubborn bastard you are.'

It was like being back in the shed. Once again the coolness of the floor left like bliss, and as I lay there, slowly I realised things were already starting to improve. Rather than being blurred and distant, Malcolm's voice sounded perfectly clear, and I noticed more than a hint of concern there as well, 'Lay off Rick, you know what I think of the kid, there's no way I'd purposely set out to harm him. It's just I didn't think it would be as bad as it obviously was. Christ, I'm just as worried about the boy as you are.'

The explosion that followed, suggested his partner was a long way from being convinced as he shouted back, 'Is that a bloody fact? Well all I can say is, if tying a boy's wrists and ankles, then hanging him by the neck until he's half bloody throttled is your way of showing you like him, then I can't help but think, God help anyone you don't get on with.'

Now appearing genuinely upset, Malcolm turned and called out to Seth, 'Carry the boy up to my bedroom, then get that wife of yours up there as well. Tell her to make sure he has everything he needs. I'll ring, and get Martin to come over and check him out. He'll be prepared to do that, without asking any awkward questions.'

But a visit from Martin, whoever he may have been, didn't prove to be necessary. My breathing rapidly improved, but I admit it took just a little longer for the trembling to stop. Doing as she'd been told, Maria appeared and started unnecessarily fussing, but only because she knew it was what Malcolm expected. So I in turn reminded her he'd said I could have anything I wanted, and what I wanted above all else, was for her to clear out and leave me in peace.

Another half hour passed, and I knew it was, because Malcolm had instructed Maria to bring my clothes and whatever up to the room so I could dress, and it meant I had my Mondia watch back on my wrist. But a slight set back, there were a couple of occasions when I felt I was going to be sick. Not all that surprising, it was as if every nerve in my body, including my stomach, was still twisted in a knot. Fortunately, that situation improved as well, then Malcolm spoilt it by strolling into the room and sitting on the end of the bed while he spoke,

'Pleased to see you looking a lot better Mathew, and thank Heaven for that. Jesus, you gave me a fright. Now is there anything you want? Just name it, because if it's anything I can manage, it's as good as yours.'

Was there anything I wanted Malcolm? You must be kidding me, just one thing really, all I wanted was for someone to do to you, exactly as you'd just done to me, the only difference being, I hoped they left you there long enough to make a thorough job of it. But comments like that weren't worth it where Malcolm was concerned, they also only happened in my dreams. Past experiences had taught me my reply needed to be a lot more laid back than that, so instead I told him the truth, 'It's no different to all the other times I've had to come out here Malcolm. All I want is the car to take me back to the city, so I can ride my bike home.'

While I was speaking I watched his face, and was certain there was something I'd never seen before. Just a hint of compassion, with a little fear around the edges. I wondered if he thought this time, he'd gone just a little too far, and he should have listened to his partner, after all. But looking on the bright side, maybe getting a fright made obstinate people a little more cooperative, because he said, 'Right, then home it is youngster, but not before you spend another half an hour here resting. Look Mathew, I'm truly sorry you got hurt to the extent you obviously did, and although I know you won't be too keen on the idea, I've instructed Lindsay to run you home in the car, well, close to your home anyway. But Christ knows what can be done about that rope burn on the side of your neck.'

I knew what he meant, I'd noticed it in the mirror when I'd used his bathroom, but there was no way I was stopping that getting me out of here, so I assured him, 'Don't worry, I'll dream up something in the way of an excuse. If there's one thing I've learnt since I've been coming out here, it's how to be a very effective liar.'

Lindsay was Malcolm's driver, and at first he'd treated me with something approaching contempt, but as his knowledge of my situation became clearer, his distaste had veered more in his employer's direction instead. Now a reasonable relationship existed, especially since he'd helped me reach a compromise with Malcolm. As long as I didn't attempt to lift my head, then they'd trust me to travel in the back of the car on my own. And I was determined to keep my part of the bargain, because although the temptation to try and glance out of the window was always there, my preference was to travel without Seth's distasteful presence beside me. I was fed up with what he subjected me to during a greater part of the journey. But on that day, Lindsay sensed that all was far from well, and finally I told him what had occurred, and how frightened I was in having to

go back and possibly risking something equally as brutal sometime in the future, as I confessed, 'So you can see the position I'm in Lindsay, I'm scared to go back, but I'm equally as scared of what might happen if I don't. You've known him longer than anyone, so do think he'd expose me by using those photos?'

His reply didn't help, but at least it was straight to the point, 'You're right Mathew, I have known him for many years, in fact I was working for him long before he met Rick, and as far as your question is concerned, just let me say he's the most vindictive man I've ever met. And as for his sordid business ventures, I admit I've just had to force myself to ignore them, but I find some compensation in the fact a considerable part of his income is derived from legitimate sources. The farm's very profitable, and he also has a license that enables him to deal perfectly legally in precious stones.'

And I wasn't surprised by the news. During one of my visits to his bedroom, I'd noticed a leather pouch on his dressing table, so with curiosity overpowering caution, I walked over and upended the contents into the palm of my hand, and guessed I was left holding around ten uncut diamonds, so I replaced them as if they were red hot, but now Lindsay continued,

'He does extensive business in Europe, but as it happens, he detests flying, so limits himself to a couple of visits a year. As far as the likes of his diamonds are concerned, he does his business in Antwerp, and when it comes to the distribution of his pornography, that's done through his connections with a paedophile ring in Amsterdam. With the cities something like two hours apart by road, it's all very compact and convenient. But as far as your situation is concerned lad, I warn you to tread very warily indeed. These people the ring deal with in Europe, are powerful and wealthy beyond what the likes of you or I could even comprehend. They insist on the highest possible quality, and specifically state the type of child pornography they want, and the likes of Malcolm and Rick do their best to provide it, and previous photos supplied mean that whether you know it or not, you've become a desired commodity lad, which means your body is worth big money, so be very careful indeed.'

And I decided, my position couldn't have been made any clearer than that. So once again having to accept my fate, for the time being, anyway, I was back sitting at the table, with a throat so painful I didn't want to eat at all, when I barely managed to avert what could have become a disastrous situation. As my mother bent forward to place my evening meal in front of me, she bent a little further forward as she said, 'Good grief Mathew, how on earth did you get that dreadful graze across your throat?'

During the split second of panic that followed, I felt my father's eyes rivet on me as well. I'd told Malcolm I'd think of an excuse, but the fact was since arriving home, and being so glad to be here, I hadn't given it a moment's thought. But during that instant of desperation, when my heart seemed to stand still, suddenly out of nowhere it appeared, a vision of Eddie Levers, as he'd ran full tilt into that clothesline, and somehow my hastily concocted explanation seemed to flow from there, 'I was playing with some of the other caddies on the lawn behind the clubhouse. One of them threw the ball we were playing with over my head, and as I turned to run back and get it, I ran full tilt, straight into their clothesline.'

Immediately my mother started fussing, in that special way that only mothers can, 'Good grief child, by the look of that nasty graze, you're lucky you didn't break your neck. I'll go and get something to put on it to help it heal, now are you sure you're alright?'

'Honest Mum, I'm fine, but can I leave some of my meal, because it still hurts to swallow?'

I was right; I had turned into a champion liar. But nothing had changed, too much pain had been experienced, too many tears quietly shed, to let it all go to waste now. Even after what had just happened, I'd see it through to the end, wherever the end may be.

Three weeks later, in the bathroom dressing, with Maria having just walked out, Rickie bounded in, with his usual manic exuberance, 'Wondered if you might want to look at these?'

He handed me a number of larger than normal photos. They consisted of a series taken of a naked boy, his wrists tied behind his back, and hanging from a rope around his neck, with his feet suspended well above the floor. As I slowly sifted through them, I found it progressively harder to accept I was looking at photos of myself. But the one I found most sickening of them all, was that showing a pool of fluid on the floor, directly under that hanging body. It was only then I vaguely remembered the sensation that had barely registered through that smothering mist of desperation and terror. I recalled that hard though I'd tried, I'd been unable to control my bladder, fear had seen to that, and I'd urinated down the front of my legs. The memories of something similar having occurred in the shed, and now this, did absolutely nothing for me at all, so after one last withering look, I handed them back.

But Rickie hadn't finished, as it so happened, there was one more. As I reluctantly peered at it, I found it even harder still to comprehend what I was seeing. It was another photo of a naked boy, but this time with a difference. He still possessed a head of thick, fair hair, but was lounging almost insolently in a large, upholstered leather chair. With one leg flung nonchalantly over one of the arms, it meant he was openly, if unintentionally displaying himself, and as my eyes moved up from his loins, they took in a smoothly muscled young body, fine tuned from a constant diet of sport. He was glancing up at the camera, and the look on his face was one of absolute confidence, as if he was saying to the world he was proud of his body, and what was more, couldn't care less who knew it. The already powerful effect was further enhanced by his smooth, tanned skin, and a pair of haunting, green eyes.

As I leant against the vanity in the bathroom, I studied that photo as I never had before; because I found the effect it created nothing short of shattering. As far as a display of raw, youthful sex was concerned, those others, devastating and cruelly sexual as I was sure those people in Europe were going to find them, in my opinion got nowhere near it. Not since I'd stood in front of that mirror in Malcolm's bedroom and studied myself wearing that garment he'd insisted on, had I been made so aware of the power of my own sexuality. Finally, I found the effect so disturbing, I put the photo down, feeling that if I didn't, I was in danger of it igniting in my fingers. And as Rickie turned, and with one last grin, walked out of the room, I breathed yet another sigh of relief. At least I had the comfort

of knowing they'd be in circulation thousands of miles away from where they could possibly cause untold damage.

And as the sound of his footsteps faded, I found myself gazing wistfully through the open door into the bedroom, thinking of the shame that occurred in there. But these days as I placed myself in the position each man demanded, automatically my eyes locked onto that paper frieze. Then when the sex started, I was no longer in that detestable room, I was down at the beach, standing on the sand, gazing out over that sparkling water, enjoying the feel of the waves as they washed in over my feet. And over and over and over again, I'd repeat that promise I'd made to myself. One day I'd have a son and I'd call him Michael, and at risk to my life, I'd guarantee no man would ever do to him, as the men who came into that room, did to me.

But time to snap out of my thoughts. Some time had passed since Malcolm had declared the session over, so now that I was dressed, and had suffered the indignity yet again, of Maria doing what she always did, which now included insisting on doing my hair, bloody stupid woman, I strolled down the hall, through that superb foyer, then down those eight stone steps to the waiting car. And it registered, another day nearer the end.

Quite a number of weeks later, apparently due to Malcolm allowing me reasonable time to recover from my experience in the barn, but inevitably the loathed message received via Bergman as usual, that approaching Saturday, my presence was once again required out at the house. But speaking of Bergman, my situation with him much improved, the time now spent in his office, almost non-existent. The thought had crossed my mind, was he tiring of me, over those months had the associated risk finally registered, after all, every month that passed meant I was that much closer to leaving school, and what would happen then? With the threat from the boys eliminated, would I attempt to expose him for what he was? If that happened, it would be his word against mine. He'd win in the end, it seemed he always did, but life could become very difficult for him during that time. There'd been a number of boys at the school who'd testify they'd been molested by him, his reputation was well known, would it finally be a case of the authorities saying, where there's smoke, there's quite possibly fire?

Due to the situation with my father, I knew that as far as I was concerned it couldn't happen, but he wasn't aware of that, and over the months the strain had been showing, there was no doubt he was a very worried man. Many questions, few answers, but I didn't know, and I didn't care, all that mattered were the indications were pointing in the direction where he'd hopefully not be involved with me at all, that our 'relationship' would be a thing of the past, that is if it wasn't already. But I still had Malcolm to contend with.

As I rode to the house, it was as if the weather was doing its best to warn me of what lay ahead. The day was cold and miserable, with persistent showers constantly sweeping across the city. There'd been no improvement as I stepped out of the car, and as I climbed those stone steps, I noticed the driveway was packed with cars, and as I walked from the bathroom into the bedroom, I could see the tar-sealed area was also cluttered with vehicles, which meant one thing; a major meeting of that strange, satanic group was in progress. Then Seth appeared and added to the misery of what was an already miserable morning.

He pulled the frame away from the wall where it was now stored, and erected it in the centre of the room. For some time Malcolm had offered it as an optional extra. The men could indulge in the sex they wanted as usual, or agree to pay a small additional fee for the use of the frame. So now all the emotions that were involved were increased yet again by the fear of also being rendered helpless. But as Seth instructed me to place myself face down in the required position, I didn't hesitate in complying, because even the slightest sign of resistance was dealt with, using a combination of violent physical and sexual abuse. And after checking my wrists and ankles were very secure, he threatened me as he strode out of the room,

'I'll warn you just once kid. Keep your mouth shut about what happens in here today. Dare to mention one bloody word, and so help me, you little bastard, I'll make sure you regret it.'

As the door closed behind him, automatically I went into my usual routine as my eyes locked onto that paper frieze. A few minutes of silence, no leaves to listen to, now the sound of male voices coming from the hall. A click from the latch as the door's opened, another as it's closed, and I sense the intruder has moved up and is standing behind me, his presence confirmed as a hand glides over my buttocks, then after a couple of seconds, 'So, we finally meet kid. Quite a few of us have admired that body of yours from afar, so we decided the time had arrived to enjoy what's on offer, like those who pay exorbitantly for the pleasure.'

Something was very wrong. Although I didn't recognise him, he could only be a member of that weird group, and Malcolm was adamant they weren't allowed anywhere near me or this room, and the fact he was here gave much cause for concern in a number of areas. The naïve twelve year old was a thing of the past, replaced by a fourteen year old who was much more versed in his understanding of the obscene world that functioned within the walls of this elegant house, and which also included being very aware of the term 'sexually transmitted diseases' and when I'd plucked up the courage to express my concern with Malcolm, he'd taken great lengths to appear understanding and reassuring.

He stressed no client ever came out to the house, unless he'd been cleared by a certain doctor he specified. Perhaps I'd thought at the time, that's where Martin's name had originated from. So apparently, no clearance from that doctor meant no boy sex. Since I'd been coming out to the house, to my limited knowledge, I suffered nothing more serious than a common head cold, so perhaps this safeguard was proving effective, but something else was telling me that detecting the presence of such diseases needed to go further than that. But with this unauthorised man's intrusion, not even that minor precaution existed, and it was possible he could sense the concern in my voice as I warned him, 'I'm telling you Mister, you'd better leave me alone. You know Malcolm has forbidden you to come anywhere near me, so you've no right to be in this room.'

But things didn't look good. As he moved into my vision, he's already removed his clothing, and there was a very casual tone to his voice as he replied, 'I accept you've done your best to protect yourself lad, but I'm afraid it's not going to work.'

He placed his clothes on the bed, and as he moved back behind, a voice called from the hall,

'Too much talking in there. Get on with it, or move aside and let a real man at the kid.'

Due to the laughter, the man had to wait for some time, before he had a hope of being heard,

'Just slow down out there will you. I've waited long enough for this, so all the more reason why I want to do it properly. So once I'm finished, just ask the kid if I know what I'm doing.'

His reply caused more laughter, with one of them thumping his fist lightly on the door, but with the act barely underway, the door was flung open as a number of other men stormed into the room, and following this unpleasant intrusion, a pattern of filthy conversation started,

'Hey, come off it you guys, at least I should be allowed to have sex with the kid in private.'

'Ah, don't be such a prude, I couldn't care less if you stand there while I'm doing it to him.'

'Now there's a thought. Maybe we can all learn something in here by watching each other?'

'Bullshit, what's there to learn, after all, what we're doing to him comes naturally anyway.'

'Don't know about that. I've seen an old Chinese book that shows numerous variations on doing it with a boy. But that position you've got him in looks good, so I'll try that.'

'For Christ's sake, hurry up. Standing here watching is making me desperate for my turn.'

'Do me a favour and shut up will you, don't spoil it for me, because I'm just about to come.'

And when he did, another immediately took his place. As his movement continued, I wondered how this could be happening, then the obvious explanation arrived. Malcolm was away, so making the most of his absence, Seth had set me up into coming out here so I would be available for them. As it went on, more men came into the room, gathering in groups, watching and laughing, continually adding to the string of crude comments as the assault went on, one finishing, another taking his place.

What was left of an atrocious morning dragged painfully on, inevitably replaced by an equally as cruel early afternoon. The bedlam seemed to be getting worse, and now additional humiliation, the higher pitches of women's voices, now mixing with those of the men. I took my eyes off the frieze, and turned to the side. At least six women were standing around watching, occasionally shouting encouragement and crudeness, equally as effectively as the men, then I noticed something that made me feel ill. Two children were standing beside one of them, the first a girl, no older than six, her eyes displaying innocent bewilderment and concern at what was occurring in front of her, the other, a boy, about four years older, and in comparison to his younger sister, he stood there shouting and yelling obscenities, and as he urged them on; the childish pitch to his voice as loud as many of the men.

Another finishes, the shudder as he ejaculates making it obvious, and immediately another takes his place, and the rhythmic movement of sex starts yet again, but he doesn't get very far towards satisfying himself. A voice blasts out from the doorway, filling the room with seething, livid fury, 'What do you scum think you're doing?' then when he sees the man desperately continuing to thrust up into me, 'Get away from that boy, get away from him I tell you, before I pull you off the kid and proceed to break your fucking neck.'

It took but seconds for the bedlam in the room to cease, and as Malcolm strode in to a point where I could see him, he looked more dangerous than I could ever recall. His eyes blazed around the room as he shouted, 'Get the fuck out of here the lot of you, before I cause some major damage and throw you bodily out of here myself.'

In no time the room was empty, seconds to remove the straps, and there was no doubt he was genuinely distressed, because he ran his hand soothingly through my hair as he asked,

'How long has it been going on kid, how long have you been here being treated like this?'

I didn't answer him, because I wasn't sure, I didn't have my Mondia watch, and what was more, I'd stopped caring. All that mattered was that it had finally stopped, and although I knew it was a bit childish, all I wanted was my mother, to see her smile, because nothing could assure me it would be alright better than that. But my mother wasn't here, thank God, so I did something I hadn't done in quite a while, I wept just a few desperately needed tears. But enough of that, they had to stop. After all, fourteen year olds weren't supposed to cry, no matter what humiliation they'd been subjected to, and also nothing had changed over the years. Red eyes meant those dreaded questions could still be asked, but never mind, I'd had that covered for quite some time. If for some obscure reason it turned out to be necessary, the problem was still so easily solved, I'll simply blame it on the wind.

Chapter 30

As I headed for the bathroom, Malcolm put his arm around my shoulders, and eased me out into the hall. After what I'd experienced, the fact he'd walked in when he had, should have made me grateful, but his proximity had the opposite effect, making me shudder instead, so I told him, 'Look, honest Malcolm, now that it's over, I can manage quite alright on my own.'

But the moment I glanced up, I knew there was no way my request was going to be granted, and therefore wasn't surprised when he said, 'Considering what I suspect you've just been through, there's no way you're anything like alright yet, so no arguments lad, you're going to take it easy upstairs.' He turned his head and bellowed for Maria, and she must have been hovering around somewhere, because she appeared as if out of mid air, 'Get upstairs and prepare the bed in the second bedroom,' then as she stood there and gaped, he added, 'Well get on with it woman, don't just stand there like an idiot, for Christ's sake exert yourself.'

I hoped for her sake she knew where the second bedroom was, because as far as I could tell after my excursions around the house, there appeared to be about ten of them. Apparently she did, because she took the hint and departed, and before too long, I found myself lying on a very comfortable bed. Malcolm stood in the doorway looking at me, but just before he turned to leave, he went out of his way to distance himself from what had happened, 'I hope you realise I had no idea of what they intended, there's no way I'd have approved such abuse.'

And there was still no way I could fathom the man. Long before I'd decided he was an enigma, who conveniently shuffled the rules to suit himself, and yet again I thought, what was he trying to prove? That it was acceptable to blackmail someone's twelve year old son, to ensure the boy supplied his body for male sex whenever he demanded. That it was acceptable to use the boy for his variety of pornographic ventures, that included stripping the boy naked, tying his wrists and ankles, then hanging him from a rope around his neck while a series of photos were taken, that according to rumours I'd heard floating around the house, had made him a small bloody fortune.

That it was acceptable that on a number of occasions, he'd demanded the boy present himself in his own bedroom, where he'd been made to wear a pair of girl's panties, while he fondled him, then demanded he perform oral sex, that was until he stripped the panties down and indulged in anal sex himself. Was it acceptable that on a couple of occasions when the boy had been told to make himself available on a Saturday, he'd been made to 'service' anything up to nine men. But although the same boy had just been the victim of gang rape, it wasn't acceptable, simply because he hadn't authorised it. Was I looking at this from a biased point of view, or could I sense a double standard somewhere?

I spent quite some time relaxing on the bed while I got some way towards recovering, then carefully eased my feet to the floor and crossed over the hall to

a bathroom, where I used the facilities to liberally soak my face in cold water, and generally clean myself up. Following Malcolm's instructions, Maria had brought my clothes, and I'd almost completed dressing when Malcolm returned. It was apparent he was still far from happy when he asked, 'I suspect I know who was behind what's just happened Mathew, but never the less, I'm still very interested to hear your side of the story. So tell me lad, who do you think was responsible for what's just occurred?'

Incredibly, even allowing for my loathing of the person in question, I still hesitated. Years of schooling had effectively ingrained me with the unwritten rule. No matter what, you never dropped anyone in it. But just in time, I remembered, that rule applied to human beings, so that meant Seth didn't qualify. Comments I'd heard while in the room confirmed Seth had been approached, and seeing the opportunity for what he considered to be easy money, had agreed to cooperate by making sure I came out to the house, and apparently had been well paid for doing so. So here goes, 'There's no doubt Seth was responsible Malcolm. He made me come out here, and they paid him really well for doing so, and there's something else.'

May as well commit myself, because there was no turning back now, 'Seth's been having sex with me, because he said he'd kill my dog if I didn't cooperate for him.'

See how you get around that lot, you heartless, double dealing mongrel.

Malcolm proceeded to turn about six shades of purple, then swung around and glared at Maria, who'd chosen a most unfortunate time to appear as he literally shrieked at her, 'Find that fucking husband of yours and tell him he's wanted in my office, and it might pay to warn him he's in danger of getting his bloody throat ripped out. Now get on with it.'

When he turned back, he was a different man as he held out his hands and pleaded, 'What can I do to make up for what's happened kid? Name it, anything within reason, and it's yours.'

Amazing, after all this time, he still didn't get it, nothing had changed, it was so simple,

'All I ask is to be able to go home, that's all Malcolm, nothing more, just let me go home.'

He stood there gazing at me, obviously thinking carefully about what he wanted to say,

'You know kid, way back I told Rick that lurking behind those choirboy looks of yours, there lingered one tough, stubborn kid, and during the time you've been coming out here, you sure have proved me right. So if that's all you want, then fine, you'll find the car waiting for you.'

I decided I couldn't care less about his assessment of me, one way or the other, so I completed dressing, but purposely quite slowly, then headed down the hall towards the stairs. Half way there, and directly outside his study, I paused and listened, and was delighted, it appeared I'd managed to time it perfectly. Voices were coming from behind the closed door, one literally strident with fury, the other, barely more than a whisper. Seth had always been far too big for me to be able to handle physically, that was something that still only happened in my dreams. But in the end and through it all, victory was finally

mine, because now there was the satisfaction in knowing, brother, was he getting his. My heart was bleeding for him, not while kneeling on that faded Persian rug in the bedroom, this time it was all over Malcolm's plush green carpet as I continued on down the stairs.

From that very first day, I'd made an accurate assessment of him. An aggressive and at times dangerous and sexually deviant bully, when it came to dominating a twelve year old boy, but a submissive wimp while trying to explain his deviousness, when confronted by his employer. Still, much as I was enjoying the one sided confrontation, best not to linger, so down the stairs and across that elegant foyer, with its magnificent chandelier, and with that wonderful old grandfather clock, still ticking away on my right. Even allowing for the house and all its atrocious memories, I still couldn't resist one last lingering look, then I closed that massive timber door, making sure it shut with a resounding thud behind me. Next, down those eight stone steps, with Malcolm true to his word, the car waiting for me on the gravel driveway, still positioned so I couldn't read the number plates. Briefly it crossed my mind, I'd run around and look at them anyway, but in the end decided not to bother.

During a previous trip in the vehicle, Lindsay had informed me during the course of a casual conversation we'd been having, the vehicle wasn't registered in Malcolm's name, and the address on the registration was in another suburb as well. As always, a smooth trip back to the city, then my final goodbye, including a firm handshake with Lindsay, and after he'd backed out and driven away, following my usual routine, I collected my bike from where I always left it, leaning against the inside of the back fence. But for this last time, purposely a small variation, because as I walked out of the property, I purposely left the gate wide open. With any luck, a large dog would wander in and hopefully tear their immaculate garden to pieces. As I rode past the park, a quick glance towards that toilet block, briefly brought back sickening memories, and as I pedalled towards home, time to make a well overdue decision. No matter what eventuates in the future, I'm never going out to that house again. Although it was a decision I'd lived in fear of making for so long, what had happened out there today meant the decision had effectively been made for me, because logic said there was no way I could risk showing my face there again. Considering the way I'd stitched Seth up with Malcolm, the moment he laid his eyes on me, Seth would kill me, mind you, that was as long as he was still employed. Going from what I'd heard as I'd passed by the study, there was a chance even that was debatable. Good riddance to bad rubbish, was a term I'd heard my father use occasionally. I decided it was more than appropriate now.

So it's back to school on the Monday, and as the days and weeks continue to slip by, they're accompanied by the stress of waiting for his next demand for my services out at the house. And when I refuse, and he finally realises I mean it, the turmoil created as those photos appear around the school, will leave me forever tainted. And as I sit in class, my mind drifts back to where it all started, and yet again I ask myself, why me, what had I done to deserve such treatment? And here it was, all this time later, and I still hadn't thought of a logical explanation. Maybe it was a penalty I was paying for something I'd done in a

past life. And that concerned me, because if that was so, then it must have been something pretty terrible.

But back to the present, only a few weeks before we break up for the Christmas holidays, then back to school for a couple of months until I turn fifteen. Over two years of shame and constant abuse I knew I couldn't have survived with, but a couple of months was an entirely different story, I could handle that alright. There might be numerous times when I'd arrive home covered in bruises from the fights I'd been in, but I knew I'd get there in the end. There had also been the question of my position with my mother during my time at the house, but I'd taken steps to deal with that as well. On the occasional Saturday when she was convinced I was caddying at the club, but had been elsewhere instead, I wondered how I could explain the absence of the fees I'd earned. It had become a standard practise for me to give her half, which she put away for me in a savings account.

However, quite early on, some of Malcolm's clients had offered me money, if only to help ease their conscience, or so I was convinced. And I'd refused point blank, feeling that accepting would have made me no different to a child prostitute, coupled with the fact that I knew Seth would take it off me anyway. But finally I'd been forced to acknowledge this other factor had to be taken into consideration, so I started taking the occasional note, but only enough to overcome that particular problem. To get the note past Seth, I'd fold it and slip it under my top lip, and it worked, because never once did he comment that my lip appeared slightly swollen.

I wished I could start work straight after the holidays, be it with my father, or if the situation exploded, somewhere else, but it was one time when looking younger than I was didn't help. But one major surprise as it was quietly announced Bergman would be leaving the school, and there was no indication as to when or if he would be coming back. I decided doing hand springs during assembly would be frowned upon, but it was close, I barely managed to restrain myself, and my delight was far more for the sake of other boys, rather than myself, because after all this time, nothing could change what I'd been subjected to by him. So finally the last day of the year; my luck holding, nothing from Malcolm's direction eventuating either. But whereas I would have to return for those couple of months in the New Year, for many of my friends, this was the final day of their schooling, which meant there was a strong chance I'd never see them again, and much to my sorrow, this included Chis. If that small amount of time spent with a certain master could be deleted, the rest could be classed as having been very successful, a combination of wonderful friends and excellent teaching. And as far as those drab buildings were concerned, maybe they didn't look like prisons after all, perhaps they were just crying out for a little affection, that's all.

Chapter 31

The start of a new year, but far more important, the start of a new life, but first, a query about my old life that needed to be determined. As my knowledge of all things sexual had steadily increased, the phrase 'sexually transmitted diseases' gave me ever increasing cause for concern. I had no trust in Malcolm's dubious medical checks on his clients, and felt it imperative to have one carried out on myself. Sure enough, the result came back, I'd been infected with Chlamydia, but after a lecture from the doctor relating to safe sex, and the appropriate use of protection, I was assured a course of antibiotics would cure the problem.

With nothing in the way of demands eventuating from Malcolm's direction, and the months of schooling required for me to turn fifteen now behind me, the way was clear to start that long awaited apprenticeship under my father, at the same time hoping our at times erratic relationship, wouldn't pose a problem. However, I found I loved the work, which included many of the menial tasks that were the lot of a first year arrival, but found I was far from relaxed, due to being in the constant company of adult males. As a result, I was sure the staff assessed me as being just a little aloof, where nothing could have been further from the truth, but yet again, I was hardly in a position to be able to clarify the situation.

A number of weeks of working behind me, lying on my bed one evening, simply relaxing and enjoying my own company, when my mother called from the other end of the house,

'Mathew, come out here, there's someone on the phone asking for you.'

And when I picked it up, that South African accent was all too familiar, as he informed me,

'You've had a reasonable break from your duties out here boy, but due to the demand that's building, I need your services urgently this coming Saturday. Although your schoolmaster seems to have suddenly departed, nothing else has changed. Your pickup point remains the same, and the car will arrive about nine o'clock as usual. Make sure you're there waiting.'

For a moment I hesitated as I checked, but it was safe, my mother was back clattering away in the kitchen, and as usual, my father wasn't even home, so I was free to let loose,

'You must be insane for two reasons, first for ringing me here like this, and second, for thinking I'd ever set foot in that house of yours again. It's over Malcolm, finished, and I want to make it perfectly clear, I'm having nothing more to do with you and your disgusting filth.'

There was a pause, and it was as if I could feel him leering at me from down the other end of the line, 'You're wrong my young friend,' he replied, 'nothing of any consequence has changed as far as I'm concerned, so think again, but this time more carefully, and definitely a lot more rationally. You seem to be forgetting about the dominant position I'm coming from.'

It registered, that arrogant I've got you where I want you attitude, which suggested there was a chance he wasn't aware I'd left school, so I didn't hesitate to ram my new position home,

'It's obvious you don't know how wrong you are Malcolm. The fact is a lot's changed, first of all I've left school, I've been working for quite a few weeks, which means that large part of your blackmail is of no further use to you.'

I could tell from the slight hesitation that followed, that had set him thinking, but knowing him as I did, and especially after being so carefully warned by Lindsay, there was no way he was going to give up that easily, and I was right, after gathering himself, back he came again,

'Alright, so school is in the past, but what about your parents boy? Some of those photos of you and James performing, are already being classed as classics of their kind, and considering the number that have been taken over the years, of two boys performing, you should feel quite proud, knowing they've become as in demand as they have, so think of your parents lad, what's their reaction going to be if they were to be shown some of those erotic examples?'

He wasn't intending to give up easily, well guess what Malcolm, neither am I, 'My mother would almost die of shock, but in the end, she'd be there for me, but my father would probably order me out of the house. But guess what Malcolm, I'm not twelve any more, I'm fifteen, and I've put away a reasonable amount of money, and that means one thing. No matter what threats you throw at me, and no matter what problems they cause, I'll survive, and that's why after all this time, I'm finally in a position to be able to tell you to go to hell. I admit, I'd rather what you're threatening didn't happen, but if I'm left with the choice of doing what you want, or leaving home, then rest assured, leaving home wins every time.'

I wanted this man out of my life, and I wanted it now right now, so my turn to threaten,

'And there's a few things you should consider. There can't be too many South Africans floating around, who own a large farm about an hour and fifteen minutes somewhere out of the city, and who also deals in precious stones. Also, remember that solicitor with that head of white hair? Some time back I found a photo of him in the Herald. So if you produce those photos you're talking of, I'll produce that one, and seeing as the subjects I'll be talking about with the police will be those of child rape and pornography, I wonder how he would stand up to an interrogation, especially considering I took a note of the days he came out to your house, so believe me when I say I'll do my best to incriminate you, you black mailing bastard.'

I was sure he knew it was slipping away, but being Malcolm, he had to have one last try,

'Look kid, I admit I'd have liked to have used you for another twelve months, especially considering you look so much younger than you are, so what say we compromise? Give me another six, not only will I make it worth your while, after that, no photos, nothing, that'll be the end, the last we ever see of each other.'

And I couldn't give him my answer quick enough, 'Malcolm, try to understand, it's over, finished, I've no intention of giving you another six seconds.'

I was tempted to slam the receiver down, but acting as the polite son I'd been brought up to be, placed it back gently on its cradle. I was back lying on my bed when my mother walked in, her arms full of washed and ironed clothing, and as she placed mine where they belonged, she asked, 'Who was that Mathew, someone who wanted you to caddie for him?'

I knew what he wanted, was a long way removed from caddying, so I simply replied,

'Something like that Mum, but I told him my caddying days were well and truly behind me.'

The house was quiet, my mother probably watching television, and in the solitude of my bedroom, I thought about my two abusers. Bergman, with his fastidious manners, neat and expensive clothing and immaculate grooming, in most areas of life a decent man, trying vainly to survive where a man with his sexual preferences shouldn't, surrounded by young boys, with the end result being, the constant temptation of the sex he desired, finally forcing him off that respectable path he normally travelled, and it was unfortunate that it was I, who, unwittingly provided the temptation for him to take the dangerous risks he did.

Malcolm, on the other hand, just the opposite. Cruel, callous and calculating, with his approach to life determined solely by financial gain, and accompanied by a total lack of remorse as to how he achieved it. People to him were nothing more than objects to use, and he remained conveniently oblivious to the damage he caused in the process. If it were possible to compare them on a list preferences, taking into consideration their sexual deviance, Bergman's would register well towards the top, Malcolm's well to the bottom. Both paedophiles, both fastidious dressers, but that was where any further attempt at comparison ended. They both lived in tainted worlds, but they were worlds that were a universe apart.

Nevertheless, although I felt convinced I'd succeeded in throwing off the shackles applied by both of them, quite a number of months passed before I was convinced I could finally relax. Then followed a brief period of self incrimination. What if I'd had the courage to stand up to Malcolm long before now, what amount of misery could have been avoided? But then followed something like sensible realisation. The only way I could have stood up to Malcolm, was from a position of mental and financial strength, and I'd only recently managed to acquire something in the region of the latter. But due to what I'd experienced out at his house, with those brutal encounters with Seth foremost in my mind, something I was now desperate to acquire was the ability to be able to protect myself to a point where such intimidation by the likes of Seth, could never occur again.

Being able to box relatively competently was all well and good, but something was telling me I needed to be able to lift myself to a level well beyond that. But where that level was, I had absolutely no idea. Judo was quickly considered, and just as quickly disregarded. Whereas it obviously suited many, I wasn't one of them, and as for prancing around in those baggy jackets;

that did absolutely nothing for me at all. However, finally through a chance encounter, I was introduced to a man, who for the next few years, was to play a major role in my life. Similar to Albie, he was quiet to a point of shyness, but yet again, lying just below that demure surface lay a lethal talent that left me spellbound with its dynamic effectiveness.

Mitsuki, was a master in the art of Jujitsu, that centuries old Japanese version of self defence. So during the years while I served my apprenticeship, I spent every spare moment training under him. The result was when I finally emerged as a qualified trades person, I also emerged as being proficient at Jujitsu to a point of being lethally dangerous. Unfortunately, those years of abuse under Seth had taken their toll, and as my new ability emerged, it did so accompanied by a pent up resentment, and I became a good example of the typical quick tempered, angry young man, with an ever present chip on his shoulder, a time bomb forever ticking, in danger of exploding at the slightest minor provocation. But gradually common sense prevailed, and I realised I was heading down a path, that unless I changed direction, could see me emerging as a junior version of the very man I detested. The thought of this happening didn't impress me, so I immediately concentrated on doing my best to get this undesirable trait firmly under control.

The apprenticeship under my father was to take around five years, the first three of which passed without any undue problems, my life saturated by a combination of work, Jujitsu and competition golf. But a major interruption appeared in the form of Compulsory Military Training. Half way through my eighteenth year an official letter arrived, demanding my presence at a military depo in Shortland Street, right in the centre of the city, where I, along with a number of others, was to undergo a medical examination. As I joined about thirty other youths, I couldn't help thinking, 'this should prove interesting' but my daydream, presumably along with a number of others, was rudely interrupted by a very military type voice, that proceeded to shout in a very military fashion, 'Right you lot, strip, then place your clothes neatly against that wall', and as around thirty pairs of eyes stared back in disbelief, he thundered, 'yes, you heard correctly, everything off, naked, understand? Now get on with it.'

The 'examinations' that followed, were conducted by two officers, both openly homosexual, and apart from a stethoscope that was casually passed over somewhere that could loosely be described as my chest, the rest of the so called medical followed something similar to what I'd first experienced in Bergman's office. Not, I decided, an overly auspicious start to life in the New Zealand Army. Never the less, around four weeks later a letter arrived, confirming I'd been classified as being A1 medically fit. My parents were horrified, I finished up highly amused. After all, I thought, if I could be passed as being medically fit with a major heart valve problem, for the army not to accept you, you'd have to be lying full length on a cold, hard slab in a mortuary. My parents insisted the decision should be reviewed, my reaction, absolutely not. The truth was, I was curious about experiencing life in the army, as it presented the opportunity of offering something quite different to my every day civilian life.

Our first day at the Papakura Military Camp, passed something like a well rehearsed nightmare. Bleak, damp, cold and miserable, it seemed the elements were determined to test us, before the army had even started. By the time the hours needed to issue us with our gear had concluded, many were considering going over the fence and rushing back to where they'd come from. But through the gloom and despondency, some words of wisdom from a sergeant we all came to admire, as he duly informed us, 'I'm aware this hasn't been a great introduction lads, but when your three months with us has expired, if you are asked to do it all again, eighty per cent of you will agree to do so.'

His words were met with much mirth, but he was proved to be one hundred per cent correct.

Chapter 32

With the ordeal of what we needed to be issued almost completed, we were shown to our huts that consisted of around twenty or so beds, with timber chests in which to store our belongings beside them, and not much else. The choice of who bedded down where, was left entirely to us, so I chose one on the right hand side, second from the far end, no particular reason, other than it looked as uncomfortable as any. After placing my gear on the bed, I left to collect one last item of clothing that due to short supply, hadn't previously been available.

When I returned, I was greeted by the sight of another young man of reasonably substantial proportions, lying full length on what I had claimed as my bed, with my belongings lying in an untidy heap in the centre of the floor. I took a deep breath. There would be those who'd attempt to dominate, some would succeed, some wouldn't. I could do without this, I'd been through it too often before, but there was no alternative, the issue had to be settled, one way or the other. I reminded myself, stay polite, but firm, 'Excuse me friend, you're lying on my bed. I'd appreciate it very much if you'd get off and place my gear back where you found it.'

Around twenty pairs of eyes locked on. He grinned, and placed his hands behind his head,

'Think you've got it all wrong mate,' he replied, 'this is my bed now, so it's up to you to claim it back, that's if you still think it's yours?'

Nothing to be gained in wasting time; best get it over and done with. I bent down, locked my thumb and finger in his left ear lobe, and pulled sharply. Didn't learn that movement from Mitsuki, I'd been taught it years before from the strange lady at Bible Class. It appeared it was as effective now, as it had been then, and as he rose from the bed, he attempted a right hand blow, but finished up flat on his face on the floor. He glanced up, not hurt, but apparently still a little surprised as to how he got there, as he asked,' Have you been trained at that martial art stuff?' I nodded. My clothes finished back in a neat pile on my bed, enough done, very little needing to be said, the brief encounter duly noted and registered by one and all. No more problems, and after a couple of weeks had passed, we finished up the best of friends.

Now some relief from what had been a strict training routine. A dance was to be held in the camp's recreation hall. Not far South were the Ardmore Hills, notorious for two things, first, the rather infamous military prison, and second, the training facility for future nurses, many of whom were only too happy to make themselves available as partners for the evening.

Also, some relaxation from the top brass, with a sensible amount of alcohol provided. Not that it's availability affected me one way or the other, having carried on what seemed like a family tradition of non drinkers, by preferring to down a Coke instead. But the evening rocked successfully on, in the process reminding me of the assembly hall at school, as the building literally pulsated to the noise from within, but the carefree tone changed slightly, as one of the boys

from my hut eased up a little hesitatingly alongside, 'Hey Colbie, one of the officers is out the back of the hall, beating the hell out of Wallace. Unless something's done about it, I tell you, it's serious enough, I think there's a chance he could finish up in hospital.'

Now Martin Wallace and I had become great pals, we were one of a kind, and accordingly, got on like a house on fire, and the fact he was being knocked around, didn't impress me at all, and as I walked around to the rear of the hall, I noticed a group standing and watching the slaughter. As far as the limited supply of alcohol was concerned, it instantly became apparent, that somehow, and from somewhere, Martin had managed to acquire a little more than what normally would be deemed as being his share. So with his fighting ability dulled accordingly, it was apparent the one sided battle had to stop, before he got even more seriously hurt than he already was.

Even then, warning bells rang, after all, an officer from the camp was involved, but that moment of hesitation lasted only until his face came into view, and there was instant recognition. He was one of those involved with that degrading medical inspection in the city. That was all that was needed as I moved in, but still exercising considerable caution. Alcohol fuelled or not, he was still an officer, and a fight with someone holding that sort of rank, offered a one way ticket to the Ardmore Military Prison, where the alleged treatment of inmates, going by the rumours that circulated around the camp, left a certain amount to be desired, and therefore, something to go out of your way to avoid. Whether this included eighteen year olds, I wasn't sure, but one way or the other, I had no inclination to find out.

Once again, stay calm, stay excruciatingly polite, 'Sir, could I suggest you back off. He's had enough, any more and he could finish up seriously hurt.'

His reply, brutally to the point, 'Fuck off, you interfering little prick, or you'll get even worse than what I'm giving to him.'

It was that 'little prick' part that really hurt. Over the last couple of years I'd caught up, and could now be considered a good average for my age, so I retaliated in kind, 'There's a good chance that's not going to happen Sir, so please, back off, or accept what happens from here,'

He declined to take the hint. For some reason one of the boys from the group who'd been watching, timed the confrontation, and swore it lasted no more than nine seconds. The following morning, on parade, standing at attention while waiting for the usual inspection, a mantle of frost covering the ground, quite usual for South Auckland at that time of the year. Eyes not wavering, looking straight ahead, the inspecting officer coming into view, and concern flickers. The right hand side of his face was raw from where it had hit the asphalt, and the sticking plaster over his nose, wasn't adding to his battered appearance either. Now standing directly in front, our eyes meet, recognition registers in his. Finally acknowledges me with the briefest of nods, pauses, then moves on, which proved he may have his faults, but he knew what a sense of fair play was. Whether it included eighteen year olds or not, I've avoided a trip to Ardmore. The day may be cold, but at least it was starting well.

Four weeks completed, meaning we're a third of the way through our compulsory training, but that morning was to have repercussions that were

destined to affect me for the rest of my life. Some excitement as we're given the news. Later that morning we were scheduled to take part in a live shoot down at the rifle range. Now all deemed to be physically fit, due to the extensive training we'd been subjected too, something I'd managed with barely a problem, much to my parent's delight, the next phase in our military life was being placed in our respective companies, be they infantry, artillery signals or ASC, the latter being the much sought after soft life of driving. However, with the full intake included, which was around one hundred and fifty boys, the top six who scored the highest points on the rifle range, would make up a select group to be trained as sharp shooters, possibly more commonly known as snipers. Those who were successful would advance to the rank of corporal.

Down at the range, the conditions considered perfect for shooting. Barely no more than a light breeze, the morning cloudy but clear, meaning no glaring sun to contend with. Having been issued with our six live rounds, sixteen of us take up our positions on the range, automatically placing ourselves in the approved firing position that had been drilled into us. Sixteen hearts thumping, caused by the thrill of anticipation, all ready and waiting for the sergeant's command to commence firing. Everything as it should be, except for one small omission, none of us had been issued with ear protection. That anticipated moment almost upon us, the sergeant shouting his final instructions, 'You will hold your positions until I give the order to commence firing. Remember, there is no time limit involved. Take the time you feel you need to fire the six rounds. Now is everybody ready?'

Not a word, not a movement, sixteen youths sighting down the barrel in front of them, their whole being registering solely on that target in the distance. Now those tensely waited final instructions, 'Right, everyone ready, then you may commence firing.'

And as he shouted that final, all important word, the explosion caused by the combined total of sixteen rifles commenced its devastating journey as it smashed into my right ear, carried on with a loud popping noise while passing through my head, then departed with equally devastating damage out of my left ear, and from that time on, I was rendered totally deaf. At that moment, I sensed serious damage had occurred, but I was left with one unintended advantage. I was now so deaf, as I fired off my remaining five rounds, I did so without the distraction of any noise, because I couldn't hear a thing anyway.

Down at the canteen that evening, still stone deaf, looking for my usual game of table tennis. One of the boys was an Auckland representative player, and every game he'd beat the pants of me, and I couldn't wait to go back for more. The following morning, some slight improvement, a little of my hearing returning, but accompanied by this disturbing ringing noise in my ears. Late morning, placed on report for disobeying an order, that being an order I hadn't heard, with the boys instantly jumping to my defence, 'Hey, come off it sarge, give him a break, he can't hear properly.'

'What do you mean, he can't hear properly?'

'Just that sergeant. Since he came off the range, he's barely been able to hear a thing.'

'Charge dismissed Colbert. Get moving, you're down to the medical officer immediately.'

The usual no hopers sitting around, convinced they're half dead because of a head cold, or something as equally as devastating. Finally my turn as I walk in, the medic peering at me through thick lensed glasses. Nothing overly noticeable about him, probably entered the army on leaving Medical School, and will depart when retirement finally beckons. He politely asks,

'And what can I do for you soldier?

'Not too sure Sir. Got my ears blasted on the rifle range yesterday, and haven't been able to hear properly since, and I've also got this weird ringing noise in my head that's bugging me.'

There was something about the change in his demeanour that concerned me. His back seemed to stiffen as he leant forward, now concentrating, looking at me intently through those thick glasses, his attitude clearly suggesting what I'd said, had for some reason, disturbed him. It was as if a wall of protection was now separating us, and it was there for the sole reason of protecting the army, certainly not me. He continued to sit for quite some seconds before he replied, and when he did, he spoke slowly and carefully, as if giving a lot of thought to what he was saying, in the process making sure that wall of protection remained intact, 'Yes, well as far as your hearing is concerned, there's no doubt it's reacting to shock, but it should return to something like normal before too long. And that ringing, time should take care of that as well. But tell me, have you received your company posting yet?'

My unease increased, my hearing should do this, the ringing should do that. All very non committal, but I was hardly in a position to argue. Not only was he the medical professional, he had an officer's superiority as well, and now he wanted to brush the problem with my hearing aside, and talk about my posting instead, so I explained, 'First of all I was posted to the artillery, but after the exercise on the range, they told me I'll be going to the infantry. Never handled a rifle before in my life, but my score was the third best recorded.'

And his reaction to that, instant and emphatic, almost suggesting a mild form of panic,

'Oh no, you're not going to either of those. As a precaution, you're to be kept away from noise for the rest of the time you're in the camp. Without a doubt, it's the ASC for you my boy. I'll fill in the required paperwork straight away. Rather than firing rifles, you're going to be driving trucks instead.'

Driving trucks? That ought to prove interesting, I'd never set foot in a truck in my life, bar that one when we shifted all those years back. No doubt about it, the army offered an interesting life, the only sad thing being, I missed out on being promoted to corporal.

So the next stage of my army life, turned out to be the ASC. The NCO who seemed to be in charge was a short little man with a handlebar moustache, a voice that made up for his lack of size, and an American Indian motorbike, that he careered around on at breakneck speed, and in the process, breaking every road rule known to mankind. We were sitting in a room, waiting for a lecture from some idiot who'd failed to turn up, lolling around, having a chat, when our little speeding non commissioned appears instead, 'What are you lot doing

here,' he thundered, 'aren't you supposed to be out there doing something, or whatever?'

One of the boys attempted to explain our situation, but got cut short instead, as he roared,

'Oh, what the hell, I've given up trying to keep track of you lot. Anyway, never mind, you're in the ASC, and believe it or not, that means you're supposed to be driving trucks, so hands up those of you who have your heavy licence.'

And when not one hand was raised in confirmation, he thundered, 'Well you're having your test straight after lunch, understand?'

We sat there open mouthed and in a mild state of shock. Surely he didn't mean it, we were all the same, never having driven a truck in our lives, in fact, there were at least a couple, who hadn't even driven a car. And if that wasn't bad enough, trucks like the old Chevy's at the camp, didn't even have synchromesh gears. One of the regular drivers had informed us, every time you had to change gear, you had to double the clutch. Doubling the clutch, as far as I was concerned, was like talking a load of double Dutch, I had absolutely no idea what it meant.

Then came a flash of inspiration, surely if we could persuade someone to let us have a truck, we could spend some time practising before we sat the dreaded test. After all, it wasn't as if there was a shortage of them, the place was literally littered with trucks, courtesy of the Americans, left here after the war, apparently more economical than shipping them back to the States. So from somewhere a truck was purloined, with the results of our practising being nothing short of hideous, until it reached a point where we sent it back, scared that if we didn't, the demolition wrought on the gearbox would prove to be so substantial, instead of driving it, we'd finish up having to push it, and it was all uphill to where it belonged.

Back to the room, mournfully preparing to accept the fate that awaited us in the form of a furious NCO who'd found he'd been lumbered with a series of idiots in the ASC who couldn't drive trucks. An hour evaporated, our nerves steadily deteriorating, another fifteen minutes, now the familiar sound of an Indian motorbike being driven at reckless speed and skidding to a halt outside, and moments later our elusive NCO appearing moustache quivering as he shouts to all and sundry, 'Sorry I'm a bit late, one of our vehicles involved in an accident in Newmarket that kept me. Now what are you lot here for, oh, that's right, testing for your heavy licences, wasn't it? Well no time left for those sort of trivialities, I've no doubt you're all very competent anyway, so leave all the necessary, like names, date of birth and addresses, you'll all have your licences in about four days from now. Any questions? No right, then that's fine chaps, due to this bloody accident I've got all this damn paperwork to contend with, so cheerio, must run.'

He careered off, no doubt with handlebar moustache still quivering. However, by the time we left the army, rest assured, we really could drive trucks, even if we did have to teach ourselves. The remaining six weeks spent in the ASC seemed to pass in no time at all, and as we sat and chatted over the numerous humorous incidents that had occurred, and the few not so funny, of

the many friends made, the extremely rare disagreements, one thing we all confirmed were those words that had been uttered by our sergeant on that very first miserable day. On a show of hands, if we'd have been offered the opportunity of doing it all again, if the paperwork had been in front of us, ninety per cent of us would have signed on the dotted line without hesitation. On returning to civilian life, if there was one word in the English language we'd never fully appreciated the importance of, but most certainly did on having spent those months in the army, it was the word discipline.

Four months on, comfortably back into life as a civilian, the medical officer right with one opinion, wrong with the other. My hearing had improved, but the ringing in my ears as persistent as ever, to a point where I was forced to contact the authorities and request a medical assessment of the problem. A few more weeks pass, an official letter arrives, confirming an appointment with a specialist in the city. Thanks to my Mondia watch, I arrive exactly on time, the waiting room deserted, not another human being to be seen. Ten minutes and a door opens, the specialist stands there beckoning to me, dressed in full military uniform, a major if I've determined his rank correctly, going by those pips on his shoulders. An ideal situation for the army, not so for yours truly, the army assessing damage to my hearing caused by the army, not as far as I'm concerned, anything like an ideal situation.

He rambles on, using technical terms I have trouble following, so I give some polite hints, I'd like to be able to understand what he's getting at, so finally he responds accordingly,

'To put it frankly young man, you're experiencing a condition called tinnitus, which relates to permanent damage to your hearing, and at this point a cure doesn't exist, and there's a good chance there never will be, so I regret to say, you're going to have to learn to live with it. However, it also renders you unfit for any possible future military service, so as from today you can take it you're out of the army.'

I make it known I'm far from happy, especially when common sense indicates that if a pittance had been spent on providing ear protection, the damage would never have occurred. He agrees, but at the same time shrugs his shoulders, clearly indicating he considers it just one of those unfortunate things, so I raise the question of compensation, and the benign smile changes to a smirk as he confirms, 'Well I wish you the best of luck if you should decide to head in that direction, but they're bound to fight your claim, so you'll find it will become a very lengthy and therefore costly exercise, and from where I'm sitting, I wouldn't be putting my money on your chance of winning.'

I take the hint, enough said, one thing I've acquired free of charge and courtesy of the New Zealand Army, tinnitus for the rest of my life, a condition I'm not looking forward to having to live with. Years later and still suffering, I couldn't help wondering what the outcome would have been if the Accident Compensation Commission had existed.

Chapter 33

But the Commission didn't exist, so I was conveniently left to make the best out of what proved to be a dreadfully debilitating condition. The time remaining on my apprenticeship passed reasonably quickly, but through it all those disturbing dreams still persisted, I'd still be kneeling in front of him, lying over that Kauri table, being cleansed by Maria in that bathroom, walking on into that bedroom, performing sex acts with James, choking while I hung from that rope in the barn, but the harder I tried, the more distant the remedy required to eliminate them seemed to become, and the confinement caused by the walls of the factory seemed to be adding to my frustration.

So after much careful deliberation, I made the decision to act on something I'd been contemplating for quite some time, I would take off, interested to have a look around the world. And I stumbled, as I attempted to explain to my father the necessity for me to be able to do so, but he stopped my ramblings, assuring me he completely understood, in fact stressed he felt it would be highly beneficial. So with his encouragement adding the final boost, another phase of my life commenced.

Similar to thousands of other young travellers from various points scattered around the globe, I chose London as my central base for exploring the endless variety of beauty and general interest that Europe offers, and while there, I always stayed at what was known in those days as The Overseas Visitors Club. Formed by a group of young entrepreneurs who'd recognised the necessity for providing reasonably priced lodgings and facilities for the seemingly endless stream of wanderers who constantly passed through that part of the world, the club offered everything that anyone in a similar situation to myself could want, clean, comfortable lodgings, reasonable food to suit all tastes, a central location and the interest provided by mixing with many other nationalities.

On my arrival, I don't deny, some short lived despair, when after being allocated a bed in a twin share room, found my roommate's accent clearly indicated he was South African. However, in a pleasing contrast to Malcolm, he turned out to be a fine young man, polite and well spoken and a pilot in the South African Airforce. During one of the many occasions when we lay on our beds and chatted, he told me of his deep concern for the future, as he saw it, for his country, as he stressed with some considerable feeling, 'One day the blacks will take over,' he said, 'the constant demand by those who've never even set foot in the country and who have absolutely no firsthand knowledge of the problems that exist, combined with the fact that the blacks out number us to the extent they do, will win out in the end, and when that happens, crime will explode out of control. Take it from me Mathew, there's big trouble looming in that country I was born in and love so dearly, but I made my decision sometime back. The reason I'm here is because I've applied to become a fighter pilot in the Royal Air Force instead. All of the flight testing and medicals and whatever,

plus all the usual never ending paperwork is behind me, so now all I can do is sit around and wait. I want this just so bad Mathew.'

Three days after our discussion, an official letter arrived, and I noticed his hands were shaking slightly while he opened it. No cause for further worry, he'd been accepted, he was in.

His ecstatic delight was contagious, so we decided to celebrate his success in the form of a steak meal at a restaurant that had become our favourite in Piccadilly, but first, there was one slight problem to overcome, we were both low on funds. Perhaps it was in some way quite fitting that our financial saviour appeared in the form of another of his countrymen. Johan was a solid, bear of a young man, who constantly wandered around the club with a smile on his face and an ever present invitation to fight. There wasn't really all that much wrong with him, other than on a number of occasions some of the boys classed him as being a bit of a pest. The terms he suggested never varied, as he'd say in his strong Boer accent,

'We both put up ten pounds man, and the first to put the other on the floor takes all.'

We were keen to celebrate that evening, and Johan cooperated by suggesting I fight him early in the afternoon, and seemed slightly surprised when I accepted his well timed invitation, especially after having had so many of the boys graciously decline. His money not only paid for our superb steak meals, but also an excellent bottle of wine to go with them.

Just over one month later, my roommate having departed after receiving his posting, and I'd just returned to London after sampling the scenic delight and general pleasures available while touring around Scandinavia. As with most of my touring in Europe, this had been financed by teaching basic self defence to those willing to pay to learn how to defend themselves simply, but effectively. However, one of my few regrets as far as my extensive travelling was concerned, was the time I'd spent in Paris, which had been marred by absolutely atrocious weather, something that in most cases, I'd been lucky enough to avoid.

But now the situation was reversed, and as I looked out over the bleakness that was currently prevailing in London, the temptation of the clear blue skies I'd been assured were waiting in France proved too tempting to resist. So with my finances bolstered by money wired to me from home, and with my self defence courses proving to be surprisingly lucrative, I wasn't slow in taking the hint that nature was offering, and it was back across the channel.

And the small, quaint hotel the travel agent had recommended so highly seemed to be living up to expectations, and with the young bell boy doing all the things that well trained bell boys should, I slipped into his discreetly offered palm what was a reasonably generous tip. Apparently suitably encouraged, as he went to step out and close the door, suddenly he turned and spoke to me, doing his best to make himself understood in his very limited version of English. Before leaving, I'd been informed my schoolboy French would prove to be next to useless when put to the test, but fortunately, this had proven to be quite incorrect, because I had found I could understand what was being said, as long as they spoke reasonably slowly, equally as well as they could understand me.

So as far as the bell boy was concerned, I went to some lengths to explain that as long as he slowed down a bit, rather than speaking with the rapidity that came so naturally to him, then there was a good chance I could fathom what he was saying if he dispensed with his attempt at English, and spoke to me in French. But when he did repeat himself, slowly and carefully as requested, I realised this ten or eleven year old was offering some female companionship for the night. Now slightly uncomfortable, I did my best to explain I wasn't in the habit of using the services of such women.

This in turn erupted in a disaster approaching major proportions, as he proceeded to inform me with considerable venom, that rather than offering me the services of some lowly lady of the night, on the contrary, I was being granted the ultimate privilege of an introduction to his much loved older sister, who it so happened, he adored like nobody else in his life. Fortunately, my hastily concocted apology managed to finally smooth some extremely ruffled feathers to a point where after some further slight deliberation, he extracted a photo from his wallet. And as my gaze settled on the slim figure at which he was pointing, it instantly became apparent his sister didn't just fall into the category of being relatively easy on the eye, because she was in fact nothing short of being stunningly beautiful.

With the time confirmed by the use of her young brother, we met later that afternoon at a café across the lane from the hotel, and any unease that existed evaporated in minutes, as in no time at all we sat sipping coffee and chatting away like old friends, a situation that was assisted by the fact she happened to speak the most enchanting, lightly French accented English. And as the sun started to settle, heralding the start of the closure of yet another perfect Parisian day, her infectious smile combined with her delightful personality swept me totally under her spell. Conveniently, she happened to be on a few days holiday from her position in the public relations division of the Shell Oil Company's Paris office, so for the next three days she acted as a guide as we toured the city's sights, but on the fourth day a wonderful addition, as we slept together that night.

The following morning I booked out of the hotel and moved into her small but tastefully decorated apartment, with this heralding the start of a mutually powerful attraction, the flames of which weren't just fanned by our sexual compatibility, but also by a series of other intangibles that are such a successful element in helping to weave that intricate spell, that only those who've been involved in such special relationships, can ever hope to understand. So we lived, loved, laughed and played together, and somehow and from somewhere Annette Raymond discovered that elusive formula that succeeded in eliminating the fear, inhibitions and guilt those years of abuse and shame had created. And as a result, we proceeded to make wonderful, unbelievable and truly unforgettable love of such a magnitude, that never had I thought such a relationship would prove to be possible.

And there were many other bonuses as well, such as escaping from the city, taking off into the magnificent countryside, occasionally hiring a boat and cruising the canals, stopping at the numerous jetties provided, strolling up into the quaint little villages where we'd wander the streets, pausing to admire the

variety of merchandise displayed in the shop windows or in the open air stalls, with the aroma of fresh fruit and vegetables, of cured meat and spices of all kinds hanging heavy in the air. But mainly we'd simply climb into her small Renault car, then after offering a prayer that it wouldn't break down, we'd take off wherever our instincts took us, stopping at the vineyards, mixing and laughing with the locals as they made jokes about my accent, and I'd laugh along with them, while sampling their wonderful wines. I may have qualified as being close to a teetotaller, but I had no objection what so ever to the occasional glass of white wine, with Annette doing her best to even the score with her preference for reds.

Those nights were spent in one of the numerous boarding houses or pensions, scattered along the way, laughing as we chose one that for some obscure reason, managed to catch our eye. The evenings were often spent lying in front of the ever present open fire, with Annette lying comfortably in my arms. Occasionally we were able to take Annette's brother with us on some of these excursions, and the boy's delight on being able to escape the city, seemed to at least match my own. It had rapidly become apparent the affection that existed between sister and brother was absolute in the extreme, with this special bond seemingly having been intensified by the absence of their parents, this being a topic that simply wasn't discussed.

So for reasons that remained tactfully unknown, at least as far as I was concerned anyway, the boy lived with his uncle and aunt, they of course being the proprietors of the small hotel the agent in London had so enthusiastically recommended, and at which I'd stayed at so briefly. Similar to any youngster his age, most of his weekdays were spent at school, but the moment he arrived home and homework was completed, the minimal time left was spent working for his relatives. The majority of his weekends were spent the same way, but every so often his uncle would relent and allow the boy some time away, and that's when we'd take off.

Early on, I'd suggested to Annette that seeing as the boy was with us, perhaps we should be sleeping apart, but she quickly laughed that off, and as my friendship with the lad continued to strengthen, I realised he was more than familiar with the ways of the adult world, because one day he casually informed me that if I hadn't have been sleeping with his sister, he'd have found the situation strange in the extreme. But as my time with sister and brother drifted pleasantly on, I found that Allain was making me long for that boy of my own. He didn't have to be as handsome as Allain, because I'd long accepted he was one of the few I'd ever met who could rival James for sheer, dark, brooding good looks, but I was also having to reluctantly accept that his sister was not destined to become the mother of my desperately needed son.

Above all else, she was a child of Paris, her adoration of the city being all consuming and total in the extreme, and it was this that placed that impregnable barrier between us. For my part, charming, vibrant, exciting and outstandingly beautiful though it was, where Annette preferred the feel of the pavements under her feet, I much preferred grass. And where she remained constantly captivated by the architecture that surrounded her, I could see even more beauty in a landscape. And probably above all else, where she thrived with those inevitable

thousands bustling around her, I needed a lot more open space. Back in her apartment one evening, after experiencing for us what had proved to be a rather hectic day, the possibility of our future together was tentatively discussed, so we sat and talked into the small hours, desperate to find some sort of workable compromise. But finally the inevitable and common sense won through, so midst a few tears and a lot of pain, we reluctantly agreed circumstances that tended to dominate our separate lives were clearly indicating the time had come to part, and as a result, the following morning I booked my return flight to London.

Both sister and brother insisted on accompanying me to the airport, and I in turn insisted they weren't to come into the lounge, being all too painfully aware the farewells were going to prove bad enough, without dragging them on and on. The taxi pulled up outside the battery of doors at the departure terminal, and even as I jumped out and collected my luggage, I noticed a traffic control officer already had us firmly in his sights. Our driver would be given no more than the allotted time then he'd be expected to move on.

And as I took Annette in my arms, she felt even more warm and yielding than I could ever recall, and we kissed with a passion that only separating lovers possess, but in contrast, Allain continued to sit in the cab, not moving, simply staring straight ahead. After another last, lingering kiss, Annette slipped back into the rear seat, but as I moved up to say goodbye to the boy, apart from a perfunctory shake of my hand through the open window, he offered nothing more. As the driver eased out into the queue of slow moving traffic, I stepped back onto the forecourt and waved, but after travelling no more than ten metres, suddenly the taxi stopped, in the process bringing four or five other vehicles to an urgent stop behind it, then the front door was flung open as the boy stumbled out. We stood there eyeing each other for a few seconds, then he charged back and flung himself into my arms, from where he wrapped his own around my neck and cried as if his heart was going to break.

So with a couple of the same in mine, I held him close and talked quietly, assuring him the pain we were experiencing in parting would soon be replaced by the memories of the wonderful times we'd enjoyed, and it was one of those occasions when I'd managed to say the right words, because the flow of tears finally stopped. And when they did, I made him promise that no matter what the future brought, he'd always look after his sister for me, which he solemnly promised he would, and as we walked back arm in arm to the cab, I nodded to the traffic warden, silently offering my thanks for his patience. So after one last hug for the boy, and the same again plus a kiss for his sister, the taxi finally cruised away.

As I stood there, I had to admit there were faint similarities to when Col had left, even if they were many years apart. Once again I found myself wishing the vehicle would swing around and come back and stop beside me, so I could step back in and return to the apartment with them, where life would simply carry on just as it had during those past, wonderful months. But instead I stood there waving as the driver headed for the freeway back to the city, with Allain hanging precariously out of the window, waving enthusiastically back, just as Colin had, and it was finally when the taxi disappeared that the realisation

flooded over me. For the first time, two people from outside my own immediate family had managed to step into a very special time in my life, and both in their own irreplaceable way, had claimed a permanent place in my heart.

Chapter 34

So it was back to London, where a letter had been waiting for me for quite some time from my mother. Although he was loath to admit it, my father's health was declining, and although the problem appeared to have been stabilised, she felt that considering the time I'd been away, which I was the first to admit had extended well beyond what I'd originally intended, perhaps she hinted, it was time to be giving some thought to returning home. Something else that hastened my decision to do so was once again the weather in London, which was as bad as the day I'd left. It was as if I'd been away for hours, rather than the months I had, so with the letter and the atrocious weather providing all the incentive I needed, I booked my flight back to Auckland, travelling via New York. A young Australian and myself had stuck up a strong friendship during our time together at the club, and with him now homesick for the family cattle station in Queensland, we decided to travel across the United States together.

However, at the last minute his departure was unexpectedly delayed, so our revised arrangement was that rather than altering my own departure at the last minute, I'd continue on, which meant I'd arrive about six days ahead of him, then wait for him to catch up with me there. As it happened, this revised arrangement worked well, Rodd had visited New York before, he'd done the sights and wasn't all that keen on doing them all over again, so just a couple of days in the city suited him fine. So the days suddenly made available before he arrived, meant I could please myself where I went and what I saw, without having to drag him along somewhat reluctantly as well.

The flight proved to be smooth, comfortable and uneventful, leaving me convinced that as far as any future travel was concerned, flying surely had to be the only way to go. In keeping with the arrangements we'd made, and once again due to fast diminishing funds, I booked accommodation for us at the local YMCA, which similar to the club in London, offered clean and reasonably priced rooms. Now settled, and with those days available to me before Rodd arrived, I was eager to take in the sights, so Radio City, the United Nations Building, The Statue of Liberty, The Empire State Building, Rockefeller Centre, Times Square, the Guggenheim Museum and Central Park were all struck off my list, along with a substantial loss of sweat and energy. At times I couldn't decide what troubled me the most, the cold and dismal damp of London, or the ninety five degree heat and one hundred per cent of humidity that was currently prevailing in New York.

Late afternoon on the fourth day, another round of sightseeing successfully completed, eager to get back, the weather as hot and humid as ever, with just the thought of a cold shower making it all well and truly worthwhile. Finally down in the shower room, relaxing as that blissful cold water tumbled down, my thoughts swinging as I contemplated the rest of my journey home. At no time during my time away could I confess to feeling homesick, but the thought of visiting familiar sights and catching up with old friends had me accepting there

was no doubt I was looking forward to it. But I was crudely snapped out of my daydream as a hand glided over my buttocks, and in a split second I wasn't in New York, I was back in that bedroom, where the same had occurred all too often.

I turned slowly, and quickly assessed him as being around my own height and weight, fair hair, a reasonable build, and unfortunately the semi sneer on his face reminded me in some way of Seth, and this became even more pronounced when he stopped eying me and spoke,

'Quite some body you've got there kid, and I wouldn't mind sampling a bit of it, you know what I mean. I suggest you just relax and accept what happens, won't take me all that long.'

If anyone knew what he meant, I did, and I certainly wasn't too sure about this kid bit. Sure, he was quite a bit older than I was, but whether the difference was enough for him to qualify as being able to get away with calling me 'kid' was I felt, definitely open to debate.

Also, I had to admit to being slightly surprised. I'd encountered a number of homosexuals during my travels, after all, there'd been at least four of them at the club, and in all cases they'd proved to be great company and only too content to keep their sexual preferences entirely to themselves, and there'd never been a hint of the aggression that was openly on display here, but as usual, that inner voice was saying stay cool, calm and collected,

'Look, just stay away from me, alright. Get another cubicle and keep your hands to yourself.'

Apparently he wasn't bothered by my hint, perhaps convinced that previous experience in matters such as this would prove to be enough. He moved in, very aggressive, and it crossed my mind, perhaps alcohol was involved, not that I could smell it on his breath.

The floor and walls of the shower room were tiled, and the decidedly higher than normal ceiling had two lights, with for some reason, the bulbs protected by metal grills. His feet travelled so high as he sailed over my head, one of the grills was dislodged, and it clattered across the floor, making a terrible racket as it bounced around until it finally came to rest.

I continuing to roll then sprung to my feet, ready for his next attempt, but a glance across the room showed my aggressor was at rest also. He was lying face down and full length, blood streaming from what had to be a severe cut on his forehead, probably sustained when he'd ploughed head first into the tiled floor. And what made the situation appear even worse than it already was, not that it wasn't bad enough already, was that being a shower room, it had been used fairly frequently throughout the day, and with many feet having assisted with the coverage, the floor was floating in a film of water, with which the blood was rapidly mixing, and in doing so, exaggerating the mess even more.

A slight noise as another youth entered the room. He stopped dead, took one look at the inert body and the rest, then turned and fled. I went across and turned him over, and as I'd expected, the cut was deep, very deep, and continuing to pour blood. There was a cabinet on the other side of the room with a number of white towels stacked on it. One wouldn't be white much longer, because I grabbed it and went back and held it against his forehead, doing whatever I

could to help stem the flow, and that was when the manager walked in followed by a couple of the local constabulary. I was taken back to my room to dress, during which my attempts at an explanation were studiously ignored, then something new but not overly pleasant, as my arms were held behind my back while handcuffs were snapped on my wrists. Now down to a waiting patrol car and with the ride proving to be comparatively short, in no time at all I found myself sitting in a holding room at the local precinct.

The place hummed with the chatter of phones and various electronic equipment apparently all doing what they were supposed to be doing, with the only problem being nobody seemed to be the remotest bit interested in me. Finally, as one of the many personnel went to walk past me yet again without even a glance in my direction, I decided a hint was required,

'Hey, what about seeing if you can get them to take these embarrassing things off my wrists? I'm not going anywhere stuck in here like this, and I can't understand why I'm here at all.' He stopped and glanced across, his expression saying he wasn't all that interested anyway,

'Just hang on a little longer,' he said, 'that's what they all say, so you're following a rather familiar pattern. What's your name? I'll try and locate the paperwork, that'll fill me in.'

He wandered off, and about twenty minutes past, during which I gave up hope of any further response. Looks like I'm set to spend the night in this cage, but at least I can see out and the room's air conditioned, which is an improvement on the last time I was incarcerated.

This had occurred in East Berlin, where I'd been wandering around with three others, and the difference compared to the West was providing quite a shock to our systems. Under the American occupation West Berlin was thriving and well on the way to returning to the vibrant, bustling city locals assured me it had been. But East Berlin was providing a morbid contrast, stark, solemn and desolate, rather than busy crowds like its counterpart, few people to be seen, and rather than enjoying the fresh air, it was as if they were hibernating instead.

After wandering around amongst this uninspiring collection of semi desolate buildings for a couple of hours, we'd decided returning to the West now held top priority, but as we headed in the direction of the Brandenburg Gate, there in front of us appeared the reason for my brief acquaintance with an East German cell. Painted in all its glory on the side of a badly damaged three story building, was a massive propaganda mural, which gave a clear indication of how low relations between the USSR and the USA had sunk. Painted in a semi cartoon fashion, the mural showed the two countries with a solitary soldier standing on them, the Russian, smiling and welcoming, the American scowling and aggressive. And added to these was the depiction of a nuclear armed missile, fired from Russia and landing in the centre of the USA, with the deadly mushroom cloud spreading outward and devastating all in its path.

I couldn't resist it; I just had to have some photos to show the folks back home. The streets may have been deserted, but apparently not deserted enough. Minutes after the photos had been taken, an East German military vehicle drove up, we were ordered to get in the back and taken to the local lockup, where they proceeded to strip out the film. Apparently to emphasise their point, we were left

to ourselves in the cell for over an hour, although I noticed they didn't even bother to lock the door. On our release, they made it quite obvious our presence was no longer required, and somehow I managed to keep a straight face until once again we were standing on friendly soil. The first two photos I'd taken were the last on the film, which I'd taken out and placed in my pocket while I installed the replacement in the camera. Those photos are still in my collection to this day, and something I was also very pleased about, my camera was handed back as well.

With it all ending happily in East Berlin, now I wanted the same result in New York, and possibly some hope, with my detective reappearing, staring intently at some paperwork,

'Seems you half killed some guy up at the YM, so give me your version of what took place.'

First I asked him to remove the cuffs, which, accompanied by his apology he did, then I told what had occurred. He gave me a nod and departed, but in no time at all he was back, let me out of the enclosure, then indicated I was to sit at a desk, from the other side of which he said,

'They've got that moron down at casualty, because apparently he's required quite a number of stitches in that cut. He's screaming blue bloody murder, threatening to press charges for assault, but the fact is some of the boys know him for what he is. They've had plenty of trouble with him before, and class him as nothing more than a bullying, perverted pest, so our opinion is it's you who should be pressing charges, certainly not him, so do you want to kid?'

I assured him nothing could be further from my mind, and minutes later, after the usual paperwork had been signed, I found myself standing alone outside the precinct. I was free, and that was all very well, but I was also very lost. While in the back of the patrol car, I'd lost my sense of direction in what was still a very unfamiliar city, and accordingly, didn't have the faintest idea where I was. It was looking like the expense of a taxi couldn't be avoided, that was until my plain clothed benefactor appeared beside me. He lit a cigarette then asked,

'You're looking a bit lost kid?' and when I confirmed as much he added, 'then just hang on, they're bringing my car around. My night's just starting, so I'll drop you back at the YM. From now on make sure you shower on your own, and I hope you enjoy the rest of your time with us. Believe me, we're not all idiots like him.'

Back in more familiar surroundings, I thought about what had occurred and it didn't please me. My response to his approach had been instinctive, but also decidedly dangerous. Protecting yourself may be one thing, seriously harming, or taken to the extreme, killing another human being, entirely another. The position of the cut he'd received proved beyond doubt he'd landed on his head, and taking into consideration the height of the ceiling, I couldn't help wondering, how far away had he been from a broken neck? In my opinion, not far at all, so a lesson learnt, there would have to be dire circumstances, before I'd raise my hand in anger against another person again. Rodd arrived the following morning, and I didn't mention what had occurred, being of the opinion the quicker the incident was forgotten, the better. Our journey across to

the East Coast; a revelation in itself, and after a stopover in Fiji, so ended my overseas' sojourn.

Chapter 35

So it was back in Auckland, and missing Annette like I couldn't believe, eight months on, a call from a valued builder client who'd developed a mutual business arrangement with one of the city's leading architects. David thrived on designing very expensive homes for the moneyed families in the area, and George was absolutely delighted to build them. There was a small problem with a house currently under construction, he'd appreciate it if we could meet on site. With an appointment confirmed for that afternoon, when I stepped inside the partly completed two storied home, it appeared almost deserted, apart from a single carpenter who was standing at a bench positioned at the foot of the stairs. I walked over, and with his head down and busy as he was, it took him a few seconds to realise I was standing beside him. He glanced up, slightly startled, then the look of shock that briefly appeared had me convinced he'd mistaken me for someone else. Passing his apparent unease off, I asked where I could find George, and a couple more seconds past before he informed me I'd locate him upstairs.

Ten minutes of discussion saw the somewhat difficult problem solved, so back downstairs, stopping briefly beside the bench, as I mentally checked I'd given the builder all the information required, and it was during that moment of hesitation that the workman reached out and placed a hand lightly on my arm. He glanced around, appearing to make sure the builder hadn't followed, then spoke softly, as if making certain only I alone could hear,

'I can imagine what you're thinking, and I don't blame you, considering what happened the last time we met. Been a few years since we've had anything to do with each other, hasn't it?'

I looked at him carefully, still convinced he must have mistaken me for someone else, I was sure we'd never met, then ever so gradually something started to stir in my memory, there was something about his eyes.

Slowly, ever so slowly, a picture started to form in my mind, and it was that of a young boy, naked, tied face down in a shed, another boy standing behind, inserting a screwdriver handle up the boy's rectum, then violently ripping it out, then when finally satisfied, moving forward and raping him. Now another, this time the same boy kneeling on some sacks, his wrists secured behind his back, his mouth open and tilted back, while the same youth stood naked in front, verbally tormenting him, that was until once again he moved forward and this time urinated in the boy's mouth. In a way I found it surprising I hadn't recognised him, the tall, gangly youth called Paul Cunningham, was now the tall, gangly adult, with those eruptions around his chin replaced by a three or four day old stubble. But those eyes of his hadn't changed one bit, they still registered as being as cruel as ever.

Old grievances briefly dominated as I took a step forward, the movement caused entirely by a long held desire for revenge, and just as instinctively he stepped back, but it ended there, that unpleasant experience in New York

guaranteed that, so as we stood beside that workbench eyeing each other, it was that, and that alone that saved him. But at the same time I felt nothing had changed since we'd faced off in that shower room at the camp. I found I still had no desire to talk to him, and it was as if knowing I now possessed the ability to break his arm in seconds was quite enough, so there was no way I was entering into some petty confrontation, caused by something, no matter how unpleasant, that had occurred all those years back. At that time he'd been barely more than a child, probably in the process of attempting to understand and unravel what he was finding to be his disturbing sexuality.

He placed the plane he'd been using, carefully on its side back on the bench, then stared at the floor, giving the impression he was thinking closely about what he wanted to say next,

'Look, I don't intend to try and find excuses for what I did, because quite frankly, there aren't any. All I can say is many of us do things when we're young, we come to regret later. I've never forgotten what you suffered in that shed, or how you tried to protect your friend, or what he did to you. Do you still have anything to do with him, the obnoxious little prick?'

I was tempted to turn and walk away, because I had no interest in answering his questions, and there was no way he'd ever know of the ramifications that had occurred, once they'd given those films to Bergman. But a sudden change of heart, he did seem contrite over what had happened those years back, so I'd answer his question, then that would be the end of it,

'The fact is I've had nothing to do with him from that day you're speaking of, and I don't deny what happened between us certainly ended our friendship. Over the years I've heard various rumours about him, but whether they're true or not, quite frankly, couldn't care less.'

That was it, I'd said quite enough, it was time to move on and let past matters rest. Ten days later, back to check the fittings we'd supplied had been installed correctly, especially considering that original problem. More than satisfied and almost out the door when he sidled up, pressed something into my hand, then glided away again.

I glanced down, and found I was holding about six photos, and there was no doubt they brought back memories, like memories of Bergman meticulously placing them one after the other, on that Kauri table. And I wondered how Cunningham had acquired copies, maybe they'd been given in payment for when they'd handed the films back to him for developing. I'd noticed the remnants of a fire smouldering out the front of the property as I walked in. George demanded nothing but first class workmanship from his staff, it was essential, considering the clientele he was dealing with, but he didn't expect them to produce it while standing knee deep in rubbish. Going by the lack of shavings, sawdust and opened cartons and whatever else, his labourer had been there earlier, cleaning up what had accumulated.

As I walked out, all that remained of the fire was a red hot circle of glowing embers, and as I strolled over I felt the heat radiating against my face, so after one last withering look, I held my hand out and allowed those photos to slip out of my fingers. They glided down and settled in the middle of that glowing circle, and for a few seconds they stayed there, as if determined to give the impression

that such filth was indestructible, that their purpose for existing was to continue to cause stress and humiliation. But finally they surrendered, as they began to curl, then with a brief flash of flame, they were gone.

While driving away, I thought about Paul Cunningham and wondered why someone would want to hold on to something like that for so long, but then realised the world would never change, and one of my lingering fears was that with those photos of James and I proving as popular as they apparently had, were some of them still in circulation out there somewhere? If so, I hoped they continued to stay as far away as possible. And one last thing about Cunningham crossed my mind. If he could hold down a job with George, then at least he'd turned out to be a decent tradesman, but over time, even that became open to question. Although I was to be involved with many more houses with George, around the Auckland suburbs of Mission Bay, St. Heliers, Kohimaramara and Remuera, and occasionally on up the Northern beaches, but mainly on the beach front at Takapuna, I never laid eyes on Cunningham again.

Chapter 36

Fortunately, that sordid part of my life was well behind me, and the future lay straight ahead, waiting to offer its variety of opportunities and challenges that life invariably presents. Just before I departed for overseas, I'd purchased a block of land, and on my return had sold it for a figure that pleasantly surprised me, because the profit had virtually paid for my time away, and now something was telling me it was time to try again. Another block had caught my eye, but this time it was covered in scrub and bracken, and for future sale, logic said it would present better if the land was cleared. While I was overseas, the opportunities of being involved in something that required some hard, physical labour, had been few and far between, so I enjoyed tackling that foliage with a bit of dedicated enthusiasm. Accordingly, the ice cold drinks the elderly lady next door insisted on supplying, were at times very welcome to say the least.

Now although I'd travelled reasonably extensively, and during that time had encountered many interesting and amazing things, one thing my journeys hadn't equipped me with, was the devious skill required to handle wily, little old ladies. So as this amiability between us continued, I remained blissfully oblivious to the fact I was no more than a pawn in this game of chess she was playing, and that game happened to include a rather large part of the rest of my life. The afternoon had proved to be unseasonably hot, and never had the contents of that glass she was offering looked more inviting, in fact it even surpassed that one the boy had been holding while sitting on those steps. It was as I was downing the last drop of that ice cold liquid, when she sprung the carefully contrived trap she'd been so insidiously preparing as she sidled up and murmured every so sweetly, 'Oh, by the way dear, while you're over here like this, you simply must take the time to step inside and meet my granddaughter.'

Even as I struggled to avoid strangling on that last mouthful, I was calculating how far back from the fence my take-off needed to be executed, basing my calculations on the knowledge I'd acquired when witnessing Jean and Eddie's successful efforts all those years back. But hard as I tried, instinct was telling me it was too late, the snare had closed, I was trapped and destined to reluctantly face the inevitable. And after all, she had been very kind but as I walked into the house, I did so with about as much enthusiasm a man could muster, as he trod those last few remaining steps up to the gallows. She was sitting in the lounge, not in the chair, but on the wide, upholstered arm, and in an instant my embarrassment relating to my dishevelled and filthy appearance was forgotten, because as our eyes met, and a soft smile flickered briefly across her face, for the second time in my life, the attraction that was there was instantaneous. There was something enchanting about the way her slightly embarrassed smile, brief though it was, had lit up the room, at the same time making it very obvious she'd been manipulated as effectively as I'd been. In some vague way, although at the time I wasn't sure how, it was like Annette all over again, the lovely hair, those clear eyes, that smooth skin, only this time we

were painting in entirely different colours. Where Annette had been so dark, this girl was just as fair.

So with the last remnants of embarrassment having effectively evaporated, we sat and chatted, and as conversation drifted on, it became apparent we possessed a lot in common, with the result that in no time at all it was as if we'd known each other for an eternity. There was a mutual agreement that we must meet again, and this we most certainly did, and as the meetings continued the inevitable happened as we preceded to fall in love. It took us no time at all to become engaged, and just over ten months since that first meeting, we married. And as I stood at the altar with my new bride by my side, I decided there was a chance that little old ladies knew what they were doing after all. A honeymoon in the warm Spring sunshine on Queensland's Gold Coast, then it was back to the commitments that arrive with marriage. A business to be run, a house to be finished, heading the list of what seemed to be a thousand and one other incidentals.

But as the months continued to fly past, no matter how I tried to ignore it, the pain that seemed to have become a part of my very being, my reason for existing, all of this caused by my desperate need for a son. I was convinced only the joy of holding him in my arms could successfully obliterate those memories that constantly haunted me. Time and time again I'd wake deep in the night, convinced Seth was there in the room watching as I lay with my legs strapped wide apart, my eyes fixed on that paper frieze, my body constantly jolting, the rhythmic movement caused by the succession of men who came into that room and indulged in the child sex they'd paid for.

There were nights when I'd wake choking, convinced I was being lowered while that noose gradually tightened around my neck, and there were memories of waiting in his office, standing in front of the Kauri table, wondering what he was going to include in his photos next. There were memories of what had occurred in that basement, and what he'd promised back at school, that nothing similar would ever happen at that house again, he'd see to that he'd said, and he was true to his word, it didn't, it happened out at Malcolm's house instead. There was the memory of walking naked into that room, with things appearing to be no different than they had many times with James, the bed covered in that white sheet, the table alongside with the variety of appliances he used resting on it, various men from the group scattered around, the services of some required, the others because they liked to watch. Then I noticed the dog.

There was the memory of catching them by surprise when I bolted, of being caught part way down the hall and dragged back, refusing to do as they insisted, then there'd been Seth's frustration as he'd lashed out, followed by Malcolm's fury, because he'd made my lip bleed. The memory of how the tears had flowed, as I'd begged them not to make me perform the acts they were intent on filming, but as always, Malcolm had been determined to get the photos he wanted, and had threatened that unless it happened, some of those photos previously taken in the basement by Kevin, would be forwarded to my father, and would also be made available for viewing at the school, and all of this accompanied by his constant reminder, 'Long ago, I learnt boys who become difficult to deal with,

aren't worth the trouble of persevering with, so be warned Mathew, cooperate, or you're as good as gone lad.'

And as always, just the thought of my father viewing those photos had been enough.

But now there was a major difference, because when I woke my wife was lying beside me, and deeply disturbed, she'd ask me time and again, why was I having such disturbing dreams? And gently I'd brush her concern aside, assuring her there was nothing to worry about, but deep down, I knew that was far from the truth, being all too aware that living with those memories and the guilt that went with them, was steadily taking its toll. I accepted nobody more than her had the right to be told, but how could I tell my new wife what had occurred in that basement, how could I explain to her what had happened in that room, that during those times I'd spent out at Malcolm's house, I'd performed the duties of a child prostitute. But as it happened, she made her confession first, it had been confirmed, she was pregnant; we were on the way to becoming parents.

And my delight at the prospect, proved to be the best remedy of them all, after all, why worry about what had passed, when you could look to a wonderful future instead. Sure, I still woke in the night, but then what was new? After all, I'd been doing it since I was twelve, so rather than looking back in dread, I'd lie there and talk softly to my unborn son, as I carefully explained the things we'd do, and the wonderful times we'd share. But far above all else, I'd repeat over and over again that promise I'd made to myself, that I'd protect him, and that at risk to my life, no man would ever do to him, as the men who came into that room did to me.

Happily, as the weeks slipped smoothly into months, the pre natal checks constantly confirmed everything was progressing normally, and finally that long awaited day arrived. Circumstances had dictated the necessity for our arrival in the early hours of the morning, and as the sun heralded its arrival with its majestic, glowing presence, the morning dawned crisply cold, with a mantle of frost covering the ground around the Waitakare Hospital.

Similar to many expectant fathers, I alternated between sitting around, or pacing back and forth in the waiting room, following to the letter what was deemed as being normal under such circumstances, and during the course of those early morning hours, the number of men in the room had steadily dwindled, until now I was on my own. The last to depart had made no effort in trying to conceal his delight at the prospect of holding his new-born baby son, making it clear I wasn't the only one who was hoping for a boy. Another twenty minutes of waiting and pacing, the situation not doing my nervous system any good at all, then my heart skipped a beat as a nurse appeared in the doorway, beckoning to me to follow her down to the delivery room.

My wife looked surprisingly well, considering our first addition had proved slightly reluctant to enter this world, but with the birth now behind her, she lay there glowing with a radiance I'd been informed so many new mothers seem to possess. I sat down beside her, we held hands and kissed, then said a few words that occasions such as this seem to produce, then I walked over and gazed down at that child lying in its crib. It was almost exactly as I'd expected, those straight little limbs, blue eyes so big they seemed to dominate that perfectly formed little

face. No doubt about it, as far as I could tell, everything seemed in perfect working order, that was except for one small thing. It was obvious somewhere in the course of things, that important message had failed to get through. Somehow, whoever it was had failed to inform her about one very important thing. She was supposed to have been a boy.

So this new experience called being a father was dulled slightly by the knowledge my search hadn't ended after all. But through it all I managed to convince myself that at this stage of our lives at least, it had been determined by whoever it was who controlled such decisions, that my son was to have an older sister, and at this time I certainly couldn't see anything wrong with that. Long before I'd decided that having been an only child, it was not a situation I wanted repeated in my own family. However, even allowing for the fact she'd been blessed with a slightly disappointed father, through it all our daughter continued to grow, straight, strong and healthy, and as I stood in our lounge and gazed at her while she played down on our back lawn, I decided if we could manage a boy who came up to that standard, I'd have absolutely nothing to complain about at all.

So more months past, but I felt, nowhere near enough, because my wife announced we were due for a repeat performance, the second addition to our family was underway, and immediately I was uneasy and sensed a problem looming. First of all, it was apparent something had gone radically wrong in the area of our so called 'family planning' because this child we were expecting, wasn't supposed to have been on our schedule for at least another eight, preferably twelve months. Quick calculations that took me all of two minutes, gave me what I knew to be the answer for this predicament, and predicament I most certainly felt it was. As we'd been warned, and our first child had confirmed, children didn't come cheap, and although I was aware the second wouldn't be quite so financially draining, it was still going to place severe pressure on our family finances. But openly expressing my annoyance at this point, didn't strike me as being overly appropriate, because the 'damage' so to speak, was already done, so best just make the most of what was developing as a very delicate situation, so I moved my thoughts to the next couple of scenarios, one of which was about to unfold in our lives.

If this 'accidental' child turned out to be a boy, my worries were over, I'd be the happiest man on the planet, however, if it turned out to be another girl, to say major problems were looming, could be classed as winning the prize for the understatement of the decade. With my wife being fully aware of my insistence it had to be a boy, the strain this unplanned pregnancy placed upon me, and no doubt my wife as well, was nothing short of intense in the extreme, and as far as I was concerned, the stress I was feeling effectively dulled most of the pleasure I would have been sharing with my wife under normal circumstances. And that was where the trouble lay, because looking at the pregnancy from where I was standing, nobody more than I was aware the circumstances were a long way removed from being normal. Hard as I'd tried, I knew I hadn't managed to eliminate all the volatility the past events had ingrained deep my system, and if this second child turned out to be a girl, then it was more than possible the situation could cause major problems within our marriage.

And so followed months of wondering, waiting and worrying, but what I was experiencing did absolutely nothing to slow down the pregnancy, and in no time at all it was another mad dash to the hospital, which no doubt similar to countless thousands before us, proved to be totally unnecessary. The waiting room hadn't changed a bit, which wasn't all that surprising, considering only sixteen months had passed since my previous visit, but this time the pacing more extensive and excruciating than ever. Yet again left on my own, then followed by another repeat performance, a nurse appearing, but staying non committal as far as that all important question was concerned, 'I've been told not to give you so much as the faintest hint', she said, 'your wife\s absolutely adamant, nobody must tell you but her.'

Her words created a burst of elation like I'd never experienced before. Only my wife knew how important this boy was, so therefore I could understand why she was insisting on being the one to inform me I finally had my son. As I followed the nurse down what seemed to be a never ending corridor, rather than walking on tiles, it was more like floating on a cloud. We turned a corner and walked on into the ward, and I could see my wife with our new-born cradled in her arms, but even from a distance, the strain of what had been a difficult birth was evident in her eyes. They looked tired, and her face drawn, and they stayed that way as I bent down and kissed her, then asked that all important question, in fact, by far the most important question I'd ever asked in my life. But surely her answer wasn't even necessary, because I couldn't wait to take my son in my arms, to hold him close, feel his warmth, then tell him his name was Michael, and it had been chosen many years before. But in an instant of dreadful agony, that unfortunately will stay with me till the day I die, that special moment shattered into oblivion as my wife whispered, 'Please try to understand Mathew, we've been given another girl.'

I stepped back as the shock registered, desperate to put some distance between me and this unwanted child, and as that cloud under my feet changed to granite, I was aware that something even harder had appeared on my face, then moved down and smothered my heart, and noticing the transformation, my wife quickly added, 'Mathew, wait, give it some time, just be patient and soon you'll find you'll love her, just as you do our other daughter.'

But my answer accentuated what had already become a dreadful situation, as that volatility surged, and now completely out of control, as I moved even further away I snapped at her,

'Oh, you think so, do you? Well listen carefully, because I'll tell you one thing and one thing only, and believe me when I say you've never been so wrong in your life. Send her back to where she bloody came from, I want absolutely nothing to do with the child.'

I didn't dare say any more, not that I hadn't said enough already. I knew I'd developed a lethal temper long before I started with Mitsu, but since then, on most occasions, especially since that episode in New York, I'd managed to keep it reasonably under control. But here, at a time like this, nothing I possessed could stop it, as it burst through with a vengeance, having reached a point well in excess of being dangerously lethal, and what was more I knew it was still climbing. I kept heading for the door, nothing was more important than getting

out of that room, out to somewhere, anywhere, as long as I could breath. Once again it was similar to that time in my bedroom, I was convinced the walls were closing in, threatening to crush me.

A young doctor was standing somewhere to my right. Possibly he'd assisted with the birth, I didn't know, and what was more, couldn't have cared less. As I strode past he reached out and placed a restraining hand gently on my arm, possibly prepared to try and take the time to make me see something vaguely approaching reason. I stopped dead, slowly looked down at his hand, then just as slowly raised my eyes until they directly clashed with his, and during the seconds that passed, I assessed it would take me about the same amount of time to break his shoulder. Fortunately, there was no doubt he sensed he was in mortal danger, and how right he was. Quickly he removed his hand, and quicker still stepped back, and in doing so, by a split second, barely avoided getting very badly hurt.

Back out through that labyrinth of corridors, no idea where I was heading, seething, cold blooded fury guaranteeing the last thing I took even the remotest notice of were the directions on how to get out of the fucking place. Finally outside, the cold morning air like ice on my face, and by more than good luck, than anything approaching good management, finally finding and getting into my powerful vehicle, driving like a man demented, passing everything in my path, whether there was room or not, horns blaring in frustration as I passed, working on the theory they got out of my road, or else, a menace on the road, and what was more, I couldn't have cared less. Now in our driveway, pulling up, my hands still holding the steering wheel in a grip of steel, now getting out, accompanied by the smell of overheated brakes, slamming the car door, vaguely realising I couldn't remember getting here, and I couldn't care less about that either. To hell with garaging the vehicle, could stay where it fucking was, could sit there and rust for all I cared. Now at our front door, fumbling in my fury for my keys, finally getting inside the house, slamming that door as well, but taking the time to make sure it was locked. This time the walls keeping me in, but far more important still, keeping the rest of the world out.

Now pacing from one end of the house to the other in a frenzy of uncontrollable rage. I knew I'd made a mistake in allowing it to go on as long as it had, but right or wrong, no matter whose fault it was, all those years of abuse, all that humiliation and pain, and the end result? Standing here tearing my soul apart, because all I'd ever asked for in the way of compensation was a son. Somehow I found myself standing in our lounge, with my hands gripping the back of one of the large, heavy chairs. Suddenly I took a firmer grip still and raised it above my head, determined to throw it through the plate glass window at the other end of the room, but caught myself just in time, and placed it back on the floor. With constant spending on the house combined with the expense of our first child, our funds were low, and I wasn't sure, considering the circumstances, if our insurance company would be prepared to cover the cost of what would have been quite extensive damage.

Through the combination of seething fury and bitterness, somehow it registered, the telephone was ringing, and possibly had been for quite some time. To hell with it, let it ring, I refused to go near the thing. It stopped briefly,

then started again, and for a while I continued to ignore it, then the incessant noise started to drive me insane, that's if in some ways, I hadn't reached that state already. Reluctantly I picked it up knowing there was some fool on the other end of the line, daring to disturb me at a time like this, didn't the idiot know, all I want is to be left alone. Now that'd be right, I should have known, of all people it was my mother in law. She'd stayed with her daughter for as long as she could, but due to the birth tending to drift on, had been forced to go home for some well earned rest. Had anything happened while she'd been away? Had anything happened, the stupid woman had to ask, God help me, it was as if everyone was determined to drive me demented.

Once again I exploded, telling her abruptly and brutally what had happened, and how I wished it hadn't, then added to that in some not very well chosen words, what I thought of the whole, useless, senseless business, then proceeded to hang up in her ear. About twenty seconds of silence, now the thing ringing again, so I take the receiver off its cradle and leave it swinging to and fro, with it occasionally bumping against the wall. To hell with the woman anyway, it was as much her fault as anyone. Why couldn't she have produced a daughter who had at least some idea of how to give birth to a boy? Just thinking about the insane and unfair irony of the whole thing left me even more violent and furious still, that's if considering my current state, that could be deemed as being possible.

My mind flashed back to an evening when I'd arrived home late, after being out with my future wife, and I was surprised to find my father still up, and it wasn't like him, he normally retired much earlier in the evening than this, so for once we sat and talked until he asked,

'You're seeing quite a lot of this young lady Matt. Any chance this could end in marriage?'

And now it was my answer that was proving so painfully ironical, as I'd replied at the time,

'I sure like her one hell of a lot, but there's one thing I'm having to give a lot of thought too. As far as I'm concerned, nothing in my life comes ahead of having a son, and as far as that family of hers is concerned, I get the impression it's just a little too top heavy with girls. So much as I think the world of her Pop, that's the only thing that's making me a bit wary.'

And now considering the situation I find myself in, his reply was heaping irony on irony,

'Don't let that sway your decision, she's a lovely girl, and she'll give you the son you want.'

For someone who, as I recall, was never supposed to be wrong, guess what, wrong again. No doubt about it Pop, lately, you must be going close to setting a record in that direction.

Suddenly I realised I was standing in our bedroom, even though I couldn't remember taking one step down the hall, but seeing as somehow our bed had become available, I sat down and gazed out at the beautiful stand of Kauris, growing down our rear boundary. The sun was filtering through the maze of leaves, and as they swayed gently to and fro in the light breeze, their shadows created a series of patterns as they danced all over the grass. So often, while

lying awake at night, I'd imagined playing out there with my son. I placed my elbows on my knees, then buried my face in my hands, and with my disappointment having reached a point of being more than I could bare, I did something I hadn't done in years, I simply sat in that room and cried, shedding tears born from total and utter despair.

Chapter 37

It took quite some time for those tears to stop, but eventually when they did, I lay back with a thousand questions creating turmoil in my head. My original concern was now proving to be all too valid, there was a major problem, and what was more, it was growing larger by the second. It was all too much to think about, my head left thick, my senses dulled along with it, and the next thing I knew I was being jolted awake by a noise from outside. I waited briefly for my eyes to clear, then the outline of my mother in law's face appeared, pressed against the glass in the door, as she frantically pleaded for me to allow her inside. That was the last thing I needed, but reluctantly accepted I was probably left with little choice. Up until now our relationship could be classed as being reasonable at best, but how you'd describe it now after the way I'd spoken to her on the phone was anyone's guess. So bloody what, in fact to hell with it, if she'd decided to take offence, then good, all she had to do was turn around and go back where she'd come from, which was what I'd wish she'd do anyway. Nothing had changed; all I wanted was to be left alone.

As I'd predicted, once inside the attempt at lectures started, just the first on that long list I knew who would be lining up, taking it in turn while they tried to make me see reason. I cut her short, brutally short, making it plain there was nothing to be gained by trying to discuss the whole disastrous, useless, senseless business. One concession, anything to get the woman out of the house. Grudgingly I agreed to take our daughter to see her mother and new sister later that afternoon, and when I did, and dutifully lifted her so she could see in the crib, nothing had changed, I didn't give what was lying in it even a solitary glance. With my so called duty done, and after a few words with my wife, I couldn't get out of that room and home quick enough. Top priority was to put as much distance between myself and this new and very unwelcome arrival as quickly as possible.

Back to see my wife that evening, far from sure of the response I could expect, considering the manner of my departure that morning. A couple of nurses eyeing me warily, probably due to having been warned of my lethal volatility. A couple of vague relations from her side of the family standing beside the bed, mouthing the usual banal rubbish only new-borns seem capable of extracting from the mouths of supposedly sane adults. Purposely I stayed well back, saying the absolute minimum possible, but logic said sooner or later it had to happen, with one of the idiots making the fatal mistake of asking what I thought of our new addition. Well, the moron had asked, so after all, what else could I do, and as vicious fury surged yet again, I told them, and what's more, very explicitly. This was followed by a lull of shocked silence, which didn't help the situation at all, and that in turn was followed by such pathetic rubbish as, 'We should all be grateful for what Jesus provides.'

Somehow I managed to hold my tongue, but was oh so dangerously close to telling them that whenever I'd asked him to provide, such as when I was twelve

years old, lying naked and tied down over a frame, waiting to be raped by eight boys, much as I'd asked, somehow he'd managed to provide me with, guess what, absolutely nothing. So for some reason, I wasn't all that surprised he'd failed to provide me with what I wanted now. Then to add to my anger, that's if it was humanly possible, one of them uttered in a tone that indicated the words should cure all, 'What does it matter if it's a boy or a girl, as long as it's healthy.'

And that set me off again. Tactlessly I pointed out that as two young and healthy adults, I'd never remotely considered the possibility of our producing anything other than healthy children, and what was more dangerously to the point, seeing as along with about ninety per cent of the population, they'd managed to produce sons, how the hell from where they were standing, did they assume the right to comment detrimentally on the way I was feeling, and it would be appreciated if they'd refrain from uttering such a load of pious, righteous bilge. At that point I strode out of the room, yet again, leaving my wife to apologise for my behaviour.

As before, driving home as if a maniac was behind the wheel, those useless, infantile discussions achieving nothing other than raising my fury to well above boiling point again. In their stupid innocence, they had no idea of the dangerous ground on which they were treading, not the faintest comprehension of the risk they were taking in daring to open their mouths and act as if they were experts on the subject. In their audacity, they dared to speak of Jesus to me. During those years, I'd lost count of the number of times I'd begged for his help, in that shed, in his office, out at Malcolm's house, and what had it achieved? I knew what it had achieved, a sweet load of nothing, was the abrupt but correct answer. I'd been involved in such things, that many preferred to conveniently think didn't exist, and those who were left, chose to ignore anyway.

Then to rub salt into what was already a terrible wound, those idiots dared to be offended by my resentment, because in the way of some consolation for what I'd experienced, all I'd ever asked for was a son, a simple request that yet again, had been refused. So, nothing different, as usual, as I'd come to expect, once again he'd let me down. People liked to prattle on about help from above, and if what I was experiencing was an example of it, then it was something I could do without until the day I died. The next morning should have seen me at the hospital, but I went to the factory instead, and on the way up to my office, caught my foreman's attention with a flick of my head, and as he walked in, cut his congratulations dead,

'Joe, make it immediately known, the birth of this child is not to be mentioned under any circumstances what so ever. The factory is to carry on as if it's never happened, and also make it very clear that anyone who deviates from this could see them out the door.'

He confirmed with a nod of his head had quickly backed out, closing the door quietly behind him. He knew it took a lot to get me angry, but on the comparatively rare occasions when it happened, it paid to duck for cover, and obviously this was one of them. As I sat at my desk and stared at the door, I tried to think of a way out of this mess that fate had helped create, and at the same time could imagine the tone of the conversations that were no doubt well

underway amongst the staff. So he wanted a boy, and got another girl, well tough luck, he's not the first man it's happened too, and certainly won't be the last. Anyway, where's the problem? All he has to do is wait for a while, then try again if having a boy is that important.

So easy for them to sort out, but only I knew how complicated it really was. A gambler looks at the hand he's been dealt, assesses the strength or weakness of his position, then plays his cards accordingly as he risks his money from there. Now I was being forced to look at the hand in life I'd been dealt, and was having to accept that considering the way the cards from previous hands had fallen, this current hand was incidental, because I'd reached a point where all bets had been lost. For most, the decisions to be made from a similar position were reasonably simple, but for myself, I knew the position I was in was hopeless. If I was prepared to take the risk and we conceived another child, if it was a boy, I'd experience ecstasy like I'd never known existed, but what would be the ramifications if it turned out to be another girl?

Many would say it was worth the risk, you'd be unlucky to strike three in a row, but not from where I was standing. Admittedly the Gossini's had a girl first, then they produced three boys, the Mc. Kenzie's had three boys, Colin was one of three boys, the twins made up a family of three boys, so from what I'd experienced, three in a row was all too common. So as far as I was concerned, if we tried again and the result was another girl, only one thing was certain, this poison that had been injected into my system would take over, I knew there was no way I could stop it, and this fury I found impossible to contain would explode to a point where it would result in one thing, and that would be the destruction of our marriage, that was if I hadn't destroyed it already. I hoped I still had a wife I adored, but I also had two girls, at least one of whom was supposed to have been a boy. But even if it was possible to look past my fury and utter resentment, nothing changed the fact I'd fathered them, and no matter how I approached what was to me a disastrous situation, nothing changed the fact I still had a responsibility accordingly.

In many ways it seemed as if virtually no time had passed since I was walking down to the gymnasium, taking care no one saw me entering his office, locking the door, removing my clothes, placing them in the storeroom, then standing naked in front of him, legs slightly apart like he insisted, hand clasped behind my head, waiting while he decided whether he wanted oral or anal sex, and on most occasions, both. Then after orally producing the strong erection he desired, lying over that Kauri table, then after his movement inside me finally stopped, being allowed to go home. Then followed the desperation of getting under the shower, scrubbing and scrubbing until my skin hurt, as I tried to wash away the feel of him and what he'd done. But the fact was I been forced to accept nothing worked, and now I was faced with another situation, where once again, nothing was working as well.

And the truth was that only now, was I fully comprehending the terrible damage that had been done. When I'd left school and started work, I'd been so convinced I'd been tainted for life, and for quite some time after, I despised even being touched, and in some ways it had stayed like that, until I'd met Annette. I left Paris doubtful if another such wonderful relationship could ever present

itself, that was until I was introduced to a girl sitting rather self consciously on the arm of one of her grandmother's chairs in her lounge. Young, vibrant, stunning and intelligent, from the time we'd married, our love had done nothing but intensify, but now I was faced with this.

If sometime in the past one of the partners in a marriage has been poisoned, there are occasions when even love can't prove to be enough. Unless other necessary steps are taken, the union struggles on until it eventually dies. And it was due to this reason, and this reason alone, that forced me to accept why I wasn't prepared to take the risk and try for another child. If fate or whatever else decreed it wasn't a boy, I knew this toxin that constantly surged inside me would once again burst to the surface, past experience had proved there was no way I could stop it, only the next time it would do so with such viciousness, the result would be a catastrophe the likes of which I never wanted to envisage. There wasn't a single doubt in my mind, I knew exactly what would happen, I'd give my wife every material thing in this world I possessed, and I'd also include my undying love, then I'd terminate our marriage. So taking into consideration the impossible position I was in, only one decision was possible, because fate along with other events in my life had decreed we simply couldn't risk trying for another child, I would be the last of the Colbert family, because that boy I wanted and needed so badly, simply wasn't going to happen.

Chapter 38

Despite her father's indifference, somehow the baby thrived, due entirely to the loving care provided by her mother, while I did my best to ignore her as often as circumstances permitted. Another two and a half years fly past, my time away from the factory taken up virtually in its entirety by working to complete a new home for our family on the city's North Shore. But then happened an incident that many would say was destined to be. The day had been progressing smoothly like so many others, my wife hanging out the washing at the rear of the house, the girls playing happily enough around the side. The day was hot, and as their game had progressed, the little one asked her sister to help her get a glass of water, but after the tumbler was filled and passed to her, it slipped and shattered on the kitchen floor.

With their mother remaining oblivious to what had occurred, she glanced up to find the younger child looking back down at her from the height of our lounge, with blood covering the front of her dress. First the fright, then the panic to get inside, but once the hand had been carefully washed, the wound, such as it was, between the tip and first joint of her right forefinger seemed to be minor in the extreme. Even so, a band aid was carefully applied, more to assist with the soothing effect, rather than any necessity, or so it appeared at the time. That evening my wife explained in detail how horrified she'd been, but I conveniently passed it off as just another frightening but harmless incident that all parents experience at one time or another, 'Buy a couple of plastic mugs and leave them in a lower cupboard where there're accessible for the kids, then tell them they're to use nothing else when they want a drink.'

In typical male fashion, they'd been my last words on the subject, as far as I was concerned, problem solved. Ten days later, eating our evening meal, my youngest daughter sitting across from me at the table, generally ignoring her as usual, that was until there was a clatter as she dropped her spoon. I glanced up, attracted by the noise, then looked again as the same thing was repeated only minutes later, and even I had to admit it wasn't like her, she'd proved to be very competent when handling her cutlery, and it was then I noticed that finger.

She was holding it straight out, and it was clear she was doing her best to avoid using it. I continued eating, but at the same time carefully watching her, and there was no doubt about it, something was very wrong. Not only was she holding the finger straight out, the end joint appeared to be turning slightly upward, so after a couple more minutes, as I confirmed what seemed to be happening, I turned and passed my thoughts on the subject to her mother,

'You'd better get that kid to the doctor, there's something wrong with that finger she hurt.' And as usual in such matters, especially regarding the girls, she was way ahead of me,

'It's already been arranged Mathew, I have an appointment for her tomorrow morning.'

So alright, big deal, the kid's pricked her finger, wasn't as if it was the end of the world, I mean, let's face it, all of them manage to do something to themselves in the way of an accident at some stage or another. Maybe there was some internal infection and that explained why she kept holding it in that strange position. Surely some antibiotics could deal with it?'

But my wife didn't think so, and the doctor agreed with her, and as she spoke to me from the specialist's office she'd been referred to, it seemed neither did he, as she explained,

'It turns out that wasn't just a surface prick as I'd thought, and in a way I'm not surprised considering the amount of blood. He's rated the risk factor at being about one in Heaven only knows how many thousand, but a thin pinnacle of glass has pieced her finger and penetrated far enough where it's severed the tendon and also damaged some nerves. Because she's so young, and the difficulties this creates, he'd hoped rectification could have been left until she was a little older, but the seriousness of the injury means he's left with little choice. He operates as soon as possible, or she's at risk of losing the use of her finger permanently.'

I took a deep breath, but decided it was no use getting agitated, after all, the child was only running true to form. It had been apparent from way back, for some reason she'd been sent here for the prime purpose of driving me insane. Surely after taking everything into consideration, I'd be used to it by now, so I finished up snapping back down the phone,

'Alright, alright, I get the bloody message, it's registered, so for Christ's sake just tell him to go ahead and do whatever is necessary, we'll worry about the exorbitant charges later.'

I placed the phone very firmly back on its cradle. Guess what, just another chapter in the book I was currently writing about the never ending worry of household and family expenses.

However, in spite of my chagrin the medical wheels turned both rapidly and efficiently. We were informed the child would be operated on the following afternoon at Auckland's Middlemore Hospital, and it would be appreciated if the child was there by nine o'clock in the morning, but due to the uncertainty as to the exact time she'd be going into the theatre, but mainly due to the speed of her admission, that had left my wife no time at all to secure the services of a baby sitter for our older daughter, it had been reluctantly agreed we were left with no option other than to leave her in the care of the hospital staff, and it was as I was driving her back home, that my wife expressed a mother's concern for her young daughter,

'Mathew, I simply detest having to leave her for so long, so is there any hope of my having the car, it's important someone should be with her when she comes out of the aesthetic?'

The speed of her admittance had also caught me unprepared. I had a string of appointments that were impossible to cancel at short notice. Another deep breath, this I could also do without,

'Look, I'm stuck with appointments, and it's impossible to cancel them, especially considering that we need all the work we can get. There's absolutely

no way I can do without the car, so leave it, I'll check when it's appropriate, and I'll go out to the hospital.'

Now hours later, all my appointments behind me, the day steadily deteriorating, with angry clouds building up over the city, but still dry as I glided into a parking space at the hospital.

An inquiry at reception provided the necessary directions, and as I walked down towards the ward I decided hospital floors hadn't changed, they still felt like granite. Now stopping outside, it would be stretching one's imagination to call it a ward, a large room was I felt a far more appropriate description, with whatever one chose to call it containing about ten cots, rather than the usual beds and accompanying equipment. Childish paintings were pinned haphazardly around the walls, no doubt the artistic efforts supplied by some of the older children, who'd previously passed through the hospital for an untold variety of reasons.

To my left a table with some equipment stacked on it, that briefly tugged at memories from some time long in the past. Beyond that again and nestling back in a corner, a large plastic container, filled to a point of overflowing with what seemed to be a collection of children's toys, no doubt all donated by a series of very grateful parents.

In front of that, a well worn Persian rug, talk about bringing back past memories, but enough of that because as my eyes continued to skim over the cots they noticed nothing, so I tried again, this time accompanied by just a little impatience. Here I was standing around, making like some stupid idiot lost in a hospital, looking for what was proving to be an elusive daughter, who I wasn't all that concerned if I found or not. Disturbing thoughts entered my head, I mean if someone had absconded with her, that meant there was room for us to try again. Couldn't understand what all the fuss was about anyway. So she'd stuck a bit of glass in her finger, and what had I come out all this way to see? Probably at most a couple of stitches in the end of her finger, and probably wouldn't even be able to see those, because of the wide band aid covering them. Still looking, still no sign of anything, so I stepped back out into the corridor and rechecked the number over the doorway, and no, I wasn't wrong, this was definitely the ward or what have you I'd been directed too.

So I stepped back inside and started again, but this time more slowly, accepting too much haste often meant much less speed, this time forcing myself to scan the cots far more slowly, and still nothing, that was until my eyes passed over, then snapped back and riveted on a cot well over on the right hand side of the room and tucked well back in a corner. It still took a few moments for it to register there was something there after all, my original searching being obstructed from this distance by what appeared to be a pillow, but beyond that, when I looked closely, definitely the outline of a little body. So I strolled over, but when I arrived and looked down at the little figure lying there, blissfully out to the world, for quite some time I struggled to accept what I was seeing.

There was no mistaking that hair so blond, it virtually blended with the white of the pillow, and in place of that band aid I'd envisaged, there was a plaster cast that encased her arm from the tip of that finger right up to her shoulder. And if that wasn't enough to shock me, on the end of that finger on

which he'd operated, was sewn of all things a plain, little white button. Without taking my eyes off her, I changed my position, moving to the side which meant I could study my little daughter more closely. That plaster cast seemed almost as big as she was, and probably due to the weight, was being supported by that additional pillow. Her hair seemed to flow like golden rain, and as I continued to stand there and study her, I knew I'd never even taken the time to appreciate just what a beautiful little creature she was.

There was a chair standing forlornly nearby, so I pulled it over and sat down. Here I was, looking down at this piece of perfection lying in this cot beside me, who happened to be my youngest daughter, and who for the better part of two and a half years, I'd gone out of my way to ignore. After a few more minutes of gazing intently while I continued to soak up that delicate, childish beauty, I bent forward and released the side of the cot, allowing it to drop away, and the faint noise caused the slightest of movements, so I ran the tip of my finger softly down her leg, and the feel of her skin could have been compared with touching a rose petal. Another fifteen minutes as I sat there, and I knew exactly how long it was, because after all this time, outdated though it was, I still wasn't prepared to part with my Mondia watch.

Now some action in the form of valiant but fruitless attempts to open her eyes, and another ten minutes past during which a nurse appeared, checked what she had to, and apparently satisfied, gave me a smile and glided away as quietly as she'd arrived. I kept on whispering my daughter's name, and finally success, my voice apparently getting through, because she looked up and vaguely gazed around the room. I was certain she didn't know who was sitting beside her, and considering what she'd been used to from a very indifferent father, decided it was probably just as well, or she'd have started crying for her mother instead. But I was wrong, she knew who it was alright, because she murmured 'oh daddy' three times, then promptly passed out cold again. So I continued to sit with my daughter in that hospital room and accepted from the day she'd been born, I'd done my best to ignore this little human being that I'd been partly responsible for creating. But now, after this time spent with her in this hospital, I wanted to take her in my arms and tell her how dreadfully sorry I was, but I couldn't, because of that plaster cast.

So instead, I continued to sit where I was while I made silent peace with my daughter, whose only mistake in her young life was having been born a girl instead of that boy I wanted so badly. So I did my best to explain to her, that although I hadn't realised it at the time, I'd always loved her, and for one very good reason, in fact probably the best reason of them all, I loved her because like her sister before her, I loved her because she was mine. And at the same time I admitted I was still no nearer understanding why, but rather than being that boy that needed my love and protection, it was my two little girls instead. I sat there for quite some time, as she continued to sleep blissfully on, and I used that time to allow that long overdue acceptance to fully register.

Finally I raised my eyes and looked around the room, and I was surprised to find the light had dulled appreciably, so I walked over and glanced out the window, and the reason was all too clear. I'd forgotten about those dark clouds that were hovering when I'd arrived, but now the patches of blue sky that had

been there, had totally disappeared, and as the first of those showers that had been threatening finally arrived, tapping with their gentle song on the window, running down, forming miniature streams that wandered around, finally terminating as a collection of small pools on the uneven ground, they were also doing something else, melting once and for all, that ice that had been surrounding my heart.

A couple more days of visiting, then the news we could take her home. The delicate operation deemed as having been most successful, considering the highly unusual damage, and the resulting difficulties that had been associated with it. When we walked into the ward, she was playing with a selection of blocks on that Persian rug, and already managing with the cast as if it had always been there. And the day before during one of our visits, I'd remembered to ask the surgeon, who'd walked in at a very convenient moment,

'Why the necessity for a white button of all things, on the end of that finger?' and he'd laughed as he replied, 'Even allowing for all the advances in modern surgery, for tensioning the tendon, I've still found nothing to beat it.'

So with that worry behind us, and also deciding I couldn't care less about his account, I scooped her up and carried her out of the hospital, and on the way to the car, I whispered to her, telling her once again just how sorry I was, and although I knew she didn't have the faintest idea of what I was talking about, she slipped her good arm around my neck and gave me a hug, and I decided it was a long time since I'd felt anything better. On that day a bond was formed with my youngest daughter, exactly as I knew I had with her sister, and a little late though it might have been, I felt there was nothing that existed, that could break it again.

Chapter 39

With the relief of knowing I'd finally accepted my second daughter as a father should, I was also very aware one hurdle still remained, because over the years I'd finally come to the conclusion I was 'damaged goods' and how I appeared to have coped as a boy, yet was struggling as an adult left me mystified. It was all too complicated, so never mind, even if those troublesome memories were proving stubborn to erase, the best way of dealing with them was to push them far back into the crevasses of my mind, where for most of the time they were inundated by the profusion of things waiting to be done.

So as few more years past, it seemed the therapy revolving around non-stop activity was working reasonably well, so if there was the inevitable reminder, such as a face in a crowd, an item mentioned through the media, or if one of those hundreds of repugnant moments flashed into my mind during an unguarded moment, then get up and do something, do anything, as long as it helped to drive those memories away, so that in turn guaranteed life with my family carried on smoothly down a comparatively trouble free path, and it continued to work, that was until the decision was made to purchase a new car, the first we'd owned to be fitted with the now compulsory seat belts.

On that first morning as I secured the restraint across my chest, it took only seconds to realise I had a problem, and I was surprised, the situation I felt was nothing short of ridiculous. There was absolutely no similarity between the strap of a seat belt and those that had secured my wrists and ankles in that bedroom. And what was more, I was in a car, for Christ's sake, not a bloody house, but finally I was forced to accept the restrictive sensation, slight though it may be, was apparently proving enough to reactivate that area of my brain that had so badly affected at that time. Those memories of being rendered helpless kept flooding back, accompanied by the click of the latch on the door, as the men entered the room, then departed as discreetly as they'd arrived. There was also the reminder of the fear associated with the fact that I never knew when Seth would take the opportunity to indulge himself as well, which was something I'd feared above all else .

I tried again the following morning, and quite a number after that, but the sensation never varied, it was as if the effects of a drug was taking over, slowly flooding my system, proving impossible to stop, and when this insidious invasion was complete, always without fail my mind would wander back to that time in my life, that above all else, I so desperately wanted to forget. So finally, for the sake of my survival on the road, and far more important still, for those I encountered, I realised it was essential I drove without the distraction caused by that belt. For quite some time I fought this, determined to be no different on the road than anyone else, but constantly an incident that had occurred at the house kept coming back, and if there was anything I detested being reminded of, it was that.

her. Then after a few moments more, lifted my head and gazed directly into her eyes, and in an instant my delirious dream of sexual bliss was shattered. What I'd conveniently read in her eyes as being desire, had been in fact just the opposite, because it was now cruelly obvious she'd been pleading to be left alone.

Not a sound passed her lips, but she was crying, the combination of humiliation and despair registering so very clearly as the tears welled out and tumbled down, finally coming to rest as they soaked into the pillow on which her head was resting. And instantly I withdrew and eased back, absolutely mortified, and now she was openly sobbing, and from that point there was only one thing I wanted, and that was to get out of that room as fast as I could. I swung my feet to the floor, then bolted for the still open door, but it seemed as always, it was Seth who got to me first. Grabbing a handful of my hair, he terminated my intended departure with a sudden, painful, backward wrench, then holding me upright to a point where I was balancing on my toes, he snarled directly in my ear as he tightened his grip even further and at the same time twisted my hair, purposely creating as much pain as possible as he threatened,

'Where do you think you're going, you little bastard? You know as well as I that you haven't completed what you were brought here for, so get back and finish it, or you'll answer to me.'

My horror at what had occurred meant any attempt at self preservation departed in seconds, so I twisted, and even with him still holding my hair, shouted directly in his face,

'You can all go to hell, can't you see, she's crying Seth, she doesn't want me, so there's no way I'm touching her again. Honest, you pack of scum belong on some distant planet, and if I had my way, you along with the rest of them, would all be dumped there and left to rot.'

Definitely not a wise comment, especially under the circumstances, and I knew from many past experiences, if you wanted Seth's violent temper to erupt, nothing achieved it quicker than defying him, which I had found to my detriment. Hauled back down the hall to the bedroom, not sure if my hair was going to stand the strain, forced to lie across the bed, one hand bearing down on the small of my back, the other undoing his belt, and as the large buckle from which clatters as his pants fall to the floor, I think as usual, this is just great.

Chosen to do what they all wanted to watch, realise the girl hasn't consented, refuse to proceed any further, which Seth conveniently interprets as directly defying him, now it's me who's going to be raped. Now thrusting himself into me, the pain caused by his erection nothing short of extreme, a reminder from the past as I clamp my teeth into the blanket, determined not to utter a sound as the brutality continues.

No telling how long it's going to go on for, when Seth is in one of his many bad moods, he borders on being uncontrollable, and that means the situation is dangerous in the extreme, but it's Maria who intervenes, abusing him and waving her arms as she pounds into the room,

'Seth, for God's sake stop what you're doing to the boy. If Malcolm hears one word of this, we're as good as finished, it won't be you who's thrown out, it'll be both of us, so stop and think for once in your life, instead of letting that

violent temper of yours dominate over everything else. If we're dismissed, where will we ever get another position that pays like this? Well I'll tell you, it isn't going to happen, so let the boy alone,' then as she turned to me as I stood painfully up and moved a safe distance from her husband, 'And Mathew, get into the bathroom so I can check you and clean you up, and for your sake, not a word of this to anyone, you understand what I'm saying, because your life could depend on it.'

It had been just another incident to add to the many I knew I'd never forget or forgive. But as the saying goes, everything comes to those who wait, and it may have taken another eighteen months, but in the end I nailed you Seth, you underhand and absolute total bastard, and what's more, I managed to make a proper job of it, that's if what I heard erupting from Malcolm's study was any example.

Chapter 40

I snapped out of yet another of my many unpleasant reminiscences, and found I was parked outside my office, which meant I'd driven virtually right across the city in the heavy early morning traffic, and could barely recall having done so. The dangerous signs were there, the seat belt had to go, but solving one problem almost immediately created another, that being the cost associated with the steadily increasing number of traffic violations received, for not wearing a seat belt. But there arrived a day when those wheels of change started turning.

Another day, and another morning of business appointments in the city, so over the harbour bridge and due to the density of the traffic, leaving a reasonable gap between my car and the vehicle in front. Now off the bridge and swinging up towards Ponsonby, some distance further up, someone stepping out and signalling for me to pull over, a man in a blue uniform, and he must have binoculars for eyes to have noticed the absence of a belt from where he was standing. Another ticket to add to the number already accumulated, could be classed as becoming a habit, and one I could definitely do without.

On his polite request, automatically reached for my licence, and an empty pocket resulted in a couple of quiet curses as I realised that for the first time in years, I'd left home without my wallet, so another couple of curses, just for good measure. But the mistake created nothing more than a minor inconvenience, being left with having to produce the document inside the forty eight hour period allowed. May as well get it over and done with, so the following day saw me standing at the counter at the central office in the city, and even at this relatively early hour, the place was a hive of activity, hinting that traffic violations earned the powers to be a small fortune.

All indications were that I could be in for quite a long wait, so I leant casually against the counter, filling in time by allowing my eyes to rove over this seething mass of humanity, all of whom seemed to be industriously heading in every direction but the one I wanted, which reminded me of my brief incarceration in New York. But a ray of hope, a man in a smart uniform heading in my direction, and going by the adornments on his shoulders, it gave me the impression he spent the majority of his time sitting behind an expansive desk in the upper reaches, rather than tending a counter on the ground floor, but he was pleasant enough as he asked, 'Well young man, and what can we do for you on this very pleasant morning?'

I explained, with some embarrassment, I'd received a violation the previous day, but found I'd left home without my licence, so was presenting it as required. He took the offending document, briefly scanned it, filled in the inevitable paperwork, all of which took around thirty seconds, then as he was handing my licence back, casually enquired, 'And may I ask, what was this violation to do with ?' and when I explained, he promptly added, 'well that was pretty foolish, wasn't it? I mean not wearing a seat belt in some situations, could easily cost you your life, so I hope you don't repeat the mistake again.'

Now even more embarrassed, I explained the problem, and his response was immediate,

'For Heaven's sake son, this ridiculous situation can't continue, so go to your doctor, get an explanatory letter and from then on you won't have a problem. So get the matter rectified as quick as you can then get back to me, I'll hold this violation, so it goes no further as well.'

As simple as that I thought, but quite often, things that appear simple on the surface, don't prove to be all that simple at all. Our doctor refused to write the letter, in his opinion a discussion with someone more experienced in such matters was far more appropriate, so rather than receiving the letter I wanted, he gave me a referral to a specialist instead. On arriving home that evening, decidedly frustrated, I expressed my annoyance with my wife,

'Can't understand what's wrong with the man, he must be demented and surely he must also be joking. I need an appointment with a psychiatrist like I need another hole in the head.'

But rather than receiving understanding I'd expected, she stated she was delighted with the outcome, and insisted I was going to that appointment she'd make for me, even if she had to drag me there herself. However, being the typically perceptive male I was, or so I thought anyway, I knew she was determined to find out what caused those disturbed nights I occasionally still suffered, and possibly the appointment with the psychiatrist offered some hope of doing so. Then to build on that, there was this total obsession with having a son, although she was aware much of that could be due to the distressing situation that had occurred within the lives of my only remaining relatives on my father's side of the family, who resided across the Tasman.

There'd been a twelve year age difference between my father and his older brother, and a couple more between my cousin and myself. We visited the families on our honeymoon, which was great as far as I was concerned, because I hadn't seen them since that trip when I was twelve. Both my uncle and cousin had married childhood sweethearts, and the intervening years had seen my cousin and his wife become parents of three delightful daughters. He held the position of head ranger in the local National Park, and this was where the family resided, in a home that was part of his employment package, and nestling deep amongst the natural beauty and tranquillity the park offered, it provided the delightful serenity they all treasured so much. On his retirement, my uncle built a cottage in the nearby township in a position right on the water, all of which left my wife and myself thinking this left the close knit families what could only be described as leading an ideal existence.

So with my uncle and aunt thoroughly enjoying their well earned retirement, and with the healthy outdoor life their son was leading, with his heavy involvement with the park seeing him as a fit and extremely powerful man, it seemed nothing could disturb their carefree lives. But due to one of those cruel and unexplainable situations that life occasionally intervenes with, fate decided it had other ideas. Out of nowhere, suddenly my cousin fell ill, and after a series of tests was diagnosed with an incurable cancer, and five months later he passed away. With my aunt having suffered from a heart condition for most of her adult life, the strain associated with her son's illness proved just too much, and she

succumbed as well. So after a comparatively short space of time, my uncle found himself having to face life without his treasured wife and son, and after trying gamely to struggle on, finally gave up the uneven battle and passed away as well.

During our visit, they were already aware of their son's terminal condition, and as we parted and due to his pleading, I made my uncle a faithful promise. The family name and bloodline would continue on into the next generation, because I was determined we'd produce a boy, little realising my promise would turn out to be a lie instead, made worse by the fact it proved to be the last communication I ever had with him. But even allowing for the situation that emerged from that tragedy, I sensed my wife suspected my desperation to father a son went somewhat further than that. So due to her absolute insistence, not to mention the matter of continuing family harmony, I reluctantly promised I'd keep that appointment, but by using my own devious approach, I'd say nothing more than was required to get my hands on that all important letter.

But I have to confess to proving to be an amateur in such matters, attempting to compete with a seasoned professional, and as he so skilfully and patiently probed, the whole unsavoury story hidden in those dreadful years was finally exposed. He cancelled a number of appointments as we talked on well into the late afternoon, then following his advice I went home and sat down with my wife and explained to her what those years had entailed. And her attitude was what I should have expected, because rather than being one of disgust, which I wouldn't have blamed her for, it was one of understanding and support, to a point where she came to me some time later and suggested, 'Considering what I now know about that part of your life and the damage that was done, I feel it's imperative we try for that boy.'

Although I admit to being tempted, deep down I knew it remained far more complicated than that. After that first appointment, many followed on from there, and although I knew there'd been a remarkable improvement, I was aware that nothing existed that could erase those memories from my mind, the fact was, medical professional or not, and whether I liked it or not, they were there, imbedded forever, and no amount of discussions and professional help could eliminate this poison I'd lived with for years. The last words the specialist had offered were, 'Write about it Mathew, put it down on paper, few things help more than that.' But as far as trying for another child was concerned, my decision not too was further enhanced by inadvertently reading an article published in a well regarded medical journal.

The subject under discussion was a clinic in Europe, claiming outstanding success in predetermining the sex of a child by carefully monitoring the future mother's food intake up to eight weeks before conception was attempted, so that the mother's system at the time, became a predominant deciding factor. A form was provided that contained a series of questions relating to the intended mother's food preferences, so I filled it out and posted it away, convinced the whole thing would simply die a natural death. But some weeks later a letter arrived at my office, containing their assessment, based on the information I'd provided, with their analysis indicating we had an eighty three per cent chance of conceiving another girl, and a seventeen per cent chance of having a boy.

Although I was aware many would look on this as being somewhat more than dubious, any willingness to try again on my part was very effectively obliterated.

Never the less, I was still determined I wanted a boy's influence around the house, so to partially get over what I assessed as being an insurmountable problem, after many in-depth discussions, we agreed the safest path for all concerned was to adopt a boy instead. And this proved to be an interesting exercise in itself. After the interviews had been completed, and having been deemed to fit the criteria required of adoptive parents, and with all the inevitable paperwork behind us, the fact we wanted a boy, in itself, warranted a celebration, apparently everyone wanted to adopt blond haired, blue eyed girls, so one up to us, no, two up to us, because we were already way ahead of them in that department. But as the weeks past, we began to wonder if we'd been forgotten, then finally the phone call we'd been waiting for, a baby boy was lying there waiting for us at the local North Shore Hospital, as long we approved of the child they'd chosen for us. The overly long wait, they insisted, was due entirely to the time they'd taken to make sure of choosing a child that complied with our preferences. We arrived at the hospital, full of the anticipation experienced by adoptive parents, not early, not late, exactly at the specified time, and sure enough, there he was, sound asleep, two ears, two eyes, a well shaped nose, ten fingers and toes and the other essentials, a perfect little boy, so right, he'll do, we'll have him.

Excellent, we could pick him up the following morning, we were duly informed, and were shown the room in which he'd be waiting for us. So we arrived exactly on time to find nobody at the reception desk, so rang the bell placed there for the purpose of summoning something in the shape of a human, not a movement, not a sound, maybe they were all out attending a funeral, because the place appeared to be deserted. Many more frustrating minutes past, still nothing, so finally my wife suggests we should go down to the room in which we'd been told the child would be waiting. If he was there, then fine, if not, perhaps the whole thing's been cancelled at the last minute?

But no, there he was, having a bit of a wail this time, so my wife changes him and picks him up, and immediately he stops crying, so we stroll back to reception with him, still nothing, so we glance at each other, say 'to hell with this' and take him home, a baby dressed in blue, rather than the pink I'd become accustomed too. Some months later, working out the front of our house, a car pulls up, the woman occupant peering intently down our drive, her intense gaze leaving me slightly curious, so I wander over and ask if I can be of any help.

'Are you Mr. Colbert', she asks, and when I admit to that sin, she adds, 'you and your wife adopted a baby boy something like nine months back. I'm from Adoption Services, just checking up, hope you don't mind the intrusion.'

'Sure, no problem,' I reply, 'like to come in and see him, he's in his bedroom sleeping.'

'Oh, that won't be necessary,' she replies, 'I can see everything's just fine. Nice to have met you Mr. Colbert, goodbye.' Welcome to adoption in New Zealand, nineteen seventies' style.

Chapter 41

The years continued to slip pleasantly enough by, life as hectic as ever, the sound of our son's laughter providing some of the best therapy I could have asked for, intermingled with the occasional growl for annoying his sisters, but then what's a brother for after all? I'm also convinced my volatility caused by those years is now a thing of the past, that meeting with Cunningham, leaving me convinced of that. If he could walk away from me still intact, considering the things he'd done, surely that was all the proof I required. But I was wrong, there was one more, and a major one at that, and it originated due to the importation of a piece of machinery from Germany.

My father and I had reflected long and hard of which unit best suited our requirements, and it was this German product that stood out above all others as being our obvious choice. The country was still locked down under the bureaucracy of the Muldoon Government, with a licence being necessary for the purchase of any overseas product. This alone took months of patience, couple with the additional time required to ship the unit from Germany to New Zealand, but finally here it was, standing on our workshop floor, waiting to be installed. The anticipation was electric, however, one problem remained, because although the unit had been exported to an English speaking country, all the installation instructions were in German.

This left us with no alternative, anyway, we felt the installation should prove to be fairly basic, even without the help of the instructions. But the noise that erupted when the unit was activated indicated something was terribly wrong. A cast alloy guide had been packed and stored in the head of the machine in such a manner, it had been completely hidden, and the only way we could have known it was there, would have been if we'd been capable of reading the instructions. With the remains of the guide carefully extracted, a close examination showed the only damage appeared to have been suffered by the guide itself, which was sitting on a bench in a number of rather forlorn and shattered pieces.

With the unit useless without it, all I could envisage was the time wasted while we waited for a replacement. The only alternative, was to find someone who possessed the ability to perform some very technical welding of a type, so I'd been informed, that had rarely been successfully achieved in the country. After numerous phone calls, as I desperately searched for someone who could help, my extensive enquiries finally centred around a small company, situated in the Western suburbs, who I'd been told, would be the only company possessing the knowledge of the welding technique required. A brief phone call confirmed this was possibly so, and their suggestion was get the guide out to them, so as they could confirm whether they could help or not.

As I stood at the counter in their office, a young man around my own age came over, and on viewing the pieces of guide, immediately recalled the conversation we'd had. He commented that at least the breaks were clean, but stressed the final decision lay with his father, who was regarded as the

undisputed expert when it came to this rare type of technical welding. Taking the fractured sections, he walked back into a rear office, and after speaking into an intercom, waited until an older man joined him. Due to a glass partition, from where I was standing they remained clearly in view, but as I stood and waited for what I hoped would prove to be a positive decision, suddenly, it was as if as inbuilt warning system was sending a faint electric current tingling through my system.

Now jolted fully attentive, and having found the young man extremely pleasant to deal with, I turned my attention to the older man and studied him more closely, and as I did, those warning signals changed from a slight tingle, to something approaching a full on red alert. My memory screamed there was something about him, and it related to those years back, that stocky, powerful build, that thinning head of distinctively crew cut auburn hair, and the more I studied him, the more certain I became, it was all too obvious, it could only be one man. Automatically I straightened as I continued watching as he turned slightly more towards me. The passing years had inevitably etched a few more lines in his face that hadn't been there before, but one thing hadn't changed, it was still as florid as ever.

Instantly I was back in that bedroom again, the memory of his hand violently twisting my arm, the attempt at a vicious slap, followed by that swinging fist as he attempted that far more violent punch. Then those days later, strapped face down on that frame, first being brutalised by Seth, then this obnoxious toad had walked into the room. The verbal taunts at my helplessness, plus the fact I couldn't talk back, followed by the application of the blindfold and ear plugs, and what happened during those next couple of hours had been sealed into my memory for life. No matter what a boy of my age had said and done, the latter due to nothing more than an automatic act of self defence, nothing excused what had happened in that room.

There were times when I wondered whether that toxin had dissolved, lost forever during the passing of time, I'd hoped so, but apparently not, because what was left was churning, my cold blooded desire for revenge escalating rapidly upward, but at the same time, after all those years and having learnt the benefit of restraint, especially after that regrettable incident in New York, fortunately that voice of reason had appeared and was saying, 'Take it easy, cool down, be rational, this isn't the place, and it certainly isn't the time.'

My thoughts swung back to that meeting with Cunningham, and my decision that I never wanted to get into a violent confrontation with another human being ever again. Well I'd been wrong, I'd forgotten, there had always been one man left, and due to one of those strange occurrences that life for some reason, occasionally manages to manipulate, there he was, standing no more than five metres away from me.

As I continued to stand at that counter and study him, my thoughts swung yet again in Cunningham's direction. Considering what had happened in that shed, out of those eight youngsters, he'd been one of the worst of them, but they'd only been boys, what had happened to me in that room had been because of this brute of a man. I'd turned my back on Cunningham, because it had been my decision to do so, caused to some extent, by the fright I'd received, due to

what had happened in New York, but one thing was certain, I sure as hell wasn't turning my back and walking away from him.

And I smiled to myself, at least this chance encounter was proving one thing, time was taking care of my volatility. Not all that far back I'd have been leaping over this counter and confronting him, and too hell with the consequences, but instead, here I am calmly standing here as I study that florid, arrogant face. My assessment was it oozed out of every pore, his business and the money he obtained from it, took up the greater part of his life, and I was in no doubt his wife and children lingered somewhere well behind. To some extent I'd experienced something similar with my own father, that no holds barred determination to succeed, no matter what the cost to anyone else. And that was fine, if that's how they preferred to live, and as far as my father was concerned, it hadn't created too much of a problem, in fact, once again I smiled as I thought about it, because my mother never appeared happier than when he was out of the house.

So due to past experience, and assessing this man like I felt I could, he'd be the first to arrive in the morning, and the last to leave at night, and from what turned out to be a highly accurate assessment as far as his daily routine was concerned, I formulated my plan of attack.

Without doubt, my number one priority was getting the guide repaired, that's if it proved to be possible, then think carefully, act accordingly, and deal with the bastard from there. But now it was a question of business coming first, because the two men had parted, my abuser from those years back, heading straight for the workshop, the younger man heading back towards the counter. The news was good, in fact all I could hope for. One of their staff had recently arrived in the country from Europe, where he'd acquired the expertise to be able to repair the guide. It would be ready in two days time, and purposely I arranged to pick it up late in the day, after all, no sense in wasting more time than proved to be necessary.

Those two days later, standing back at their counter on which the beautifully repaired guide was resting, along with the account. I glanced at it, then looked again more closely, confirming the extortionate figure they'd charged, but wrote out the cheque without hesitation. Anything was worth getting our new acquisition into production. On leaving their factory, I headed back to the local shopping centre, and quickly locating a telephone box, contacted my wife, 'Look, it's me kid, I'm going to be home a little later than usual. Some important business has suddenly cropped up that I have to attend to, so put my meal in the oven and tell the kids I hope to be back soon enough to be able to read them their bedtime story. This has been hanging around for quite some time, and it means a lot to me to be able to get it sorted out, so after that, I'll get home as quick as I can. Yes, alright, see you soon.'

Now back to the factory, which was one of around six or eight that were part of a light industrial development, and previously I'd paid close attention to the one adjacent to theirs. It was unoccupied, and as I drove back in I swung around and parked close in beside the building and directly behind a wooden fence. With my vehicle being dark bronze in colour, it blended in perfectly with the surroundings, and was parked in a position that even allowing for the fence, still

left me with an unobstructed view of their front entrance, and in the half light of early evening, I sat there and waited.

Twenty minutes past, and I knew it was, because I kept checking my Mondia watch, with the shades of the approaching night getting slightly darker by the second, which suited me perfectly. He must have plenty of work, even allowing for his exorbitant charges, because there was no doubt they were working some overtime, the lights coming on in the factory confirming that. Another forty minutes, the lights being gradually extinguished, then a flurry of activity as one by one, cars appeared around the side of the building and drove away, leaving just two standing out front. It all added up, he'd mentioned he had a son around my own age, so the odds suggested it had been his son who'd served me. Another ten minutes and sure enough the young man appears, unlocked his car then climbed in and sped away. Couldn't say I blamed him, after a day of being confined in the factory with that father of his, he was probably almost as keen to see the back of him as I'd been.

Twelve minutes more, not all that much in the way of daylight left, my patience finally rewarded as one by one the lights in the front of the building extinguished, another few seconds and he appears; that stocky, unmistakeable figure bending as he activates what is probably a deadlock. I eased out of my car, then stopped at the end of the fence while I check up and down the road, not a soul in sight, the area inundated with the sound of absolute silence. And I'd been determined to make sure it stayed like that. Purposely I'd left the door of the car ajar so as to avoid making even the slightest noise, the soft soles of my shoes soundless as I glided up and stopped about three paces behind him.

Once again he was bending slightly, this time unlocking his car, and it was as he straightened that he finally sensed my presence, so he spun around, peering at me through the late evening light, or what was left of it, then that familiar aggression flared as he snarled,

'Who the bloody hell are you? Shit you gave me a fright, standing there like that. What the fuck do you want? Better still, piss off while you've got the chance, before I call the cops.'

I'd worked hard for quite some time, being determined to erase any resemblance of the proverbial angry young man, and there were times when it had proved harder than I thought, but the responsibility of a wife and children had helped take care of most of what was left, but much as I was reluctant to admit it, I'd reached a point where standing in the street and facing up to this man, even though it seemed a bit sadistic, I was going to thoroughly enjoy this.

'So, you're going to call the police are you? Well don't know if I'm missing something, but I have to say that hard as I'm trying, buggered if I can see a phone handy anywhere in the immediate vicinity, so as far as that phone call's concerned, I wish you the best of luck.'

The tone of my voice, which I did absolutely nothing to disguise, offered all the warning he needed. His naturally aggressive instincts were telling him he was in deep trouble, and accordingly was left with two choices, either turn and attempt to bolt, which I was sure he'd assessed as not being an overly viable option, or stand and fight. Not surprising for him, he chose the latter, and as he charged I let him come, being determined it was he who'd throw the first punch,

and he did, a roundhouse vicious swing, that if it have connected, could have caused some serious damage, because all those years on, he was still a powerful man. But fortunately, one thing that hadn't changed all that much, were those reflexes Albie had installed in me all those years back, and which had been toned close to perfection by Mitsu. Time guaranteed I was slower than I'd been then, but I was still fast enough. As I swayed back, his punch swept past my face, and now deep satisfaction as I retaliated, moving in close, driving my elbow with all the force I could muster, into a point just left of his stomach, as I aimed for his kidney. He let out a sharp cry of pain, his face, unpleasant enough, now even more distorted by the pain he was experiencing as he sagged forward. But even as he did, the palm of my right hand was travelling up, on past his stomach, brushing his chest as I'd been taught, terminating with sickening force, directly under his chin.

His head snapped back, and as I knew it would, his balance went with it, so by the time he was staggering half way back towards his car, he was moving very quickly indeed, but by the time the back of his head collided with the division between the doors, he was practically airborne. The severity of the impact meant he literally bounced back towards me, and that's when the blade of my hand descended, landing with brutal velocity on the bridge of his nose. Now another, if anything harder still, striking a point at the base of his neck and fractionally behind his left ear. Briefly, somehow he straightened slightly, then fell forward, hitting the ground with quite an audible thump, and I knew he wouldn't be in any condition to be able to stand unaided for quite some time to come.

I was certain he had a very broken nose, because the flow of blood was already seeping out beyond his face and onto the asphalt on which he was lying. But to some extent, minor though it was, it appeared his thick neck had saved him from even more severe damage. As I reached down and rolled him over, and he let out a slight moan, and as I grabbed his tie and wrenched his head up, I sensed he was lucid enough to comprehend what I was saying,

'Remember you asked me who I was?' and as his eyes got reasonably close to focusing, I continued, 'well just listen carefully and I'll tell you. Cast your filthy mind back to a large house out in the country, and I'm sure you recall walking into a bedroom where a boy was waiting, made available for you to use in any perverted way you wanted, but only after you'd paid a considerable amount of money, so as to be able to indulge in child sex.

Similar to all the others who entered that room, you'd been informed the boy was not a willing participant, and this was done on purpose, because it had been decided it added to the anticipation of what they intended to subject the child too. Do you recall trying to slap and punch him, and the boy retaliating and punching you instead? Now cast your mind a little further forward, once again walking into that room, but with the boy strapped face down on a frame, naked and helpless, exactly as you'd demanded, only this time very effectively gagged as well. Do you recall verbally taunting him, then fixing a blindfold over his eyes and inserting ear plugs as well, and I'm sure you recall the sexual highlights you achieved from what you did to that boy over the next couple of hours. Well guess what, if there's one thing that young boys have a habit of

doing, it's growing up, so do you still need to have it explained even more explicitly, exactly who I am?'

I stood up, and at the same time released my grip on his tie, and as his head dropped back I turned to walk away, but taking one of my business cards out of my pocket, I flipped it in his general direction. Rather fittingly I felt, it fluttered down and finished lying between his outstretched legs, and this somehow encouraged me to have a few more final words,

'I know we've just done business together, and because of our past, there's a large part of me that wishes it hadn't been necessary, but if you feel like pressing charges for assault, then please, be my guest, that card may save you some time if you wish to give my particulars to your solicitor. However, there's one last thing I want to stress, and that is there are few things I'd enjoy more than having my legal representative standing in court and telling all present about your filthy sexual preferences. And what's more, I'd make sure he described down to the finest detail, exactly what you did to me while I was lying on that frame.'

His eyes flickered, but if there was meant to be any form of a signal, I had no inclination to find out what it was, so I turned and crossed over to the still open door of my car, and as I drove slowly away, he was still lying exactly where I'd left him.

Not all that far into my drive home, when the trauma associated with the evening's events hit me. As I was passing Western Springs, a vacant spot appeared on the side of the road so taking the opportunity offered, I pulled over beside the curb. I held my hands up in front of my face, and they were trembling, probably not surprising, considering what had happened. Sitting behind the wheel of my stationary car, I allowed my mind to wander back to where it all started. Seeing as I wasn't happy driving, not much else to do anyway. There was that fight with Wallace, well, hardly a fight, a couple of punches, with my being hurt the most. He'd collected a smack in the mouth, I'd finished up with a badly cut knuckle. Why had it happened? In a word, the result of bullying. Then there'd been those couple of fights with Arnold. He wasn't all that much of a bully, he just wanted to impose himself, and after having given him that bit of a bloody nose, his mother was convinced someone had half killed him, which was all very well, she should have seen the bruises he left me with after that first uneven encounter. Then had followed that brawl with Ivan, and if Smithie hadn't intervened, they'd have carried me home in pieces, once again due to bullying, and there'd been fights at High School, due to refusing to be bullied. There'd been that fight with Christopher Hull, all carefully controlled and legal, and it resulted in what had been accepted as the most brutal caning ever administered at the school, and who had swung the cane? A man who was nothing more than an unpleasant, over sized bully. So why had I succumbed to Bergman's and Malcolm's threats, because of an inbuilt dread of being subjected to years of inescapable torment and bullying. Yet those who claim to know it all say children simply have to learn how to deal with the problem, just part of growing up they say. From where I'm currently sitting, who do they think they're kidding?

Back to reality, I hold my hands up, still a slight tremor, but at least everything is well on the way to settling. Not bad considering the state I'd left him in, but still nothing to be proud of under normal circumstances, but only he and I knew the circumstances were a long way removed from normal. In the state he'd left me in, it was only Seth's intervention that had saved me from serious and possibly lifelong damage. It turned out to be the only thing I'd thanked him for, during all the unpleasant time I'd known him. As I'd waited across the road from the factory, I'd convinced myself I couldn't get my hands on the man quick enough, but now sitting quietly, with the unpleasantness behind me, I knew this was the end, I'd never hurt another human being to that extent ever again.

I glance out of the side window and vehicles continue to flash past, and due to a shower of rain, their lights briefly cause sparkling and dancing patterns to flicker across my windscreen, until they speed off as they head for home, or wherever else circumstances dictate they need to be going. I check my hands again, not a movement, not so much as a quiver, my recovery complete, now time for me to continue on home as well. My wife and kids, how I adore them, and the last thing they need is the stress of a husband and father being charged with aggravated assault. The question of legal action had been mentioned on the spur of the moment, now I wished I'd shown some restraint. Too late now, he'd either go down that path or he wouldn't, it was no more complex than that. Just have to wait for a sensible outcome, but one thing was certain, my threat to make sure he was exposed for what he was, was no idle threat. He'd be a fool to risk it.

Time to start the car and continue my journey home, the purr of the engine somehow soothing, and a gap appears in what seems to be an endless flow of traffic, so I ease out and join the seemingly never ending procession. Glad I remembered to phone my wife and warn her I'd be late, it didn't happen all that often, and after the time spent sitting and recovering, I'll still be home earlier than I anticipated. I bet my life the kids will still be up, patiently waiting for their bedtime story, it had become such a ritual, these days there was no hope of getting them into bed without it. Last I recall, I was on a pirate ship, floating down the Zambese River, helping to fight off a hoard of spear throwing natives who were determined to have us for dinner. Doubt if I'll be able to top that effort tonight. The boy would be there, forever in the thick of it, that's unless he'd been banished to his room for starting a fight with his sisters. Oh, the joys of parenthood. He'd blended well into our family, but he was barely over a week old when we got him, so no reason why he shouldn't, I guess.

Now swinging into then up and over the Harbour Bridge, all strapped in and legal, that small problem well and truly behind me, getting closer to home by the second, and how I need that familiarity even more than usual. For some reason those two important promises I'd made, and how they'd affected my life slipped into my mind. The first to Adrian's mother, and I had stayed true to my word as I did my best to protect her son, and look what I'd received in return, and the second, those last words I had with my uncle. After having promised him I'd father a son, for a reason I've never been able to comprehend, fate intervened, and decreed that what I said turned out to be a lie instead, and with it, our family

bloodline ending forever. But one advantage appearing out of the carnage, surely this placed our adopted son in the best position of all. Rather than being responsible for terminating a family, he'd have the privilege of starting a new one instead, and to me that sounded good, in fact, what could be better than that?

Chapter 42

Now many years have passed, and included amongst them a decision to move our family to the sunshine of Queensland, on the mutual understanding between my wife and myself, that if we didn't take to our new environment, we could always go back. And there was no doubt some agreed, 'you'll be back here inside eighteen months' some of our neighbours had declared, and in doing so, proved it wasn't only my father's predictions that could be proved so wrong. That was well over twenty five years ago, and somehow the urge to return hasn't erupted yet. But a few years back, what did finally erupt was that troublesome heart valve.

Due to the best of medical care, it held out far longer than the medical experts had predicted, which was due, so they insisted, to the fact I was a non smoker and consumed a very limited amount of alcohol, but the time finally arrived, and just as that doctor who'd attended to me after that cross country run had predicted, heart valve replacements had become comparatively common, and with the preliminary procedure required before the main event completed, the specialist wandered into the recovery ward and asked,

'Well, what do you want first, the good news or bad?'

'Either way, please yourself.'

'Alright, the good news is your arteries are perfectly clear, no need for a bypass, but that valve is rubbish, and in my opinion, should have been replaced long before this, so have you given any thought to what you prefer, artificial or tissue?'

The fact was I'd had ample time to consider this issue, and what had lodged foremost in my mind was an artificial valve meant I'd be on blood thinning medication for the rest of my life, where as a tissue valve wouldn't last as long, but would function without the necessity of those drugs, so I'd made up my mind long before, as far as I was concerned, tissue was the only way to go. After all, knowing myself as I did, I was bound to forget to take the pests of things anyway. And this decision left me with the only aspect in our lives that I have with Mr. Kevin Rudd. Removed from the highest office in the land by the devious Julia Gillard, then regaining same in a similar manner, where I'm just one of the masses and as Liberal as the day is long, once again he's the Labor Prime Minister, so that solitary thing we have in common? We're both kept alive, courtesy of a heart valve, generously donated by a cow.

There's no doubt our time spent in Australia has proved interesting in the extreme, with my business encounters with some of the local land developers immediately coming to mind. One thing I can't complain about is their ethics and honesty, because logic says it's impossible to complain about something that's non-existent. But through it all we've managed very well, and somehow, although I'm not sure how, Malcolm's house must have made a lasting impression in more ways than one. My wife and I reside in our own Colonial style home, surrounded by an expanse of lawns and gardens, with the mandatory

two vehicles parked on the gravel drive out front, with the river running down to the sea behind.

That little girl who originally I wanted nothing to do with, is now a mother with two daughters of her own. The first with hair so dark and shining, it's an exact copy of her father, with this being in direct contrast to her younger sister, who's as golden blond as her mother. Also that boy I always wanted has finally arrived, even if the happy event occurred one generation too late. Nicolas Michael is the son of our older daughter, and his likeness is exactly how I imagined our own son would be, with hair as blond and thick as his grandfather's was at the same age, but with eyes as blue as the sky, rather than that green I detested so much. And now another male addition in the form of handsome young Dylan, courtesy of our son and his wife, who brings the variation of some male dark hair into the family, just as his father did all those years back, the blond hair in their family supplied courtesy of his two adorable sisters.

And as far as my life is concerned, like any other human being, there are aspects I'd change if I could, but one of those would never be my wife. Nobody more than I realises how fortunate I've been to have her by my side, with the combination of her love, honesty and common sense constantly backing me up through good times and bad, and I will continue to adore her until I close my eyes for that final time.

But I must confess that just occasionally, when I hear the laughter of our grandchildren echoing around the house, my mind drifts back to what has long past, and what might have been, and what I would give to banish some of those dark memories from my mind. But if I find the pain becoming just a little too intense, my preferred remedy is to step outside onto one of our verandahs and enjoy the serenity a typical Queensland evening so often offers, just as I'm doing now. And as I lift my eyes and gaze up into the slowly darkening sky, in some slight ways there's a similarity to when I was in that shed, looking down into that imaginary bottomless pit. But rather dwelling on the unpleasantness that occurred there, I force my mind in an entirely different direction until I'm back at the beach, standing on that golden sand, enjoying the motion of the waves as they wash in and over my feet.

Then a blond headed boy appears, and as he slips his hand into mine, we take off together. And as we wander along, I point out those rolling waves that provided so much fun for us to water ski over, and also describe some of the wipe outs it created, and I show him the creek where we used to go spearing flatties, and I mention the eels that insisted on swimming between our legs, and finally we look at those cliffs from where I'd had to help Adrian down, because he'd been so ill. But somehow I also failed to mention that on many occasions when we reached the top of those cliffs, we'd spend a few misbehaving minutes chasing the sheep. And those few minutes spent with my imaginary son have succeeded, because they've left my mind totally at peace, and once that state of contentment has been reached, that signals it's finally time for him to leave, so with a quick wave, in an instant, he's gone.

So back to reality, and as I once again turn my eyes to the sky, I realise the time for me to depart is fast approaching as well. A storm is threatening, with

the ominous cloud bank spreading rapidly across the horizon, with the upper most reaches constantly highlighted by the intermittent flickering of lightning, immediately followed by the warning broadcast by the ominous rumble of thunder. Another few minutes spent watching this awesome and brilliant display being provided by nature, and now the wind has arrived, blustering wildly in, stripping the leaves from the trees, hinting at another job looming. Fortunately, Seth isn't here with his rake, which means I'll be only too happy to tidy the property in the morning.

Now a distant roar warns of heavy rain fast approaching, drumming on the roof tops like the beating of many drums, until it heralds its violent arrival, with the first of the large drops starting to darken the timber deck at my feet, at the same time offering an undeniable warning that it may be prudent to step back inside. And as I reluctantly turn and head for the door, if mixed fleeting thoughts and memories of things past, have caused my eyes to turn slightly red, then never mind, it's of no concern, over the passing years nothing has changed, I'll simply blame it on the wind.